Music in American Life

*A list of books in the series appears
at the end of this volume.*

Theodore Thomas

THEODORE THOMAS

America's Conductor and Builder
of Orchestras, 1835–1905

EZRA SCHABAS

With a Foreword by
Lady Valerie Solti

UNIVERSITY OF ILLINOIS PRESS
Urbana and Chicago

Publication of this book was made possible in part by the
substantial generosity of Brena and Lee A. Freeman, Sr.

This book is printed on acid-free paper.

Library of Congress Cataloging-in-Publication Data

Schabas, Ezras, 1924–
    Theodore Thomas : America's conductor and builder of orchestras,
1835–1905 / Ezra Schabas ; with a foreword by Valerie Solti.
        p.   cm. — (Music in American Life)
    Bibliography: p.
    ISBN 0-252-01610-6
    1. Thomas, Theodore, 1835–1905.   2. Conductors (Music)—
United States.   I. Title.
ML422.T46S3 1989
785'.092'4—dc 19
    [B]   88-38072
                                                                  CIP
                                                                  MN

To Ann

Contents

Foreword   xi
Preface   xv

Introduction   1
1 From Vocation to Mission   4
2 Spreading the Gospel   24
3 Musical Shrines   48
4 A Chastened Prophet   69
5 Escape to Middle America   85
6 The Warrior Returns   101
7 Undisputed Ruler   121
8 From Boastful Dream to Catastrophe   147
9 More Catastrophe and Picking Up the Pieces   168
10 A Vote of Confidence   181
11 Debacle at White City   195
12 Mission Accomplished   213
13 A Building for the Future   234

Chronology   259
Notes   261
Bibliography   285
Index   297

Illustrations follow pages
68, 146, and 212

Foreword

Theodore Thomas, the German-born conductor and visionary, was a giant in the musical life of nineteenth-century America, a pioneer who introduced Americans to Wagner, Strauss, Elgar, Saint-Saëns, and Bruckner, often performing their compositions before they had been heard in Europe. Through his carefully planned programs he hoped to educate the public and encourage the rapidly growing immigrant population to appreciate classical music. His finest achievement, however, was the founding of the Chicago Symphony Orchestra and the building of its permanent home, Orchestra Hall. Upon his death in Chicago in January 1905, impassioned tributes were paid to him by the leading musicians of the day—Nikisch, Weingartner, Richard Strauss, Lilli Lehmann, and Paderewski. Yet, within a short time of his death, oblivion descended, although his orchestra flourished.

I first became aware of Thomas in 1975, when I was researching the life of Cosima Wagner. Diana Haskell, the ever-generous librarian of special collections at the Newberry Library in Chicago, suggested that I look at the Theodore Thomas Papers for correspondence concerning a commission for Richard Wagner to write a festival march, to be conducted by Thomas, for the American centennial celebration in 1876. I was immediately intrigued and surprised that I had never heard or read anything about Thomas. My initial inquiries revealed little, apart from his connection to the CSO. I resolved to put my research on Cosima Wagner to one side and learn as much as I could about Thomas.

It was like tracking down a ghost. I began by reading through Thomas's letters and press reports, as well as the substantial memoir written by his wife, Rose Fay Thomas, after his death and his unfinished autobiography, which reveals much about the conductor's character and ideals. With the help of Evelyn Meine and Ken Utz at Orchestra Hall, I located Thomas's desk, an old and neglected piece of furniture that has since been restored and is now in daily use in the CSO executive director's office. A full-length portrait turned up in Cincinnati and now hangs in the upper lobby at Orchestra Hall. A framed baton in the Glessner House in Chicago and music scores in the Newberry Library and Orchestra Hall were also found. Evelyn Meine discovered a jeweled silver and gilt baton and a silver laurel wreath at the back of an old safe in Orchestra Hall, both of which had been presented to Thomas by musical organizations he had worked with in the Chicago area. Some cardboard boxes held a collection of dolls—replicas of the entire Thomas orchestra, complete with instruments. Mrs. Thomas's autograph book, signed by the great musicians of the time who had been guests of the Thomases while in Chicago, is in the Newberry Library, together with Thomas's personal library, which includes his books on music and gardening (his other love).

Perhaps the most remarkable discovery was of the Theodore Thomas Memorial, unveiled by his daughter Minna Thomas Sturgis in 1924 on a site facing Orchestra Hall. The memorial, which consisted of a classical statue, *Ode to Music*, backed by a frieze, had been removed during construction of the Art Institute, but nobody seemed to know where. The statue was found in Grant Park, but the frieze, with the dedication to Thomas, appeared to be lost. Then, quite by chance, Joyce Idema, the CSO director of public relations, read a newspaper report that a man exercising his dog on a Chicago beach had noticed some marble columns sticking out of Lake Michigan, along with some granite tablets. We went to investigate, and the tablets were indeed the missing frieze. The task remains to reassemble and resite the memorial, and a committee has been formed with that aim.

The more I learned about Thomas, the more I admired this man of tireless energy and enthusiasm who had elevated the orchestral musician from little more than a hired servant to a respected citizen. Beset with financial problems throughout his life, Thomas was often criticized by those who could not understand his pursuit of excellence or his refusal to compromise. He was a virtuoso conductor, well respected in the musical world, but not always appreciated by the American public. A practical genius, he never wasted his time and energies on self or social advancement. Yet Thomas's correspondence with the town planner and architect Daniel Burnham shows him to have been a Renaissance man in the truest sense. With Burnham he dreamed of creating a physical expression of the democratic ideal by transforming the Chicago he loved into a metropolis that would enrich the lives of its inhabitants with facilities for the arts and recreation.

Theodore Thomas was not a flamboyant conductor and hence did not attract to himself the anecdotes and attention that preserve and fuel the memory. His death came too soon after he had realized his dream of a permanent orchestra in its own hall, yet his legacy is a rich one. Lilli Lehman described him as "a rough diamond to whom I would like to erect a monument." While history has been unfair to Thomas, this excellent and much-awaited biography by Ezra Schabas will show that, as nineteenth-century America's premier conductor and builder of orchestras, he deserves to be remembered well and with gratitude.

Lady Valerie Solti
London, England

Preface

This biography of Theodore Thomas stems from research begun more than twenty years ago on the social history of the North American symphony orchestra. The research led to several papers and four one-hour talks aired by the Canadian Broadcasting Corporation. In the course of this work, it became apparent to me that Thomas was nineteenth-century America's seminal figure in symphonic music, the first American conductor to train fine orchestras and teach audiences to appreciate the music of the masters.

Resolving to learn more about Thomas, I read his brief autobiography and George P. Upton's "Reminiscence," which were published together after Thomas's death in 1905. I went on to read *Memoirs of Theodore Thomas* (1911) by Thomas's second wife, Rose Fay, a lengthy, informative, and, like Upton's, blindly affectionate account of the conductor, as well as Charles E. Russell's *The American Orchestra and Theodore Thomas* (1927), a more probing if overly credulous story of Thomas's life and achievements. I then studied other Thomas material: profiles, interviews, articles, concert reviews, his letters, his views on conducting, composing, repertoire, teaching, and musical life generally, and his concert programs—he kept nearly all of them—which show sequentially how American musical taste developed.

Clearly, North American orchestras owe much to Theodore Thomas for setting high standards of performance and patterns for orchestral growth and public support. Our classical music tradition is European-based and, in Thomas's time, was slavishly German. Yet there are now over 1,500 American orchestras, some among the best in the world. Thomas laid the groundwork for this American story.

This biography is the first since Russell's (there have been two dissertations in the interim, by H. S. Whistler [1942] and T. C. Russell [1969]). It interprets

Thomas's life and times from a late twentieth-century stance. The Chronology will help the reader follow the main events in Thomas's life, and the Notes and Bibliography will, I hope, encourage scholars and interested laypeople to extend their study of this remarkable man.

Acknowledgments

I have had much assistance in preparing this biography. The staffs of the Newberry Library (the main repository of Thomas's papers), the Chicago Historical Society, the Cincinnati Historical Society, the Library and Museum for the Performing Arts of the New York Public Library at Lincoln Center, the Music Division of the Library of Congress, the library of the Faculty of Music and the reference, interlibrary loan, and microtext sections of the Robarts Library of the University of Toronto, the Chicago Symphony Orchestra, and the Archives of the New York Philharmonic have all been most helpful. Special thanks go to Diana Haskell of the Newberry Library and to Archie Motley of the Chicago Historical Society, Laura Chace of the Cincinnati Historical Society, Richard Jackson of Lincoln Center, Wayne Shirley of the Library of Congress, Kathleen McMorrow of the University of Toronto music library, and Evelyn Meine of the Chicago Symphony.

I am indebted to John Steinway, grandson of William Steinway, for allowing me to study his grandfather's diaries and to Richard and Theodora Schulze for giving me access to the Felsengarten Collection. Others to whom I am grateful for providing me with important material and/or helping me arrive at new insights about Thomas include Sydney Beck, R. W. H. Binnie, Arnold Broido, Dena J. Epstein, Diane Hallmann, Philip Hart, Joseph E. Holliday, Ralph Locke, Anne McKinley, Phillip Morehead, Carl Morey, T. C. Russell, Leon Stein, Jacklin Stopp, and Thomas Willis. I am especially grateful to the several readers of my manuscript for their many good suggestions: Mordecai and Irma Bauman, Ray Laakso, Lawrence Leonard, Paul Schabas, and Gwendolyn Setterfield.

I thank Judith McCulloh of the University of Illinois Press, who urged me to make several painful but necessary revisions of the manuscript. Jane Mac-Donald was a valuable secretary and clerical assistant in the early stages of my work, and the editing of John Parry and Theresa L. Sears was most important in the final stages of the manuscript's preparation. German letters were translated by Eckehart Catholy, Wilfred Renard, and the late Hans Wiebe. Grant support from the Canada Council and the Office of Research Administration of the University of Toronto made much of the research possible. Additional support was provided by the Cincinnati Historical Society. Finally, and most of all, I thank my wife, Ann, who read, edited, advised, and helped me in every conceivable way to put this volume together.

THEODORE THOMAS

Introduction

The Chicago Orchestra, Theodore Thomas conducting, gave the dedicatory concert for Chicago's new Orchestra Hall on December 14, 1904. "Millionaires and toilers" had contributed "ten thousand dollars to ten cents" to show the world that "commercial and material-minded Chicago" cared enough for its orchestra to give it a permanent home.[1] No Chicagoan, however, was more proud of the new hall than the orchestra's founder and conductor, Theodore Thomas. Since its inception thirteen years earlier, he had directed it at the enormous Auditorium a few blocks away, but he craved a more intimate setting. Seventy years old and in failing health, Thomas had convinced the Orchestral Association that the hall was a necessity. The association went to the people of the city for help, and they responded willingly. They knew Thomas well—he had conducted concerts for them for over three decades.

Thomas had been at the center of American musical life for half a century. Its leading conductor and musical organizer, he had helped not only orchestras to grow and prosper but audiences to develop and refine their musical taste. German-born but raised in New York, Thomas was first a violinist, then a concertmaster, soloist, and chamber player. In 1862, at the age of twenty-eight, he became an orchestral conductor and, over the next thirty years, led the Theodore Thomas Orchestra and the New York Philharmonic in more than 2,000 concerts from the Atlantic to the Pacific, from Maine to Louisiana. He was musical director of both the Philadelphia Centennial in 1876 and the World's Columbian Exposition in Chicago in 1893. Founder of the biennial Cincinnati May Festival, he directed similarly impressive festivals in other major cities and even ventured briefly into opera as director of the short-lived American Opera Company. The audiences he cultivated in his popular annual summer series at New York's Central Park Garden and later at Chicago's Exposition Building became the symphonic devotees of the future. Thomas also spent a good deal of time urging the United States, a country that looked to Europe for its art and artists, to develop schools of its own.

The man's extraordinary energy brought him failures as well as successes. The Chicago Fire of 1871, followed by personal financial ruin at the 1876 centennial, caused him years of hardship. Full of zeal, Thomas became the first director of the Cincinnati College of Music, where he hoped to build a Leipzig of the West, but he was thwarted by provincial outlooks and narrow-minded materialism—in Gilded Age America, education in the arts had low priority. His American Opera Company tried to build a troupe of American singers performing operas in English and a tuition-free National Conservatory of Music to train young singers, but administrative problems and a recalcitrant public wrecked both ventures, and the company went bankrupt. For an exorbitant fee he commissioned Richard Wagner to write what turned out to be a shoddy march for the opening of the Philadelphia Centennial, and he got caught in the piano war at the Columbian Exposition (Ignacy Paderewski's right to play was questioned, and Thomas's plans for music at the great fair were undermined and ultimately failed). Finally, he never secured financial support for a permanent, full-time New York orchestra, which the Philharmonic was not.

Thomas's conducting was a revelation at a time when this art was in its infancy. He chose his players carefully and demanded accuracy, fine tone quality, precision, and above all musicianship. He rehearsed his orchestras note by note, phrase by phrase, relentlessly seeking clear and honest interpretations. Stern and unwavering on the podium, none knew better how to mold a hundred musicians into an ensemble that spoke as one. Orchestras did as he commanded and liked it, for he was a natural leader in a young country. North America today is "orchestra land" because of him.

Orchestra Hall in Chicago was to have opened on November 4, 1904, to start the Chicago Orchestra season, but it wasn't ready. For Thomas, irritated and impatient with delays, time was of the essence. During the previous summer, he had become deaf in one ear and partially blind, and his chronic cough was getting worse; he had premonitions that he might not live long. When the hall was finally dedicated, it was cold and drafty, the cement and plaster were still damp, and the doors and windows were only half-fitted. At rehearsal, Thomas had thought the acoustics good, but the sound of the orchestra changed drastically when the hall was full. Not only Thomas and his audience but also the press began to have doubts about the hall. He conducted two more concerts there and the audience response improved, but he was not completely reassured. Was the hall a mistake? Would his hopes for this crowning achievement of his life be shattered? Thomas caught the grippe, pneumonia soon set in, and he died on January 4, 1905. Orchestra Hall remains, to this day, the home of the Chicago Symphony Orchestra, and though it has been renovated twice, it is still essentially as Thomas knew it.

Puritanical in outlook and principled to a fault, Theodore Thomas was characteristically reserved, enigmatic, elusive, and remote. We know little about his parents, family, and upbringing or about his first wife and his children—his personal life was very private. He saw great music in terms of its ethical content and moral force, and he lived his life to conform with the belief that great music built character and fostered enlightenment. High-minded and devoted to his mission, Thomas was also a man of contradictions, a microcosm of the hypocritical Gilded Age from which he had sprung. He could be inconsiderate and intolerant, and his ego and vanity took him down false paths to sorry endings. His unswerving pursuit of his goals made him controversial at every turn. How these controversies were resolved tells us much about the nineteenth-century United States, how it grew, the pervasive false values and standards of its cultural and artistic life, and the struggle that Thomas's music had in finding a place in it. This volume is about Theodore Thomas: his importance in his own time and his significance today.

1

From Vocation to Mission

New York in 1850 was a thriving, cosmopolitan center with a population of over half a million, the largest city in the United States and the seventh largest in the world. The Empire City—already its sobriquet—led the country in trade and commerce. Its broad avenues were lined with large commercial buildings and up-to-date, commodious hotels and restaurants, and its many well-dressed people gave it an air of prosperity and optimism. It was also a melting pot for many nationalities.

Actors, musicians, and dancers flocked to New York looking for work, for the opportunities only that city, as the country's leading center in the performing arts, could offer. There were more than twenty theaters, vaudeville houses, and other halls to entertain the city's diverse population, and its theatrical life rivaled London's. In 1850–51, theatergoers could attend *School for Scandal* and *Othello* at the Broadway Theater, an adaptation of *David Copperfield* at the Burton, *Macbeth* at the popular Bowery, and the famous Booths, J. B. and his gifted son Edwin, in repertory at the National. New York audiences were enthusiastic and notoriously partisan, with especially strong views on the respective merits of English and American actors and plays. Their feelings ran high—so high, in fact, that they contributed to the notorious Macready-Forrest riots at Astor Place in May 1849.[1]

Serious music did not generate such passions. Only a few theaters mounted operas, and these were sung mainly in Italian, even if their librettos were in French, German, or English. Interest had declined in opera sung in English and, even more so, in operas by English composers. As for American opera, it was almost nonexistent and the few works that had been produced were poorly received. The 1,800-seat Astor Place Opera House, completed in 1847 and the favored site for Italian opera, produced in the fall of 1850 *Il Franco arciero (Der Freischütz)*, *Norma*, and *Lucia di Lammermoor*. Some minor operas in French were given at a much smaller theater, Niblo's Garden, and several light operas in English were presented at other theaters during the season. Opera's total audiences were small when compared to drama. Italian opera, the most popular, was a toy of the rich. Its audiences were mainly concerned with beautiful singing; the words mattered little, and few understood them anyway.

If opera made little impact on the life of the city, classical music made even less. Solo recitals, chamber music, and orchestral concerts attracted small audiences. The Philharmonic Society of New York, founded in 1842, was the city's only orchestra, and it gave but four concerts a season. Prominent solo artists from Europe had visited New York, notably violinists Henri Vieuxtemps and Ole Bull in 1843 and, a few years later, pianists Leopold de Meyer and Henri Herz, but such visits were the exception rather than the rule. The first real chamber series was begun in 1851 by Theodor Eisfeld, one of the Philharmonic's conductors.

The possibilities that New York and, for that matter, other large American cities held for good music had not gone unnoticed by several small European orchestras that traveled to the United States between 1845 and 1850. The most important and influential was the Germania Society, a group of twenty-three young musicians who, discontented with conditions in Germany, had banded together in Berlin in 1848 to emigrate to America. The society was self-governing and members shared their earnings equally. Mottos like "Equal rights, equal duties, equal rewards" and "One for all and all for one" guided them. These idealists proclaimed proudly that they were *ensemble* musicians committed to playing the music of the great German masters as it should be played, that they would have nothing to do with the cheap show-off music one heard so often from the leading traveling virtuosi of the day.[2]

The first appearances of the Germania Society were tantamount to a musical revelation. Unlike the Philharmonic, also a cooperative organization but usually unrehearsed for the few concerts it gave, the Germanians were thoroughly prepared and performed with uncommon dedication. Unfortunately, they had not reckoned on New York's "uneducated" musical public, which only minimally appreciated their efforts. Discouraged, the group finally disbanded in 1854, its members settling in New York, Boston, and other American cities, many to become musical leaders in their adopted communities.

More successful with the public was Joseph Gungl's orchestra, also from Berlin. It came to the United States around the same time as the Germanians, but its approach was more practical—it did not expect too much too soon from the public. Gungl, an oboist and director of the Fourth Austrian Artillery band until he formed his own orchestra in 1843, balanced light and serious music— he wrote over 300 marches and dances during his lifetime—and thus gained much favor with his concert audiences. He took a dim view of American musical life, however, and wrote revealingly in the German periodical *Neue Berliner Musikzeitung* that music "lies still in the cradle here, and nourishes herself on sugar treats. The American business man may surpass those of most European nations but in the fine arts—but especially in music—he is behind all and not capable of enjoying instrumental music. It is a matter of course that only the so-called anti-classical music can in any degree suit the taste of an American public . . . waltzes, galops, quadrilles, above all, polkas. There are exceptions, but only a few, a very few."[3]

One exception was Jenny Lind, who was "sold" to this same public through effective promotion in 1850. Managed by master showman Phineas T. Barnum, the "Swedish Nightingale" had an impressive American tour. She sang operatic and oratorio excerpts and songs at ninety-three concerts that grossed an astonishing $712,000. Later, her reputation secure, she severed her connection with Barnum and gave concerts independently in North America until May 1852. Her enormous popularity gave good music a welcome boost —she was clearly as good as Barnum said she was—and encouraged public concertgoing generally.

The most important boost to concert attendance in the United States— and especially New York—came from the growing German-American population, whose numbers had reached new highs at mid-century. Many knew a great deal about music, particularly those who fled Germany after the Revolution of 1848. They were independent spirits who valued freedom, their cultural heritage, education, and the arts. In general, they opted for drinking in public on Sunday—not readily acceptable in fundamentalist America— and enthusiastically maintained German-language theaters, singing societies, and newspapers, many of which were as liberal and forward-looking as the most progressive American journals. In all, six million Germans emigrated to the United States between 1830 and 1900 to become one of the country's largest national groups.

It was mostly middle-class Germans who supported orchestral and chamber music concerts. They played musical instruments, sang in choirs, and held amateur choral festivals, called *Sängerfests*, where thousands sang in massed choruses. German musicians settled mainly in New York, because it offered them the most opportunities.[4] They, in turn, along with the German immigrant population provided the impetus, in the second half of the nineteenth century, to make New York one of the world's musical capitals. German music was played far more than the music of other nationalities, not only in New York but in cities like Boston, Cincinnati, Pittsburgh, St. Louis, and Chicago, and the musicians who performed it were and would be largely German-born or German-trained until World War I.

Johann August Thomas, the *Stadtmusicus* of the small town of Esens in East Friesland in northwestern Germany, emigrated to New York in 1845. A musician of no great distinction, in Esens he had played and taught wind and string instruments, organized musical groups, provided music for town holidays and state affairs, and led the band of the Schützen Corps, the local shooting society. Despite the prestige of the latter position, he was paid poorly for his work, which had much to do with his decision to leave the country.

Thomas's eldest child, Christian Friedrich Theodor, born on October 11, 1835, in Esens, had begun studying the violin at age three. Theodor, as he was called, showed great talent—he read music with ease and had absolute pitch. Johann August took him to the Hanover Court when he was seven; he made such a favorable impression that he was asked to stay on and study under Heinrich Marschner, the court music director and one of Germany's most prominent composers. But Theodor's parents turned down the offer, preferring to keep their son at home. A happy, playful, typically mischievous child, and a good student at school, Theodor returned to the Hanover Court frequently to play for Marschner, who retained a keen interest in him.[5]

Theodor was ten when the family embarked on the strenuous voyage across the Atlantic, which took six long weeks since they traveled under sail. (Steamships, introduced a few years earlier, crossed the ocean in two to three weeks.) New York City was overwhelming, after Esens with its mere 5,000 people, and Johann August quickly set out to find work. To help feed his growing family—there would be five children in all—he pressed young Theodore —the "e" was added once in North America—into service. Father and son played together, mainly in theater orchestras, groups of about twelve players each, which performed incidental music for plays and filled scene changes and intermissions with overtures and other short pieces; larger groups were used for opera. Their widely varied repertoire provided good training for Theodore and improved his sight-reading. Also, it was in these theaters that he developed a life-long affection for Shakespeare, thanks to watching the Bard's plays day after day. But becoming a professional musician so early in life meant the end of Theodore's formal schooling, which he was to regret later.

In 1848, following a prolonged period of unemployment, Johann August and Theodore went to Norfolk, Virginia, to join the Navy Band as first and second horn, respectively. (Theodore had learned the necessary horn-playing skills from his father.) While in Norfolk, they also played in orchestras in the surrounding area, with Theodore on the violin, to earn additional money. Their band duties were not arduous, and in the process Theodore learned much about wind instruments, which helped him later as a conductor.

After a year, the Thomas family's finances improved, and Johann August returned to New York. Nothing is known of his subsequent activities, and Theodore never mentioned him again. Obviously the elder Thomas had trouble earning a living, either because of limited ability or lack of work. He was also not sufficiently aggressive to make his way as an independent musician. Being a *Stadtmusicus* in a paternalistic society was not the best preparation for success in New York's rough-and-tumble laissez-faire musical world.

Theodore Thomas would not follow in his father's footsteps. At age fourteen, he knew how a musician must get along in the United States, how to create one's own opportunities in order to succeed. He went south, a wandering fiddler in search of adventure, traveling from town to town with his violin strapped to his back.

> I do not remember taking anything with me but my fiddle, my little box of clothing, and some posters which I had had printed, announcing a concert by "Master T.T." I kept a supply of these posters in my trunk, and when I had no money I first obtained permission to use the dining hall of a hotel for a concert, and then I went around on the day before the concert took place and put up my posters with tacks. When the time for the concert arrived, I would stand at the door of the hall and take the money until I concluded that my audience was about gathered, after which I would go to the front of the hall, unpack my violin, and begin the concert. Sometimes I played with piano accompaniment, but oftener without. I have yet in my possession a set of variations on "Home Sweet Home," which I wrote down some years later as a souvenir of those days. I did not have printed programmes.
>
> Often I sent my trunk on ahead, and travelled on horseback alone—if possible at night—carrying with me plenty of cigars and a pistol, hoping to be attacked on the road by bandits! I remember one place in Mississippi where, after I had announced a concert, I was ordered by the authorities to leave town, because they believed the devil was in the fiddle! On one of these trips I carried my violin in a bag, and, lying down on the ground in the woods for a rest, suddenly jumped up and stepped on it, breaking it, of course. I then went to a carpenter shop, took off its top, pieced it, glued it on again, and played on it the next day. All this is not so easy without the help of tools made for the purpose, and how I managed to place the sounding post I do not know—probably with a string.[6]

After a year, Thomas realized that his peregrinations were not helping his musical development, and he returned to New York, intending to go on to Europe for serious study. But it was now 1850. The Germanian Society and Joseph Gungl had made their impact, other impressive and cultivated

German musicians had emigrated to New York in his absence, and Jenny Lind had sung there. In short, the city's musical life had matured. Why go to Europe, Thomas asked, when New York held such promise? He would learn on the job instead of through formal instruction at a European academy or conservatory. Although he did not know it as yet, this practical education was ideal training for the future. From it, he would learn the "business" of music and what the musical public wanted.

Soon Thomas was giving solo performances, the first as "Master Thomas" at the Dodworth Musical Festival at Metropolitan Hall on February 20, 1851. He played in orchestras, including with the Germanians when they accompanied Jenny Lind ("exceptional . . . compass, technique and warmth . . . a sense of grandeur," he said of her voice), soprano Henriette Sontag, contralto Marietta Albani, and other great singers later in the decade like tenor Mario (Giovanni de Candia) and dramatic soprano Giulia Grisi, all of whom he admired for their beautiful vocal line, breath control, phrasing, and style. Instrumentalists of the time played too dryly, technically, and did not sing through their instruments, but he approached violin playing with singing in mind—although he was frequently accused of playing coldly—as he did conducting.

Several conductors influenced Thomas's development. The most important, he said, was Karl Eckert, who directed Sontag's touring orchestra. Eckert "was a man of the world and had moved in good society . . . educated . . . a gentleman, a high-grade musician, violinist, composer and last but not least the only really fully equipped and satisfactory conductor who visited this country during [the early 1850s]. All of the rest were more or less 'time beaters.' "[7] Thomas credited him with laying the foundation for his career. Eckert made great demands on his players, maintained unusually strict order at rehearsals, and gave principals responsibility for their sections. He appointed Thomas principal second violin, giving the ambitious young musician the opportunity to lead others for the first time. Thomas showed sound judgment in his admiration for Eckert, who subsequently became kapellmeister of the Vienna State Opera and later the Berlin State Opera.

Another conductor from whom Thomas learned much, even if he was reluctant to acknowledge it, was the eccentric Louis Antoine Jullien, who came to the United States for several months in 1853. Musically brilliant, the French musician was also a bit of a poseur, with absurd airs and pretensions. He dressed flamboyantly—he always wore white gloves—used a jeweled baton, and stood on a crimson podium edged with gold. Jullien brought a cadre of outstanding European players with him and, together with the best musicians he could find in New York, put together an orchestra of 100 that eclipsed even the Germanian Society in quality. Thomas, a member of the first violin section, was so put off by the conductor's bizarre behavior, however, that a half century later, unsoftened by the passage of time, he labeled Jullien a "musical charlatan." He was, of course, the exact opposite of Jullien. Staid and reserved, he carried himself even as a young man with great dignity and loathed attracting attention to himself. Thomas was equally reserved when conducting, which led some to say that he lacked temperament. He would not be the last of the "unflamboyant" masters of the podium to suffer this criticism.

Jullien went in for spectacles, the "Fireman's" Quadrille being the most notorious. At the beginning of a concert the audience was told "that there might be some startling effects . . . but no one need be afraid, all would end well." Then, when the audience was effectively lulled into "reposeful security, the clang of real fire-bells was heard; people jumped from their seats. . . . fire and flames were . . . bursting from the roof." As the audience calmed down, firemen stormed into the concert hall carrying hoses and ladders, which they duly climbed. They squirted water, broke glass, and did everything possible to give a realistic air to the proceedings. In the meantime the orchestra played "fortissimo through every possible diminished seventh that could be raked up out of the musical scale." The noise and confusion of the "Fireman's" Quadrille caused near panic. Some people fainted, others laughed. "Finally the fire was put out, the firemen with their machines retired, and the orchestra artistically prepared the audience for a song of praise and thanksgiving which came in the shape of Old Hundred (the Doxology), played and sung and joined in by the well-pleased audience. It was a *ne plus ultra* of realistic music."[8]

Excessive showmanship notwithstanding, Jullien knew what to do with an orchestra. He popularized good music with a fine group of musicians and a prudent mixture of the serious and the light, much like Gungl had five years earlier. Houses were full wherever he played. In Boston, he gave all-Beethoven and all-Mendelssohn evenings; he believed—accurately—that the city was up to it. He also programmed a number of American works at his concerts, more in his one short visit than the New York Philharmonic did in its first ten years. The *New York Herald* spoke glowingly of his orchestra's variety in dynamics and tone color, which, evidently, other New York groups lacked: "Jullien extracts not only a *piano* passage but a *forte*. A *forte* is not simply loudness, but it is a great body of sound balanced and varied in its resonance."[9] He whetted the public's appetite for orchestral music and effectively dropped seeds for orchestral growth in America's hinterlands. Young Theodore Thomas was on hand to see it done.

In 1854, when Thomas was nineteen, he was elected to the Philharmonic Society of New York. The society was made up of the cream of the city's players, and he was proud to be given a place in its first violin section, but from the beginning he was critical of the society's policies. Now in its twelfth year, it still gave but four concerts annually; he thought that it could and should give many more. Members were known to skip rehearsals and concerts with impunity if more lucrative jobs beckoned—a cavalier approach to concert giving that was unacceptable to the serious young violinist who was developing his own ideas on how orchestras should function and progress. Thomas made his feelings known to his colleagues, thus beginning a long and controversial relationship with America's first orchestra.

Soon after his election to the Philharmonic Society, Thomas met pianist William Mason, and the two musicians became fast friends. Six years older than Thomas, Mason was the son of Lowell Mason, the Boston composer, organist, and music educator, and had had all of the advantages of being brought up in a musical, cultivated, and well-to-do New England family. He had just returned from abroad, where he had studied with Moscheles, Liszt, and other leading pianists and given recitals in Weimar, Prague, and Frankfurt. Mason wanted to present chamber music concerts in New York similar to Liszt's at Weimar. With the city's taste maturing, the time seemed ripe, and he asked Thomas to be his first violin. Thomas accepted eagerly.

Mason invited three impressive local players to be in his chamber group: Joseph Mosenthal, second violin, a pupil of Spohr at Cassel, a member of the Philharmonic, and an organist and choirmaster (he later conducted New York's Mendelssohn Glee Club); George Matzka, a German violist who would subsequently play with Thomas's orchestra and be its deputy conductor; and cellist Carl Bergmann, who had led the Germanians from 1850 until 1854, when he was elected co-conductor of the Philharmonic. Thomas, who already had mixed feelings about not having studied in Europe, thought himself inadequate next to these well-trained, sophisticated musicians with such enviable European backgrounds. Yet his skill as a violinist was clearly evident. He showed instinctively fine musical judgment as an ensemble player and helped to set programs that audiences liked, displaying at the age of twenty some marked leadership qualities that Mason, sponsor of the chamber concerts, welcomed and used. At first called the Mason and Bergmann Concerts, with Bergmann, the oldest and most experienced musician of the group, serving as director, they were renamed the Mason-Thomas Concerts after a two-year lapse. Thomas, with Mason's approval, took over from Bergmann, and the concerts flourished. Mosenthal and Matzka lived with this happily; Bergmann, understandably, had reservations.

The five musicians gave their first concert in New York on November 27, 1855. Mason and Thomas, determined to succeed, handed out programs on Union Square, the center of musical and theatrical activity.[10] Their efforts paid off, as several hundred people attended the concert—no small feat considering the music's limited appeal. Not only did the concert mark the debut of New York's most important chamber series for the next thirteen years, but it featured the American—and perhaps the world—premiere of the Trio in B Major by Johannes Brahms, one of Europe's brilliant young composers. Mason had obtained a copy of the work immediately after its publication the year before. As expected, the three musicians played with loving care. They knew what the lengthy work was about—its varied moods, freshness, and vitality—and approached it with romantic exuberance. Schubert's D Minor Quartet ("Death and the Maiden"), the "Evening Star" excerpt from *Tannhäuser*, a song by Otto Nicolai sung by tenor Otto Feder, and short piano pieces by Chopin and Heller preceded the Brahms.

Dwight's Journal of Music, a conservative Boston weekly that closely scrutinized American musical affairs from 1852 until 1881, credited Bergmann with training Mason's spirited young group, liked the Brahms, and noted about the Schubert that "it was the first appearance of the Quartet in public and after only six weeks of practice together I was prepared to make allowances for them. These, however, were unnecessary; in light and shade, in delicate pianissimos, careful diminuendos and crescendos, in boldness and vigor, the rendering . . . surpassed anything I have heard in America." [11]

Programming was Mason and Thomas's strong point: there was something for everyone—songs, piano pieces, and chamber works—but it was nearly always good music and was performed well. The concerts attracted a chamber music public whose taste improved steadily. For example, in 1861 the group had no compunction about programming complete quartets by Mozart and Schumann as well as Beethoven's Piano Sonata op. 31, no. 3 on the same concert. Its final New York program on April 11, 1868 (it continued to give concerts in other centers) consisted of Mozart's Quartet in D Minor K. 421, Beethoven's Sonata for Piano and Cello op. 5, no. 2, Schumann's Sonata for Piano in G Minor op. 22, and Mendelssohn's Octet.

In the spring of 1856, Bergmann, encouraged by the response to the Mason and Bergmann Concerts and the growing interest in serious music generally, conducted a series of orchestral programs with Thomas as concertmaster at the City Assembly Rooms on Broadway in Lower Manhattan. The hall was truly makeshift—the few good concert rooms in New York were too expensive for adventurous, impecunious conductors who had to take full responsibility for their concerts—but it did not dampen the orchestra's zeal to play well. Bergmann chose works similar to those played by the Philharmonic—Mozart symphonies, Schubert's Symphony in C Major, Beethoven's Symphonies no. 2 and 7, and works by Mendelssohn, Haydn, Nicolai, and Wagner. Happily, the audiences were large and appreciative, and although the series was short-lived—one spring season only—it was an orchestral feast reminiscent of the days of Louis Jullien.

The Bergmann series was important for Thomas, whose success as soloist in Mendelssohn's Concerto at its April 13 concert put him in the very front rank of the city's violinists. As the orchestra's concertmaster, he worked closely with Bergmann and learned much about conducting from him. Bergmann was a natural musician with superior intuition, and Thomas was aware and appreciative of this quality, although he was disturbed that Bergmann was so relaxed, genial, and permissive with his orchestras. Thomas thought that such behavior by a conductor encouraged careless and undisciplined playing. He saw the conductor as more of a martinet who kept a distance from the musicians and whose word was law.

Years later, intentionally or not, Thomas disassociated himself from Bergmann, who had become an alcoholic, and was accused of not acknowledging his debt to the older musician and of failing to help him when help was needed. (Frederick Bergner, the principal cellist of the Philharmonic, replaced Bergmann in the Mason-Thomas group in 1861.) The two men were worlds apart in conducting, life-style, and demeanor. Thomas admired self-control, which Bergmann decidedly lacked. A realist, Thomas dealt positively with problems, while Bergmann was impractical, a dreamer. An achiever concerned with self-realization and having a meaningful life, Thomas, in the end, may have lacked compassion.

By the end of the 1850s, Thomas was leading a rich and varied professional life. He played regularly with the Philharmonic and other orchestras and was the concertmaster of the Italian opera orchestra at the new Academy of Music on Fourteenth Street, whose doors had opened for the first time on October 2, 1854, with a performance of Bellini's *Norma*. The elaborate hall seated well over 4,000 people and would be New York's principal opera house —and, on occasion, concert hall—for the next thirty years. Located on prime real estate, the academy's backers (wealthy local businessmen) promised to run it on a nonprofit basis for the good of the city's artistic life, if the city granted them special property concessions. In fact, the owners proved to be greedy landlords who charged lessees exorbitant rents and demanded gratis a large number of boxes for their own use, for all attractions. Because of this, lessees rarely realized enough income from ticket sales to meet expenses, much less make a profit.

There was no resident opera company as such in the Empire City. Instead, enterprising, profit-seeking concert managers formed makeshift companies for which they booked theaters like the Academy of Music. Managers took the financial risks themselves, much as orchestral conductors like Bergmann did. Depending on their knowledge, skill, and luck, opera managers could make or lose a fortune in a season. Opera was "show business."

Bernard Ullman, Thomas's employer at the academy, had made his managerial reputation in 1846 by directing the first American concert tour of the Austrian-French pianist Henri Herz. One of the more successful American impresarios, the imaginative and volatile Ullman put Thomas in charge of hiring and firing his orchestra's musicians. Thomas, who knew good playing from bad, took to the job, and Ullman's orchestra thus sounded first-class at all times. Cleverly, Thomas deliberately engaged newly arrived musicians from Europe who were usually in dire straits and thus gained their lasting respect and loyalty for giving them their first opportunity in the United States. Some would make up the nucleus of his own orchestra a few years later.

In addition to gaining experience in managing orchestras, Thomas's work at the Academy of Music taught him about the inner workings of opera and that a company's success or failure depended far more than it should have on its principal female singer(s). The public adored them in much the same way it does film and television stars today. Good or bad box-office returns hinged on the prima donna, who earned disproportionately large fees compared to other company singers. Performances were, inevitably, geared to presenting her in a favorable light, and in general she sang as she wished, adding vocal pyrotechnics—often with little discrimination—to please her public. If conductor, orchestra, manager, and the rest of the company did not agree with the prima donna—or worse, did not obey her—she might walk off the stage, cancel contracts, or join a rival company. Under the circumstances, presenting an opera as a valid representation of the composer's and librettist's intention was a secondary objective of an opera manager. Thomas, much as he admired great singers—and most prima donnas of the time were great singers—resented their power and especially their abuse of it. This colored his attitude toward opera and, even though he would conduct it in later years, he may never have believed in it enough to do it convincingly.

Luigi Arditi, an Ullman conductor and composer of the famed "Il bacio," was a virtuoso pianist and competent violinist who had trained in Italy and conducted in Havana, Cuba, before coming to New York in 1854. Arditi believed that singers did their best if they felt unencumbered by conductors and orchestras. If he did not like what they were doing, he would find a mutually agreeable middle ground, but for him it was the singing that mattered. Thomas, who learned much from Arditi, mistook his deference to singers for servility. Arditi's reasoning and musical dedication were too subtle for Thomas, who saw the conductor as the central musical figure in any ensemble, commanding at all times. Later, when Thomas conducted singers, he would constantly be criticized for his inflexibility and lack of rapport with them.

Another Thomas teacher was Carl Anschütz, who also conducted for Ullman. A native of Koblenz, Germany, Anschütz conducted in London before coming to New York in 1857. Although his strength was German opera, he knew Italian opera well and shared his knowledge willingly with his ambitious concertmaster. Anschütz explained to Thomas the principles behind bow markings in string parts, doubling of instruments, and other "tricks of the trade."

And, finally, there was Theodor Eisfeld, formerly kapellmeister at Wiesbaden and later director of the Concerts Viviennes in Paris. Eisfeld shared the Philharmonic's conducting with Carl Bergmann until 1865 and evidently showed Thomas all of the things a conductor should *not* do. According to Thomas, Eisfeld buried his nose in the score, kept time mechanically, and lacked authority.

Obviously, learning to conduct meant on-the-job training; it was all that Thomas could hope for. Formal training did not exist; as an art and a craft, conducting was still in its infancy. Thomas's classroom was the orchestra, where he observed and assessed the strengths and weaknesses of his conductors. It was an uncommon route to the podium, since most aspiring conductors were pianists—an instrument Thomas never learned to play—who coached singers and subsequently conducted them in opera houses or concert halls. Orchestral conducting was more typically an ancillary activity for conductors, and not many did it well.

There were advantages in coming out of the orchestra, namely, Thomas learned the importance of effective orchestral rehearsal procedures and the need for good intonation, precision, balance, and blend, as well as how to achieve them uncompromisingly. Orchestral musicians value conductors who make much of these matters. Thomas's orchestral experience also taught him the fundamentals and importance of programming for the time in which he lived. As an orchestral violinist who played a great deal of music of all kinds, good and bad, he took note of how audiences responded, of how factors like pacing a concert program, mixing the serious and the light, the fast and the slow, and so on, affected their responses. No other conductor in his time would have a surer instinct for pleasing the public without pandering to it.

Like all great conductors, Thomas was a natural leader who, even as a young man, exuded authority on and off the podium. He would "rule" his players, however benevolently, throughout his entire career and brook no interference from anyone, even unions. A benevolent despot, Thomas had early developed a jaundiced view of "democratic" orchestras because of his work at the Philharmonic, which had improved little in its first twenty years because it had no conductor who insisted on consistently good and disciplined playing and 100-percent attendance at rehearsals and concerts. The society elected its conductors by ballot on an annual basis, and if Philharmonic players considered a conductor's behavior too autocratic, they might not re-elect him. Younger and more musically demanding musicians like Thomas pressed for better leadership, but to no avail; the "old guard" would not change its ways. However, its attitude helped clarify and firm up Thomas's views on the subject as he approached his debut as a conductor. Implementing these ideas would set a pattern that other conductors of American orchestras followed for almost a century.

On April 20, 1859, Theodore Thomas replaced Carl Anschütz as conductor at the Academy of Music just minutes before the curtain was to go up on Donizetti's *Lucrezia Borgia*. The composer's *La favorite* was originally scheduled to open that evening, but for undisclosed reasons it was postponed. (William Mason said that the first opera Thomas conducted was Halévy's *La Juive*, on December 7, 1860. Mason was present when the message came from the academy asking Thomas to conduct the work: "[Thomas] thought for a moment, then said 'I will'. He rose quickly, got himself into his dress suit, hurried to the Academy . . . and conducted the opera as if it were a common experience." [12] Mason may have had the circumstances right but the opera and date were wrong. George P. Upton claimed in his *Musical Memories* that Thomas actually conducted a performance of "Consecration of the Temple," Anton Emil Titl's cantata, in Chicago in March 1859. [13] When did Thomas first conduct? The mystery remains unsolved.)

This initial appearance, a personal triumph for Thomas, led to more formal assignments, the first being on April 29, 1859, when he did *La favorita*. However, conducting Italian opera was not his strong point, and he mainly deputized for other conductors at the academy for the next three years. His strength lay in orchestral conducting, and his debut, although far less dramatic, was not long in coming. Without any financial backing, Thomas rented the two-year-old Irving Hall, a nondescript, already rundown building just off Union Square, to conduct an orchestral concert on May 13, 1862. He hired an orchestra of forty, engaged several soloists and an amateur choir, the Teutonic Choral Society, and, thanks to his experience with the Mason-Thomas concerts, directed the advertising and ticket selling. The concert notice that Thomas prepared, so awkwardly Victorian in its style and content, said in part, "To this concert [Thomas] would beg leave to call your attention, as it is his determination to make it one of the finest as well as the most popular Vocal and Instrumental Concerts of the Season." Of the program it said, "In alluding to these novelties [new or rarely heard music], the [sponsor] scarcely considers it necessary to say that the solos will be rendered by Vocalists and Instrumentalists of the most established reputation." [14]

The program was typical of what Thomas would present for years to come —a mixture of daring and prudence that would not just please the public but challenge, educate, and uplift it. The daring part was the first American performance of Wagner's Overture to *The Flying Dutchman*. Wagner was already the most controversial composer of the day and would be so for at least the next two decades. Much of the New York press thought his music unattractive, yet the *World* grudgingly agreed that Thomas had chosen wisely: "Most of the audience expected dreary wastes of dissonant harmony and were agreeably surprised to find not merely defined ideas but actual bits of melody." [15] The *New York Daily Tribune* disagreed: "It was ingeniously destitute of melody. Ghastly rumpus was its main feature. The violins should have been four times as numerous to outweigh the brass, and bring out the rapid passages distinctly." [16] The latter comment was well taken, but a small string section was all Thomas could afford.

Both the *Tribune*—the most influential morning daily—and the *Herald*—the morning daily with the largest circulation—offered unqualified praise for Thomas's performance of excerpts from Meyerbeer's *Struensee*. [17] (Meyerbeer's reputation was at its zenith in both the Old World and the New.) As for Thomas's conducting in general, the press seemed to agree that he knew what he was doing and had matters under control. It was noted that Irving Hall was only three-quarters full, despite a substantial number of complimentary ticket holders, and there was speculation that the one-dollar admission price was too high. All in all, though, the *New York Daily Transcript* summed up the evening as "undoubtedly the most intellectual and artistic musical offering of the season." [18] Encouraged, Thomas booked a repeat concert for four months hence, again at Irving Hall (which was slated for renovation over the summer). [19]

The hall's improvements, an orchestra augmented to sixty players, lower ticket prices with a fifty-cent maximum, and the May concert's press reviews resulted in an almost full house for Thomas's second concert on September 19. He did a symphony of the little-known C. P. E. Bach, composed in 1776 and described as "a venerable old composition of an *Allegro, Largo,* and *Presto*—and the model Haydn loved, and which has come down to this day only somewhat extended by other composers." [20] *Dwight's Journal of Music,* which considered itself expert in authentic performance practices, would have preferred "to hear the work played by a small orchestra of twelve instruments *obligato,* as intended by Bach," but was otherwise pleased. Choir and orchestra did the Meyerbeer excerpts again (Thomas was to use choirs frequently, for they provided variety in the program and helped attendance). Mme. d'Angri replaced Mme. de Lussan, a French opera singer and teacher, as the vocal artist—"she received full encores in both," *Dwight's* reported [21]—and William Mason, the piano soloist, did a transcription of Meyerbeer's "Schiller" March and his own "Concert Galop" to round off the evening.

The two concerts left Thomas exhilarated and inspired him to set his course for the future. He said, forty years later, "[I planned] to devote my energies to the cultivation of instrumental music." What the country needed "to make it musical was a good orchestra and plenty of concerts within reach of the people." [22] He produced both. His orchestra would travel across the land giving programs at once interesting and full of variety, highlighting contrasts in mood, tempo, style, and color. He would play music of composers, both old and new, who would capture the listeners' fancy—on first or repeated hearings —and avoid those who would not or did not. Audiences would respond to his programs; they would be programs that "worked."

The young conductor's new fame catapulted him into the leadership of the Brooklyn Philharmonic Society, for which he conducted three concerts in its 1862–63 series. Brooklyn was still an independent city with several fine theaters and its own Academy of Music, completed in 1861, that surpassed any New York opera house or concert hall. Its largely middle-class, educated population avidly supported good music. Formed in 1857, the society functioned much like the Philharmonic Society in London (the Royal Philharmonic after 1912): its members subscribed annually to a fixed number of orchestral concerts at which a conductor, engaged by the society's board, presided over an orchestra of his own choosing.

Brooklyn's Philharmonic took its work seriously. Thomas could not have agreed more with its charter, which expressed well the prevalent Victorian views of art and morality: "The first duty of every community is to advance its own moral and spiritual well-being, and that every plan and purpose of material prosperity should be made to harmonize with this object and to promote its accomplishment." To this end the society promoted "pure and elevated recreations for the people [to further] art, which when removed from vicious association and consecrated to the utterance of noble sentiment, is lifted out of the category of mere amusements, and becomes an educational influence of the highest order."[23]

The society thrived from the start. Its conductor, Theodor Eisfeld, with players from the New York Philharmonic, gave concerts of music by Haydn, Mozart, Beethoven, and other German masters—symphonies, overtures, suites, and assorted short pieces for soloists and orchestra. Apparently, Eisfeld was unavailable for the complete 1862–63 season, and so the society turned to Thomas. Thomas used his Irving Hall orchestra, which helped give the group some degree of permanence. He conducted Beethoven's Symphonies no. 1 and 5 and Mozart's Symphony in G Minor, K. 550 (at least one major work per concert), along with shorter pieces, much as Eisfeld did. In one concert he played Beethoven's "Kreutzer" Sonata with pianist Robert Goldbeck, proving that he was still an active violinist worthy of attention. Although by today's standards the programs seem like a potpourri, they were well planned, substantial, and gave Thomas the much-needed opportunity to conduct before a serious and critical audience.

Teresa Carreño, a gifted nine-year-old Venezuelan pianist, was the soloist at Thomas's first Brooklyn concert, on December 13, 1862. Destined to be one of the great artists of her generation, she had made her debut at the New York Academy of Music on November 25, and the overwhelming audience response led to five more recitals there. It was the same in Boston, where she was booked for two concerts and then gave twelve. A singer, composer, and, on occasion, conductor, she would marry four times, three to brilliant musicians: violinist Emile Sauret, baritone Giovanni Tagliapetra, and pianist Eugen d'Albert. Her fourth husband was Tagliapetra's younger brother Arturo.

Thomas had met Carreño shortly after her arrival in New York. He played the violin frequently with the child at her home and evidently was moved to tears by her extraordinary musicianship.[24] He was not alone in this. Her performance so enraptured the usually reserved Brooklynites that they kept her playing encores until after midnight. They liked their new conductor, too, and it was a heady time for both artists. When their paths crossed again in later years, they recalled well the pure joy of this early association.

The enterprising Thomas gave his Second Annual Vocal and Orchestral Concert at Irving Hall on May 9, 1863, almost a year to the day since his debut concert. His reputation had grown in the intervening twelve months, as had Irving Hall's, which, with its renovations, was now a busy concert venue. The young conductor enlarged his orchestra to eighty and programmed Beethoven's Symphony no. 5 and the first American performance of Berlioz's *Harold in Italy*. The Beethoven performance was lauded; he was everyone's favorite composer, and Thomas clearly did his music with feeling, understanding, and dedication. His choice of *Harold*, however, like Wagner's Overture the preceding year, reflected his policy to do new music of quality even if some might not like it at the outset. Thomas had identified the genius of the uneven Berlioz and boldly brought him before a public oriented to German music. The violist was Eduard Mollenhauer, who, like several other outstanding instrumentalists, had come to the United States with Louis Jullien ten years earlier and stayed. As anticipated, the press had reservations about *Harold* as a fully realized work but was grateful to Thomas for programming it.

Public response to the evening was sufficiently impressive to convince Thomas to launch a full-blown series of popular musical matinees on ten Saturdays at Irving Hall, commencing October 24, 1863. Admission was set at fifty cents. The programs would contain a careful mix of good music and soloists, and the inspired Thomas chose the Creole pianist and composer Louis Gottschalk, then at the height of his popularity, as soloist for the first three concerts. Born in New Orleans, Gottschalk had studied in Paris and toured Europe, North and South America, and the Caribbean during his short lifetime (he died in 1869 at age forty). An impressive performer, he also had good looks, grace, and crowd-pleasing affectations. For Thomas, he played his own works and transcriptions to a receptive audience.[25]

The matinees caught on, and tickets sold well. Some of the music was undeniably frothy and light—"Oberländler" for two violins (Thomas was one of them) and the waltz "Hydropathen," both by Gungl, and "The Dearest

Spot" by Wrighton, with Jenny Kempton, soprano, as soloist—but Thomas began each concert, except the first, with a major work such as Mozart's Symphony no. 39 and the *Haffner* Symphony, Haydn's *Drum Roll* Symphony, and Beethoven's Symphony no. 2. By the time the season concluded on December 26, he had done three symphonies by Mozart, three by Beethoven, one by Haydn, and two by the Danish composer Niels Gade, as well as three overtures by Beethoven, three by Weber, and several others by a variety of composers. Transcriptions of operatic excerpts were given at almost every concert, as were works—thirteen in all—by the popular Strauss family, including Johann, Sr., Johann, Jr., Joseph, and Eduard. New York had not heard orchestral programs of such diversity and played so well since Jullien's time. Thomas's fellow musicians gratefully gave him a testimonial concert in April 1864, the first of many such tributes.

In the midst of Thomas's other successes, the Mason-Thomas concerts had been extended to nearby cities, particularly to Farmington, Connecticut, where Karl Klauser, the music director of Miss Porter's School for Young Ladies and a close friend of Thomas, diligently promoted the cause of good music. It was at Miss Porter's, in 1864, that Thomas met Minna Rhodes, a young and cultivated member of the teaching staff and the daughter of a prominent Brooklyn Episcopalian minister. William Mason wrote:

> [Thomas] asked me to take a short walk with him, as he had something serious to talk to me about. I could tell from his manner that he was in a very serious mood. We had walked only a few steps before he turned and asked me what I thought of Miss Rhodes . . . as a possible wife for him. I was astonished at the question and told him immediately what I thought. "Your education has been so different from hers," I said, "that I don't know whether you will be happy or not. Miss Rhodes is thoroughly American—for instance goes to church on Sundays—and I don't believe that you ever went to church in your life. It seems to me that your rearing has been too different for you to be happy." But they were married, and I am afraid that Mrs. Thomas had some hard times at the outset. Thomas was very determined and firm then, although he grew softer in later years.[26]

The wedding took place on August 30, 1864, when Thomas was almost thirty. Years later, his second wife, Rose, described Minna as

> a remarkably brilliant woman [who] had received the most thorough educational training of the day. Her fine mind and accurate knowledge . . . attracted Thomas, for he was always an admirer of intellectuality, rather than beauty, in women. "I don't care for so-called pretty women," he said. "What I admire is character and intelligence. If a woman has these, she does not

need beauty, but I will confess that if a woman of character and intellect has beauty in addition, it is like a lamp shining through an alabaster vase. But this is a rare combination."[27]

Whether Minna Rhodes Thomas was beautiful or not, the union was a happy one. It helped to "Americanize" the young conductor, changing him gradually from a rough-and-ready "Dutchman" to a refined gentleman. His fellow musicians saw less of him socially, thus leading some to accuse him of being snobbish, especially when he reproved them for crude behavior on or off the concert platform. Generally, he did not get along with people easily and gracefully. He was markedly stern, aloof, and impersonal, a very private person, although on rare occasions he could let his hair down with a flourish. William Mason was his first real musical friend and one of the few—if not the only one—in his lifetime to call him by his Christian name. Mason penetrated Thomas's formidable reserve but knew how far he could go. Thomas accepted friendship but not camaraderie. It was easy to respect him but hard to love him.

Thomas was especially private about his family and rarely spoke of them to others. As a result, we know practically nothing about them. The same was true of his parents, brothers, and sisters, of whom he saw little as he grew older. Minna Thomas never complained about her husband's long absences because of concert tours but remained discreetly in the background, in keeping with her role as a well-bred mid-century Victorian wife and mother. She bore him three sons and two daughters and was forever sympathetic and dutiful. Thomas neither confided in his wife nor sought her counsel, which might have eased his suffering, given the infighting of the musical world. She might also have helped him to be more mellow, less candid and outspoken, less brusque and impatient, especially with the press. Nineteenth-century newspapers were notoriously partial, and Thomas's behavior made him fair game. He was praised by the press for his achievements, but it was often faint praise. Thomas resented bad reviews of his concerts more than most performing artists, and later in life he foolishly claimed that he did not read the reviews, thus annoying the press all the more.

With his first matinee series behind him, in January 1864 Thomas tried his hand as conductor of the newly organized English Opera Company. The company's future looked precarious from the start, with opera in English having been in decline for some years. *The Bohemian Girl*, by the popular Irish-born British composer Michael Balfe, opened the season at the Park Theater in Brooklyn on January 4 to a mixed reception, mainly due to mediocre singing and poor orchestral playing. Thomas's conducting, however, was deemed exemplary, although "even his experienced baton failed now and then to keep the instruments steady. [He] labored felicitously to assist the *debutantes* so far as lay in his power and by his attention and coolness exerted a beneficial influence over the entire performance."[28]

Thomas's growing reputation and prowess as a conductor did not prevent the company from getting more unfavorable reviews in New York later in January. It seemed as if nothing the group did could please the critics. At the root of the company's problem was that, as far as the press and, to a degree, the public were concerned, opera in English could not be as good as opera in Italian. Such attitudes resulted from Europe's pervasive influence over American musical life—one heard Italian music in the opera house and German music in the concert hall. Irish-born William Vincent Wallace's *Maritana* followed *Bohemian Girl* but did no better, closing in mid-February.

The English Opera Company reorganized in the spring and, again with Thomas conducting, produced *Notre Dame of Paris*, a new opera by the American composer William Henry Fry. Fry's first opera, *Aurelia the Vestal*, was never produced; his second, *Leonora*, was presented in Philadelphia in 1845, possibly the first public performance of an opera on the "grand" Italian scale, à la Bellini and Donizetti, by an American. *Leonora* lacked dramatic impact and failed miserably at the box office; and it did no better when it was revived in Italian in 1858 with Carl Anschütz conducting. Fry wrote a number of other works and was also a journalist with the *New York Daily Tribune* for some years. The series of lectures that he gave in New York in 1852–53, in which he urged American composers to break free of European domination and look to the New World for inspiration, attracted wide attention.

Notre Dame, Italianate in style, opened promisingly on May 4, 1864, at the American Academy of Music in Philadelphia, an attractive new hall seating 2,900, with excellent acoustics. The opera used large forces that were controlled magnificently by Thomas: a chorus of 100 with "amateur aid," an orchestra of 60, a military band of 35, and a ballet and auxiliary corps of 165. The production had elaborate scenery, including a church organ "loaned and erected" on the stage of the academy. There was great interest in the performance, and the publicity was well managed. Appeals to nationalism were used shamelessly to attract the public, but to no avail. Audiences were small, and the press was unfavorable; at best, the opera was a succès d'estime.[29] Fry, embittered, died a few months later.

Despite his increasingly busy conducting schedule, Thomas retained his connection with the Philharmonic Society of New York, playing occasionally in its first violin section. The relationship became awkward, however, because of the society's concern over the excellent public response to Thomas's matinee concerts and their effect on its own subscription series. Still, it asked him to be soloist in Mendelssohn's Concerto at its November 6, 1864 concert. Thomas played faultlessly and, it seems, with more expression and emotion than usual. *Dwight's* commented: "We have sometimes fancied that it was as if he were afraid lest his hearers might suspect that he also felt as a man feels —and ought to hide it—but on Saturday, as Beethoven was accustomed to say, he '*Knopfte sich auf*' and in future his reserve will be useless, for now we know he is not made of stone." [30]

The press, well disposed as it was to Thomas, had little praise for the Philharmonic, which had had to raise its subscription prices to help meet the higher rents of the Academy of Music, where it had moved that fall from Irving Hall. Newspapers felt the increase unfair, especially since they thought the playing inferior to Thomas's matinee orchestra. Thomas was the kind of leader the Philharmonic needed but would not seek out. And so, after two decades of allegiance, large numbers of the society's supporters chose to subscribe instead to Thomas's concerts. He represented the future of music in New York—no one was more sure of that than Thomas himself.

2

Spreading the Gospel

Theodore Thomas made a significant step forward in his development as a conductor and a leader of American musical life in the fall of 1864 by initiating an evening concert series, or symphony soirees. At the matinees, he had shown his conducting skill, the high quality of his orchestra, and his ability to bring music to life better than any other conductor of his day. But these concerts were only a first step in achieving his goal of bringing great music to the people. At the soirees, he would address *serious* music almost exclusively.

Full of self-confidence, thanks to the success of the matinees, Thomas beat the drum loudly and somewhat immodestly on behalf of his new five-concert series. Advance notices promised an ensemble "the proficiency of which cannot be surpassed," programs "as effective and attractive as possible," and concerts "in every respect worthy of the Metropolis of America." [1] Given that these promises might very well be fulfilled, the series competed seriously with the Philharmonic's five concerts for the symphonic subscriber's dollars, especially since Thomas charged only five dollars for a season subscription while the society charged eight. In addition, Thomas planned premieres of eight new works (compared to none by the Philharmonic): Part 2 of Berlioz's *Romeo and Juliet*, Beethoven's Triple Concerto, Mozart's Symphony *Concertante* for Violin and Viola, and shorter works by Schumann, Bach, and three lesser-known composers—Joachim Raff (Thomas would do his music frequently in the future), Franz Lachner, and Frederic Ritter, an Alsatian musician who had settled in the United States. Thomas's orchestra was considered superior in performance to the Philharmonic, which the soirees would underscore.

After two brief rehearsals—Thomas wanted more but could not afford to pay for them—the series opened on December 3, 1864, with three major works: Beethoven's Symphony no. 8, *Romeo and Juliet*, and Chopin's Piano Concerto in F Minor, with Sebastian Bach Mills as soloist. As if the program were not long enough, the soprano Fanny Raymond, Frederic Ritter's wife and a writer and translator of some repute, also sang several short vocal pieces. The orchestra, not unexpectedly, played raggedly, but the press, in a positive mood, still found good things to say about the intent young conductor. The *New York Herald* praised his adventurous programming, and *Dwight's*, noting that the audience was prestigious musically and critically, predicted that with more rehearsal "his mission would be satisfactorily fulfilled." The *Times* took another tack. Relishing the opportunity to stir up a feud between Thomas and the Philharmonic, it complimented him on his use of *two* harps in the Berlioz while noting that the "stingy" Philharmonic usually did not bother to provide even one when it was required.[2]

Thomas's first soiree series coincided fortuitously with the final winter of the Civil War. The growing optimism in the North as the terrible conflict drew to a close was reflected in increased activity in the performing arts, including music. The preceding three years of war had not lessened attendance at plays and concerts in New York—full houses had been more the rule than the exception, thanks to the material prosperity that the war had brought to the city—but now people were thinking more concretely and constructively about building for the future. The growing serious music public saw Thomas's efforts to build an orchestra and concert series in this light. It liked his missionary spirit: he was the exemplary Victorian—noble (a favorite word of the time), sincere, disciplined, and an idealist concerned with teaching music to others and bringing to life the latent musicality he ascribed to all Americans.

Responding to Thomas's growing popularity, New York's *Playbill*, a theatrical weekly, did a "Musical Portrait" of him on January 11, 1865. It credited him not only with improving the musical taste of the community but with outdoing native-born Americans in "progressive impulses. . . . An enemy to routine, active, enterprising, sanguine, [he brings] courage to any undertaking in which he thinks he can advance the interests of art." *Playbill* lauded him for his talent and, significantly, for his "respectability of character."[3] The *Orpheus: A Repository of Music, Art and Literature*, a monthly journal that had begun publication in 1865, was also pleased with his work and praised his programs for their length (short), "unity of character," and balance between classical and romantic. It liked his pioneering spirit and values generally, concluding that "personal hard work and great sacrifice of labour and money have enabled Mr. Thomas to be the regenerator of concert programmes in this city."[4]

The young conductor seemed to have few if any shortcomings, until one in particular was singled out by critics: his inability to compose and, by extension, his lack of a European musical education, which would have assumedly taught him this skill. Important soloists and conductors of the day were expected to compose. Was Thomas, therefore, really important, or was he just some New World musical upstart who knew how to train an orchestra but otherwise was not to be taken seriously? Not that Thomas didn't try to compose. He wrote a number of short works in the ensuing years, but all were received badly. He did, however, show talent for transcribing keyboard works for orchestra, a case in point being his orchestral version of Bach's Toccata in F Major ("first time in America"), played at the second soiree on January 7, 1865. That led to other transcriptions, several of which could well be revived today.[5]

The second soiree, which took place a month later, was better prepared than the first. Besides the Bach, Thomas did Schumann's Symphony no. 2 (he loved Schumann's orchestral works, despite their faults) and Beethoven's "Emperor" Concerto, with Carl Wolfsohn as soloist. Wolfsohn, a leading German-born Philadelphia pianist (he later moved to Chicago) played chamber music frequently with Thomas. The *Herald* was rapturous: "Soirees are musical luxuries which leave one in a dream of melody for the interval elapsing between them." Other New York dailies were of the same opinion, although they expressed it more prosaically. *Watson's Weekly Art Journal*, however, criticized Thomas for letting Wolfsohn and soprano Jennie Van Zandt do solo pieces on the program without orchestra.[6] Thomas took note, and it was not long before nonorchestral pieces virtually disappeared from his programs, as they did increasingly from orchestral programs of other groups.

Thomas's major work at the third soiree was unfortunately the American premiere of Joachim Raff's *An das Vaterland*, an eighty-minute symphony that had been composed between 1859 and 1861, when Germany seemed on the brink of unification. It had won first prize over thirty-two other major symphonic entries in Vienna's Musikfreunde symphonic competition. In the program note, Raff offered his opinion that "Few Germans who have feeling and enthusiasm for their nation have been left by the events of these last years without a deep impression. . . . [The music] describes the lofty flight of the mind, deep power of thought, purity and gentleness and perseverance unto victory, as important elements in the natural disposition of the German."[7]

Pro-German as the musical press was, its members almost unanimously condemned the work as overblown, pretentious, and even dilettantish. The symphony was, although none said it, all too typical of the lengthy compositions emanating from central Europe by competent, unimaginative symphonists. Did Thomas, by programming the work, cater excessively to the German Americans among his subscribers? Most of them retained a love for their native land and hoped that it would soon be Europe's leading nation. The *New York World*, not interested in such speculations, observed mischievously that the members of the orchestra seemed delighted when the final notes of the tedious work were finally sounded.[8] To add to the concert's problems, Frederick Bergner, the cello soloist in Beethoven's Triple Concerto, had taken sick moments before he was to play, and another cellist had to be called in to sight-read the solo part. Thus, the third concert was a low point in the series; however, the final two, given later in the year, mirrored the success of the first two.

When the season concluded, colleagues and friends gave Thomas a testimonial concert with the admission receipts set aside to help pay outstanding soiree bills. One of the sponsors was William Steinway of the Steinway Piano Company. Already a Thomas advocate, Steinway would extricate him from several financial entanglements and related crises in the future. Another sponsor was Gustav Schirmer, the music publisher, who helped channel new European scores to Thomas before they reached other conductors. A third sponsor was Harvey Dodworth, member of a well-known New York musical family and leader of a prominent wind band, who had appreciated and counseled the talented young Thomas when he returned from his travels through the South in 1850. L. F. Harrison, the manager of the English Opera Company, Max Maretzek, the opera conductor, and Carl Anschütz were also there. Five soloists and sixty orchestral players donated their services, and Thomas himself conducted the orchestral pieces and also played the "Kreutzer" Sonata with William Mason. Clearly, Thomas had reached new heights in popularity with the musical fraternity and the public.

The soiree orchestra was soon known as the Theodore Thomas Orchestra, and its reputation grew. Now Thomas had to keep the orchestra together if it was to improve as an ensemble and become the cohesive, responsive instrument he envisaged. This meant finding work for it, even if the work was not all ideal. The group's next venture, therefore, was a series of summer concerts —the orchestra's first extended engagement—at Belvedere Lion Park, where it played three times weekly from June 4 to September 20, 1865. The concert hall was well ventilated, a must given New York's hot, humid summers, and had the ambiance of a German beer garden, with liberal supplies of beer and sausage. The concerts caught on, even though the audiences, which lived downtown, had to make a long journey north in slow, horse-drawn omnibuses (Belvedere was in Harlem, still a farming community).

Belvedere could afford only a thirty-piece orchestra, which played for about two and a half hours nightly, with two intermissions. On opening night, Thomas took no chances and did mainly light music; the "heaviest" works included "Fantasia" from *Tannhäuser*, a selection from Donizetti's *Don Sebastian*, an aria, "Cujus animam," from Rossini's *Stabat mater* (no soloist was mentioned; it might have been transcribed for orchestra), and the overtures to *La gazza ladra*, *Oberon*, and Auber's *Le domino noir*. The remainder of the program consisted of a march, a waltz, a polka, a potpourri, a galop, and a quadrille. In the next few concerts, Thomas squeezed in a Beethoven or Mozart symphony, hoping for an encouraging response; but it was not forthcoming, and the programs reverted to light music for the rest of the summer. On August 10, there was a special program with two orchestras taking part in a musical-military tableau, "A Day in Camp, or Recollections of the War"— not exactly high art.

Thomas was pleased with his Belvedere summer. When the series concluded, the orchestra played with far more polish than it had three months before. The concerts had exposed the group to thousands of listeners, many of whom would be attending more serious Thomas concerts in the fall. Start them with polkas and galops played well, and in a few months they would be asking for Beethoven and Schubert, said Thomas, and he was right. The summer concert would be an invaluable source of new audiences for the Thomas Orchestra for the next twenty-five years.

During that same summer of 1865, the Thomas Orchestra accompanied the Arion Society Choir at its annual picnic. The Arion was one of two leading New York German-American amateur choral societies—the other was the Liederkranz—and Thomas was eager to cement his relations with both, since their members were avid concertgoers who represented the cream of the German community (for example, William Steinway was active in the Liederkranz and one of many society members who generously supported worthy civic and cultural causes). Also, both choirs were excellent, and Thomas, looking ahead, planned to use them at his winter concerts.

In mid-July, Thomas was a judge at a week-long *Sängerfest* at the New York Academy of Music. This choral competition/festival of German-language choirs from all parts of the eastern United States, sponsored by the Arion, Liederkranz, and other German choral groups, attracted several thousand singers. Thomas was impressed by its scope, as he had been earlier by the more formal festivals of the Handel and Haydn Society of Boston, where the great oratorios of Handel, Haydn, and Mendelssohn were done. The Boston society's first festival had been held in May 1855, with a chorus of 600 and an orchestra of 78. Now, in 1865, following Abraham Lincoln's assassination, it held a still larger festival, with a theme of peace, unity, and healing. It lasted five days and played to thousands. Such large-scale festivals, so inspiring, set Thomas thinking: Why not a Thomas festival with the Thomas Orchestra and both English- and German-speaking choirs? Little did he know—or did he?— that he would be leading music festivals from coast to coast in less than two decades.

After Belvedere, Thomas took on a variety of miscellaneous engagements in order to keep his orchestra working. One involved accompanying the English soprano Euphrosyne Parepa and her fiancé, German violinist Carl Rosa, in several concerts. It was an important contact for Thomas, for Parepa and Rosa later formed the Carl Rosa Opera Company in Britain, a group that would commit itself to performing English opera. Its work would influence Thomas when he became similarly involved in American opera in the 1880s.

Thomas announced, with some self-effacement, the second soiree series in October. The notice summarized the soiree's first year, thanked supporters for their "liberal encouragement," and explained the series' progressive programming policy: "Whilst selecting freely from the great masters, the conductor has again adhered to the plan [of] submitting to public approval not only their lesser known works but others which belong to the modern school and have never been played in this country. . . . The latter represent the growth and effort of our own times, and are eclectically interesting for that reason. Their intrinsic merits, also, give them the right to be heard."[9] Thomas was talking primarily about Wagner, Liszt, and Berlioz. Convinced of their genius, he intended to perform their music as frequently as he saw fit, regardless of criticism.

Such boldness would not have had its reward without the orchestra's undeniably fine playing, for new music must be done well to be received well. On February 10, 1866, Thomas conducted the long-awaited—at least for Wagnerphiles—Prelude to Act 1 of *Tristan und Isolde*, its first reading in North America. As expected, the work stirred controversy. (The complete opera was not staged in New York until twenty years later.) The *Times*'s reaction was devastating: "It is absolutely without significance and unintelligible to the eye and unmeaning to the ear. Stripped of orchestral colour it would exhibit mere puerility. . . . That Wagner was thrust out of Munich after Tristan seems natural. No people can be expected to stand for it. We see nothing but pretentiousness, and that tendency to over-elaboration which always precedes decay."[10] But other defended it. Wagner himself became the central figure of strenuous debates in New York's musical circles, and the more Thomas played his music, the more vociferous were the debates. Thomas, sure of Wagner's genius, saw how much Beethoven had cast his symphonic spell over nineteenth-century German composers and thought it was unhealthy for so many of them to ape the master. Much as he revered Beethoven, he was convinced that composers of "new music" were needed to keep musical life viable, and he took it upon himself to put their work to the test. With a musical public at once more mature and catholic in its taste, this policy could not but make Thomas more popular.

Wagner and new music aside, Thomas's main concern was to find enough work for his orchestra to make it a permanent, full-time group. A summer series in 1866 at Koch's Terrace Garden, a recreation site cum restaurant, was a first step. Located on Third Avenue, between Fifty-eight and Fifty-ninth streets, Koch's was more central to the expected audience than Belvedere's and was partially enclosed, so that concerts could be given rain or shine. Thomas scheduled 100 programs there that summer, 70 more than at Belvedere. Proprietor Koch provided the site and the food and drink, while Thomas collected the concert admission fees, from which he paid the orchestra.

The situation was risky for Thomas, who credited himself with being a better businessman than he actually was. He was competing with Carl Bergmann's orchestra at Belvedere and Harvey Dodworth's concert band in Central Park (bands were already a popular alternative to orchestras at summer concerts), and he was charging higher prices, too. Fortunately, with an assist from the enclosure and Koch's superior beer and cigars, Thomas's concerts were the most popular. Bergmann and Dodworth simply lacked his commitment, dedication, and "touch"; nor were their groups as skillful as Thomas's. A Thomas beer garden concert was intended to be pleasurable *and* purposeful; talk or other distractions might well earn the culprit a rebuke from the platform.

The format for Thomas's summer program, which had evolved at Belvedere and was refined at the Terrace Garden, typically included twelves pieces in three parts: (1) march, overture, waltz, and operatic selection; (2) overture, symphonic movement, symphonic movement, and fantasia or solo; and (3) overture, waltz (or ländler), polka or solo, and quadrille, galop, or operatic selection.[11] An attention-getting piece began each part to alert the audience, who would usually be chatting away while drinking beer and munching pretzels. Overtures by Mozart, Beethoven, Weber, Mendelssohn, and Wagner were common. The Strausses were Thomas's favorite waltz composers and a reliable source for polkas, galops, and quadrilles, so popular with summer audiences. Offenbach, Kéler-Béla (Albert von Kéler), Joseph Gungl, Benjamin Bilse, and other good composers of light music also found their way into Thomas's programs. The three-part pattern, with occasional variations, was the norm at his summer concerts for years to come.

In keeping with his mission to develop ever-growing audiences for great music, Thomas programmed more challenging works at Terrace Garden than at Belvedere. Excerpts from operas by Verdi, Meyerbeer, Weber, Rossini, Gounod, Offenbach, and Donizetti were common, as were shorter movements from symphonies of the classical masters, which whetted the listeners' appetite for the next season of soirees. Thomas presented a "Mendelssohn Night," a "Beethoven Night," and a "Mozart Night," each time presenting several of the featured composer's works. The *Herald*, a steadfast Thomas supporter, reveled in the "enthusiasm . . . of the listeners, such genuine life and spirit in the playing of the performers, and such crowded audiences" as well as in the prominent public the concerts attracted: "On Friday night there were nearly two thousand persons present, the majority of whom were of a class whose rank might easily be determined from the number of equipages drawn up at the entrance, from the respect and attention paid to the music and the order that prevailed."[12] Notwithstanding these observations, class lines broke down at the informal Terrace Garden concerts, where the rich, the poor, and the middle class together enjoyed a summer evening of good music.

In his autobiography, Thomas could not resist recalling humorous incidents at Terrace Garden. "On one occasion . . . while playing the 'Linnet Polka,' I requested the piccolo players to climb up into the trees before the piece began. When they commenced playing from their exalted position in the branches, it made a sensation." On another occasion, in the "Carnival of Venice," his tuba player had gone into the shrubbery behind the audience. When he began to play, the police mistook him for a practical joker and tried to arrest him! "I shall never forget the comical scene, as the poor man fled toward the stage, pursued by the irate policemen, and trying to get in a note here and there, as he ran."[13]

As Thomas found more engagements for his players, he tightened his hold on them and increased his demands on their time. He required their attendance at all rehearsals, at a time when musicians customarily sent substitute players to rehearsals if scheduled times clashed with actual jobs in other places. Most conductors tolerated the use of substitutes, since rehearsals were not in-depth sessions but primarily for checking the accuracy of the orchestral parts and making sure that the orchestra could cope with the music without breaking down at the performance. Rehearsals were routine and uncreative, and conductors thus scheduled few of them, failing to see the need for more. But not Thomas. He was the first American conductor to rehearse music meticulously, to strive for appropriate style and expression, to show the orchestra how to get across his conception of the work at hand, no matter how long it would take. An efficient rehearser, he made his points with dispatch. And his musicians, instinctively sensing what he wanted, helped the process.

Successful as he was in giving rehearsals the time, attention, and attendance they deserved, Thomas failed in his attempts for exclusivity—that his orchestra members play for him and no one else. Rather arrogantly, if not without reason, he felt that other conductors let their musicians play without discipline, carelessly, sloppily, and that the ill effects rubbed off on their work for him. His plan was based on a doubtful assumption and destined to fail, especially since he could not as yet provide work on a year-round basis. He never gave up trying, however, and finally imposed an exclusivity of sorts on his players in his Chicago years, even though by then he had relaxed his views on the subject. One wonders what Thomas would think of present-day orchestras, which have an annual round of guest conductors to spell their resident conductor, who is usually guest-conducting elsewhere.

By the fall of 1866, it was clear that the Thomas Orchestra had become a fixture in New York's musical life and needed a *real* concert hall. This was provided by America's leading piano manufacturer, Steinway & Sons, whose instruments would win an international prize in Paris the next year. Steinway Hall was built to publicize the Steinway name, get the public to the company's showrooms adjacent to the hall on Fourteenth Street, opposite Irving Hall and the Academy of Music, and have great artists play the Steinway piano, thus endorsing its excellence. The hall had 2,100 seats, and although its stage was a marginally satisfactory sixty feet wide, its meager thirty-foot depth would be a constant problem for orchestras. Rumor had it that, in exchange for a pledge to always use Steinway pianos, Thomas was helped financially by Steinway. Although the latter did, in fact, lend or even give money to Thomas over the next twenty-five years, and offered preferred rates whenever the orchestra used Steinway Hall, it was never proved that Thomas made such a deal. The Steinway was undeniably the finest piano in the United States, and Thomas likely used it for that reason alone.

On October 30, 1866, Thomas conducted a gala concert to open the new hall. It was a disappointing evening, however, as there were serious shortcomings in the acoustics and the stage's size. Also, the hall was drab, its decor colorless; in fact, the Spartan confines made it seem more like a New England meetinghouse than a metropolitan concert hall. (Within two years, it would be renovated.) Yet Thomas was only mildly concerned with the hall's problems. What mattered was that he now had a home base, where he would experience his busiest season to date, and it put him on the way toward achieving his "permanent" orchestra.

Thomas fulfilled a staggering number of concert commitments. In addition to fifteen Wednesday night concerts at Steinway Hall and eleven Monday night concerts at the Brooklyn Academy of Music, he started a series of thirty-six Sunday night popular concerts at Irving Hall. The irreverent *Herald* welcomed this latest intrusion on the Lord's Day: "It is a relief to have some rational enjoyment on a Sunday evening without being obliged to listen to some Puritan individual droning out the hundredth Psalm, or undergoing the ordeal of a sermon with fifty subheads."[14]

Despite these popular concerts, Thomas had not forgotten his mission as great music's standard-bearer, which meant continuing his soirees, the proving ground for his orchestra and his programming, even though he lost money on them. One highlight of the 1866–67 series was a performance of Beethoven's Ninth Symphony, and he did both the "Eroica" and the Seventh Symphony later in the season. On the fourth soiree, he did his transcription of Liszt's "Mephisto" Waltz for the first time. When the audience hissed and booed the unfamiliar piece, Thomas turned to them and said, "I will give you five minutes to leave the hall. Then we shall play the waltz from beginning to end. Whoever wishes to listen without making a noise may do so. I ask all others to go out. I will carry out my purpose if I have to stand here until two o'clock in the morning. I have plenty of time."[15]

As if he were not busy enough, Thomas was appointed musical director of the Brooklyn Philharmonic for this same season. It meant still more work—and money—for the orchestra, as well as the opportunity to share rehearsals and performances of some of the big works he did at the soirees. There were five concerts, with public rehearsals preceding each one. The public rehearsals, common at the time, were in fact concerts, although the conductor could (but rarely did) stop the orchestra to review sections of works being done. These rehearsals were usually held in the afternoon and catered primarily to women; tickets cost less than for the actual concert. The press often reviewed a public rehearsal in lieu of the concert, although some conscientious critics would attend both if an important new work was being presented.

The Brooklyn programs had great variety, from Beethoven and Berlioz to "Lo, Hear the Gentle Lark," sung by Mme. Parepa-Rosa. An ample budget allowed for prominent American singers Thomas could not afford at his own concerts, such as mezzo-soprano Minnie Hauk (fourteen years old and still singing light soprano arias), soprano Clara Louise Kellogg, who would write disparagingly of Thomas's conducting in her memoirs, and mezzo-soprano Adelaide Phillips, as well as the French violin virtuoso Camilla Urso. The concerts went well, and the Brooklyn Philharmonic invited Thomas back the next year—and, in fact, each year until 1891, when he left New York for good.

All in all, it had been an astonishing year. Thomas had led his orchestra in over 200 concerts between September 1866 and April 1867. His musicianship, conducting skill, stamina, and staying powers had all been put to the test successfully. The same could be said of the Theodore Thomas Orchestra, which dominated the entertainment pages of New York's daily press, particularly in view of the 100 concerts it had given the previous summer. On March 13, 1867, there was yet another testimonial concert for Thomas, and, at the end of the season, the Brooklyn Philharmonic gave him a silver baton as a going-away present. Thomas was off to Europe for the summer to listen to orchestras, meet musicians, and in general broaden his horizons.[16]

Just before his departure, Thomas became embroiled in controversy at the annual elections of the New York Philharmonic. The society had recently changed its bylaws to allow Dr. R. Ogden Doremus, a popular chemist and nonmusician, to be nominated for president. Without warning, Thomas nominated George Bristow, a violinist in the orchestra, a competent organist and choirmaster, and a prolific composer who was bitter that the Philharmonic ignored his works as it did all American music. Thomas, who conducted what American music there was whenever the opportunity arose, reasoned that with Bristow as president, the society's attitude toward American music—and a number of other areas—might change. Thomas himself might then have greater influence at the Philharmonic, perhaps even replace Bergmann as conductor and lead the society out of its musical—and financial—doldrums.

If he did not think all these things when he nominated Bristow, others did, and they wondered if he was too ambitious, seeking too much power too soon. When Doremus won the election easily, Thomas realized he would have to wait to change the ways of America's oldest orchestra.[17]

Thomas's visit to Europe gave his ego a great boost.[18] He was delighted to find that his reputation had preceded him and that he had access to the continent's leading composers and conductors. He was particularly inspired by Johann Strauss, Jr., who conducted his own works, such as *The Beautiful Blue Danube*, while Thomas was in Vienna. Thomas had had a way with Strauss waltzes in the past, but after observing Strauss in action, he approached the waltzes with new ardor. In the years that followed, the Thomas Orchestra was unsurpassed when it played them. It was said that even Strauss knew this.[19]

During the trip, Thomas was unable to get an audience with Richard Wagner, in spite of being the master's leading North American disciple. He settled instead for the German pianist, conductor, and composer Hans von Bülow, the former husband of Wagner's new wife, Cosima. Thomas could not have done better, if one of his reasons for going to Europe was to meet important and stimulating personalities. He and the brilliant and articulate von Bülow not only had mutually penetrating and informative discussions but also found that they were kindred spirits: they approached music with the same fervor and unwillingness to compromise quality; and they both revered Beethoven, saw Wagner as the standard-bearer of music of the future, and shared a dislike for prima donnas and pretense generally among musicians. Similarities ceased when it came to temperament, for von Bülow was volatile and notoriously irascible, while Thomas was reserved and controlled. Neither man suffered fools gladly.

One lasting memory of his European trip was Thomas's meeting in Paris with the aging Berlioz, who thanked him for promoting his music in the United States and gave him an autographed copy of his *Requiem*. While in Paris, Thomas also heard the famed Pasdeloup Orchestra, considered one of the best in Europe. It was unimpressive, when compared to his own orchestra, and he noted that its problems were much like those of New York's orchestras: fluctuating personnel and insufficient rehearsal time. Orchestras in France were not subsidized by the state, as they were in Germany and Austria-Hungary, and it showed in their ill-prepared concerts. Thomas was surprised to find that orchestras in German-speaking Europe served opera first —symphonic concerts were "extras" in their schedules. Even the Vienna Philharmonic, founded in 1842, the same year as the New York Philharmonic, was primarily an opera orchestra.

Thomas returned home in high spirits, convinced that he was on the right track. European orchestras were no better than his. His approach to orchestras as primarily symphonic organizations was sound and uniquely American. Opera's roots in the United States were still tentative, but orchestras, as Thomas saw it, were already a fundamental part of the country's musical life. Looking to the future, he was confident that it would be America where people would go to hear great orchestras perform symphonic music. Opera would become more important—the same could be said for bands— but orchestras would be at the country's very heart. As for his own conducting, his assessments had been overly modest: his methods and the results they achieved were as effective as those of the leading conductors he had observed in the Old World.

Attention was now turned to building audiences. The second Terrace Garden season was already under way with George Matzka having conducted the orchestra in his absence. Upon Thomas's return, the programs became more serious, more symphonic. Would the public respond, or would it go elsewhere? It was not in Thomas's nature to rest on his laurels; there must be great music even at summer garden concerts, and if he had to lose money in the process, so be it. But the audiences seemed to like hearing the occasional substantial work, and attendance held up. Some of Thomas's more ardent admirers even got the newspapers to ask why the city did not help Thomas, why it did not give him a civically supported site for his summer concerts to ease his financial worries. Alas, it was all talk and no action. Toward the end of the summer, Thomas advertised in his Terrace Garden programs that "the Orchestra may be had for Fairs, College Commencements, Balls, Weddings and Private Parties. Orders received FOR ALL OCCASIONS when Music of the highest order is required FOR ANY NUMBER OF INSTRUMEN- TALISTS, F. L. Eben, Business Manager."[20] For the Thomas Orchestra to become a mere entertainer was a melancholy prospect. Was this the price for keeping the orchestra together?

The orchestra's 1867–68 season included several popular series, the soi- rees, and the Brooklyn Philharmonic, although not as many engagements in total as in the previous year. There were even fewer in 1868–69, when Thomas first did out-of-town concerts at Vassar College, in Poughkeepsie, where Frederic Ritter had been appointed professor of music, in Albany, and in a few other small centers in nearby states. Because these were well received and financially successful, Thomas, who had thought of his orchestra as a New York group serving the Empire City and its environs, now saw that there were huge, untapped audiences in other cities and towns. How to schedule them and get to them were problems—rail travel could be uncomfortable— and where to play was still more problematic—there were not many theaters or halls suitable for symphonic concerts. It was clear to him, however, that he must work these things out.

In the meantime, Thomas addressed other activities. The Peabody, Oberlin, Boston, New England, and Cincinnati conservatories, and the Chicago Academy of Music (later the Chicago Musical College), were all founded between 1865 and 1867. They were privately run and self-supporting, with a few, like the Peabody, helped by wealthy donors. New York did not as yet have a music school of quality. Thomas, with his colleague William Mason, now a successful piano teacher, rose to the challenge and announced the organization of a new school under their direction at Fifth Avenue and Twentieth Street, to be opened in the fall of 1867.[21] Fortunately for Thomas, who already had more work than he could handle, the school never got off the ground.

Thomas realized that he would have to give up his violin-playing commitments if he were to carry out his grueling orchestra schedule effectively. Thus, not unexpectedly, he dropped the Philharmonic. But the Mason-Thomas concerts were another matter. They had a secure following, the programs were challenging for performers and audiences, and dropping them would mean an irreplaceable loss for the city. True, the concerts had lost money from the very beginning, but few chamber concerts then or now pay their way. Besides, William Mason had quietly covered what deficits there were. However, with Thomas wavering, Mason gave in, and the two concluded their labor of love in New York on April 11, 1868. The concerts at Miss Porter's School continued until 1870, undoubtedly for sentimental reasons. In all, there were sixty Mason-Thomas concerts in New York over a fifteen-year span, as impressive a series of chamber programs as the United States has ever seen.

Thomas officially ended his violin career with the New York Philharmonic on April 18, 1868, a week after his last Mason-Thomas program, as soloist in the first movement of the Beethoven Concerto. It was evidently a good performance, and the Philharmonic thanked him later for his "very acceptable and valuable services."[22] Although he would not be directly involved with the society for the next eight years, he continued to cause it problems.

Central Park was soon to play a pivotal role in Thomas's life. In 1856, New York City had purchased land for the park—a site extending from 59th Street to 110th Street, between Fifth and Eighth avenues, for about $5.5 million. It was America's first major venture into urban park planning. Frederick Law Olmsted, one of the two landscape architects chosen to design the park, supervised the plan's actual implementation. He gave the city a lasting claim to good town planning and was so successful that similar commissions subsequently came his way from other cities.

New Yorkers loved Central Park. It lured them uptown to enjoy the greenery, the walks, and the open spaces; it was a place to breathe more freely. By 1868, the great metropolis's population was approaching one million, nearly all of whom lived between Forty-second Street and the Battery at the southern end of Manhattan. The burgeoning tenements of the Lower East Side greedily swallowed up newly arrived poor immigrants, the affluent moving north to escape the squalor. Public transportation improved and became more accessible. For over thirty years, horse-drawn carriages that seated about twelve had plied the city's main streets at three to five miles per hour, crossing from one curb to the other, picking up and discharging passengers. Fares were high, and only the well-to-do used the omnibuses freely. Then, in the 1860s, horse-drawn streetcars with their own right of way appeared. They were faster and cheaper than carriages and put trips to Central Park within reach of the average city dweller.

Immediately south of the new park, on Seventh Avenue (just one block away from where Carnegie Hall would rise over two decades later), a restaurant and open-air beer garden with a small, informal auditorium and stage opened in the spring of 1868. Called Central Park Garden, it was a larger and more elaborate version of Terrace Garden, was in a better location, and had one of the best cuisines in town. It also had one other formidable attraction: nightly concerts by the Theodore Thomas Orchestra. The "unrivaled" group of forty players promised to perform music to suit every taste for the hundreds of listeners who would be dining and drinking in the delightful setting.

The *New York Democrat* enthusiastically described Central Park Garden as

> a brilliant place. . . . 200 feet on Seventh Avenue and 150 feet deep. As the street car passenger arrives at Central Park Garden he [sees] hundreds of little bright gas lamps adorning the front of the large edifice, giving it the appearance of one of the grand music halls of Vienna and other German capitals. The grand music hall, which is the central building, is very handsome, with an interior of 100 by 75 feet. At the rear is the main stand from which Theodore Thomas' unparallelled band of 42 performers discourse the music. . . . The floor is taken up with small tables where the visitors are seated, drinking music and wine in the same breath, [and] the surrounding gallery [has] 22 private boxes. A handsome hall leading from this gallery gives entrance into the large dining room. . . . And from this up one flight of stairs are the ladies parlours and retiring rooms. . . . The cafe or bar connects with the Music and is the largest and most elegant in the city. The Garden is in the rear of the building, provided with fountains, flowers and greenery and is surrounded by numerous little arbours.[23]

The *Herald*, interested as always in social tone, predicted that the Central Park Garden would be a "favorite trysting place of all New Yorkers," a model of gentility, "especially adapted to administer to the mental and physical enjoyment of the cultivated and refined, who alone can aesthetically appreciate good music, good wine and rare cooking." Ladies could attend "without fear of unpleasant associations."[24] At twenty-five cents for a single admission or ten dollars for a season's subscription, New York's high society could at last mix cultural pursuits with pleasure in an appropriate setting.

Thomas's Central Park Garden concerts were to be a landmark in New

York's musical life. What he had learned about presentation and programming at Belvedere and Terrace Garden was applied with infinitely greater skill at this new, sophisticated, fashionable venue. His orchestra played there daily for eight consecutive seasons, each four months long, for a total of 1,127 concerts. (The New York Philharmonic, in contrast, gave a total of 260 concerts in its first fifty years.) Here, in this "Palace of Beauty," Thomas built New York's audience for symphonic music.

At first, Thomas's programs leaned heavily on the usual light music; within two or three seasons, however, he was conducting full symphonies and concertos as a matter of course. He would devote evenings exclusively to the music of one composer: Mozart, Beethoven, Schubert, Schumann, Wagner. Over the years, he did all nine of Beethoven's symphonies, the four symphonies of Schumann, the principal symphonies and the Octet of Mendelssohn, the serenades of Brahms, and works by Cherubini, Gade, Glinka, Anton Rubinstein, and Raff. New works by Wagner, Liszt, and Berlioz were played as soon as they became available.

In effect, the Central Park Garden *made* the Thomas Orchestra, providing, for a third of the year, a setting in which it could hone its skills and broaden its repertoire. Thanks to these concerts, New York became the English-speaking capital (if not *the* capital) of the symphonic world. August Manns in London and Jules-Etienne Pasdeloup in Paris led their orchestras in many concerts, but neither group had the finish of Thomas's ensemble. The famed Leipzig Gewandhaus Orchestra, conducted by Carl Reinecke, did not give anywhere near as many concerts year-round. Niels Gade, Ferdinand Hiller, and Max Bruch led orchestras in major European cities, but, according to all reports, these groups did not play as well as Thomas's. As for summer concerts, prominent European conductors such as Strauss, Kéler-Béla, Gungl, and Joseph Lanner did well but lacked Thomas's high motives —they were, purely and simply, entertainers who did light music only.

While Thomas was charming his public uptown in his first season at Central Park Garden, Steinway Hall was undergoing extensive interior changes. The Thomas Orchestra was the headliner when the hall reopened in October 1868, no longer "one of the ugliest concert rooms in New York" but now quite attractive.[25] William Steinway had engaged Henry Rick, a European architect —the results *had* to be good—to redecorate the hall. Rick did it in Renaissance style, the effect being both "sober and impressive." Improved or not, it continued to be Thomas's principal concert hall. In the 1868–69 season, he gave Sunday concerts there, in addition to others at Lyric Hall on Twenty-fourth Street and Sixth Avenue. The Central Park Garden concerts continued through October, followed by matinees there until Christmas, an experiment that was not too successful.

The soirees, now in their fifth season, remained Thomas's principal outlet for serious music. He conducted thirteen New York premieres in five concerts, although to hedge his bets he had a work by Beethoven on four of them, including the sixth and seventh symphonies and the Piano Concerto no. 4, with Ferdinand von Inten as soloist. There were nine new works for chorus and orchestra, the result of Thomas's having taken over the musical direction of the Mendelssohn Union, a large amateur singing society. For several years, he had wanted to build his own chorus to work with the orchestra, but since he insisted on compulsory attendance, it was not an easy task. He prudently chose unadventurous choral works for the group's first season under his direction: Beethoven's *Choral Fantasy* and shorter pieces by Palestrina, Bach, Mozart, Schumann, and Mendelssohn. The new works for orchestra were Anton Rubinstein's *Faust*, Niels Gade's *Frühlings Phantasie*, with solo voices and piano, Liszt's tone poems *Tasso* and *Prometheus*, Bruch's Symphony in E-flat, Robert Volkmann's Festival Overture, and *Fantasia* for piano and orchestra, composed and played by an immigrant German pianist, Otto Singer, who had impressed Thomas. (All the composers other than Singer were top-ranked contemporaries.) Despite such programming, Thomas lost more money than he could afford, and it was clear that he would need a subsidy from the local government or from New York's wealthy in order to continue. Neither was forthcoming.

The management of Central Park Garden, which had made a profit in its first year, was loath to repeat the prescription of the Thomas Orchestra and good music only. For the 1869–70 season, therefore, it engaged Jules Levy, a popular cornet virtuoso, as the orchestra's resident soloist and "box-office insurance." A man of astonishing endurance, Levy played at every one of Thomas's 160 concerts. He was a master of the usual froth: "show-off" pieces by Rossini and Charles De Bériot and Paganini's *Carnival of Venice*. He also performed a number of his own compositions. Thomas, who detested cornet music, stoically accepted the inevitable—cornetists were the rage—but resolved that it would be for one season only.

The audiences were larger than ever that season, but Thomas did not share in the profits: the management paid him a straight fee. So the problem of paying his orchestra for the rest of the year did not go away. He saw that there was a limit to the number of popular concerts he could or wanted to give in New York—if anything, he was overexposed in the great city—but what could he do? The answer was obvious: tour.

Thomas had traveled with solo artists and orchestras in the 1850s throughout the East and the Midwest—it was called the West then—and had experienced the trials and tribulations of the road. Now, a decade later, he remembered that tours were usually profitable for managers, soloists, and conductors. He had to admit that travel conditions had improved, trains were more comfortable and efficient, and hotels were less primitive. Special rates for his orchestra could be negotiated with railways and hotels, and even the concert halls might be better than expected. He thought he could depend on receiving 80 percent of the concert income, the balance going to the local manager, who paid for advertising and renting the hall.

A wave of prosperity in the United States made Thomas sanguine about the prospects of touring. His public in the hinterlands had turned out in droves for his concerts and had paid well for them. Why not again? Despite its unpredictability, touring was better than facing another New York season. True, it would mean abandoning the soirees, but he could not afford them anyway, and the other local concerts were increasingly becoming break-even propositions. He would have to give up the Brooklyn Philharmonic concerts, which after the soirees meant the most to him, but he had no alternative. Thomas needed financial help, but he was too proud to ask for it; instead, he went out on tour, hoping to stimulate orchestral life and bring great music to new audiences in cities and towns across the land, while solving his financial problems and, most important of all, keeping his orchestra together.

Thomas planned to travel with the orchestra for seven to eight months of the year. The tours he mapped out with local managers followed the railway lines that connected American cities and towns from east to west and became known as the "Thomas Highway." If the orchestra's ultimate destination were Chicago, it could give at least twenty concerts along the way, in cities like Boston, Buffalo, Cleveland, and Detroit. It was the same from St. Louis to New York, the returning leg of the circular route he would take, with stops in Louisville, Cincinnati, Pittsburgh, Washington, D.C., Baltimore, and Philadelphia.

The two main reasons the Thomas tours were successful—why the houses were full and the audiences, most of whom had never heard an orchestra before, were thrilled—were programming and the orchestra itself. Thomas custom-tailored his concerts, in some cities doing all light music, in others mixing in more serious works, much like at Central Park Garden. His intuition and his sense of time and place were unequaled. When he returned to a center for a second or third time, he did more serious works than on the previous occasion, thereby educating his audiences, not merely entertaining them. As for the orchestra, Americans had never known a group with such outstanding tone quality, precision, and ensemble technique, and they were overwhelmed by its excellence. For the musically sensitive, life was never the same after they heard their first Thomas concert. Audiences had, in the past, clamored for virtuoso pianists, violinists, and cornetists. Now they clamored for a virtuoso orchestra. For the next thirty-five years, Thomas's name on a marquee was synonymous with the finest orchestral music in the United States.

Touring did have its problems for Thomas and his men. There were snowstorms and rail breakdowns that played havoc with the schedule, for Thomas booked daily concerts in order to meet expenses (as such, there were practically no days off). Railway cars, pulled by coal-burning locomotives, were often dirty beyond belief, and the orchestra had to stay in hotels with grossly inadequate heating and plumbing. As for good food and good wine— both of which Thomas enjoyed—they were almost nonexistent other than in major eastern cities. Illness dogged the players, who grew homesick for New York and their families, and there was no time for rehearsals or for individual practice. The result was that the orchestra thoroughly disliked touring after the first month; by the end of the season, the players loathed it, as did Thomas. Yet the tours continued and would remain part of Thomas's professional life.

Thomas's first tour began on October 6, 1869, in Poughkeepsie, followed by concerts in Albany, Hartford, and Waterbury (Conn.). Then the orchestra went to cultivated Boston for three nights—more performances than in any previous stay. The "Athens of the New World," considered the most musically sophisticated city in America, had seen its own Handel and Haydn Society give impressive performances in 1867 of Beethoven's Ninth Symphony, Handel's *Samson* and *Messiah*, and Haydn's *Creation*. Its conductor, Carl Zerrahn, who would lead the group from 1854 to 1895, was an original member of the Germanian Society and in the top rank of American conductors, just a notch below Thomas. It was the most important stop on the tour for Thomas, and he had carefully primed his group for it.

Bostonians were overwhelmed by the excellence of the Theodore Thomas Orchestra. John S. Dwight wrote with acuity: "Boston has not heard such orchestral performances before. [There was] perfect understanding with their leader and each other . . . admirable discipline . . . superiority in every part. . . . There was nothing which our people, our musicians needed so much as to hear just such an orchestra." [26] He had hit upon one of the most important reasons for the group's influence on American orchestral life: a fine ensemble is not only admired but also sets an example and a standard for local groups and musicians wherever it appears. The *Boston Advertiser* praised the orchestra's "precision and accuracy [and] wonderful vitality which fills and permeates all its performances. . . . A spirit of intense life seems to animate it in every part." The *Journal* observed: "For once, at least, New York has taught Boston a good lesson." Its description of composers on one of Thomas's concerts is a good example of florid musical journalism of the day: "What a range of sweets from Bach to Weber . . . the wanderings of Wagner, the fancies of Meyerbeer, the delightful vigor of Strauss, the airiness of Mendelssohn, the pomp of Bach, the melody of Liszt, the dreamy measures of Vogt, the finish of Vieuxtemps and the harmonic richness of Weber." [27]

Thomas was a versatile conductor, as comfortable with a commonplace piece as a Beethoven symphony. He put the required effort into each piece he conducted and was enough of a showman to know the importance of sufficiently captivating an audience through one means or another to help it identify with him at future concerts. In Boston, Thomas first presented his memorable arrangement of Schumann's *Träumerai*, a lovely melody that became his signature tune. He scored it for strings only, without double basses, and in the final section added mutes, which he said made for "an effective *diminuendo . . .* finishing with a *piano, pianissimo, pianississimo, a la* Ole Bull."[28] Unlike Bull, who, in performing his "Arkansas Traveler," moved slowly to the back of the stage, playing softer and softer, Thomas's men stayed in their places. The effect was enchanting; when *Träumerai* was over, one could hear a pin drop. The work received accolades everywhere and became a must on Thomas programs.

After Boston came New Bedford (Mass.), Providence, and Portland (Me.), and then, by popular demand (Thomas had to reschedule the tour), Boston again for two more concerts. The orchestra moved on to sixteen other eastern and midwestern cities, the longest stay being five days in Cincinnati. Cleveland, like Boston, booked extra concerts. The *Cleveland Plain Dealer*, searching for superlatives, described Beethoven's Fifth Symphony as "delicious." The *Buffalo Express* called the orchestra "the most complete combination ever seen in this part of the world." The *Detroit Free Press* said it produced "the most remarkable musical entertainment." Cincinnati's audiences, considered among the more musical, "were lifted up and inspired as never before."[29]

The *Pittsburgh Evening Chronicle* gushed with superlatives as well, but, much like *Dwight's*, it underscored the beneficial and lasting effect the Thomas Orchestra would have on local musical development:

> Thomas infuses music and poetry into an orchestra. . . . The music is controlled, lifted up into gorgeous volumes of sound or refined away into impalpable realms where the least faint sound lingers trembling on the ear, and [we] begin to comprehend why it is that the genius which evokes such spells is hailed with the acclamations of enraptured audiences. . . . We will now have a standard by which we can judge critically hereafter. Wherever Theodore Thomas and his orchestra go they will sow seeds that will bring forth good fruit . . . inspire a love for a high order of music [and] promote local organizations. . . . All honor then to the accomplished gentleman and his admirable assistants for what they have done and for the golden promise of what they will yet do in building up true music taste in America.[30]

Several amusing incidents occurred on this first tour, indicative of the rudimentary state of American musical knowledge at the time. One was related by George P. Upton, music critic for the *Chicago Tribune* from 1861 to 1885, prolific author of books and articles on music and concertgoing, and later Thomas's long-time friend and collaborator. In an Iowa city after a concert that included Boccherini's Minuet, the mayor, according to Upton, said with considerable emphasis, "'You should have played it louder.' 'But,' said Mr. Thomas, 'it is marked pp.' 'No matter if it is,' replied the municipal critic, 'such a pretty tune deserves to be played louder.'"[31]

In January and February 1870, the orchestra gave concerts in cities close to New York but none in its hometown. A spring tour followed, with the young German pianist Anna Mehlig as soloist. Whereas orchestra members had been soloists for the first tour—an economy measure—Thomas now felt that he could afford a soloist of reputation. The pretty and energetic twenty-one-year-old pianist may not have known what trying times were in store. The tour began in Boston with concerts on seven consecutive evenings plus a Saturday matinee, and Mehlig appeared in all but one of them. She fearlessly took on, in addition to solo pieces in several of the concerts, the following taxing works: Beethoven's Concertos no. 3 and 4, Weber's *Concertstück*, Chopin's Concerto in E Minor, Schumann's Concerto in A Minor, Gade's *Frühlings Phantasie*, and Liszt's Concerto in E-flat.

Thomas and the local sponsors were so sure of their Boston public that they charged one dollar per ticket, a very stiff price, and bravely programmed full-scale works by Beethoven, Schumann, and Berlioz. There were full houses in Boston and most of the other major cities. Clearly, symphonic music was in great demand, and improvement in public taste was inevitable. Thomas would be the public's teacher, his programs its textbooks. His continued effectiveness now depended on frequent and widespread touring.

It was significant that Thomas's first two tours and most of those that followed were financially successful. He either worked out a percentage split with a local sponsor or got a guaranteed fee (unfortunately, full details on the deals he made have never come to light). Concerts turned a profit because of Thomas, his orchestra, and his programming, but also because of sensitive ticket pricing and extensive revenues from program advertising. The latter reveals much about contemporary music life: notices for Albert Weber pianos (but not Steinway), the Mason and Hamlin cabinet organs made by William Mason's family, brass instruments from the Boston Musical Instrument Company, and Paganini strings from S. Bauer & Company. Sheet music firms also placed advertisements, one of which noted that a piano version of *Träumerai* was available only from the Edward Schuberth Company of New York.

It was during the Chicago stop of this second tour that Thomas met George Upton—a bizarre encounter that tells us much about both men. Upton had a letter of introduction from Adolph Dohn, a prominent Chicago musician and friend of Thomas. He later wrote that Thomas had greeted him "most cordially, with a strong grip of that powerful hand, and then with that peculiar smile of his, which had so many different meanings, said in a brusque way: 'I am glad to meet any friend of Mr. Dohn's, and will be pleased to have you come and see me while I am here. You must not expect me to call upon you, for I am too busy, and besides, I never go into newspaper offices. I have no need to cultivate the critics, for I know my work. I do not care to read what they write, and would not have time if I did.'" On recalling this "new experience," Upton explained: "I had been so persistently visited by advance agents, business agents, artists, and even impresarios of concert and opera troupes, that it was refreshing to meet a musician who did not care to see the interior of a newspaper office."[32] Not all critics and newspapers would be as tolerant of Thomas's outspokenness and vanity as Upton was.

With a surfeit of pioneering concerts and strenuous travel behind it, the Thomas Orchestra gratefully returned to Central Park Garden in 1870 for a third summer season. The happy occasion merited a premiere, this time Thomas's own "Inaugural" March—unfortunately, an innocuous work with dull, conventional harmonies, singularly lacking in imagination. Despite this poor start, the season was to be the best yet at the Garden. Even Thursday nights, set aside for serious works, sold well. The most notable was an all-Beethoven program to commemorate the 100th anniversary of the master's birth, at which Thomas conducted the complete "Pastoral" Symphony.

Travel commenced again in October. This time the orchestra gave ten concerts in Boston, equally divided between symphony and popular. Two were all-Beethoven concerts, the first of which had the "Eroica" and the Piano Concerto no. 4 (with Anna Mehlig) before the intermission. Even that most fervent of Beethoven lovers, John S. Dwight, complained about the concert's excessive length. Thomas did the Septet in the second half with a full string complement instead of the string quartet, for which it was originally written —one of the first conductors to do it this way. Again, Boston showered praise on Thomas. Where else in America or, for that matter, in Europe could one hear Beethoven done so well? Thomas was called an "unconquerable battler" for good music and likened to a "votary of Apollo, a harmonious Don Quixote and a musical Hercules cleansing the Augean stable of much trash."[33] The appreciative press and public aside, Thomas felt a compatibility with Boston's intelligentsia in general, with its life-style and its heady mixture of puritanism and transcendentalism. Indeed, he would gladly have moved there if there had been a Boston Central Park Garden.

Following the 1870 Boston engagement, the orchestra took the "Thomas Highway" west, with one sellout after another. Extra concerts were booked and florid reviews written. It seemed as if the Thomas Orchestra could do nothing wrong, as if its music were reaching all the people in just the way Thomas had hoped. The *Cincinnati Daily Gazette* reported on the "grand reception" the orchestra got, unlike the half-full houses of the previous year. Not only "the elite and wealthy" attended, but "hundreds who could not claim a place in this class . . . filled the places in the upper gallery." [34] Thus reassured, the orchestra moved eastward, giving daily concerts with no days off and no unions to tell Thomas to ease his grueling pace. The men arrived home on Christmas Eve exhausted.

A group of Thomas's supporters pressed him to give at least a few concerts in New York during the winter, and he squeezed two Steinway Hall programs into his schedule in January 1871. Enthusiastic New Yorkers noted the improvement in the ensemble, thanks to its having played together without break since the previous summer. As one, they said that Thomas must have what he wanted, a permanent orchestra, and that it behooved the nation's leading city to make it possible. [35] But would they support it on a continuing basis? A great orchestra—which New York now realized it had—could not survive otherwise. Whether it was Thomas's fault—he was away again until May— or that of his friends, the idea got scant attention once the glow of the two Steinway Hall concerts had disappeared.

Soon, Thomas had to cope with a totally new problem: a potential rival, an ambitious German conductor of considerable ability named Leopold Damrosch. Born in Posen in West Prussia, Damrosch, who held a doctorate in medicine from Berlin University, had had excellent musical training. He had been the solo violinist in the Weimar Ducal Orchestra, had conducted the Breslau Philharmonic Society, and had toured with Hans von Bülow and Karl Tausig. He also knew both Liszt and Wagner. Damrosch's aristocratic Prussian wife and his wife's sister, who accompanied him, were both accomplished singers.

An invitation from the Arion Society to head its chorus had brought Damrosch to the United States in May 1871. It was hardly an appropriate position for a man of his background and ability, as everyone (including Thomas) knew, and he was soon looking for more challenging musical outlets. Damrosch was outgoing, impetuous, and volatile, and Thomas resented his eagerness—some thought him pushy—to make himself known in a city that Thomas increasingly felt to be his private preserve. Although the story could have been apocryphal, Thomas was alleged to have said at their first meeting, "I hear, Dr. Damrosch, that you are a fine musician, but I want to tell you one thing: whoever crosses my path, I crush." [36] Given their personalities and their situations, it was not surprising that the two conductors had little affection for each other from the start. Yet Thomas did voluntarily play Damrosch's Festival Overture at two Central Park Garden concerts in June. And Damrosch did lie low for several years before getting involved in orchestral music and, ultimately, becoming a thorn in Thomas's side.

After its fourth summer at the Garden, the Thomas Orchestra headed for Chicago, where it was scheduled to open the newly renovated Crosby Opera House on October 9, 1871, the first of ten concerts there. Unfortunately, the trip was a rendezvous with disaster. It had been a rainless year throughout much of the United States, and on October 7, two days before the Thomas concerts were to begin, a large fire broke out on Chicago's west side. Before it was checked, it had caused an estimated $1 million in damage. The next night, as the story goes, Mrs. O'Leary's cow kicked over a lantern, and the result was the world-famous Great Chicago Fire, which raced through the heart of the city, destroying everything in its path. When the calamitous fire had run its course, approximately 300 people had been killed, 100,000 left homeless (Chicago's population was 330,000), and property damage exceeded $200 million.

One of the fire's structural victims was the Crosby Opera House. George P. Upton had seen it lit up for the first time since its renovation on the eve of the opening and sadly wrote that "two or three hours later it was ashes."[37] He had been waiting for Thomas's orchestra, which arrived at the Twenty-second Street rail depot at the height of the fire. Forced to leave the train, the musicians headed nervously into the city on foot, carrying their instruments and other possessions. Soon they were turned back and had no alternative but to flee Chicago and entrain for nearby Joliet, where they would stay until their next engagement, in St. Louis on October 21. The fire meant that the orchestra would have no work and income for twelve days. Thomas, distraught, persuaded the St. Louis managers to move up his opening there to October 18, but he could find no other engagements for the orchestra to fill the canceled Chicago dates.

It was Thomas's first real setback. Before the fire, he had planned concerts and tours and they had happened, for better or worse. He now saw that there were some events that he could not control, that were not predictable. Later, he was to reflect, "Providence evidently wished to discipline me a little more. I was still too young, too presuming and had too much vitality."[38] In the end, he himself paid the orchestra's wages for the lost days. He was not obligated to—there was a force majeure clause in his contracts with his players that relieved him of liability for their salaries and expenses—but he felt that he must honor his commitments regardless of circumstances. Thus, his sizable "reserve fund," which he had built up over several years of concert-giving, was wiped out in one week, leaving him plagued with grievous financial problems for the next decade.

The remainder of the tour was uneventful, and the orchestra returned to Boston. There, Thomas included in one of his concerts an orchestral setting of the "Love Death" from *Tristan und Isolde*, which had been meticulously rehearsed during the wait in Joliet. William Apthorp, one of America's leading critics, wrote in the *Atlantic Monthly* that, "In spite of its great beauty, it was hardly suited to the concert-room."[39] Thomas, whose passion for Wagner's music was as great as ever, repeated it in New York the next month. The *Times* and the *Tribune* spoke well of it, as did the public, which, like Thomas, was being seduced by the wizard of Bayreuth.

Concerns about composers, their works, and their reception were put aside temporarily, now that Thomas had to earn still more money to maintain his orchestra. He decided to try new territory and thus toured the South from January to May 1872 with an enlarged orchestra of sixty players. Expenses were greater and earnings less than expected for the eighteen-city tour. Small centers such as Mobile (Ala.) and Macon (Ga.) were happy to have the orchestra but either balked at the high prices or, because of a small hall, could not meet expenses. Reserved seat prices were sometimes raised to two dollars and then lowered because of public resistance.

Profits were pitifully small. Yet in terms of spreading the Thomas gospel, the tour's effect on the musical life of the South was long-lasting. Most of the cities visited had never before heard the Thomas Orchestra; some, in fact, had never before heard any orchestra. Cities like Charleston had the orchestra for four concerts in three days. The *Atlanta Constitution* referred to one concert as "a musical treat the like of which has never been equaled in the musical annals of Atlanta." An extra concert—four had been scheduled—was added to the New Orleans schedule, even though all five took place just after Mardi Gras. The *New Orleans Picayune* carried a front-page story on the city's good fortune at having such an "expensive" group so far from its home base (an oblique reference to the two-dollar top Thomas invoked) and happily quoted the opera impresario Max Strakosch, who claimed that no European orchestra equaled Thomas's.[40]

The southern tour was the most tiring yet for Thomas and his men. The usual problems of bad halls, unpalatable food, poor accommodations, and dirty trains had worn them down more than usual. Opportunities for much-needed rest were absent, and the pressure showed—Thomas, for one, looked much older than his thirty-seven years. He rarely saw his wife and had few opportunities to show his devotion as a father. He was clearly on the horns of a dilemma: touring provided the income and exposure the orchestra needed, but sooner or later it would have to be cut to a minimum or brought to a halt altogether. If Thomas stopped touring, he would lose his orchestra; if he continued touring, he might eventually lose it anyway, since he had pushed his players to their limit. He wanted his own orchestra on his own terms, yet the alternative to touring was a more supportive New York, still a fond hope at best. Would another city, or cities, take on the Thomas Orchestra, or at least give it some long-term work? And what about his conducting career? Was he growing musically, barnstorming as he did around the country, giving concerts every day, with few opportunities to appraise his work and learn new scores? The answers would come in due time.

3

Musical Shrines

In 1870, Cincinnati was one of the five largest cities in the United States and the leading center of culture west of the Alleghenies. Large numbers of German immigrants had settled in the "Queen City" and by 1872 comprised at least one-quarter of the population, making it an almost bilingual community. Music, too, was an important part of Cincinnati's life, and the city claimed a number of choral societies, a Conservatory of Music, and at least one orchestra. A huge *Sängerfest* had been held in Cincinnati in 1870, in the commodious, barnlike Exposition Hall, and many thousands of enthusiastic German Americans had attended. The question was, could Cincinnati support an English-language festival? One local couple, Maria and George Ward Nichols, thought so.

Maria Nichols, a charming young woman with a fine temperament and considerable imagination, was a member of the prominent and wealthy Longworth family. Her husband, George, was a writer, art educator, and vigorous entrepreneur/administrator who had begun his career as a journalist in Boston. He had fought with the Union army and served as a lieutenant-colonel under General Sherman and as his aide-de-camp in the March to the Sea (Nichols's *The Story of the Great March* was published in 1865 and had sold 60,000 copies within a year). Married in 1868 when Maria was nineteen, the Nicholses took up residence in her native Cincinnati, where they founded an important School of Design (which eventually became part of the Cincinnati Art Museum).

Theodore Thomas had first met the Nicholses in the spring of 1872, when the Harmonic Society, of which George Nichols was president, sang with the Thomas Orchestra.[1] The Nicholses and Thomas, fired with dreams of grandiose festivals, made plans for a Cincinnati music festival, to be patterned after Boston's and held in 1873 at the Exposition Building. It would feature the Thomas Orchestra, the Harmonic Society, and other selected choirs from Ohio, Indiana, and Illinois. The choirs would study the festival's music well in advance, under the direction of their own choirmasters; then, immediately prior to festival time, Thomas would take over. Also, Cincinnati instrumentalists would augment the Thomas Orchestra in large works. It would be as much a local Cincinnati event as a Thomas festival, and, significantly, it would give Thomas a $5,000 fee and the Thomas Orchestra a week of guaranteed income. George Nichols would be the festival's administrator and principal fund-raiser, and Thomas its musical director. They were a formidable pair —strong, willful, and ambitious. Surely, the festival would prosper.

With the festival in mind, Thomas returned to New York for his fifth season (1872) at Central Park Garden, where he went from strength to strength, drawing even larger audiences than in the past. The orchestra was increased to fifty players and, for a benefit concert on June 20, to sixty. As the quality of music improved and audiences grew more attentive, Thomas became even more insistent on silence during concerts and more adamant about refusing to do encores—unscheduled and complete repetitions of works. For him, sequence was all-important, and encores upset the shape of a concert. Further, encores unnecessarily prolonged a concert and could not only fail to hold the audience's attention but fatigue the performers.[2] George Upton cited an observer at a June benefit concert who wrote that Thomas, in refusing persistent demands for an encore, had left the podium and "quietly took a seat in a corner of the orchestra until he had carried his point," at which time he resumed the scheduled program.[3]

During the 1872 season, the *Philadelphia Evening Bulletin* described well a night at the Central Park Garden:

> The concert commences at eight, when but a handful are present. Thomas takes the stand with his accustomed quiet confidence and dignity. Car load after car load arrive, and by the time the first part is completed the scene is a very different one. The fashionable and middle classes and various nationalities . . . are represented—the New Yorker, Philadelphian, Bostonian and Jerseyite; English, French, German, Cuban, and Italian; Christian and Hebrew, Grantist or Greeleyite. At each interval the stage empties its half a hundred geniuses amid the indiscriminate throng at the bar, shouting for lager, and seizing the frothing glasses which are hastily supplied to it. At length a roll-call on the drum restores orchestra and audience to their places, and those couples lingering in the garden who have relapsed into personal sentiment take up again the more general one which the next musical composition inspires.[4]

Encouraged by Thomas's ever-growing popularity, twenty leading New Yorkers formally asked him to resume the soiree concerts that he had abandoned in 1869.[5] Thomas, who had never doubted that he would return to

New York during the winter season, quickly agreed—too quickly, as it turned out, for he did not pin them down as to how they would support the concerts (i.e., how much money they would guarantee and for how long). These worthy gentlemen did not intend to make any sort of firm commitment, yet Thomas went ahead on his own, as in the past, gauging his prospects from the success of the Garden concerts. The formal symphony concerts in stuffy halls in the dead of winter would be far different from the informal summer evening concerts, however, and might well lose money after soloists' fees and orchestra salaries were paid. Obviously, this was something Thomas could ill afford.

Before his New York winter "return," Thomas did a fall tour, including a week at the newly built Aiken Theatre in Chicago, where his followers were reminded how much they had missed their favorite conductor and his orchestra. Then came Steinway Hall, glittering for Thomas's homecoming. The full house was not disappointed: press and public as one applauded the musicians.[6] George Osgood, an American bass, sang Wotan's "Farewell" from *Die Walküre*, the first of a number of Wagner's new works that Thomas would put on to enhance his, and Wagner's, popularity. The competing New York Philharmonic, although larger than Thomas's group by some twenty-five players, suffered again by comparison. The trials of the year before—the exhausting tours, the Chicago Fire—were gradually forgotten as Thomas prepared for 1873, one of his best years.

In the spring of 1872, Jacob Grau, an American concert manager, had gone to Vienna to engage Anton Rubinstein, the great Russian pianist, composer, and conductor, for an American tour. Founder of the Imperial Conservatory at St. Petersburg, Rubinstein had played in all the leading concert halls of Europe and rivaled Liszt in virtuosity and popularity. He outlined his terms with Grau: 200 engagements for $40,000, half to be paid before signing and in gold only. He also demanded that he not be "obliged to play in establishments devoted to purposes other than artistic ones" (i.e., garden concert sites, tobacco establishments, and cafés), and he insisted on ample protection from "savage" Indians.[7]

Grau knew Rubinstein's value but lacked the $20,000 down payment, so he wired his nephew, Maurice Grau, and instructed him to ask William Steinway to sponsor the tour. Steinway agreed promptly, on condition that, while in the United States, Rubinstein play a Steinway piano with the Steinway name emblazoned on its right side for all to see. Maurice Grau hurried to Vienna to close the deal, since his uncle had been taken seriously ill, and was confronted by Rubinstein, who now proposed to lighten the formidable schedule of daily concerts by having the Polish violinist and composer Henryk Wieniawski share the tour. (Wieniawski was almost as well known as Rubinstein and held the coveted post of solo violinist to the czar of Russia.) The younger Grau had no alternative but to agree, although the new scheme's financial implications were unclear. Neither Rubinstein nor Wieniawski knew that Grau, concerned about their drawing power, would engage two singers to boost ticket sales for concerts in smaller centers.

The two artists nervously departed for America in September 1872. New Yorkers greeted them at dockside with a serenading ensemble from the Philharmonic, the first such welcome since Jenny Lind's arrival two decades earlier, and their debut recital at Steinway Hall was an enormous success. Rubinstein and Wieniawski found the hall excellent, the audience knowledgeable and appreciative, and the Steinway piano unsurpassed. After a rigorous tour, they joined the Theodore Thomas Orchestra on New Year's Eve, as Steinway had arranged. Rubinstein performed his own Concerto in G Major and, without orchestra, Schumann's *Kreisleriana* and Chopin's Ballade in G Minor and Scherzo in B Minor; Wieniawski did a solo work of Rubinstein's, his own *Polonaise* and the first movement of Beethoven's Concerto with his own cadenza.

It was a memorable concert, earning a front-page review in the *New York Times*.[8] Public response was such that, even with three more concerts planned between January 2 and 9, 1873, in New York and Brooklyn, another two were added. Thomas, forever on the move, squeezed in two orchestra-only concerts in Albany and in Norwalk (Conn.) on January 6 and 7. On January 11, Rubinstein played in Thomas's revived symphonic series at Steinway Hall. Then, their professional relations secure, conductor and soloists parted company for a few months, to meet again in Chicago on March 18.

First in Cincinnati and then, on March 31, in New York, Rubinstein conducted his newly revised *Ocean* Symphony with the Thomas Orchestra. The latter concert, once announced, brought Thomas's feud with the Philharmonic into public view. Rubinstein had played with the Philharmonic the preceding November and been booked to conduct the new *Ocean* in its New York premiere on April 19 for an outrageous fee (at least for the Philharmonic) of $1,000. (The Philharmonic had done Rubinstein's original version of the work in 1871.) Thomas, who did not mind irritating the Philharmonic, had gotten Rubinstein's permission to include several movements of the work in one of his January concerts in New York. But the orchestra's March performance of the entire work—Rubinstein must have felt that Thomas's group could do it more justice—was the last straw for the society, and it considered canceling Rubinstein's concert. Only after conductor Carl Bergmann, society president George Templeton Strong, and other members had heatedly debated the matter did the Philharmonic proceed as planned. The affair intrigued New York's musical circles and, of course, helped concert attendance. Thomas supporters had a good chuckle about how their favorite conductor had stolen a march on the stuffy old Philharmonic.

Although the *Ocean* Symphony was a dull work, Rubinstein's conducting was another matter. The *Daily Tribune* described him as having "an abundance of nervous energy in his motions. . . . He never looks at the score. . . . Standing in an attitude of command before his men, he guides them with quick but not at all ungraceful gestures using both hands, and conveys unmistakable signals with the eye and the head. He knows exactly what every separate instrument has to do. . . . [His] secret . . . is in the magnetic power of the man—a power which cannot be explained, cannot be described, can only be felt."[9] Later, when John S. Dwight heard Rubinstein conduct, he suggested that he would be competition for Thomas—whom he enjoyed deflating on occasion—if he conducted more often.[10] Rubinstein, as much a musical magician on the podium as at the keyboard, had a great impact on Thomas and other contemporary conductors. The Philharmonic musicians so admired his gifts, in fact, that they buried their grievances, forgot about Thomas's coup, and elected Rubinstein an honorary member of the society.

Thomas, Rubinstein, and Wieniawski continued to tour together in the East until the end of April 1873, when they played at Thomas's first choral-orchestral festival in New York. More touring followed. Their last concert together was in Philadelphia on May 12 (Thomas was due to start at Central Park Garden two days later). Such was Rubinstein's following that at his final recital in Boston, prior to his returning to Europe, his "very clothes were rent by enthusiastic admirers in search of souvenirs. Women rushed on the platform and embraced him, and the entire audience yelled 'Come back again! Come back again!' "[11]

The collaboration between Thomas and Rubinstein yielded rich dividends for both men. At a farewell dinner given him by William Steinway, Rubinstein said that not only had he never expected to find an orchestra like Thomas's in the United States but that there was none in St. Petersburg, Vienna, Berlin, Paris, or London to compare with it:

> When he accompanies me with his orchestra, it is as though he could divine my thoughts, and then as though his orchestra could divine his. It is as perfect as the work of some gifted pianist accompanying a singer with whom he has often rehearsed. I know of but one orchestra that can compare with that of Theodore Thomas', and that is the orchestra of the National Conservatory of Paris [Habeneck's Conservatoire Orchestra], which was established by the first Napoleon in the year 1808, into which only artists, when young, are admitted; and they may have any number of rehearsals until they arrive at *absolute* perfection. It is that orchestra alone which is as perfect as Theodore Thomas'—but, alas, they have no Theodore Thomas to conduct them.[12]

The admiration was mutual. Thomas, as was his way, tersely summed up the Rubinstein-Wieniawski contribution to American musical life: "Programmes of works of the highest standard, rendered by such artists and such an orchestra, were a revelation everywhere, and made a lasting impression. They gave this country the great artistic impetus for which it seemed at last to be ripe." [13] He said nothing about his personal relations with the two men, although some years later William Steinway said that Rubinstein, whom he revered, and his good friend Thomas had become "dearer to each other almost day by day." [14] In truth, Rubinstein and Wieniawski showed Thomas that performers do not necessarily sacrifice their integrity when they allow music's expressive demands to take precedence over the written page. As a result, his readings became more "human."

Prior to the first Cincinnati May Festival, Thomas gave his first New York choral-orchestral festival. Undeterred by the financial risks involved—he had limited backing—he was confident of success because of the great popularity of oratorio. Victorian audiences in England and North America listened to oratorios by Handel and Mendelssohn with deep affection, almost ritualistically, as if they were worshiping passively in a secular setting. A contemporary writer explained why when he perceptively compared opera and oratorio:

> The opera appeals to the individual, the oratorio to the mass. The one is warm, passionate, eager—the other profound, sombre and majestic. . . . As [opera] portrays the passions and weaknesses of the individual, so [oratorio] mirrors the affections and aspirations of a people or a tribe. Essentially grand and massive, oratorio legitimately deals with those more awful themes of religion, the use of which in opera would be intolerable. [It expresses] the awe, the helplessness, the yearning for supernal pity, that all mankind sometimes feels in common. [15]

Thomas showed an instinctive flair for large-scale choral music for the first time at this festival, which in fact had not started out as a festival. (He had invited the 500-voice chorus of the Handel and Haydn Society of Boston, by far the best in the United States, to sing Beethoven's Ninth at his final symphony series concert on April 26. The group's enthusiastic acceptance prompted him to ask it to do other major works while in New York, hence the festival.) It taught him how a large, first-class choir functions, which would help him in Cincinnati the following month. The festival included big works—Mendelssohn's *Elijah* and Handel's *Israel in Egypt*—at both the New York and the Brooklyn Academy of Music, and Thomas willingly shared conducting duties with Carl Zerrahn, director of the Handel and Haydn Society. (Rubinstein and Wieniawski also played at two festival concerts.) Discerning New York critics praised Thomas's choice of music and thanked him for not emulating festivals in the Gilmore tradition (i.e., extravaganzas that bandmaster Patrick Gilmore had directed in Boston in 1869 and 1872 involving mammoth orchestras and choirs that numbered in the thousands). [16]

Beethoven's Ninth closed Thomas's revived symphony series, as it did his first festival.

His trial run over, Thomas now gave his undivided attention to the Queen City festival, which, as he was soon to find out, was not his but Cincinnati's. He would have to work with committees and boards composed of rich, powerful, philanthropically minded community leaders. A festival committee had begun fund-raising in September 1872 and in less than a month had amassed $30,000 from individuals, large corporations, industrial firms, music houses, retail stores, and breweries. In November, the required funds secured, the committee announced publicly and reassuringly that there would be a festival the following May, "for the purpose of elevating the standard of . . . music, and to bring about harmony of action between the musical societies of the country and especially the West." [17]

With Thomas's help, the committee pursued its goal with uncommon zeal. Whenever he was in Cincinnati during the next eight months, Thomas missed no opportunity to speak at local meetings and to the press about festival plans. He even went so far as to praise the barnlike Exposition Building and Sänger Hall's acoustics, which were, in truth, poor. He played up shamelessly to local and regional pride and promised that Cincinnati and the Midwest would soon be national leaders in festival enterprise. The *Cincinnati Times and Chronicle* responded gratefully, stating that "the selection of Theodore Thomas as the director is a guarantee that what is to be done will be done," while the *Daily Gazette* called him "The Prince of Musicians." [18]

Thomas's main problem, from the outset, was George Ward Nichols, who managed the festival's administrative details without salary and not to Thomas's liking. Worse, Nichols meddled in areas Thomas clearly felt were in his domain. For example, the latter chose the soloists, all of national reputation, but Nichols, keen on making the festival a local effort, tried to convince him to add a Cincinnati soprano from a prominent family. Thomas, who thought that she was not up to the standard required, said no, although he eventually gave in, admonishing Nichols that it was his (Nichols's) "own risk." [19]

Full of ideas, Nichols also proposed a vocal competition, which a reluctant Thomas said he would accept as a "necessary evil" if festival authorities insisted (they did not). Nichols asked that local school choirs sing at a matinee concert, but Thomas, although well aware of the appeal such choirs had— "The singing of the public schools I recommend by all means. A popular move like that is justifiable if put in the proper place."—emphasized that a festival of great music was not "the proper place" for such choirs. The children sang anyway—one of Thomas's compromises—with varying success.

Nichols knew little about the rehearsal time needed to prepare concerts or how much orchestras could do in a day and still do it well. Thinking of box-office returns, he asked Thomas to program a matinee concert on the same day as an evening performance of Beethoven's Ninth. Thomas replied laconically, "It is easier to make and announce programs than it is to rehearse them." Nichols won: the festival was four days in length, with four evening concerts and three matinees (the children's concert was the fourth matinee), a killing schedule for Thomas and the orchestra.

The festival chorus was, as Thomas feared, difficult to prepare and manage. Nichols organized the amalgam of 800 singers, who came from twenty-four local and regional choirs, got the festival music to them for study in the winter and spring, kept in touch with their choirmasters to see how they were faring, and, finally, made arrangements for them to attend massed rehearsals with Carl Barus, the festival's chorusmaster, in Cincinnati. It soon became clear that many of the smaller choirs outside Cincinnati were not up to singing the difficult repertoire Thomas had chosen—eventually most of the chorus was drawn from Nichols's Harmonic Society and other city groups—and that chorusmaster Barus was not skilled enough to prepare the program. A month before the festival began, Thomas replaced Barus with Otto Singer, a German-born pianist he had introduced to New York several years before. (Singer remained in Cincinnati after the festival and later tried—and almost succeeded—to undermine Thomas's position as director.)

Thomas did not easily accept his role as festival music director in absentia, without financial authority and dependent on a willful administrator. He had to get approval from Nichols and the festival committee before signing any contracts, and Nichols spared no opportunity to remind Thomas of this. The two men were bound to clash, for Thomas had trouble sharing authority with anyone, much less the equally authoritarian Nichols, who thought Thomas knew nothing about administration and was unable to comprehend the kind of festival Thomas wanted. While Nichols saw it first as a local community effort and second as an artistic event of national importance, Thomas could not, in principle, bring himself to make artistic compromises for the sake of the community festival concept. In the end, Nichols learned that Thomas held the trump cards, that the musical director programmed all the concerts, decided on the solo artists, fixed the rehearsal schedules, and approved the many other details of concert giving. Given this understanding, Thomas learned to live with Nichols, who, ultimately, did what was expected of him.

During the spring, Nichols arranged for an organ to be installed at Sänger Hall and had the stage enlarged to accommodate both chorus and orchestra. Thomas himself laid out the orchestral plans—a festival orchestra composed of fifty-two Thomas players, thirty-five members from the "celebrated" Cincinnati Orchestra, and a dozen or more prominent players from such cities as St. Louis, Louisville, and Chicago.[20] With the festival imminent, the committee dressed up the Exposition Building beyond all expectations. The bleak and cavernous interior promenade, where the concerts would be given, was "decorated with long festoons of evergreens between columns." There was "an immense pyramidal display of hothouse plants and flowers, twenty feet in diameter at the base and rising to a height of twenty feet or more, probably the finest display in the country."[21] To accommodate the well-dressed audience, wide wooden walks were built from the street gates to the doors of Sänger Hall to cover the rough gravel walk. Good and plentiful food and drink were planned for the half-hour intermissions. (Thomas had urged that there be no beer, to avoid the lighthearted, gemütlich atmosphere of *Sängerfesten*, but he did not get his way.)

The local press, behind the festival from the outset, whetted the public's appetite with a plenitude of detail about what was coming. Ticket orders poured in, rail and boat lines stepped up their services, and the city was decked out with flags, bunting, and signs. The *New York Daily Tribune*, which considered Thomas tantamount to a musical saint, wrote that much more could have been done by way of preparation had Thomas not been against "show and noise." The *Tribune* felt that music festivals should be publicized with modesty and restraint, in keeping with their serious musical content.[22]

The long-awaited date arrived—May 6, 1873—but the weather was not on the festival's side. Despite sultry conditions (it also rained every day but one that week), some 6,000 people—a near-capacity crowd—arrived in formal dress for opening night. The orchestra was center stage, with the chorus on each side. Windows in the gas-lit hall were pried open for relief. Everyone was tense with excitement—there was "triumph in the air," as if those present knew that this was to be the first of many May festivals in the next hundred years. Finally Thomas appeared, and the huge chorus rose to sing. Orchestra, organ, and voices responded in turn to his baton in Handel's "Dettingen" Te Deum. The festival had begun.

It was, all in all, a good first concert. However, the large hall was kinder to Thomas, who was at his best, and to the orchestra and chorus than it was to the soloists. The *Detroit Tribune* mercilessly pecked away at tenor Nelson Varley's short stature and "shrill" notes, which made his "Sound an Alarm" from Handel's *Judas Maccabeus* at the first matinee the next day seem much like "the chant of the bantam in the poultry yard."[23] Local soprano Emma Dexter, so assiduously promoted by Nichols, made her debut at the second evening concert singing "With Verdure Clad" from Haydn's *Creation*—she also performed at several later concerts—and was applauded loudly by loyal townsfolk but totally demolished by the out-of-town press. The *Chicago Times* recommended that she would sing better "if Cincinnati spent less time petting her and gave her more time for practice."[24] Even George P. Upton, who praised everything Thomas conducted, had to confess that Dexter was "a good society singer only."[25] Nichols was silent.

Among the vocal high spots was the American bass Myron Whitney, an oratorio singer of repute, who had to encore "Rolling in Foamy Billows" (*Creation*) because his first attempt, appreciated as it was, was almost drowned out by the torrents of rain that mercilessly pelted the roof of Sänger Hall. The contralto Annie Louise Cary, a leading American singer who had studied with Pauline Viardot in Germany and sung in prestigious European opera houses, triumphed with excerpts from Gluck's *Orpheus*.

Michael Brand, a young local conductor, directed the children's chorus with a local orchestra on the third matinee, and the packed house could not resist such "a spectacle of grace, beauty and fascination. . . . The girls, about 600 in number, were dressed exclusively in white with blue and red sashes in alternate rows. . . . The effect of colour was singularly beautiful especially in its strong contrast between the dark background of boys and the variegated spring colors of the immense audience in front." [26] The *Chicago Times*, aware of Thomas's objections to the concert, mischievously alleged that Thomas had promised to conduct the children and then "snubbed the whole arrangement. . . . He declined to permit his orchestra to play for them. . . . The Cincinnati players spent most of their time playing in the Thomas orchestra as extra players and thus were unprepared. Thomas is charged with selfishness in seeking to make his own portion of the Festival as successful as possible, and that part of it belonging to Cincinnati as nearly a failure as possible." [27]

Thomas persevered, and his Beethoven's Ninth on the third evening was such a triumph that it made all that followed seem anticlimactic. On the one clear night of the week, even the soloists got full marks, for the Ninth not only sounds hard to sing but is hard to sing. One paper described the rapturous response of the audience, which

> rose *en masse* and went wild with enthusiasm. People mounted their seats, and hats and handkerchiefs were waved. Cheer upon cheer rent the air; and they were not all masculine voices either. Thousands of shouts for "Thomas!" "Thomas!" "Thomas!" went up all over the great hall, until Thomas appeared, and again and again bowed his acknowledgements, and then followed loud calls for Cary and others. It was an intense, deep, significant, all-pervading enjoyment, that told more in the glistening eye, the flushed cheek and the radiant face than in outward demonstrations. It thrilled one through and through in every nerve and fiber.

The writer confessed, unashamedly, "My eyes unconsciously filled with tears, and I was not alone. Was it unmanly? If so, I plead that you have not heard the Ninth Symphony as I heard it last night. Utter strangers grasped each other by the hand and exchanged congratulations. Friend clasped friend, and said: 'Wasn't it glorious!' and the warm responding pressure told volumes that words could not utter. Cincinnatians were jubilant, gloriously jubilant, over the musical success, and the financial aspect, good or bad, seems to be entirely forgotten for the time being."[28]

Lest anyone doubt the power of great music played well for a receptive audience, when Nichols came to the stage at the final concert and asked if the festival should be an annual event, the crowd responded with "a resounding aye."[29] Then Thomas said cryptically: "If I had the ability to speak I should have a great deal to say." Clearly, he had spoken through his music, for the upstart Cincinnati festival was compared favorably with the Handel and Haydn Society festivals by the press in the Midwest and the East. Much of the success was due to programming: only instrumental works were performed in their entirety—symphonies, tone poems, suites, and overtures—excerpts from oratorios and other choral works were the staple, and the matinees were "lighter" than the evening concerts. Thomas, America's musical educator, was not rushing Cincinnati's development of musical taste. He was elated by the public's favorable response to the weightier music programmed, which clearly suggested that more would be welcome at future festivals. Few, if any, noticed that there was only a sprinkling of French and Italian music and no American, except "The Star Spangled Banner" and the children's "America." It was a festival of German music—much like the Handel and Haydn festivals —performed in Middle America.

The Cincinnati festival also received praise for its decorum. The *Indianapolis News* noted that there was "no excessive drinking or hilarity. Decency and order [were] ensured." The *Detroit Tribune*, in the same vein, described festival behavior as "Boston order in Cincinnati halls."[30] For its part, the public liked the long intermissions, which added a relaxed grace to the evening concerts.

Thomas and his orchestra could now call Cincinnati their second home, not a mere touring stop. Local musicians appreciated his high standards, even if they could not as yet meet them. The Queen City had, thanks to Thomas, taken a huge step forward musically, and the local and regional press generally boasted about Cincinnati's cultural accomplishments. In fact, the festival had given the entire Midwest much-needed self-esteem. As for practical matters, box-office income met all expenses, a remarkable feat, and the guarantors —Thomas was one of them—got their money back within a few days. Art, business, and the community had joined forces and succeeded. It was the American way at its best.

With his reputation at new heights, during his sixth season (1873) at Central Park Garden, Thomas boldly convinced the management to raise prices on Thursday nights so that he could enlarge his orchestra and do full-scale symphonic works.[31] To elevate the "tone" of the concerts and teach his audiences more about music, he provided them with a major essay on music and short news items in the printed programs. Whether this was too much of a good thing for Garden audiences remained to be seen. The essays were important, since they reflected Thomas's views, and although he probably did not write them—their authors were not identified—they must have crossed his desk before publication.

The first essay read like a sermon about Thomas and his mission, reminding readers that the Thursday concerts would have been too ambitious a few years back, that Thomas was "a teacher as well as an entertainer," and that, although he did not intend "to make the concerts mainly a study," he would exclude "whatever is not sound and wholesome." It also spoke proudly of the orchestra's symphonic series at Steinway Hall and its adventurous programming. The second essay a week later was lighter on self-praise, stressing the need for a permanent orchestra hall "to put New York in respect of orchestral music on a level with the musical capitals of Europe."[32]

Another essay injudiciously compared the Handel and Haydn Society's performance of Beethoven's Ninth with the Cincinnati festival's and claimed that the Cincinnati Chorus sang the last movement better because it was "trained and drilled for this occasion, first by an accomplished chorus master [Otto Singer], perfectly possessed of Mr. Thomas' views, and, finally, by Mr. Thomas himself. [It] had nothing to unlearn to sing the symphony according to his intentions." The writer felt that Carl Zerrahn's preparation of the Ninth, which Thomas ultimately conducted in New York, was unlike Thomas's conception. Rather patronizingly, the piece added that the Handel and Haydn "had its own traditional method of singing the symphony," that "the methods of no two conductors in such music are identical," and that both performances were in fact "meritorious."[33]

More hints of Thomas's views on music and musical life in the United States were revealed in a eulogistic essay praising Wagner's music and crediting his growing popularity to the "persistency of the one man [Thomas] to whom the introduction of Wagner is mainly due in this country."[34] The writer had obviously forgotten that Bergmann had conducted first performances of excerpts from *Rienzi, Tannhäuser,* and *Lohengrin* in the 1850s (Thomas had actually played at some of these concerts) and that he frequently had programmed Wagner at his Philharmonic concerts, despite opposition. Such immodest and pedantic articles did not, however, help Thomas and his cause. It was puffery, poorly concealed in Gilded Age rhetoric, noble artistic concerns expressed in florid and tedious prose. Was success going to Thomas's head? His admirers reveled in his achievements but worried about such panegyrics.

As the Garden season drew to a close, the nation reeled badly from a financial panic that began on "Black Friday," September 19, 1873. The immediate cause was railroad speculation, but its roots lay more generally in the Civil War, the Austro-Prussian War, the Franco-Prussian War, and the unstable business conditions each created. European recessions, the Chicago Fire of 1871, and the Boston Fire of 1872 had stretched insurance companies beyond their limit and many went bankrupt. The problems of the entire post–Civil War period seemed to be catching up with the American people. Although the nation was on the road to recovery by mid-October, economic depression and widespread unemployment continued for the next three years. Concert life suffered, as did artistic life in general.

Thomas nevertheless decided that this was the time to bring to a head his need for a permanent orchestra in New York and a home for it. Even if the country had lost its buoyant optimism of the early 1870s, he was convinced it would support him. Accordingly, Thomas prepared a lengthy proposal for a practical yet imaginative new hall.[35] Because of New York's dependence on box-office income, the proposed hall would seat 2,500, making it larger than most European halls. Portable partitions, removable for summer concerts to increase seating space and make room for tables, would separate the hall from the adjacent foyers. Refreshments would be served, as at the Central Park Garden, at summer concerts and be available in the foyers for the formal winter events. The seventy-piece Thomas Orchestra would be resident for the entire year, with thirty players added for the six-month winter season. Daily concerts and Saturday matinees would be given in summer and four concerts a week in winter, with two-week vacations for the players between the winter and summer seasons.

The proposal also included a unique scheme to develop new audiences: weekly matinee concerts for young people. (It would be ten years before this was realized.) Looking ahead to a time when Americans would staff his and other orchestras—perhaps 80 percent of his current players were German immigrants—Thomas proposed that a music school for advanced orchestral students be quartered in the new building and promised that the school's orchestra would, among other things, play works written and conducted by student composers. But it all came to nought. The plan received short shrift from civic officials and businessmen, and by the New Year it was dropped altogether.

Thomas was successful that same autumn in forming an American Wagner Union. Similar to several in Europe, it would sell expensive subscription tickets for the first Bayreuth Festival in 1874 at the new Festspielhaus that Wagner was building in Germany, where *Der Ring des Nibelungen* would be staged. Thomas's relationship with Wagner dated back to 1871, when he had asked the composer for permission to do excerpts from the still incomplete *Ring* and Wagner had turned him down. Undeterred, Thomas turned for advice to Hans von Bülow, who suggested that Thomas see Wagner in Europe to make his case. According to von Bülow, the composer was interested in the United States and knew that Thomas was a leading Wagnerian, and he predicted that Wagner would say yes after meeting Thomas. Although the meeting never took place, at a Wagner night during the 1872 Central Park Garden series, Thomas conducted from manuscript the American premiere of the "Ride of the Valkyries." Did he get the music through von Bülow, or did Liszt have it copied without Wagner's knowledge? The full story remains a mystery. As for the "Ride," it made a stunning impression, an incomparable crowd pleaser with which Thomas was to become identified. He vividly recalled the work's initial reception: "the people jumped on the chairs and shouted."[36]

Wagner's refusal to have his *Ring* music done in the United States had more to do with American copyright laws, which failed to protect foreign composers sufficiently, than with artistic concerns. He was always on the lookout for the best possible return and thus needed to work out a legally firm American royalty arrangement. Given the circumstances, Wagner trusted Thomas no more than anyone else, despite the conductor's good intentions, which were evident on and off the concert platform. Thomas, for his part, trusted Wagner and, with the help of two benefit concerts put on by the Thomas Orchestra, sent a substantial donation of $10,000 to the composer in October 1873. Wagner cloyingly thanked Thomas and the Wagner Union but said nothing about the imminent postponement of the Festspielhaus's opening until 1876.[37]

Thomas took to the road again, still the only sure way of keeping his orchestra together, but his joy in bringing great music to the hinterlands and creating new audiences was at a low ebb. He resolved that this would be his last tour, that even if New York would not build him his hall, it would at least back his permanent orchestra. Alas, he was wrong on both counts. Good times or bad, the city government was not ready to subsidize serious musical enterprises like symphony orchestras. Also, Thomas had made some enemies in high places who could and did hurt his cause. To many, he seemed unnecessarily stubborn, taciturn, and abrasive—a musical emperor who wore his crown too boldly and expected more from his subjects than was his right. He was, after all, from a poor immigrant family, a self-educated man who had risen from the ranks and was still rough around the edges. The rich and the privileged expected him to be more humble, more grateful for their help, if and when it was forthcoming.

In December, Thomas returned to the Brooklyn Philharmonic after a six-year lapse, his New York series continued, and he gave other concerts, all well received. He was, in short, still on top. Richard Grant White, the Shakespearean scholar, writer, and philologist, mounted Steinway Hall's stage unannounced at a Thomas concert in April 1874, thanked Thomas for improving the public's taste for good music, and then presented him with a check for $3,500, a gift from "society ladies [and] contributors from every class."[38]

The gift, too small to bring his building plans to fruition, did help to clear up Thomas's Chicago debts. The orchestra was back in Central Park Garden in May 1874, entreating its patrons at every program to have a "resident" orchestra, not a "traveling" one.

The Brooklyn Philharmonic, as appreciative of Thomas as White and his friends, thanked him profusely at a testimonial concert on April 22 for his "long and arduous exertions for the cultivation of the public taste."[39] Pompous Philharmonic members went on at length in this vein, talking about the goodness of music and Thomas's contribution to its propagation and betterment as if referring to the Scriptures. One asks why music—particularly German symphonic music—was listened to so self-consciously, why it was burdened down with pseudophilosophies and implications of moral goodness. Was Beethoven to blame (consider his *Heiligenstadt Testament*) or was Wagner? Couldn't music be enjoyed for what it was instead of being assigned extramusical tasks like building character? "Ordinary" people too often avoided serious concerts because of their artificial, snobbish ambiance and because of the rabid music lovers in attendance who deified German composers and listened to their music as if it had come from God.

Howard Shanet addresses this issue from a twentieth-century vantage point:

> Musicians of the serious type—Rubinstein, for example—were frequently referred to by the German title Herr, even when they were of other nationalities. Repelled by the very commercialism which gave their society unprecedented opportunities for enjoying music, they tried to be noble in art, above sordid money making, avoiding the vulgar "trash" that satisfied lesser souls. These self-righteous attitudes were shared by a small but determined part of the listening public, who sometimes seemed to constitute a semi-religious congregation; by a large number of performing musicians who functioned as artists-priests; and by certain composers, who, if we carry our figure a bit further, seem inescapably to have aspired toward some degree of divinity. . . . As in any cult the public did not always come for pleasure, and the practitioners did not always come for profit; indeed, they seemed often to be participating in an artistic penance.[40]

The end result of this Germanic influence was an American public with fragile and unstable musical underpinnings. Serious music was enveloped in mystique, and though it was fashionable to be a cognoscente, a member of the intellectual and social elite, the supposed listening demands of the music kept the bulk of the population at a distance. But the success of the Central Park Garden concerts—unaffected, down to earth, however light most of them were—proved that there was a substantial public for good music, even among those who equated attendance at symphonic concerts with church-going. Thomas's plan for audience development—from light to serious music in gradual stages—would have been more effective if he had not cast himself as the standard-bearer of the German connection, a symbol of the artificiality and hypocrisy of the times. Music's message is in the music, but Thomas too often thought otherwise.

The Handel and Haydn Society engaged the Thomas Orchestra for its Third Triennial Festival in Boston in May 1874. Thomas amicably shared the conducting with Carl Zerrahn, who did an abridged version of Bach's *St. Matthew Passion*, its first North American performance. Zerrahn used a typically huge Victorian chorus of 600, an orchestra of 90, and a boys' choir of 60. Thomas, who was just discovering Bach's choral music, made note of Zerrahn's efforts and the forces used in this masterpiece.

Also programmed was a new oratorio, *St. Peter*, by the American John Knowles Paine, which, in the prevailing German academic style of the time, made little impact. Paine, born in Portland, Maine, in 1839, was the senior member of a group of German-trained American composers of the second half of the nineteenth century. An organist, he began teaching at Harvard in 1862 and became its first professor of music in 1875. Among his students were John Alden Carpenter, Arthur Foote, Edward B. Hill, Frederick Converse, Henry T. Finck, and Daniel Gregory Mason. Thomas admired Paine's craftsmanship and premiered many of his works over the next three decades. The two men also became good friends, the cultivated Paine showing Thomas affection and respect that the latter could not help but appreciate.

Thomas, who was almost as interested in Brahms's music as in Wagner's, used the festival to introduce the former's *Variations on a Theme by Haydn*. He might have wished that he had not, if he chose to believe the press. The *Boston Traveler* called it an "abstruse and irrelevant arrangement," and the *Transcript* declared: "It was a mistake to admit Brahms, as a disturbing element, in such an otherwise delightful programme. If this composer must juggle with musical themes he should take those of his own composition rather than meddle with the beautiful ideas of a master mind like Haydn."[41] So much for first impressions and for Brahms in 1874.

Plans for the 1875 Cincinnati May Festival moved ahead purposefully. Otto Singer evidently knew Franz Liszt well enough to invite him—with Thomas's permission—to attend. After an exchange of letters, Liszt declined because he felt that the trip to Cincinnati would be too strenuous (he was then sixty-three years old), but the invitation stirred up rumors (perhaps started by Singer) that Liszt would supplant Thomas as the festival's music director.[42] Thomas made no comment and took no action against Singer. He was pleased that the festival was now permanent and that its committee had been legally incorporated as the Cincinnati Music Festival Association (CMFA), with

Nichols as president. On September 19, 1874, as requested by the CMFA, Thomas outlined his proposals for the May 1875 festival in a public letter: two full-scale choral works—Cincinnati was ready for them—as well as several symphonies.[43] Like a field marshal, he referred proudly to the first festival: "Today we are victors. We fought the fight and have come out from the conflict without a scar." He urged the chorus to work hard and do "justice" to the music planned. "Each work is a lofty embodiment of the genius of its author," he reminded them. It was heavy stuff, tractlike, but it probably suited the time and the occasion, for the CMFA replied in the same spirit and stressed the need for "united and earnest action."[44]

The CMFA's management of its affairs would serve as a model for other American music festivals for the next century. During Thomas's years, not only did its artistic goals have top priority, but it responded conscientiously to community needs and met its responsibilities to festival guarantors without compromise. After a sound appraisal of the finances of its first festival, it boldly guaranteed $60,000 for 1875. Sänger Hall was enlarged to 5,000 seats, with standing room for 3,000 more—a wise move, since, as it turned out, more tickets were sold on the day the box office opened than during the entire 1873 festival. Prior to the festival's opening, the town again was resplendent with flags and banners, houses were decorated with evergreens, portraits and busts of composers were in shop windows, and even triumphal arches were built on main avenues.[45] One "stopper," perhaps inspired by Thomas's martial declamations of the previous September, was a large poster of a battle scene with Liszt, Wagner, and Schubert pouring "a destructive fire of musical notes upon the assailants below. . . . [Musical notes] are exploding in every direction. Theodore Thomas, mounted upon a prancing steed, is leading up a solid phalanx of fiddlers to the assault, and a heavy battery of trombones and ophicleides is hurling bass notes into the forts."[46]

In his element, Thomas ruled masterfully over the festival. Calm and composed with the orchestra alone, he was quite the opposite when conducting the chorus, bursting with physical energy and inspiring the amateur singers to rare levels of excitement. One newspaper described him as "violent in gesture, imperious, impetuous, striking with his baton, beating out with both arms, stamping his feet like a big drum, even shouting out the word of command."[47] Highlights were Mendelssohn's *Elijah*, Bach's *Magnificat*, in a romantic scoring for large orchestra and chorus by the song composer Robert Franz, and Beethoven's Ninth, the performance of which was so moving that Cincinnati was said to suffer from "Ninth Symphomania."[48] Thomas generously let Otto Singer conduct Liszt's *Prometheus* at the final concert, and to make everyone happy, *he* conducted the children's chorus, the last time it would appear on the festival program. Again the festival made a profit, and the guarantors got their money back.

Thanks to a retired Cincinnati merchant, Reuben Springer, the festival was not put on hold for the next two years. Springer, born in Frankfort, Kentucky, of relatively humble stock, had married well, built up a profitable wholesale grocery business, invested wisely in real estate and railways, and eventually amassed a huge fortune. Now, profoundly impressed by what he had seen and heard, he proposed to the CMFA that a permanent festival music hall be built and that a new society be formed to run it.[49] The proposal, entitled "Some Views about a Music Hall Building," went into great detail about where the hall would be, how it would be managed, who would use it, and how it would be financed. Springer designated a large city-owned lot for the hall and for additional exposition buildings. He stipulated that the hall must be leased to the society at nominal cost and used solely for the public good. Rental fees would be as low as possible, just enough to keep the building in first-rate condition and defray expenses.

Springer's proposal stressed that the community must be involved in running the hall. He envisaged a society made up of interested townspeople who would pay an initiation and annual membership fee and in return get preferential treatment in purchasing tickets for hall events; the society's board would be chosen by the city council. He also recommended that "the Society should not commence the enterprise with less than $250,000," and its expenses should not exceed this amount, "so that the Society should start clear of debt." The frugal millionaire wanted the building to be "plain, but very substantial; and care should be taken not to lavish money on mere ornamentation. The attempt to make it fireproof [an expensive and therefore controversial innovation in new buildings at the time] should not be even entertained."[50] Springer promised to donate half of the target sum, pending the proposal's acceptance. He wanted no special credit for his role and no part in the hall's management; he wanted only to be known as one of the hall's donors.

Cincinnati jubilantly accepted the offer. The project moved slowly at first, with disputes surfacing between musical and industrial interests because of the adverse effect the new hall might have on the existing Exposition Building. To smooth matters, Springer offered an additional $50,000 for the erection of adjacent exposition wings if citizens would raise an additional $200,000 for the same purpose. He added still another $20,000 in November 1875 when the entire project seemed in jeopardy. On January 3, 1876, the Cincinnati Music Hall Association became an incorporated share-capital company, and three months later the city conveyed the land to it tax-free. Complicated delays in construction necessitated postponing the 1877 festival until 1878. When the exposition wings were completed in 1879, the complex covered an area of 142,000 square feet at a total cost of $497,000; the music hall's organ, the most expensive in the country, was an additional $32,700. Pressed to have the hall named after him, the "quiet, unostentatious and modest" Springer emphatically refused.[51]

Thomas could now look ahead confidently to bigger and better things in

Cincinnati—his own hall, a supportive public, work for his orchestra, and a chorus the equal of any in the United States. New York was a different story. The 1875 Central Park Garden season, Thomas's eighth, had failed miserably. He had recklessly scheduled more esoteric concerts than the public could bear, and attendance dropped sharply. When he engaged Dudley Buck, his organist at the Cincinnati festival, as assistant conductor in order to give himself a break from daily conducting duties, attendance dropped even more. The public had paid to see and hear Thomas, not Buck or anyone else, and it construed his absences as lack of interest.

Adding to Thomas's problems was the unexpected and formidable competition from Gilmore's Garden, formerly known as the Hippodrome. The enormous theater had been transformed during the spring into a mammoth arcade, with fresh grass plots, bright banks of flowers, and beautiful shrubs growing everywhere. It had 2,000 seats and promenade space for several thousand more. The musical attraction was Gilmore's Band, 100 players strong (40 more than the Thomas Orchestra). New Yorkers liked its engaging director and the band's popular and wide-ranging repertoire.[52]

The worst blow, however, came in July with the mysterious disappearance of Thomas's old friend Edward Koch, owner of Central Park Garden, who left behind a raft of unpaid bills. Thomas had no choice but to take over the operation in order to finish what would be his last summer series at the Garden. Undeterred by a bad storm, his followers turned out in droves for the final concert, a benefit in his honor. The principal work was Beethoven's Fifth. After eight years, New York had tired of Thomas's Garden concerts, and so had Thomas. Clearly, he would have to look elsewhere for summer work.

More financial setbacks were in store for Thomas that winter, even though he and his men were as busy as ever. Concert attendance continued to decline, costs went up, and Thomas's growing family was stretching his resources to the limit. Minna had borne him five children, three boys—Franz, Hector, and Hermann—and two girls—Minna and Marion—and although Thomas spent little time with them, he was determined, in the time-honored "American tradition," to provide them with the best education possible and a life free from want, neither of which he had had as a boy. The family lived in a large rented house on East Seventeenth Street, then a fashionable residential area, and its upkeep worried Thomas constantly. He knew he had been too extravagant in view of his circumstances. Then, to his great embarrassment, a suit against him for bad debts—he owed about $20,000—was written up in the press that winter.[53] Fortunately, loans from friends like William Steinway tided him over. The proud conductor tried desperately to solve his financial problems, to no avail.

And then there was Leopold Damrosch. In the four years since his arrival in New York, he had not been idle. During Anton Rubinstein's 1872–73 visit, Damrosch had discussed his frustration at not being able to start an orchestra of his own because of Thomas's popularity and his iron grip on orchestral players. Rubinstein advised him to form an Oratorio Society, to avoid conflict with Thomas, and predicted that eventually other things would come from it.[54] Damrosch followed this advice, and a mutual assistance pact with Thomas was the result. For several years thereafter, the Oratorio Society and the Thomas Orchestra would appear jointly at concerts, and, depending on the repertoire or the sponsors, either Damrosch or Thomas would conduct. Damrosch did Mendelssohn's *St. Paul* and Handel's *Messiah* at society concerts, and Thomas did Beethoven's Ninth at his Steinway Hall series.

Despite their collaboration, the musical world knew that the two men were not friends. Thomas was self-conscious, defensive, and often rude with Damrosch, whose education, elegance, and worldliness he resented; he thought him pretentious and disliked the way he spoke constantly about his prominent European friends. Thomas also was irritated because Damrosch had won over a number of leading New Yorkers to back his enterprises. As for Damrosch, he considered Thomas inflexible, crude, and boorish. He resented Thomas's presumption that all concert music in the city was Thomas's domain, and he was equally dissatisfied when Thomas supposedly threatened to discharge any player who worked for other conductors, especially Damrosch. Further, Damrosch thought that Thomas's knowledge of music was poor and that his conducting was stiff and lacking in interest. As often happens between rivals, each failed to appreciate the other's good qualities.

Sam Franko, the American violinist and occasional concertmaster for Thomas in the 1880s, wrote perceptively of the two men:

> There could scarcely be a greater contrast than the personalities of Thomas and Damrosch: Damrosch, small and lively, didactic and talkative, given to enthusiasms, free and daring in his conceptions—Semitic; Thomas, much taller, practical and matter of fact, taciturn, unimaginative, literal-minded —Nordic-Germanic. Dr. Damrosch was not so popular with his orchestra as Theodore Thomas was with his. He simply was not one of them. He talked over their heads. The musicians were easily disposed to criticize him, while they stood in awe of Thomas. At rehearsals Damrosch was hypercritical, making the orchestra nervous. When the time came for the actual performance, he was often the first to change his own previous instructions.[55]

In 1875, Thomas's darkest year to date, Damrosch had a stroke of good fortune. Hans von Bülow, whom Thomas had met in Europe seven years earlier and had corresponded with intermittently since then, had been engaged by the Chickering Piano Company for an American concert tour similar to Rubinstein's Steinway tour three years earlier. To emulate its formidable competitor, Chickering had built a concert hall, and the German pianist was slated to give the "housewarming" concert. An orchestra was needed to accompany him, and von Bülow apparently recommended or at least approved that Damrosch organize and conduct it. Naturally, Thomas was troubled. Wasn't his orchestra the best in the country, and didn't an artist of von Bülow's stature merit the best? Thomas assumed that von Bülow's Old World connections with Damrosch meant more to him than Thomas did, orchestra or not. He never considered the more reasonable explanation, whenever it was mentioned, that Chickering could not promote its cause with a conductor who was associated with Steinway.

As for von Bülow, after his first New York concert he wrote glowingly to his mother about the United States, its people, the Chickering piano, his old friend Damrosch, and the Damrosch Orchestra.[56] This early infatuation with all things American also led von Bülow to write to his former wife, Cosima Wagner, "I have found my real Fatherland here [and] am now taking the first steps to obtain citizen's rights in this free country."[57] Later, he would change his mind, after playing only 139 of the 172 concerts scheduled and complaining bitterly all the while of concert conditions and audience behavior. He was not as tolerant—by his standards—of the primitive halls and backward audiences he played for as was Thomas or, for that matter, Rubinstein. Von Bülow accused Chickering of exploiting him, and at a rehearsal in Baltimore he removed the Chickering sign from the piano, threw it on the floor, and gave it a hardy kick. The intemperate pianist did not make many friends with such behavior, and Thomas's chagrin changed to relief as reports of such incidents found their way back to New York.

Theodore Thomas at age fourteen,
when he toured the South with
his violin strapped to his back.
(Courtesy of the Newberry Library)

Theodore Thomas at age twenty-
two, already a prominent New
York violinist. (Courtesy of the
Newberry Library)

The Mason-Thomas ensemble, circa 1861. From left to right: George Matzka, Joseph Mosenthal, Frederick Bergner, Theodore Thomas, and William Mason. (Courtesy of the Newberry Library)

The program from the first Philadelphia Centennial concert by the Thomas Orchestra, including works done at the inaugural ceremony. (Courtesy of the Newberry Library)

The program of Rubinstein's final Philadelphia concert, one of several "finals" he did before leaving the United States. (Courtesy of the Newberry Library)

Sänger Hall, site of the First May Festival in 1873. (Courtesy of the Cincinnati Historical Society)

The opening concert at Cincinnati's new Music Hall, May 14, 1878. (Courtesy of the Cincinnati Historical Society)

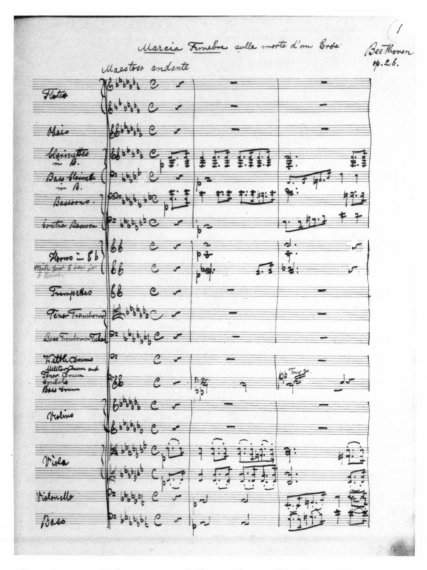

Thomas's autographed transcription for large orchestra of Beethoven's Piano Sonata, op. 26, second movement, *Marchia funebre* sulla morte d'un 'Eroe. Note the full percussion section.

A page from Thomas's autographed transcription of Chopin's *Polonaise in* A♭, op. 53. He altered the key to A Major and must have been confident that the strings would manage the difficult run.

Theodore Thomas in an informal pose prior to a May Festival concert, circa 1894. (Courtesy of the Cincinnati Historical Society)

4

A Chastened Prophet

In 1876, the United States celebrated the 100th anniversary of its birth with a grand international exhibition in Philadelphia, home of Independence Hall, where the Declaration of Independence had been signed and the Liberty Bell rung. The state of Pennsylvania contributed $1.5 million, and the federal government almost $11.5 million, or 1 percent of the country's annual budget, to the exhibition. Despite the importance of the occasion, some cautious congressmen viewed the fair as a "gaudy extravaganza" that the government had no business subsidizing in hard times.

In a sense, they were right. The economic depression was at its worst, and the country had a graft-ridden government and a doubtful president in Ulysses S. Grant. American politics had been described as a "meaningless dance to a tune played by an invisible orchestra."[1] Henry Ward Beecher of Plymouth Church, Brooklyn, one of the country's leading preachers, had been accused of adultery, and the scandal that ensued shattered any illusions Americans might have had about their high standards of morality. Reconstruction in the South had failed and state governments were in disorder and disarray. Blacks were as oppressed as ever; whites were as supreme as ever. Indians were rebelling on the Great Plains in this year of Custer's Last Stand, and immigration was down sharply.

Nevertheless, plans for the Centennial moved ahead. Some 167 buildings were erected on 450 acres in Fairmont Park to accommodate the fifty countries that participated. During the six-month celebration, an estimated eight million of the country's forty million people paid their way to see their nation's strengths: American mechanical and engineering achievements like the Corliss engine, the Bell telephone, and the Otis elevator. It was the beginning of a great industrial era. William Dean Howells said that "no one can see the fair without a thrill of patriotic pride,"[2] and few disagreed.

Theodore Thomas, America's leading musician, was—appropriately enough—the Centennial's director of music. He had taken the position for at least three reasons: he was fervently patriotic; the millions expected at the fair would give enormous impetus to symphonic music nationally and help to build new audiences; and he needed the work. Thomas's first Centennial contact was with the Women's Centennial Executive Committee, organized in 1873 to promote the exhibition and activities of interest to women, including the music program (exhibition authorities thought a women's group could best deal with music). The committee's president was Mrs. E. D. Gillespie, a Philadelphia socialite and a direct descendant of Benjamin Franklin; she was also Reuben Springer's niece and had helped to persuade her uncle to fund Cincinnati's new music hall. Described as "brilliant, witty, fascinating, courageous and strong of mind," Gillespie, a committed supporter of Thomas and his orchestra, was behind the arrangements that brought him to the exhibition.[3]

Thomas had first met Gillespie at the National Sanitary Commission's music festival in Philadelphia in 1864. Eleven years later, they renewed their acquaintance in Cincinnati, where they discussed his potential involvement with the Centennial. J. R. H. Hassard of the *New York Daily Tribune* recommended that Thomas be appointed music director for the celebration because his orchestra was the best in the country—indeed, there were "only two that seriously rival[ed] it in the entire world." The Thomas Orchestra was, according to Hassard, "one of the most interesting products of our aesthetic culture and a triumph of American enterprise. . . . Thomas has a remarkable talent for organizing great celebrations and producing magnificent effects by throughly artistic means."[4] Like George Upton in Chicago, Hassard idolized Thomas and was eager to help him find a needed summer engagement for his orchestra in 1876.

Quite unexpectedly, the committee changed its collective mind and asked Patrick S. Gilmore and his band to play at the Centennial's inauguration, the first musical assignment at the fair, and to give concerts there throughout the summer. *Watson's Art Journal* urged Gilmore to accept the invitation, but the good-natured conductor, with rare professional collegiality, wrote to the editor, Henry C. Watson, asking, "Who, in the profession, is best fitted for so important a position? Who will reflect the highest credit upon the country in that position? And whom would the cultivated musicians and the true lovers of the divine art elect to that office could they have a voice in that selection? I answer these questions, when I say the unanimous choice should and doubtless would be THEODORE THOMAS." To appoint Thomas the Centennial's music director, said Gilmore, would be "a fitting recognition of his eminent services in the cause of art."[5]

The women's committee, confronted with such generosity of spirit and deed, had no alternative but to ask the Centennial's directors for funds to present the Theodore Thomas Orchestra. The committee had considerable clout because of the growing suffragette movement, which, in a sense, it represented, but in the end the directors agreed to pay the Thomas Orchestra for the inauguration concert only. If Thomas wished to give concerts during the exhibition period, sites on the grounds would be recommended. So much for America's "debt of gratitude" to its leading conductor and symphony orchestra. Thomas made his own plans accordingly, thanking the committee for its promise to help—prematurely, as it turned out—by proclaiming that "art and culture in this country can look for support and encouragement only to the women! The majority of men are only taken along."[6]

In the hope that exhibition leaders might yet recognize the importance of good music, Thomas asked the directors to commission two works by American composers, to be performed at the inaugural ceremonies: a hymn by John Knowles Paine to words by John Greenleaf Whittier, and a cantata by Dudley Buck, a German-oriented composer like Paine, to a text by Sidney Lanier. Whittier and Lanier were true poets of the Gilded Age who recaptured the lost innocence of the past; they were good choices for the nostalgic centennial year. The women's committee supported Thomas's request and was charged with raising the money needed for the modest commissions.

Thomas also made a startling request—that Richard Wagner be commissioned to write a work for the opening ceremonies. He felt that having a composer of Wagner's stature so represented at the American Centennial would attest to the international importance of the exhibition and, further, would dramatize the Centennial's inauguration, especially since Thomas, America's leading Wagnerian, would conduct the latest composition from the pen of the greatest composer of the day. Thomas envisaged a brilliant celebration-type march in the style of the ceremonial marches in *Tannhäuser* and *Die Meistersinger*.

The women's committee approved Thomas's plan, and he wrote to Wagner in mid-November. The composer replied encouragingly, "I will say that it is quite possible that for the opening of the American National Festival something may occur to me—perhaps in broad March form—that I can make use of, although I have not written a note of music for a long time, and have quite got out of the way of so-called composing, which you will easily understand." Anticipating the money he might earn from these rich Americans, Wagner continued, "I shall expect, in return, that the Americans will behave well towards me, especially as regards the furtherance of my festival dramas, which I have postponed with special reference to them, to the second half of August, at the cost of considerable trouble in regards to the singers."[7]

Wagner's coy acceptance was as vexing as his marching orders to American Wagnerians to attend the first Bayreuth Festival. The Wagner Union had already promised it would and had raised a large sum toward the building of the Festspielhaus. Why, then, did Wagner blame the postponement on them? In effect, his comment was sales talk; the "hurt" composer wanted to be appeased with a generous commission fee. Wisely, Thomas sidestepped the Bayreuth issue and had Otto Federlein, his business manager, ask Wagner for terms. Wagner then proposed that Thomas and his colleagues either pay an appropriate fee for the piece, leaving copyright and future royalties to Wagner, or purchase the manuscript outright. Since American copyright laws ruled out the former, Federlein asked the wily composer how much money he wanted.

On February 8, 1876, Wagner wrote to Federlein, praising Thomas for his efforts on behalf of German music and promising a composition "of the calibre of my Kaiser March"—hardly a masterpiece—to be delivered by March 15 to a banking house "against the payment of $5,000." In return, he would relinquish all American rights to the work; his publisher, B. Schott, would retain European rights, although Wagner promised that it would not be published until six months after the American version. Knowing that the fee was exorbitant for such a short piece, the "potentate of Bayreuth" claimed that its owners would undoubtedly make huge profits because of his reputation and that he had been offered $2,250 by a Berlin publisher for a similar work (evidently, he saw nothing wrong with asking Americans to pay over twice as much). Verdi, whom Wagner did not consider in his league, had received $10,000 for his *Requiem*, and Wagner implied that he was worth half the sum for a five-minute march.

To Wagner's surprise, if not astonishment, Thomas and the committee accepted his terms. They had convinced themselves that they could recover the fee—maybe more—by publishing the march in piano transcription, which was immensely popular at the time, for the thousands of amateur pianists across the country. Thomas, who would do the transcription himself at no fee, explained the scheme in a follow-up letter to Wagner. The composer immediately took umbrage at such impertinence (even though the committee was within its rights), alleging that Thomas had promised there would be no American transcription. Thomas, of course, had made no such promise, and the reason for Wagner's pique was soon apparent: Schott had already prepared a piano version of the piece, which was enroute to the United States and would soon be on sale in the country's music stores. On being confronted with this violation of their agreement, Wagner said that Schott had acted without his knowledge. Then Wagner had the temerity to offer Thomas exclusive performing rights for the march, which the committee had just purchased.

The score arrived in due course, and with it a letter from Wagner. "I presume," he wrote, "that part of the honorarium was contributed by the Directors of the Exposition and that Mr. Thomas has, moreover, the exclusive right of performance for the United States." Wagner then proposed that the score be published in Europe at the same time as in the United States, despite the original agreement. In the end, it was not, but the affair pained Thomas enormously. Wagner's mercenary attitude, hypocrisy, and downright dishonesty were terribly disillusioning. From then on, Thomas confined his admiration of Wagner to his music only. As for the "Centennial" March, it was little more than a trite potboiler; even Wagner said later that the only good thing about it was the fee. Yet Thomas, inexplicably, thought enough of it to perform it frequently, following its premiere. But he never talked about it or how it came to pass. As for Wagner, he was left sufficiently fascinated to consider moving to the United States and using the $5,000 as "start-off" money, proclaiming that "the best German stock was in the New World." Later, he thought that he would use the money for a visit only. In the end, he took his family on a sumptuous holiday to Italy.[8]

Thomas's travail with Wagner was on top of a bad winter, during which the beleaguered conductor worked furiously to earn money and keep his creditors at bay. His poor judgment in the Wagner negotiations was a result, in part, of his preoccupation with financial problems. His piano version of the Centennial March was published in April by John Church and did not sell well. Thomas had little time to recover from the unpleasant affair before the Centennial opened.

Over 200,000 people attended the opening of the exhibition on May 10, 1876. The day was hot and humid; rain threatened but held off until the afternoon. Many national leaders were present: President Grant, members of Congress, justices of the Supreme Court, and several aspirants for the Republican presidential nomination—James G. Blaine, Roscoe Conkling, and Hamilton Fish. The Thomas Orchestra, augmented to 150 players, and a Grand Centennial Chorus of close to 1,000 Philadelphians, played and sang to the huge crowd. Sad to say, they were heard by but a few thousand who sat close to the speakers' platform. Thomas, resplendent in a morning suit and a silk top hat, looked every inch the circus ringmaster as he led the orchestra and chorus in a potpourri of national airs and tunes representing twelve countries in all. The bustling crowd, which knew little about what was going on, applauded the familiar songs—"God Save the Queen," "La Marseillaise," "Hail Columbia"—and sat on its hands for the others. For President Grant, Thomas struck up "Hail to the Chief."[9]

Wagner's march, which followed, drew considerable comment. As expected, the press praised the piece to the skies. According to the *New York Herald*, the "noble work" brought everyone to silence. Its "grand structure . . . built out of the simplest materials [had] musical electricity. All honor to the Women's Centennial Union that gave to America a musical work worthy of its greatest anniversary . . . that will live until America's next Centennial."[10] The *Daily Tribune* lavishly described the march as "a rich and elaborate text. . . . We know of no other composition in which the essential ceaseless bent of the march has been combined in such an extraordinary manner with the Symphony." It compared the work favorably with *Die Meistersinger* and *Tristan und Isolde*.[11] The *Philadelphia Press*, having noted Wagner's dedication to the Women's Centennial Executive Committee on the title page, said that the march reflected the "feminine loveliness, noble natures, and pure mental activity of American women [and] told of a world of souls communing together in universal concord and exulting together over the marvelous achievements of the just closing century."[12] Only the iconoclastic *New York Times* came close to the truth: the march was "a scholastic treatment of a single theme." It rightly added that a brass band would have been better suited for the inaugural ceremonies than the Thomas Orchestra.[13]

The chorus next sang the Paine/Whittier "Centennial Hymn," followed by the Buck/Lanier "Centennial Meditation of Columbia." Although both works got scant notice in the press, a few critics observed with some surprise how good they were.[14] Whittier's text was labored but mercifully short; Lanier's fared better—it had substance, and baritone Myron Whitney sang the solo part so impressively that he was forced to encore it.

President Grant addressed the crowd, delivering a speech that was refreshingly free of cant—extraordinarily so for the Gilded Age—and was understood all too well by Thomas and other American pioneers in the arts and sciences:

> One hundred years ago our country was new and but partially settled. Our necessities compelled us to chiefly expend our means and time in felling forests, subduing prairies, building dwellings, factories, ships, docks, warehouses, roads, canals, machinery, etc. Most of our schools, churches, libraries and asylums have been established within a hundred years. Burdened by these great primal works of necessity which could not be delayed, we have yet done what this exhibition will show in the direction of rivaling older and more advanced nations in medicine and theology; in science, literature and the fine arts; while proud of what we have done, we regret that we have not done more.[15]

Grant then declared "the International Exhibition now open," as a huge American flag slowly rose over the main building and foreign banners were unfurled. The attentive Thomas took his cue, and the chorus rose to sing Handel's "Hallelujah Chorus" at the top of its lungs, accompanied by the huge orchestra.

Thomas's concerts for the Centennial were given at the Edwin Forrest estate, an attractive setting of landscaped grounds and buildings several miles from the exhibition at Fairmont Park and still further from downtown Philadelphia. The park would have been a more desirable venue, but the grounds closed at nightfall, and, in any case, no tickets could be sold for "special entertainments" like concerts. Travis Quigg, a concert manager and journalist, had purchased the Forrest property early in 1876 and had built there an elegant summer concert hall, which he called Women's Centennial Music Hall, his way of thanking the women's committee for promising to sell $100,000 worth of tickets. The estate gardens had been laid out anew, the main house had been converted into a public restaurant, and the Forrest Art Gallery, a smaller building on the grounds, was designated a deluxe eating place, with a French chef in attendance. The Exhibition Transfer Company promised to transport guests expeditiously to the estate from Fairmont Park, as did Philadelphia transit authorities from downtown. To conclude the arrangements for what promised to be a great summer, the sanguine Quigg engaged the Thomas Orchestra for the duration of the Centennial at $3,300 per week, from which Thomas would personally earn $800. This was three times more than the group had earned at Central Park Garden the previous summer and for fewer performances, since the "City of Brotherly Love" did not countenance Sunday concerts.

The season opened on May 11, the second day of the celebration. Committee members, as guests of the management, were prominently ensconced in box seats, and there were an estimated 3,000 people in the audience. The opening concert was proudly called the "grandest musical performance ever given in a music hall in Philadelphia."[16] Alas, from that night on public attendance steadily declined. Exhibition visitors clearly preferred resting in their hotel rooms after a day of exhibit-viewing over making the long trip to the Forrest estate. If they did go out, they chose the lighter entertainment and "novelties" showing in downtown Philadelphia. There was, after all, other music at the exhibition during the day, notably Gilmore's free band concerts.

The poor attendance stunned both Thomas and Quigg, who, by the end of May, were each blaming the other for the catastrophe. Quigg said that Thomas's repertoire was too serious for summer concerts and that the conductor's insistence that people remain seated during concerts hurt restaurant and bar sales. Unlike Central Park Garden, with its ample space for listening, socializing, and drinking, the Forrest aisles were so narrow and the seats so close together that waiters could not unobtrusively take drinks to people at their seats. Without libations, the notorious Philadelphia humidity seemed worse than it was.

Thomas, not disposed to compromise, simply accused Quigg of poor management,[17] and with both men at an impasse, the situation looked hopeless. The denouement came in the third week, when Thomas mounted the podium at the start of the concert and told a dumfounded audience that there would be no concert unless the management complied with his demands, which were, as was later revealed, that Quigg make good the orchestra's fees. Thomas then walked off the stage, leaving the public to witness a bizarre spectacle—a debate on stage between Thomas's lawyer and a Quigg representative as to the rights and wrongs of the case. Eventually, cash refunds were given to all present, including (mistakenly) seventy-two people with complimentary tickets.

Several days later, after charges and countercharges were presented, the concerts resumed. Quigg, angry that the Women's Centennial Executive Committee had failed to deliver the promised customers, renamed the hall Forrest Mansion.[18] His advertising stressed popular and informal concerts in superb surroundings, the "most desirable Summer Resort in the Country." On June 8, a concerned New York Daily Tribune reported that Thomas was paying the orchestra out of his own pocket and conducting without fee.[19] It lamented that his misfortune could have been avoided if New York had given his group a home for the summer season. On June 21, in a foolhardy move, Thomas took full financial responsibility for the concerts, the same day that Jacques Offenbach launched a series of concerts and operettas downtown. Attendance at Thomas's concerts continued to decline.

Offenbach, France's leading operetta composer, had arrived in New York in May to conduct at Gilmore's Garden for a much-publicized, extraordinary fee of $1,000 a night. Admission was twice what Thomas had charged at Central Park Garden, and the box office was poor. Audiences had expected to see the famed cancan, but all they got were musical excerpts from Offenbach operettas—well done, to be sure, but hardly novelties. Offenbach then moved on to the Booth Theater, where he gave complete performances of his operettas and won over New York's public and, significantly, its musicians. Before his departure for Philadelphia, his admiring orchestra honored him with a banquet and several imposing gifts that attracted wide attention in musical circles: a marshal's ebony baton with an agate set in one end, an amethyst in the other, and, in the middle, a massive golden lyre with Offenbach's initials on it; and a white satin tablecloth embroidered with appreciative comments from his players.[20]

Rumor had it that Thomas was annoyed and jealous. Soon a war of words ensued, manufactured mainly by the press, though Offenbach chose to include most of it in his written account of his American visit. For example, when Thomas was asked to do an Offenbach piece, he was alleged to have said: "Never will I do anything so degrading." Nothing could have been further from the truth; Thomas had performed many a work by the Parisian composer. Offenbach, who chose to believe what he heard, replied: "Please tell Mr. Thomas that I will not be so particular. I shall be most happy to conduct any composition of Theodore Thomas when he reaches the dignity of becoming a composer."[21]

Offenbach would write later that Thomas was a mediocre violinist who had turned to conducting to make more money and had subsequently developed his reputation by being a Wagner specialist. Although he grudgingly conceded that "one must do [Thomas] this justice—he has succeeded in bringing together an excellent orchestra [of] the best musicians in America and pays them very well. . . . His orchestra stands for really marvelous ensemble playing," Offenbach went on to say, "I saw him lead his musicians in some so-called light music . . . without fire and without rhythm." (Clearly, he mistook Thomas's quiet grace and control on the podium for a lack of emotion and a cold approach to conducting.) Offenbach continued: "When he does happen to put energy into conducting he waves both arms at the same time and looks from the rear exactly like a big bird attempting to fly." Finally, in a petty and nasty vein, he commented: "It is significant that [Thomas] has a special affection for the music of the director of the Paris Conservatoire, my good friend Ambroise Thomas; he rarely fails to program a piece by the composer of *Mignon*. Three-fourths of the time the public is under the impression that it is the conductor Thomas who wrote the work."[22] In fact, Thomas did not play Ambroise Thomas's music any more than was deserved or appropriate.

On the state of the arts in the United States, Offenbach wrote with more probity and insight: "The soul of a country is art, the expression of thought in its most elevated form. In New York there is no permanent opera. . . . The directors and their companies are all nomads. So are the leading artists who, for the most part, are birds of passage coming from the old world and bent upon returning there." Public subsidies for theaters and conservatories were needed, so that "students of today" would be "masters" twenty years hence. America would then truly be artistically independent, and the world would seek out talent in America.

The composer's views received wide attention; and Thomas, for one, was in complete agreement with him. The United States had no cultural traditions of its own that it recognized and valued, particularly in the performing arts. It looked to Europe for artists and standards, lacking confidence in itself as a nation and as a people. Americans did not see the importance of planting and nurturing the seeds for an artistic life of their own; their insecurity, their quest for material wealth, and their adulation of things foreign plagued them. Certainly, the American spirit had not yet been expressed musically.

Offenbach's engagement at the Centennial was at the Alhambra Theater, renamed Offenbach Gardens for the occasion. He did a week of *bouffes* that dealt the Forrest Mansion concerts a lethal blow. On July 31, the public was told that the Thomas evening concerts would be discontinued and that "holders of package tickets can have their money returned."[23] The women's committee had sold a grand total of $95 worth of subscriptions, Quigg was left with a mortgage of $78,000, and Thomas was $20,000 in debt. The sheriff seized Thomas's library, including the Wagner march, his baton, and his inkstand, all to be sold later at auction for $1,400. The purchaser, Dr. Franz Zinsser, a Thomas supporter from New York, had heard of the conductor's misfortune and made certain that items like the irreplaceable library did not fall into other hands. Zinsser subsequently returned everything to Minna Thomas and asked her to persuade her husband to accept it without payment.[24]

Thomas had worked to the limits of human endurance for five years to clear his debts, only to sink into deeper financial trouble. There were rumors that his orchestra would disband and that, his spirit broken, he would give up music. Neither came to pass. Thomas refused to accept the terms of bankruptcy and, determined to repay all his debts, rode out the crisis.[25] With his players remaining loyal to him, he firmed up the New York Steinway series for 1876–77 and gave ten concerts in Philadelphia in September under the auspices of the Women's Centennial Executive Committee (thanks to Mrs. Gillespie, who felt obligated to help him after the summer's debacle). When Thomas was asked to direct at the Centennial's closing ceremony on October 31, he quoted a healthy fee of $2,300, to which the exhibition directors agreed. As for the future, Thomas still had no sponsor for the New York hall planned three years earlier and no stable income for his orchestra.

The New York Philharmonic was also having difficulties that threatened its future. When Dr. R. Ogden Doremus had become president nine years earlier, in 1867, he enlarged the orchestra to 100 players, raised Carl Bergmann's salary—he had become the Philharmonic's sole conductor in 1865— and engaged leading soloists like the French violinist Camilla Urso to increase ticket sales. He also saw that more new music was done, including Liszt and Wagner. Then Doremus led an audience-building campaign among the well-to-do, who could afford the hefty prices the Philharmonic charged. There were well-placed advertising and ingenious ploys like auctioning off the series' box seats, which gave the concerts a fashionable aura and snob appeal. In Doremus's second year, the Philharmonic gave six instead of five concerts, and ticket receipts went up from $14,061 to $23,636.[26]

Then, in 1870, George Templeton Strong, a prominent attorney, amateur organist, and staunch advocate of Beethoven and other pre-Wagner German composers, succeeded Doremus as Philharmonic president. Strong's taste was reflected in the Philharmonic's conservative programs, which pleased the increasingly elitist subscribers and resulted in the best sales ever. Reserved seats were introduced, and audience behavior improved (latecomers were not admitted until a work was completed). But Strong and his colleagues irritated

New York's daily press by cutting down on advertising and being parsimonious with complimentary tickets for its music critics. The press retaliated, called the society greedy, and claimed that money meant more to it than art, that its programs were designed to please a small clique, and that it gave its best seats to "pet subscribers."[27]

After the financial panic of 1873, sales declined rapidly, as did the quality of the orchestra. Bergmann was losing his grip, and players of the "old guard," who no longer could handle their parts, were bringing down the group. In the spring of 1876, Bergmann, a hopeless alcoholic, died, and a replacement was sought. Philharmonic directors had approached Thomas in 1874, when Bergmann's drinking problem had grown worse; now, the need was urgent, and Thomas was invited to take over as conductor. Eager to earn more money, he agreed, but with several conditions: to continue his own Steinway Hall concerts with the Thomas Orchestra; to have the weaker players in the Philharmonic released; and, unlike Bergmann, to have the final say in the orchestra's programming.

The Philharmonic board might have sorted out the membership and programming demands—Thomas was neither unreasonable nor lacking supporters in the society—but it could not countenance the formidable competition of the Thomas Orchestra. When Thomas stood firm, the Philharmonic was forced to look elsewhere. Inquiries were made in Europe, with no success. Then the directors approached Leopold Damrosch, who promptly accepted. Such recognition was long overdue. Damrosch had been in the United States for five years and had had few opportunities to conduct orchestral music, despite his considerable experience in this field in Europe. The appointment pleased a public looking for new heroes and left Thomas shaken by the support his talented adversary had received.

Thomas, now forty-two-years old and penniless, vowed to make New York's symphonic audiences his own on *all* fronts. He started a second, lighter series of concerts at Steinway Hall in October 1876, to balance his heavier series. Newsy programs were distributed, much like those he had made available at Central Park Garden, that kept the public informed of what he and other New York musicians and groups were doing. One early program praised the Philharmonic for resuming its three open rehearsals in addition to its six concerts and for engaging "a throughly competent and conscientious conductor in Dr. Leopold Damrosch who, it is to be hoped, will put fresh vim in the Society." The program also noted that the Philharmonic had "very wisely avoided clashing with Theodore Thomas' symphonic concerts this season."[28]

Damrosch's programs were interesting and varied. He included a number of American premieres—excerpts from *Die Walküre* and *Die Götterdämmerung*, works by Saint-Saëns and Goldmark, selections from Berlioz's *Les Troyens*—and even played the solo part in Beethoven's Violin Concerto.

But instead of being pleased, Philharmonic subscribers were upset. They remonstrated that the programs were too serious and earnest, and they stayed away in droves. Poor Damrosch, he could do nothing right; if Thomas had conducted the same works, they would, in all likelihood, have praised him. The musical public, resenting Thomas's rule over New York's symphonic life, had welcomed a new leader, but once the honeymoon was over, it preferred Thomas in spite of his self-confidence and—some felt—arrogant and overbearing ways. The Philharmonic Society's 1876–77 season was a disaster, its total income of $8,000 the lowest in fifteen years. Players earned a meager dividend of $18 each, $7 less than in its very first year.

The Philharmonic once again approached Thomas, in June 1877, and because he was in a stronger bargaining position than the year before, he made a new and more far-reaching demand: to *merge* his orchestra with the Philharmonic and then use a somewhat reduced Philharmonic as the touring Thomas Orchestra. It made sense, for a large number of players were already in both groups, but what would happen to the twenty-four Philharmonic players Thomas wanted to replace with his own men? Thomas's financial demands were modest: in lieu of a fee, he asked for nine shares of the dividends, on top of his entitlement to one as a member of the society, thus tying attendance to potential earnings. In return, he promised to abide by the Philharmonic's bylaws and the rules pertaining to its conductor—that is, he would not be, as many members feared, the "dictator" of the orchestra.

The Philharmonic Society proceeded with its annual elections for conductor: Thomas got thirty-nine votes to Damrosch's nine. Damrosch was promptly nominated to honorary membership in the society, a diplomatic way of dispensing with his services forever, and negotiations with Thomas resumed.[29] He urged the Philharmonic to accept his twenty-four musicians as members and to waive the requirement that potential members play a trial concert with the orchestra before being accepted. Compromises followed, the end result being that eighteen Thomas players were elected to membership along with three other nominees. To everyone's surprise, Thomas seemed pleased and accepted the conductor's post, although he did not merge his orchestra with the Philharmonic.

For the rest of his days in New York, Thomas led two orchestras and would constantly confuse them when he talked about "his" orchestra. No one minded, since he identified equally with the Philharmonic and his own group. It was having the name Theodore Thomas on marquees and billboards that was important, for that is what sold concert tickets. He had brought the Philharmonic Society to its knees, but once done, his loyalty to it was total. The orchestra, at first ambivalent, was soon as devoted to him as was his own group. When all was said and done, there was a feeling of inevitability in the Philharmonic's appointment of Thomas. The society had meant much to him when he had joined it at the age of nineteen, and now, despite two decades of frequent and deserved criticisms of its work, it still did. Even in the 1860s, when Thomas was starting out as a conductor, many said that he was the man to lead the Philharmonic. His positive attitude and superior ability certainly dispelled any doubts about the wisdom of the society's choice. Where Bergmann had been a talented and at times inspiring conductor, Thomas was a gifted conductor with the tools to make the orchestra his instrument as few others could. America's first orchestra was now led by America's leading conductor.

Together, Thomas and the Philharmonic would have years of prosperity, although the Philharmonic, despite its prestige—a result of its place in history as much as its deeds and influence—would never be the permanent New York orchestra Thomas wanted so badly. In his first year, receipts increased from $841 to $6,402, and players' dividends increased from $18 to $82.[30] The new Damrosch concert series, liberally sponsored by wealthy Damrosch supporters, was well received but did not hurt attendance at Thomas's Steinway Hall concerts during their final season or at the Philharmonic concerts, and the Theodore Thomas Orchestra, his elite group, carried on as such.

The Philharmonic appointment did not mean the end of Thomas's four-year-old dream of a new concert hall. The Thomas Garden Concert Corporation, formed in 1877, proposed to the city that Gilmore's Garden, centrally located between Madison and Fourth avenues on Twenty-sixth Street, be the site. Thomas unveiled a plan for the building's renovation, patterned after Milan's Vittorio Emanuele Galleria, a two-story "iron and glass" structure remarkably ahead of its time. The first floor would be an indoor arcade-promenade with shops, restaurants, and the like. The concert hall would be on the second floor, bordered by two acres of gardens—"grass, flowers, palms, fountains, and a multitude of little refreshment tables." There would be ample room for walking and, from the gallery promenade, "a full view . . . of the entire scene below. In Summer we shall have an open-air garden, in winter a conservatory; and thus the symphony concert will provide a new attraction in the charm of fresh air."[31]

Either the proposal was too daring and expensive or the public was not sufficiently interested. In any case, the building never got beyond the blueprint stage, leaving Thomas with another unrealized dream. His winter seasons of 1876–77 and 1877–78 were much as before: New York, Brooklyn, and touring. The Philharmonic was added in 1877, brightening that year somewhat, and the 1877 summer was, as we shall see, a marked improvement over the Centennial ordeal, thanks to a long engagement in Chicago that had significant ramifications for the future and profitable shorter engagements in St. Louis and Cincinnati.

Thomas was looking for a permanent home for his orchestra, and Chicago proved to be an attractive alternative to New York. This vibrant and most

American of American cities had recovered fully from the fire, was developing at breakneck speed, and would soon be America's second city. Several of its new buildings had already been cited as outstanding examples of contemporary American architecture, and more were to come. Signs of prosperity were everywhere. Best of all, Chicago admired Thomas.

George Carpenter, a Chicago concert manager, proposed that Thomas give a summer series in 1877 in an imposing, barnlike Industrial Exposition Building, two city blocks long, that had been constructed in 1871 on the shores of Lake Michigan in downtown Chicago. Designed to accommodate up to 50,000 people, the hall had been the site for many large-scale events in the Windy City. It seemed like a mad idea, an acoustical nightmare. To make things worse, the building itself was next door to Chicago's downtown railway yards, with their noisy trains, ringing bells, and cars being shunted from track to track, all of which were sure to drown out any orchestra, no matter how large.[32]

Yet Carpenter—and Thomas—were right: concerts there *were* possible. The two men decided to tolerate the trains and address the acoustics. To provide a satisfactory orchestral sound audible to several thousand listeners, Thomas designed an innovative thin wooden sounding board, thirty-two feet high by fifty feet wide, that leaned forward at an angle of thirty degrees. The stage had four levels, for the strings, woodwinds, brass, and percussion,[33] and the public sat on "common wooden chairs" close to the orchestra at fifty cents a seat, with tables and promenade space in the rear. Potted plants and shrubs dressed up the stark interior of the building, while lake breezes kept everyone cool.

With hard work and luck, Chicago's "Summer Night Concerts" promised to do for that city what the Central Park Garden concerts had done for New York—namely, introduce great music to thousands of listeners who were to be the serious audiences of the future. Chicago's musical taste had, in fact, progressed because of Thomas's pre-1877 visits, thus permitting his programs in his first year at the Exposition Building to be comparatively more advanced than at his first Garden season nine years earlier. The conductor stuck to his principles—the concerts had to have educational value, regardless of sales—and used such program themes as "Composer Nights" (Beethoven, Mozart, Wagner), "Symphony Night" (complete major works), "Ballroom Night" (waltzes, ballet music, polkas, galops, quadrilles, ländlers, even saltarellos), "Modern Composers Night" (Berlioz, Liszt, Wagner), "Une nuit Française" (Méhul, Auber, Rameau, Gounod, Berlioz, Saint-Saëns, Massenet, Giraud—demonstrating Thomas's sensitivity to the attractions of French music), "People's Programs," "Popular Gems," and "Popular Matinees."

Carpenter had shrewdly suggested "Request Nights," which Thomas took to readily and which caught the public's fancy. Audiences were asked to suggest encore performances of works done during the season, and Thomas not only complied with the requests (600 to 1,000 weekly) but used them to guide him generally in his programming.[34] Frothy works prevailed the first season: Mendelssohn's "Spring Song," Ghys's "Amaryllis," Strauss waltzes, Gounod's "Ave Maria." Years later—the concerts lasted for fourteen seasons, with only a few gaps—the increasingly sophisticated Chicago public chose compositions by Bach, Beethoven, Brahms, and Wagner.

Philo Adams Otis, a leading Chicago musical patron, described a typical summer night concert: "The young and frivolous gathered about the tables among the evergreen trees, partaking of lemonade and ice while enjoying the strains of 'The Beautiful Blue Danube'. Spectacled young women and grave young men sat in the 50-cent section and listened reverently to Bach, Beethoven and Brahms. . . . The informal Bohemian character of the interior, the low prices of admission, with the charm of Mr. Thomas' programs all combined to make the concerts very popular."[35] Evidently stronger refreshments like Kaiser and Pilsener beer were also served, as were sandwiches, buttermilk, lady fingers, and Liston's Iced Bouillon.

Thomas liked Chicago audiences as much as they liked him. He wrote a group of prominent Chicagoans that after eleven seasons of summer night concerts New York had not "supplied" his needs and had "induced [him] to try the West." He found Chicago's people to be "open-hearted, generous and enthusiastic. . . . Chicago is the only city on the continent, next to New York, where there is sufficient musical culture to enable me to give a series of fifty consecutive concerts."[36]

Another highlight of the summer of 1877 was a three-week engagement at Highland House atop Mt. Adams in Cincinnati, which helped to consolidate Thomas's position in the Queen City. Cable cars took people from the center of the city to the attractive site, and attendance never dropped below 2,500 for any of the twenty-three concerts. Railways arranged special excursions for concertgoers from central Ohio, Indiana, and Kentucky. Cincinnati treated Thomas warmly, as one of its own, and the feeling was mutual.

In contrast to 1877, the summer of 1878 was nightmarish. Chicago's Exposition Building was unavailable, and Thomas, in desperation, booked his orchestra into a refurbished Gilmore's Garden in New York. Not only did he hate the setting, but, to add insult to injury, he had to alternate on the concert platform with the Seventh Regiment Band and the Dodworth Band, because the management wanted continuous music, and was required to have a cornet soloist. Only those close to the bandstand could hear the orchestra, but Gilmore's public did not mind—it preferred bands. How ironic that, despite recent successes like the Cincinnati festival and the Philharmonic, Thomas had to undertake such demeaning work to keep his orchestra together.

Financial troubles, frustrated dreams—the strain was showing. Shortly after the Gilmore concerts began, Thomas fell into a deep depression. He was listless, disinterested, and remote on the podium; deputies conducted frequently. Preoccupied with doubts about his own work and his future, he asked himself if things were any better than they were ten years earlier. Was his obsessive wish to keep his orchestra together worth the price? Should he leave New York and start anew elsewhere? Could any other city, even Chicago, support a year-round orchestra? What *should* he do?

5

Escape to Middle America

Theodore Thomas turned to Cincinnati for the answers to his questions. There, he might realize his dream of a permanent orchestra with its own home, thanks to Reuben Springer's new Music Hall, the site of Cincinnati's third and, to date, most important May Festival. The impressive edifice loomed imposingly over the Queen City, vintage High Victorian–Gothic architecture, its red brick façade ornamented with Romanesque round arches, corbeling, and towers—a hodgepodge of styles, but evidently just what Cincinnatians wanted. As for Thomas, he was more concerned with the building's interior, which did not disappoint him: attractive large vestibules, spacious corridors, and numerous points of entry and exit to the main auditorium (a reflection of the growing attention to fire safety in American theaters), along with the most up-to-date ventilation devices to cope with Cincinnati's hot summer evenings.

The auditorium itself was large—approximately 4,200 seats—perhaps too large for orchestral concerts, but certainly ideal for choral events, given prevailing views on the forces needed to perform Handel's oratorios and similar works. It had wooden walls, which warmed the sound, and a huge stage, with space for an orchestra of 100 and a chorus of 700. There was also a massive organ with no less than 81 stops (some said 94), 6,287 pipes, and 4 manuals —the largest organ in the United States and surpassed only by the organs at Albert Hall and the Church of Saint-Sulpice in Paris.[1]

Thomas and the public liked the Music Hall, even though inside it was plainly decorated and a trifle austere for a concert hall/opera house. Springer had promised Spartan simplicity and had not broken his word. He did, however, provide an unexpected bonus—a small auditorium on the third floor designed for chamber concerts, lectures, and rehearsals, to supplement the activities of the large auditorium. Together, Music Hall and the planned Exposition Building would be one of the earliest municipally owned community centers for the arts and industry in the United States, an accomplishment for which Springer rightfully deserved the credit. The Cincinnati Music Festival Association (CMFA), to show its appreciation, had his picture on all of its advertising, usually flanked by reproductions of composers like Beethoven and Schubert.

In spite of the excitement attached to having the 1878 festival in a new hall, preparations were more troublesome than for the two previous festivals. The chorus, drawn primarily from Cincinnati choirs, was the principal source of contention. As usual, attendance was a problem at rehearsals, and George Ward Nichols was accused by choristers of not giving a hoot for them, of being unnecessarily stingy in granting travel funds for out-of-town choirs. Chorusmaster Otto Singer, ready at once to criticize Thomas behind his back, let both the chorus and the CMFA board know that Thomas had chosen works too difficult for the chorus—Gluck's *Alceste*, several of Wagner's choruses, the *Messiah*, Beethoven's Ninth. Singer had requested Liszt's *Missa solemnis*, not an easy work. When the local *Sängerbund* asked to join the chorus well after rehearsals had begun, Thomas turned them down, prompting Singer to tell the German community that Thomas preferred local Anglo-Saxon groups to German ones. Singer tried to incite the Germans still more when Thomas declined to use local instrumentalists—nearly all were German—in the festival orchestra because of inadequate rehearsal time.[2]

Problems arose also with the soloists. Nichols pushed a local contralto of dubious distinction, Louise Rollwagen, to sing the Liszt instead of Annie Louise Cary (who compounded the problem by asking for $1,500 instead of the expected $1,000, which Myron Whitney, the leading baritone, had accepted; soprano Eugenie Pappenheim was getting $1,200, but she was from abroad!). Thomas, vexed by Nichols's machinations—he was in cahoots with Singer—got his way in the end, but after much travail. As for Singer, he failed to get the CMFA board to raise his fee from $2,500 (half of Thomas's fee) to $3,000. The board itself was split in its loyalties—Nichols and Singer versus Thomas—which contributed to a number of its members resigning after the festival.

These internal disputes had little effect on Cincinnati, however. Its citizens, other than those in the German quarter, overflowed with enthusiasm, with the desire to hear good music. Shopkeepers and hoteliers were equally enthusiastic at the prospect of the business in store for them. An appreciative Chamber of Commerce, cognizant of what the festival brought Cincinnati, fielded a huge banner, "Commerce Is the Handmaid of the Arts"—a maxim for future festival planners, in Cincinnati or elsewhere.

Opening day arrived, with an estimated (probably exaggerated) crowd of

6,000 in attendance. Every seat in the new hall was taken, the aisles over-flowed with standees, and scalpers sold $2 tickets for up to $100![3] The doors opened an hour before concert time to allow early arrivals to tour the building. Even so, there were latecomers, Thomas's pet peeve. His excerpts from Gluck's *Alceste* were poor choices that wore heavily on the audience, leading one to wonder about his usually infallible instinct for good programming.

The official opening ceremonies followed, with Springer, almost an oc-togenarian, slowly making his way to the platform amid cheers from the audience. He spoke briefly, almost inaudibly, disclaiming personal praise and credit and promising "that when this building is completed no debt will rest upon it. Honor to whom honor is due—[to] the architects moved by the very spirit of harmony [and to] the laborers, hodcarriers and workmen of all kinds, who did not appear to work merely for their daily wages. They moved as if their heart and soul were in what they were doing, and I may say with truth that from the highest to the most humble, it was a labor of love."[4] Honor, duty, pride in one's work—the audience cheered still more. Then came "Fes-tival Ode," composed especially for the opening by Otto Singer. A hastily written setting of a pedestrian poem by F. A. Schmitt, its final three lines, sung by 700 voices, stereotyped the hopes of all present:

> May purest art this place adore—
> Ye graceful muses, leave it not,
> For ever—evermore!

The great occasion and the festival concerts that followed inspired solo-ists, chorus, and orchestra to outdo themselves. The matinee programs, as usual, were given over to short solo and orchestral pieces, while the evenings addressed works such as the *Messiah*, Beethoven's Ninth, and Berlioz's *Romeo and Juliet*. There was a special surprise too—Thomas emerged again as a violinist, delighting festival-goers by playing a transcription of Handel's well-known *Largo*. Standing room only prevailed at all concerts, and when the festival was over, the jubilant CMFA bragged not only about its great concerts but about its box office—$70,000, as compared to $40,000 in 1875. The Chamber of Commerce also verified that hotels had been full, stores busy, and all means of transportation—streetcars, railroads, river packets—used to capacity. "For a whole week one object seemed to animate every one, to hear music and to spend money, and at the end of the week Cincinnati was much richer than at the beginning."[5]

Thomas was in full command of Cincinnati's musical feast. He had con-ceived the festival six years before, had set its artistic standards, had scorned halfway measures, and was now reaping the rewards. The townspeople had identified his goals even if they had not fully understood their substance. His and their needs were mutually consummated by a wedding of music and community action. The Queen City may not have been the equal of Boston or New York in its musical taste—its love of pomp and ceremony, bigness and bombast, was also a bit much—but it had created a festival and a hall and had much that it could teach other American cities. For his part, Thomas never appreciated Cincinnati more than in May 1878. He had directed his kind of festival in his kind of hall, the type he coveted for New York but could not have there. His orchestra was better than ever, and the chorus was trained to his satisfaction. The press was, by and large, laudatory, his two adoring critics, George Upton of the *Chicago Tribune* and J. R. H. Hassard of the *New York Daily Tribune*, sending ecstatic accounts of his triumphs to their respective dailies. Thomas was eager for New York and Chicago to know what he had done.

In July, when Thomas was two months into the wearisome Gilmore engagement in New York, George Nichols wrote to him that he intended to start a music college in Cincinnati "which will not be inferior to those celebrated in Europe" and that he wanted Thomas to be its musical director. "Are you not tired of carrying the weight of that orchestra? Will you not accept the opportunity of firmly fixing yourself for life in a position which you can if you choose make distinguished and successful?" [6]

The proposal, so unexpected, could not have caught the depressed conductor at a better time. Thomas replied cautiously, saying that he was reluctant to leave his orchestra, New York, and touring, that he had operatic aspirations and was considering a European career. Nichols wrote a second letter with fresh bait: "[We would] widen the school so as to make it a school for orchestra. . . . Just how much of your Eastern life and work you could keep is a matter for consideration. . . . We will make this the musical center of the United States." The wily Nichols threatened to go to Germany for a director —Raff, Joachim, "or some other big fish"—if Thomas said no. He also reminded Thomas of the daily grind of travel and concerts, of his need for a fixed salary and "honourable station." In early August, Nichols suggested a handsome annual salary of $8,000 to $10,000 "for five or more years," which would be lowered if Thomas wished to keep up any of his New York activities.

Nichols, who had taken the lead in establishing the college, was a typically American mixture of idealist and materialist, a practical doer who would stop at nothing to achieve his goals. There was a lot of Nichols in Thomas, and vice versa, which may have explained their mutual antipathy, dating back to the 1873 May Festival. Two weeks after Nichols made his salary proposal, twenty-two leading Cincinnati citizens, including Reuben Springer and Julian Dexter, after whom Music Hall's smaller auditorium had been named, extended a formal invitation to Thomas to become the college's director.

Thomas weighed the pros and cons carefully and unhurriedly, or so he thought. Was it an appropriate position for the conductor of the New York Philharmonic, the Thomas Orchestra, America's musical educator? How clear was he on the points Nichols had raised concerning his being in Cincinnati year-round? Should he have more details about the college itself? Nothing was said as to how it would be financed other than that a number of rich men would be behind it. Then there was Nichols, who intended to play a key role in the school. In view of past difficulties, could Thomas really work with him at close quarters—Nichols as president, Thomas as musical director? The strong-willed, independent conductor might well be put at Nichols's mercy if he was not careful. Of course, Thomas could not know that Nichols, who piously stated that a music school should serve the community, did not understand what this meant, that his concern was primarily to run it cost-effectively.

There were several reasons for Thomas to consider Cincinnati favorably. A generous salary ($10,000) and financial stability would enable him to clear up his debts quickly. He could bring his best instrumentalists with him from New York as player/teachers, and, in a year or two, he might have as fine an orchestra as his present group, with a fine concert hall in which to play. Touring, which had become so intolerable, would be either drastically reduced or dropped. Cincinnati, not New York, would be the musical center of the United States, much as Leipzig, with its conservatory and Gewandhaus Orchestra, not Berlin, was in Germany. Thomas would have a rewarding musical/academic life, with time for study, for arranging music, and for playing. And he would, at last, have the time to be a husband and father to his family. There was also, lurking in the back of Thomas's mind, the concern that Nichols *would* bring a prominent European to Cincinnati if he turned down the offer. Singer, who was close to Nichols, had the contacts, Nichols the determination, and the college the money for such a move. The salary would tempt any fine international musician, and, whoever it was, he might ultimately take over the May Festival.

Weary and disheartened, exhausted by a summer at Gilmore's Garden, angry with New York for not giving him a permanent orchestra and a hall, and feeling sorry for himself far more than he should have, Thomas signed a five-year contract with the Cincinnati College of Music on August 22, 1878. He agreed to live in Cincinnati, to organize an orchestra under the overall direction of the college, to conduct all of his concerts through the college, and to lend his valuable library of several thousand orchestral works at no charge to the college. He would "give his entire professional services solely to the said College other than six weeks vacation." The college, hoping to earn back a good part of Thomas's salary, would keep all profits derived from his Cincinnati orchestra concerts and would take 20 percent of his fees on all of his outside conducting engagements. The contract was, in sum, all about money and how the college would make it through its star attraction. So, too, with Thomas: all he was interested in was the money and the security the position offered. He showed no concern for the college's educational policy, other than that it would emphasize orchestral studies and related activities and how it would be set and financed. If he had asked questions in this regard, he might never have gone to Cincinnati.

On this last point, one must not be too harsh with Thomas. Conservatories and colleges of music—Peabody, the New England Conservatory, Oberlin, and the Chicago Musical College—were new to the United States and groping for policies. Some were heavily endowed, others self-supporting or nearly so. Thomas had never studied at a music school or taught music, except through his conducting, and he knew nothing about running a school, setting a curriculum, or dealing with student problems. (Two years later, George Carpenter was to reveal that he had tried, that same summer, to persuade Thomas to go permanently to Chicago with his orchestra. There had been a misunderstanding in the negotiations, and, according to Carpenter, Thomas had impulsively accepted Cincinnati instead.)[7]

The news of Thomas's appointment broke on August 26. The *New York Daily Tribune* bemoaned the city's and the nation's "irreparable loss," the disbanding of the Thomas Orchestra. It described the Cincinnati college as a "complete musical university," with an orchestra school and a professional orchestra that students would join when qualified. "The directors are confident of making it self-supporting almost from the start."[8] The *Times* reminded its readers that Thomas had informally recommended such a school for New York for some years.[9] The weekly *Music Trade Review* argued that Thomas did not have "literary ability" and "refined tastes," was not an "intellectual man," and did not compose—in its view, all prerequisites for a music school director. It berated Thomas for feeling aggrieved by New York's treatment of him, asking why the city should back a full-time symphony orchestra when there were very few even in Germany. Bilse's orchestra in Berlin, for example, the precursor of the Berlin Philharmonic, gave concerts for seven to eight months annually but played light music almost exclusively. What was good enough for Berlin, the journal commented, was surely good enough for New York![10]

It appeared that Gothamites had tired of Thomas's lamenting that they, unlike the residents of Boston, Chicago, and Cincinnati, did not appreciate him. Was he "too good" for the largest city in the country, its cultural capital? He had conducted there far more than anyone else, had led the oldest and most prestigious symphonic society in the land, and had overwhelmed Damrosch, his only formidable competitor. Fully accepted as good music's standard-bearer, why did he keep asking for more? His foes urged him to be on his way as there were other conductors waiting in the wings. Some of

New York's orchestral musicians, who knew that he could act impulsively and probably had, and who also knew that he needed money, predicted that Thomas would be back soon. In the meantime, the men of his orchestra, other than the few who would go with him to Cincinnati, would work for other conductors. With the coast clear, Damrosch announced that his New York Symphony Society would play at Steinway Hall on the dates originally booked by the Thomas Orchestra.[11] William Steinway, businessman that he was, helped Damrosch to arrange the concerts.

Thomas went about settling his New York commitments. On the day he signed the Cincinnati college contract, he wrote to the Philharmonic Society: "I have been offered an engagement for a long period upon such terms as that I have felt it a duty to my family and myself to accept it. . . . I regret very much that I am obliged to take such a step, but I think I am justified in coming to the conclusion that New York will not support a first-class orchestra."[12] The timing for his resignation (late summer) was poor, and the Philharmonic, which had risen from the depths to unsurpassed prosperity, thanks to Thomas, was clearly upset. It combed the field for a new conductor and eventually turned to Adolph Neuendorff, a thirty-five-year-old German-born, American-trained, experienced opera conductor.[13]

Some of the gloom among Thomas's partisans lifted when the Brooklyn Philharmonic announced that he would conduct the Thomas Orchestra as planned in its 1878–79 series. Brooklyn claimed that its season had been set before Cincinnati approached Thomas and that Thomas would honor his commitment. It needed him especially badly, for its treasurer, J. C. Beale, had recently absconded with $7,000 in society funds.[14] Thomas's presence assured it of good ticket sales. Under the circumstances, the college had to give its approval.

The Empire City paid several tributes to its departing conductor. The New York Philharmonic, respectfully if not affectionately, gave him a gala benefit concert. William Steinway hosted a formal dinner at Delmonico's, one of New York's leading restaurants. And "prominent citizens of New York and Brooklyn" sponsored a farewell concert at Steinway Hall with Thomas conducting. Sensitive to the significance of the occasion, Thomas programmed an important premiere, the first American performance of Brahms's Second Symphony. With Brahms already recognized as one of the greatest living composers, Thomas would give New York something to remember him by. (Damrosch had given the American premiere of Brahms's First the previous December, beating Thomas for the honor by a few days.)[15]

First hearings of great works are not always received well by the press. The *Herald* said that "the *Allegretto* is the best of the four movements [applause was such that Thomas had to repeat it] and is the only one at which there is any attempt at melody."[16] Thomas himself, as well as the symphony, did better with the *Tribune*: "a leader of quick perceptions, unusually clear head, and magnetic power of command. . . . The marked favour with which the symphony was received was a compliment to the interpreter no less than to the composition."[17] The *Times*, irritated with Thomas for his unkind words about New York, noted caustically that Steinway Hall was two-thirds empty and added, "Perhaps in view of the position he has lately assumed towards this community it was significant." It said that Thomas was "cold and stiff, wearing almost the appearance of an indifferent spectator. This want of geniality which he has been apparently cultivating of late will not add much to his popularity."[18] Within a week, Thomas and his family left for Cincinnati.

Thomas had no sooner moved his wife and children into a large house in East Walnut Hills, one of Cincinnati's more attractive districts, than he was organizing his new orchestra—a few New York principals, the remainder local players—and practicing the violin. If he was concerned about leaving New York, it did not show.

The college had rented quarters on the third floor of Music Hall and used both auditoria for concerts. The first term began on October 14, 1878; it would be five weeks in length, followed by three terms of ten weeks each. The college's prospectus, which Nichols had prepared (one assumes with Thomas's approval), was a smorgasbord of courses catering both to professional students and to those who simply wanted musical instruction and could pay for it.[19] Thomas objected from the outset to mixing professionals and amateur students at the college—he had intended and expected it to serve only the talented and serious—but apparently he had not made this clear to Nichols.

The prospectus only vaguely described the college's instructional procedures. Students would study their major instrument in classes of two and three or work in "different ways," and students wishing private lessons could apply to the treasurer for rates, there being an open-ended fee structure. Some orchestral instruments would not be taught because there were no teachers for them, but the prospectus promised that appointments were imminent. There were detailed biographies of some teachers, a few words on others, and nothing about the rest. The listing of Signor La Villa of Palermo, Italy, as a master of bel canto was accompanied by a testimonial from a little-known New York voice teacher. The school seemed to be administered amateurishly and unsure of its goals.

In truth, Cincinnati had a college of music without a curriculum, and this was Thomas's fault. Students were not told which subjects to take or the number of hours weekly they should spend on classes, private instruction, and rehearsals. There were no examinations, required recitals, or diplomas, the college absolving itself from these obligations with the statement, "No definite time can be fixed for the graduation of a student. This will depend upon the studies undertaken and the progress made."

For the first time in his life, Thomas felt like a mere figurehead, and within six weeks of his arrival, he considered resigning.[20] He had not set the college's academic policy and had generally left too much to Nichols, who, as president, arbitrarily declared all matters "business" and thus in his domain. As for the college's finances, Thomas did not know how the budget was formulated, or if there even was a budget. He knew for certain that a *good* music school could not pay its way but that this institution was determined to prove that it could.

Amid the gloom, there were a few bright spots, thanks to Thomas. At his insistence, all students were required to attend a "chorus class," which evolved into "sightsinging" in the best sense—students studied the fundamentals of music through singing and, at the same time, improved their actual singing. Thomas, who had never sung in a choir in his youth, thought singing important in developing musical sensibility.

Another innovation was the college's twelve orchestral and twelve chamber concerts planned for the year, which Thomas hoped would attract national attention. The orchestra won much praise—he had created a group of the first rank after only a few weeks—and included musicians from the "Cincinnati Grand Orchestra" as well as members of the college faculty (former Thomas Orchestra principals) and a few advanced students, among them twelve-year-old Max Bendix, who would become Thomas's concertmaster in New York eight years later. August Wilhemj, Wagner's concertmaster at Bayreuth, was soloist with the orchestra for its third program and stayed on for several months at the college as a visiting violin teacher. A string quartet was formed, with Thomas alternating as its first and second violinist, and gave concerts truly reminiscent of the Mason-Thomas ones a decade earlier. In order to improve his violin playing, Thomas purchased two new instruments from George Gemünder, a well-known New York luthier. (He thought them so good that, three years later, he pressed publicly for the creation of a violin-making industry in the United States.)[21]

Despite its faults, the college saw its enrollment grow rapidly, reaching 500 by the end of its first year, June 1879, even though there were already two other music schools of modest size in Cincinnati. Thomas's reputation and the fine groups he led had projected a positive image, and his concerts were well received, albeit by small audiences. The student chorus that Thomas conducted had mushroomed to 200 students and had earned favorable press notices, thanks to a strict study program and rigorous rehearsal discipline. He himself learned a great deal about choral singing during the year.

Thomas learned also that one's social life is more visible in a smaller city. His antics during and after a rip-roaring dinner party hosted in his honor by the Musical Club of Cincinnati early in the year were widely reported in the press. Held at the new and exclusive Queen City Club, it was a happy occasion and the speeches were "models of post-prandial oratory."[22] Afterward, Thomas and several other unsatiated party-goers moved on to a cheap all-night beer hall to indulge in drunken revelry until dawn.

The *Cincinnati Enquirer* wickedly related the evening's events to its avid readers: "[Thomas] concocted a 'pancake' in his hat from beer pretzels and other condiments" and then ceremoniously emptied it into the hat of Professor Andres, who responded, predictably, with great irritation. Then some members of the Musical Club sang some questionable songs, and "Mr. Thomas smashed a bottle or two on the table, and was imitated by several of his admirers." There were "maudlin orgies," with Thomas's associates proclaiming that "he was the greatest Musical Director who had ever lived." Having made it clear that Thomas and his friends had had a rough and ready evening on the town, the *Enquirer* then forgave him: "Beyond the fact that Thomas did debauch his own and a Professor's beaver and smash several dollars worth of table and window glass, paying promptly for the amusement," there was no "gross offense against decency."[23]

Cincinnati, pleased that its musical leader could let his hair down occasionally, chuckled at one poet's rendition of the event. "Musical Mash" began:

> Herr Theodore Thomas came out from the East
>   Our College of Music to run,
> So the Musical Club prepared him a feast,
>   And that is what started the fun.
> The banquet was planned a recherche affair,
> But it ended, you see, in a glorious old "tear."

It concluded some eight stanzas later:

> The dawn of the morning was tinging the east
>   When the Musical Club got enough,
> And they all went to sleep wherever they dropped—
>   That's the truth though it sounds pretty rough.
> But now this sure knowledge forms part of their joys;
> Herr Theodore Thomas is one of the boys.[24]

One aspect of Thomas's work in Cincinnati concerned the state of serious American composition. He, Leopold Damrosch, Carl Zerrahn, and the late Carl Bergmann, among others, had been greatly responsible for German music dominating American symphonic life. (The Italianization of American operatic life had been due to the success of attractive operas—mostly Italian—sung in Italian by great singers, opera companies managed by clever impresarios like Max Maretzek, Bernard Ullman, and Max Strakosch, patronage by the rich, and other factors too detailed to enumerate here.) American composers had gotten short shrift in the first three-quarters of the nineteenth century because of "foreign" domination. After the Civil War, when German culture generally took hold with a vengeance in Britain and America, would-be American composers consciously aimed to write like their German contemporaries rather than develop their own indigenous school of composition; in fact, most of them went to Germany to study. The end result was a group of American symphonic and choral composers who were pale shadows of Mendelssohn, Schumann, and Brahms. They were talented but self-conscious, technically adept but lacking in inspiration, and, worst of all, unaware of their American heritage—its popular music, from which so much serious music is derived, and other American sources of inspiration. Their music was, as a result, rarely performed.

Such was the state of serious American composition when George Nichols proposed in 1878 that the Cincinnati Music Festival Association sponsor an American composers' competition.[25] Entrants, who must be native-born Americans, would be asked to write a large work for chorus and orchestra; the winning selection would be presented at the 1880 May Festival, its composer to receive a cash prize of $1,000. There would be five jury members: Thomas as chairman, Singer, Damrosch, Zerrahn, and Asger Hamerick, director of the Peabody Conservatory. Four of them had been born in Germany, and only Thomas had not been trained there.

Opposed in principle to competitions, Thomas was nevertheless in favor of this one, since it would help American composers to gain recognition in their own country through the good offices of America's leading music festival. By the October 2, 1879, deadline, twenty-four works had been received. The identities of the composers were, of course, kept from the jury, although Thomas recognized several of the most prominent from their handwriting, as did other jurors, especially Damrosch and Zerrahn. One such entrant was Dudley Buck, Thomas's friend and his former deputy conductor. Thomas's private opinion, after reviewing the scores, was that Buck had written the best work. As chairman, Thomas could abstain from voting, and thus not be accused of favoritism, if the other jurors felt the same way.

On January 30, 1880, the CMFA announced that *Scenes from Longfellow's Golden Legend*, for chorus and orchestra, was the winning composition and would be performed on the final night of the festival, at which time the composer's identity would be disclosed.[26] It was no secret, however, that the work was by Buck; the jury had cast three votes for Buck and two for George Whiting, the organ teacher at the Cincinnati College of Music. It was also no secret that Thomas had been the one to break the tie in favor of Buck. He was accused, as anticipated, of knowing which work was Buck's and of using his influence to persuade Singer to vote for Buck. A bitter Whiting said that Thomas had even had Buck alter his work to please Singer.[27] Only after such unpleasant allegations had been spread throughout the country was it revealed that Whiting had not abided by competition regulations in the first instance—he had failed to submit both a full score and a piano reduction as required and should have been disqualified.[28]

Other important events during Thomas's first year in Cincinnati included the Brooklyn concerts, his only contact with New York. They proceeded as planned, but Thomas, truly mindful of his obligations to the college, engaged a deputy to lead Brooklyn's preliminary rehearsals, appearing only for the final one and the actual concert. If the Brooklyn Philharmonic objected, it said nothing, since its series was a sellout, with many New Yorkers among the subscribers. Those in attendance agreed that it was well worth the onerous ferry ride across the East River.

Thomas had not been forgotten, and to prove it, on April 30, 1879, it was announced that, only six months after becoming the Cincinnati college's director, he had been unanimously elected conductor of the New York Philharmonic for the 1879–80 season. Both New York and Brooklyn had agreed to dovetail their dates so that Thomas need make only six trips from Cincinnati during the season. He would use virtually the same orchestra for both series and, because of limited rehearsal time, would give almost the same programs. New York's concerts were to be on Saturday nights; Brooklyn, ever obliging, changed its concerts to the preceding Tuesday, even though midweek concerts were less popular. The press scoffed that the Brooklyn series would be a rehearsal ground for New York, but both societies insisted that the normal number of rehearsals would be held for each. No small matter was that New York would give Thomas twenty shares of the receipts, ten more than in his first year, with a $1,500 minimum. Clearly, he intended to pursue his Philharmonic(s) career, music college or not. "Thomas returns," said the New York press.[29]

The college's board said nothing publicly about Thomas's Philharmonic appointment and would have had little to complain about in any event, for Thomas would be away from Cincinnati but a few days more than he had been in his first year. The college could, if it wished, extract its commission from Thomas's New York fee, although uncertainty remains as to whether it did. To calm those who worried that he was readying an exit from the Queen City, Thomas stayed on in Cincinnati for July and August and conducted the college's orchestra in summer concerts for the ridiculous fee of fifty dollars per concert. He could have gone to Chicago and earned a great deal more, but he felt that he should work with his new group.

Thus Thomas began his second year at the college in September 1879. He had not lost his zeal—at least not yet—to improve professional musical education. One of his first innovations was an orchestra training class. While other conservatories were concentrating on soloist preparation, Thomas, with admirable foresight, addressed the practical needs and realities of the music world by giving his students extensive coaching in orchestral repertoire and routine. Further, he insisted that women join the orchestra classes and become active in a field heretofore totally dominated by men.

Although Thomas derived some satisfaction from his teaching and conducting, his position at the college was becoming increasingly onerous. Overall poor public attendance in the first year resulted in the college's chamber and orchestral series being reduced to eight concerts each, with lower ticket prices. The orchestra, after its initial successes, had made little progress. The players rehearsed long and hard, but their lack of ability was severely limiting, and many of the key players Thomas had brought from New York had already left. He found that being resident in Cincinnati made him too accessible to the festival's board, whose members continually sought him out on the most picayune matters. Finally, there was the college administration, especially Nichols.

In January 1880, Thomas took the bull by the horns and recommended fundamental changes in college policy.[30] It was Nichols who urged that the college continue its "open door" policy by not imposing entrance requirements and that it continue to expect the school to be self-supporting. Thomas said simply that the college must put academic priorities ahead of fiscal ones and, more frankly, he wanted to be director of the college in fact as well as in name. He asked for four changes: (1) The academic year should consist of two terms of twenty weeks each instead of four terms of ten weeks each —even though the four-term scheme was more profitable financially, since the less-serious students registered more frequently for shorter terms. (2) The musical director should have complete authority over student admissions and teacher appointments, assignments, and examination duties—students were being admitted regardless of talent, and teachers conspired to get them admitted in order to enlarge their classes. (3) The orchestra should be separated from the college and a fund established to pay qualified members full-time salaries, thus attracting leading New York instrumentalists to Cincinnati and keeping them. (4) All matters pertaining to the college should be referred initially to the musical director, not to Nichols.[31]

Thomas's recommendations may have sounded like commands to the board, but they were eminently reasonable. He had come to Cincinnati to make the city, the college, and offshoots like its orchestra central to American musical life. To achieve these goals, he needed proper authority and a cooperative board. Nichols, who represented everything that stood in his way, must either leave or be neutralized. Either goal would be hard to accomplish, since Nichols was, after all, the founder of the college and belonged to the city's establishment. He was also very close to philanthropist Reuben Springer.

The board, composed mainly of practical, hardheaded, self-made businessmen, doubted Thomas's sincerity—Was he just looking for an excuse to break his contract and return to New York?—and, not unexpectedly, appointed a review committee. After a polite interval of several weeks, the board spoke against the recommendations. Undeterred, Thomas reiterated that if he were to be responsible for the "musical conduct" of the college, he must be entrusted with its "*exclusive* direction," that his position should be like that of a college president and the board's like a college's trustees. He felt that he could handle his administrative duties as "president" with the help of a secretary and a clerk for only a few days at the opening of each term. In Thomas's view, Nichols did not behave as a president/board chairman should; rather, he was more like a super-director, bypassing Thomas when it suited him.

Thomas addressed this second round of recommendations to A. T. Goshorn, the committee chairman, who did little to explain them to the board, knowing that it was not interested. The board was concerned that Thomas's displeasure with the administration might hurt the college's image and income. Its most influential members disliked Thomas and closed ranks to protect Nichols, which led to the decision that Thomas must go. The board hoped he would go quietly.

To effect Thomas's departure and absolve the board of blame, Goshorn —polite, firm, Machiavellian—tried to demolish Thomas's arguments. Goshorn asked him why he had not submitted a curriculum for professional students as promised, and he wondered about inconsistencies in Thomas's line of reasoning on the two-term/four-term issue. Salaries for orchestral players would, he said, be kept under advisement. As for Thomas being director "in name only," Goshorn asked for specific examples, which he knew Thomas could not provide. He maintained that Thomas already had more power than a college president, that he alone made professorial appointments and held no faculty meetings to seek his colleagues' views on academic matters. The board did not challenge Thomas's autocratic rule and would welcome his administering of college affairs, such as teacher-pupil assignments, but it doubted that he had the time. If he could "fix and observe such regular office hours as will be necessary for the proper performance of this work . . . it will be completely in your hands." Goshorn believed, however, that such duties were too menial and time-consuming for a director of Thomas's importance. He also stated that any approved changes would not be implemented until the next school year.

Clearly, Thomas was ill prepared to lead a school or give it the attention required. The college needed a competent academic administrator who would report to a board—and especially its chairman—that would determine policy and stay out of school operations. But the present board had no policy and its chairman/president meddled in school operations. No matter, the board trusted only one of its own kind to guard its investment, not a temperamental and arrogant musician with a German accent, even if he was famous. Thomas, infuriated with Goshorn and the board for not supporting him on the Nichols issue, recognized that some of the criticisms of his work were uncomfortably valid. Without fully weighing the consequences, and without documented cause or explanation, he obliged the board by resigning on March 4, 1880, to be effective October 1.

In the press interviews that followed—there had, quite naturally, been leaks during the negotiations—Thomas spoke nastily of Nichols and his work, whereupon Nichols resigned as college president. In a letter to Reuben Springer, later made public, Nichols wrote that he had stayed at his post against his own wishes because of his obligations to the stockholders, nearly all of whose "stock subscriptions were obtained at my personal solicitation." Thomas abhorred "business," an important element in the school's operation, and, wanting to leave Cincinnati no matter what, had used him, Nichols, as a pretext. Nichols was resigning out of self-respect and to give the board "liberty of action."[32]

Springer, who felt that the board had behaved impeccably, wrote to Thomas, suggesting that he or his authorized representative confer with the board concerning the time and terms of his "withdrawal." Springer wanted Thomas out immediately; his salary would terminate on April 8. He also wrote sympathetically to Nichols of Thomas's lack of candor in his correspondence with the board, all of which, he added, was now available to the public. Springer praised Nichols's work and explained why the board would not accept his resignation. Nichols thus swallowed his pride, rallied to the cause, and continued as president.

It is doubtful that Thomas really wanted to leave Cincinnati, for he had a workable arrangement with New York and Brooklyn vis-à-vis the college and earned good fees from all three, not to mention the May festivals. He liked and believed in the work he was doing at the college, but when he was unable to convince the board that he knew what was best for the school, his position became untenable. It would be neither the first nor the last time that American artists would clash with moneyed sponsors and lose. Thomas's wife and children liked Cincinnati, and he had just renovated sections of his home there at great expense. His New York residence had been leased for four years, and if he were to return to that city, he would have to look for new quarters, not an easy task with a large family. When he said in press interviews following his resignation that he was not sure where he would go next—Europe, maybe New York—he meant it.[33]

Thomas could have stayed at the music college if he had negotiated—a word he did not know the meaning of—temperately and prudently. He had wanted to build a great music school and he had the vision for it, but he was too single-minded, impatient, and intolerant, too prone to criticize others without taking a hard look at himself. Had he acted petulantly? Had he quit because he could not have his own way? Had he thought of the welfare of the students or the teachers? In the end, with their support, he might have won his war with the board, for the meddling Nichols was generally disliked by students and teachers. Thomas could have been a pioneer in a field where he was much needed, but perhaps it just wasn't for him.

The board's judgment, too, had been clouded by its animosity toward Thomas and his background, concern about money, threats to its authority, and lack of knowledge about what constituted a good music school. As for Nichols, after Thomas's withdrawal became public, the festival chorus greeted its conductor at rehearsal with a standing ovation. All 600 voices read aloud a letter urging the unloved Nichols to resign as the festival's president—he did so promptly—and calling for Thomas's reinstatement as music director of the college.[34] Thomas's supporters then moved to buy up the college's shares and take control of the school. The newspapers helped by publishing a list of stockholders and the number of shares each held (Springer had the most). But after a few days, Thomas, convinced that nothing could be done to wrest the college from its board, discouraged further action. Talk of starting an orchestral training school also came to nothing. Other ways of keeping him in Cincinnati were explored, but, by the time Thomas left in mid-March for his monthly conducting stint in New York, they, too, were dropped.

6

The Warrior Returns

Theodore Thomas slipped quietly into New York on March 14, 1880, dined with friends, and went to a Philharmonic rehearsal, where the players gave him a standing ovation. Reporters asked why he had left the Cincinnati music college, and he explained succinctly that the board had refused to understand that a good music school did not pay its way, that it had failed to agree to a fixed term of study for students, and that it had never intended to provide adequate facilities, equipment, and music. George Ward Nichols had promised the community a great school. Under the circumstances, Thomas wished to have no part in the deception.

As the full story of Thomas's withdrawal unfolded, he began to win new friends and even regain some former ones. The experience had, in fact, a cathartic effect on him: he now looked at life in New York more reasonably, with more realistic expectations. Exciting projects were waiting for him in his favorite city; indeed, he was entering a dramatic phase in his life. The same press that had sent him off to Cincinnati with bitter words, now forgave and forgot. The *New York Times* wrote whimsically: "Our minstrel has returned. He set gallantly forth upon his art crusade; he has traveled far; he has labored much; he has done battle with the infidels in the city of the unclean beast and now he returns, weary and war-torn, yet cheerful, to the place of his early love, and asks a welcome. He should be welcomed and will be welcomed. We are united once more, and it may be pretty safely assumed, from the favorite conductor's account of his experience, that we shall not be parted again very soon or very readily." [1]

His "homecoming" accomplished, Thomas went back to Cincinnati for his final college concerts and to make preparations for the May Festival. Unfortunately, the usually supportive Cincinnati dailies were irritated by the fuss New York had made over him and considered it an indirect criticism of the Queen City for failing to hold on to its musical lion. Civic pride, so much a part of American life in cultural as in other matters, clouded their judgment enough to make Thomas's dismissal of Otto Singer as chorusmaster of the festival seem to them an attack on a favorite son by an arrogant visitor from the East. In truth, Thomas had for two years considered discharging Singer but unwisely chose to do so just prior to the festival.[2] Singer had viewed Thomas's presence in Cincinnati as a threat to his own local position and had malevolently stirred up bad feeling against him. Their differences came to a head when Thomas canceled Singer's festival performance of Rubinstein's *Tower of Babel* at the last moment to make room for a second performance of Beethoven's *Missa solemnis* (the latter had had extensive preparation, and Thomas thought it a pity to do it only once). Singer said publicly that the cancellation was due to Thomas's jealousy of him, thus leaving Thomas with no alternative but to dismiss him. Singer stayed on at the college, where any enemy of Thomas was welcome.

With the Singer problem resolved, the Cincinnati Music Festival Association announced its plans for the 1882 festival just one week before the 1880 festival began. It reassured the public that Thomas would continue as musical director in spite of his departure from the college and, additionally, would conduct the festival chorus in the *Messiah* at Christmas 1880. Thomas felt such intermittent performances in the two-year interval between festivals necessary in order to keep the chorus together and in good vocal condition. The plan, as the CMFA had anticipated, raised hackles at the music college, which had during the previous two years sponsored *Messiah* performances with Thomas conducting. Rumor had it that the college board might even serve an injunction to stop the festival's *Messiah*.

As a result of the Thomas-Nichols dispute, Cincinnati's leading citizens had aligned themselves with either the CMFA or the College of Music and would continue to do so for the next few years, until the imbroglio was forgotten and Nichols was no longer on the scene. During the spring of 1880, however, the local press, which welcomed the feud, made capital of any event —in this case the Singer and the *Messiah* disputes—that fanned the flames between the two men and their groups. Thomas, essentially blameless, got caught in the crossfire. As always, he expected the press to support his actions because, in his view, they were for the good of music. However, some newspaper reporters felt differently and said so. Then Thomas, who rarely accepted alternative courses of action, reared up, imprudently fought back, and lost more in the end than if he had said nothing. Adverse press comments pained the thin-skinned Thomas as deeply at forty-five, when he was in his prime, physically and mentally, with enough energy for several men, as they had ten years earlier or would twenty years later.

Thomas's difficulties with the Cincinnati papers did not seriously alter the gratitude he felt toward the city for giving him the chance to collect himself psychologically in the eighteen months he had spent there, to grow musically, and to pay off old debts. He had learned new scores, and his festival programming had improved in scope and depth. This was evident on the festival's opening night, when he did his reorchestrated version of Bach's cantata *Ein' feste Burg* with contemporary instruments instead of the baroque trumpet, oboe d'amore, viola d'amore, and viola da gamba (which were almost always played badly). He reasoned that abandoning authenticity in favor of expert performances on modern instruments that suited the large halls he played in was artistically defensible. (The contrary may be true today, but that does not affect the validity of Thomas's view.)

His major feat at the 1880 festival, and one that he would not have tackled without being resident in Cincinnati for the year, was Beethoven's *Missa solemnis*, one of the most difficult nineteenth-century choral-orchestral works. (Singer told the festival chorus in rehearsal that it would be impossible to sing and said Thomas was wrong to try it.)[3] Thomas had learned the work thoroughly and coped with its vocal problems for both soloists and chorus with uncommon skill. He cleverly eased the strain on the four soloists by having an extra soprano and tenor for the first performance and a full second quartet for the second. Audiences would remember for many years how the mass's lofty choruses resounded in the furthest corners of Music Hall.

Back in New York at the end of May, the Philharmonic reported that 1879–80 had been its best season ever because of Thomas's magic name, his programming, and his conducting. His success was all the more astonishing since he did nearly the same programs in Brooklyn a few days before the New York concerts. Each one included a symphony: Beethoven's Fourth, Fifth, and Seventh, Schubert's Ninth, Schumann's First, Rubinstein's Fourth (the "Dramatic"), plus a short Haydn symphony on the Schubert program. Four programs had vocal and/or instrumental excerpts from Wagner operas, and there were vocal or instrumental soloists on five of the six concerts. With such a fine season behind him, Thomas could have asked for the moon from the Philharmonic, and probably gotten it. Instead, he generously set a maximum personal salary of $2,500 for 1880–81, even if his twenty shares exceeded that amount (which they had in the season just completed).

Nichols and the board of the College of Music seemed even more in the distant past when Thomas unexpectedly heard in late spring that Yale University had recommended him for an honorary doctorate in music. Unable to attend the ceremony, at which President Rutherford B. Hayes was also honored,[4] because of prior plans to visit Europe, Thomas nonetheless proudly accepted the distinction, although he never used the title. Here was a typically

American success story, not in science, industry, business, or politics, but in music—a poor immigrant boy who had become a great conductor and was now honored by a great university. No musician stood higher in the nation's esteem.

Recognition by Thomas's peers also came unexpectedly. The night before Thomas sailed for Europe, Julius Hallgarten, the Philharmonic's president, entertained him at his home. At midnight, the two men heard "the long and thrilling note of the cornet" that begins the Overture to Wagner's *Rienzi*. The Philharmonic had assembled outside, on West Forty-ninth Street, to give Thomas a bon voyage serenade, its way of thanking him for a good year. Many friends were also there to pay him tribute. The special midnight concert that awakened the entire neighborhood without a word of complaint continued with short works by Bach and Beethoven. Thomas was evidently moved more than he ever cared to admit by this show of affection from colleagues.[5]

Because their New York home was unavailable, Thomas and his wife decided that she and the children would spend the next few years in Europe. The children would reap the benefits of European education and culture, which Thomas had sorely felt the lack of since his youth, and he could visit them in the summers. But this trip, his first to Europe since 1869, was also undertaken for professional reasons, and he kept a careful diary of his activities.[6] In London, he attended a performance of *Lohengrin* at Covent Garden with Hans Richter conducting. Richter had led the *Ring* during the first season at Bayreuth and was considered *the* Wagnerian conductor. Thomas's comments were revealing: "A very able conductor but, like all other European conductors, he does not drill his orchestra. The intonation was poor, tone color, precision and phrasing mediocre, and the whole orchestra, but especially the wind choir, seemed to have no idea of *sostenuto*. The chorus was miserable." He concluded rhetorically, "And this is the best material in London!"

To convince himself that Richter was not all he was supposed to be, Thomas went to one of his orchestral concerts three nights later. There he noted that the famous conductor took Schubert's Unfinished Symphony too fast. He was even more critical of the rapid tempos in Beethoven's Seventh —the close of the final movement was "hurried to pieces." In comparing Richter to Carl Bergmann, now four years dead, Thomas wrote that, although both had the same talent and education, Bergmann had the more "refined conception." Thomas liked Richter's Wagner but thought that his reading of Beethoven's Ninth was haphazard and lacked thought. Knowing that Richter was initially a French horn player, Thomas commented: "It appears to me as if he himself had never played any stringed instrument, for the string choir of his orchestra played as it would without attracting his attention. No two of the violinists bowed alike, but each man bowed as he pleased." Thomas had long advocated uniform bowing and marked his scores and parts accordingly, leaving no margin for error.

Many years later, Sam Franko, the American violinist, was to remember a conversation he had with Thomas in London at one of Richter's concerts. Thomas "spoke contemptuously of the Faust Symphony performance and of the concerts as a whole. I tried to excuse the performances on the score of lack of time and money for the necessary rehearsals, but he said explosively: 'I don't care how many rehearsals you've had. I pay my money and expect a good performance. At home in New York I rehearse the Philharmonic Orchestra as often as I want, until I can offer the public a finished performance.' " Franko heard Thomas the next year and thought his performances "technically perfect but rather conventional. His musicians told me that on his return from London he had completely altered all the tempi in the Beethoven Symphonies."[7]

Richter was not completely to blame for his "poor" concerts, if indeed they were poor. Quite simply, the German conductor was unable to get leading London instrumentalists for his concerts because opera and theater work paid better. There was no Theodore Thomas to organize London's symphonic life, to find money for good orchestral players who would play great music well. It would be almost another half century before the British capital could claim even a full-time symphony orchestra.

Significantly, London's Handel Festival at the Crystal Palace, with the "immense" sound of its massed choruses, thrilled Thomas, as he noted in his diary: "At last I have learned the proper way to perform Handel. One must come to England to understand him. There is nothing in the world which cannot be criticized and many things here also need improvement. Nevertheless, the performance was generally good enough that one lost sight of all shortcomings." The work was *Israel in Egypt*; the conductor, Sir Michael Costa, a leading Handelian and a stern disciplinarian whom Thomas liked. He commented, more eloquently than usual, "Here at last I find a tradition which realizes my own ideals. Come here, ye modern composers, and learn with what simple means pure music can be made! I am coming to a different conception of things and believe that music healthy for the soul ended with Beethoven. What good does it do to double intervals to such an extent that the original character is lost? And the modern harmonies and harmonic resolutions, which begin with the chord of the ninth, and end with the chord of the twenty fifth, but always without foundation!"[8]

Was Thomas, the supposed advocate of new music, turning reactionary? With two season tickets in hand, a gift from the Handel Festival's directors, he went on to a "slipshod" performance of the *Messiah*. Chorus and conductor Costa each went their own way. Disappointed with what he heard, Thomas was nevertheless overwhelmed by the attendance at the festival, an astonishing 79,000 for three concerts and an open rehearsal.[9]

Thomas received a flattering invitation to become the permanent conductor of the Philharmonic Society of London, prompting him to write in his diary, "London needs a man to take charge of musical affairs in general. . . . If I will take the position it is mine." He spoke at length with the society's directors and pondered the proposal, explaining to his friend Lawrence Maxwell in Cincinnati, "I do not want to leave America. At the same time, if you could see how grateful the British people are for good music, and how enthusiastic, you would certainly think it worth my consideration."[10]

Eventually, Thomas turned down the offer. His second wife, Rose, was to say later that it was because he loved the United States so much and wanted to complete his work there. But London also paid smaller fees than New York, which could be a nuisance, since Thomas liked to live well; maintaining his family in Europe was costly, and he still had some debts to repay. He also knew that the London Philharmonic was more like Brooklyn's than New York City's —it sponsored concerts with the orchestra assembled by the conductor as needed. London's orchestral players were proficient but undisciplined and sent deputies to rehearsals and concerts whenever better-paying jobs came up. Prestigious as the post was, Thomas saw that it would mean starting over again and that it would take many years to develop a London orchestra to equal the quality of the Thomas Orchestra or the New York Philharmonic.

Thomas's next stop was Paris, where he met Saint-Saëns, who had already agreed to judge the Cincinnati festival's 1882 composer's competition. Thomas heard him play his Piano Concerto no. 4 with Richter and thought Saint-Saëns a "remarkable artist." The French musician's reputation as a piano and organ virtuoso was at its peak, as was his extraordinary prowess for reading music at sight. His compositions, however, were only just beginning to gain recognition. Thomas and Saint-Saëns had great respect for one another.

Weimar and Liszt were next on his itinerary. Thomas arrived in Germany on June 29: "It is very nice but a little too quiet for me and does not come up to my expectations. Now I am really in Germany—but, oh, how far I am from home." The following day the aging Liszt received him. "At first I instinctively looked *up* to meet his eye," Thomas wrote in his diary, "and could hardly believe my own when I found myself as tall as he—perhaps a half an inch difference! His geniality was beyond all expression and this meeting with him was, in itself, worth the journey from New York. . . . Now I am very glad to have seen the giant, for the world looks so much smaller to me." The two men discussed music in the United States, and Liszt said how "very kind" Thomas was to play his works so often. Liszt complained of feeling old and stated that he would write no more. This was to be their only meeting, for Thomas declined Liszt's invitation to hear his students play the next day. He wanted to hear the master himself but was too polite to ask.[11]

Joachim Raff, the director of Hoch's Conservatory in Frankfurt, and Joseph Joachim, the great violinist, were next on Thomas's list. In Berlin, he attended a performance of *Tristan und Isolde*, conducted by another eminent

Wagnerian, Herman Levi, and wrote brashly, "I do not believe this music will ever be popular." After hearing the *Ring, Die Meistersinger,* and *Tannhäuser,* he praised the sets but criticized the singers and orchestra severely. Quite unprophetically, Thomas wrote, "I do not believe that opera with German singers would be a possibility in New York. The only chance of success for good operatic performances in America would be opera with American singers." A few days later, on July 31, he took passage home.[12]

At dockside in New York, Thomas was interviewed by a *Herald* reporter. Unusually jovial and spirited, he discussed the new music he had brought back from Europe, some of it still in manuscript, commenting smugly that he had chosen works that "have met with the endorsement of the best living critics. . . . they shall be known to the public only when they are perfectly rehearsed; no . . . score shall be . . . hastily prepared by an incompetent orchestra . . . [to convey] an imperfect and crude idea of the work. The first impression is generally a lasting one."[13]

The trip abroad had helped Thomas to understand better his life at home. When the *Herald* reporter asked him to compare American and English musical life, he replied,

> Here we are really years ahead of them. Our programs are better, our musicians play better, the people listen more intelligently. The enthusiasm of the English audience carries away its judgement completely. I have seen an audience applaud wildly a crude performance of a hackneyed selection, as though its rendering were perfection. What can you expect under such circumstances? Musicians grow careless, the public's fine musical sensibilities are dulled, and the standard falls imperceptibly at the time, but surely and steadily. Then, again, the London musical season is brief, and orchestral pay is not sufficient to warrant the constant rehearsals we undergo here. I have heard music given there in very rough form compared to the finish it should have had, and discovered readily on inquiry that the cause lay in insufficient rehearsal.

Having gotten to the root of Britain's difficulties in orchestral performance, Thomas added that he had found things better in France. He liked the *Aida* he had attended in Paris, with its "sumptuous mounting" and "superb orchestra"—Parisian orchestras were the best in Europe, thanks to conductors like Jules-Etienne Pasdeloup, Charles Lamoureux, and Edouard Colonne. What was clear to *Herald* readers, and gave them cause for pride, was that their favorite conductor thought that his orchestras surpassed those in Europe in proficiency, discipline, style, and general excellence.

Thomas also was asked what he thought of P. T. Barnum and millionaire Cornelius Vanderbilt's scheme to demolish the Hippodrome (Gilmore's Garden), build an enormous museum on the site, and, as Barnum had suggested, have the Thomas Orchestra play there. He rejoined, with rare humor, that he appreciated the site's attractiveness but wondered about the "giants, dwarfs, Circassian women and roaring lions. . . . How near the tropical garden and how far from the lions will the band be, and would it be considered one of the cages of animals or an accompaniment to the flower show?"

A buoyant Thomas, relishing New York afresh, announced on September 8 that he would form a chorus, with required choral classes, to meet at the New York College of Music.[14] He intended to put to the test in his home city what he had learned about choral singing in Cincinnati and, if successful, would perform works like those done in the Queen City and attract similarly large and enthusiastic audiences. Three classes, based on those he had given at the Cincinnati College of Music, were fixed: "Elementary Instruction and Chorus Singing," taught by George Bristow; "Vocalizing," by Signor J. Tamaro; and "Advanced Choral Classes," by Thomas himself. A board of directors was put together, presided over by Carl Schurz, the influential German-American politician who had just become editor in chief of the *New York Evening Post*.

The chorus gave its first public rehearsal—in effect, a concert—on January 22, 1881, at Steinway Hall, followed by a "complimentary" concert with the Philharmonic in April. Public response to its work was good. The soloists in the April concert were the twenty-nine-year-old Hungarian pianist Rafael Joseffy and contralto Annie Louise Cary. Joseffy, a pupil of Karl Tausig and Liszt, already had a considerable reputation in Europe when he made his American debut at a Damrosch symphony concert in 1879. He would be a leading performer and teacher in New York for the next thirty years and a frequent performer with Thomas and the Philharmonic, always without fee.[15] Cary, only forty and at the height of her career, would retire the following year. The two were among Thomas's favorite artists.

That spring, Thomas wrote an article, "Musical Possibilities in America," for *Scribner's Monthly*.[16] Taking advantage of an opportunity to voice his views on the musical condition of the country in an influential and widely read journal, he wrote frankly and convincingly about the needed improvements. For example, New York was the only city in which an orchestral player could earn a decent wage, "and even here he must give lessons or play at balls and parties, thereby losing or injuring [his] finer qualities." It was even worse in other cities, he said, where the orchestral musician eked out a living by playing in beer gardens and saloons. This was an intolerable condition for the musician and for the art and community he served, and Thomas saw as a solution permanent orchestras, where musicians could grow artistically and survive financially. It has taken a century to realize Thomas's "possibilities." There are now over fifteen such "permanent" orchestras in a like number of major cities in North America with seasons of forty-eight to fifty-two weeks and four times as many orchestras with seasons ranging from thirty to forty-five weeks. It was Thomas who first articulated the reasons for them and provided the blueprint.

In this same article, Thomas addressed musical education in the public schools—its pupils would be tomorrow's audiences—and lashed out at unconcerned classroom teachers of music, some of whom were unable to hold a tune and others of whom allowed children to "scream" rather than sing. Much money was being spent on school music, he said, with little improvement in public taste. Children "learn like parrots and soon forget the little which they have learned." Thomas felt that classroom singing teachers should *not* use the piano when teaching and thus force children to find pitches independently, through their ears; it would also help them to develop greater sensitivity to tone quality and intonation. To aid the process, he recommended that the French fixed "doh" (*solfège*) be used instead of the English movable "doh."

Thomas wanted great music to be more accessible and widespread, to appeal to all classes, not just the cultivated upper and middle classes. Music, he firmly believed, uplifted the human spirit, but he sadly reported that "the general public does not advance in music, partly from want of opportunity, partly from the habits of the people. The average American is so entirely absorbed in his work that when he goes out in the evening he looks for relaxation in some kind of amusement which makes little or no demand upon his intellect, and he has no difficulty in finding it."

Protestant church music was dealt with harshly: "trifling or sentimental . . . a sort of patchwork—a little piece from this composer and another piece from that, put together by an amateur." Thomas condemned the use of inferior music to attract worshipers and felt similarly about theater music and orchestras. He described a typical theater orchestra as "a blatant cornet or trombone, drums, bells, wood and straw instruments, everyone making the greatest possible noise, headed by an important conductor, with a baton in his hand instead of a violin bow." He recalled that, in his youth, there was better music as well as groups with performing conductors to play it. Why, he asked, have music of "lower standing than is in keeping with what is presented on the stage?"

Most of Thomas's solutions to contemporary musical problems—he even touched on American singers studying in Europe, where they should learn voice production and languages—are as applicable today as they were 100 years ago:

> We want home education of a kind suited to the needs and demands of our people, and calculated to promote the new life which we hope is opening before us. We want an end of amateurism in teachers and other professionals.

Those who present themselves to guide the people must have thoroughly studied music, not dabbled in it. We need some provision for the talent which is developing every day—we need institutions, well endowed, which will not be obliged to adopt a mere commercial standard for want of means of support. We need the influences coming naturally from such institutions. We need them, not only to give instruction to pupils, but to keep up a high standard of excellence. We need them for our earnest teachers to come to from time to time, to rub off the rust of teaching, and refresh themselves by contact with those who live in a musical atmosphere. The greatest enemy to fight is mediocrity, and an institution of standing is the only defense against it.

Thomas concluded his *Scribner's* article by asking schools to teach instrument making. The noted violin maker George Gemünder claimed that certain American woods were ideal for the making of string instruments, and Thomas, who had had violins made for him by Gemünder, urged instrument makers to recognize and use these woods, for it could be the beginning of a great string instrument manufacturing industry. "Nature has done her part generously; it remains for us to do ours," he declared. No one took up the call. Although the United States has manufactured good yet cheap string instruments, it has not matched the quality of the better European instruments of the past.

Barely a month after the appearance of Thomas's wide-ranging article, a startling announcement was made that Boston would have America's first permanent orchestra, thanks to the patronage of one man, Maj. Henry Lee Higginson. A wealthy Bostonian, Higginson, who had studied music in Vienna and later was wounded while serving in the Union army during the Civil War, planned to engage an orchestra of sixty men and a conductor, "paying them all by the year," and would personally cover an anticipated deficit of $50,000 annually.[17] The musicians would be contracted for full-time orchestral duties at adequate salaries and not be allowed to take additional engagements during the season. Ticket prices would be lower than Thomas charged at his annual concerts in Boston, and programming would be predominantly German, or, more precisely, Viennese—Haydn, Mozart, Beethoven, Schubert. Higginson himself would choose the conductor, who would receive a substantial $10,000 annual salary and be in complete charge of the orchestra. Higginson, who would also fix the players' salaries, stipulated that there would be no pensions, and symphony members would not be permitted to belong to the musicians' union.

Once the initial excitement had died down and the conductor—Georg Henschel, a distinguished German-Polish baritone—had been appointed, many asked why Higginson had not chosen Thomas. Did he think that a foreigner (Thomas was considered an American) would impress the public more? Perhaps he feared that the strong-willed Thomas would have contested his leadership or that Thomas would have insisted on keeping up his other commitments. Maybe the public-spirited philanthropist felt that Thomas was needed more in New York. Whatever the case, Thomas said nothing. Henschel, who had little conducting skill (and even less experience) and lacked leadership qualities, was a doubtful choice. The new orchestra progressed slowly and would not be an ensemble of note until 1884, when Wilhelm Gericke, an Austrian conductor who followed Thomas-like procedures (i.e., disciplined rehearsals, careful programming) took over.

Thomas ceased giving concerts in Boston. Even when the newly formed Philharmonic Society of Boston invited the Thomas Orchestra to the "Hub" for a series of concerts during the Boston Symphony's second year and promised to relieve Thomas of all personal financial responsibility, Thomas said no. In fact, he no longer booked tours in New England. Whether this was a practical move or not, he viewed the region as the Boston Symphony's territory—which cost him some of his most faithful audiences.

Boston aside, Thomas had a surfeit of good fortune in the first months of 1881. The public liked his new chorus and his Philharmonic concerts in New York and Brooklyn, and the Thomas Orchestra gave a fine series in Chicago. One Chicago concert in particular endeared him to the public and was long remembered. Because of a crippling snowstorm, only a handful of people attended, and Thomas was urged to cancel. But he showed his mettle by refusing to do so: "It will not only be given, but I shall try to make it an especially good performance, for the people who have braved such a storm as this to hear us must surely be true music lovers and deserve the best we can give them." [18]

Thomas's good luck continued. The orchestra had a well-received, profitable summer season: concerts in Cleveland, six weeks at the Industrial Exposition Building in Chicago, then Milwaukee. In Chicago, he played twenty different works by Beethoven, eighteen by Wagner, and sixteen by Mendelssohn. That Thomas was considered a high priest of music who had behaved as a priest should was underscored at the final concert when David Swing, a prominent minister, lecturer, and writer, thanked him on behalf of Chicago with a rhapsodic barrage of period prose: "A captain of musicians. . . . Amid many temptations he has stood true to a pure and noble ideal and has steadfastly asked the multitude to come up to his height." [19]

To end the summer of 1881, the orchestra had a week at Highland House in Cincinnati, where Thomas caught up with CMFA affairs and attempted to mend some fences. He had directed a lackluster *Messiah*—the one the

College of Music had tried to stop—the previous Christmas with a poorly prepared chorus and local orchestra. Two months later, in February 1881, George Nichols stole a march on Thomas and launched a most successful opera festival, with a New York–based Italian opera company; and his plans for a second season in 1882 looked even more promising. After Thomas had left the college, Nichols engaged Max Maretzek, the New York operatic conductor and impresario, to head up an opera department at the school and to help him prepare the festival. (Surprisingly, opera was considered too worldly a subject for instruction in a music school by a few "moral" and God-fearing Cincinnatians, whose objections, as is usually the case, received far more coverage in the press than deserved.)[20] Maretzek knew what he was doing and, to a great extent, was responsible for Nichols's success.

Obviously, if the CMFA were to do another *Messiah* at Christmas 1881, it would have to be outstanding. Hoping to steal some of Nichols's thunder, the CMFA and Thomas sought in the fall to engage the *prima donna assoluta* of the day, the American-born Adelina Patti, as soprano soloist. It would be an extraordinary assignment for the thirty-eight-year-old diva, whose forte was Italian opera, not English oratorio, about which she knew little. Her voice was at the height of its powers, brilliant and clear. Although many thought her musically shallow, Thomas had heard her in London the previous year and been very impressed. Patti had been Europe's leading coloratura soprano since the early 1860s, and this would be her homecoming year.

Negotiations with Patti were conducted in a cloak-and-dagger atmosphere so that Nichols, who hoped to have her as the main attraction at his 1882 festival, would not get wind of them. An unusually tractable Thomas took on the difficult task of getting her to sign the CMFA's contract with somewhat more relish than expected, given his dislike of high-priced, egocentric prima donnas.[21] Telegrams flew back and forth between Thomas and the CMFA board, which monitored and approved each step in the proceedings. Patti's name was never mentioned for fear that a telegraph operator might reveal it to the "enemy." With two sponsors from the same city fighting for her, Patti raised her fee accordingly, and the CMFA finally agreed to pay her an incredible $6,000 for one appearance, $1,000 more than she usually received for an operatic performance. In comparison, Annie Louise Cary, who would be the alto soloist, would receive $500, and the other two soloists, $200 each.

By mid-November, everything was set except exclusivity—that Patti sing for the CMFA but not for Nichols's opera festival. Patti had already committed herself to Nichols for February—he had promised to pay her an equally outrageous fee—so she and Thomas cleverly arrived at a compromise, which, in the end, allowed her to accept both engagements. Publicity for the *Messiah* would not mention future engagements in Cincinnati, and Nichols would not publicize her operatic appearances until after the *Messiah*. The Opera Association had no alternative but to agree, as the CMFA and Thomas chortled with unseemly delight.

After all this chicanery, one might have expected a first-class *Messiah*, but evidently it was not; nor was it an especially proud moment for Thomas, who was an enthusiastic accomplice in this doubtful marriage of art and business. Patti had fixed ideas about how her part was to be sung and, as in the opera house, expected her word to be law. Thomas, of course, refused to be intimidated. After the performance, Patti got back at him by telling the press that he was "full of vanity and conceit. . . . He really thinks he is a God. . . . He has remarkable energy and handles his orchestra and chorus well but his *tempi* would destroy the efforts of any soloist." She defended her phrasing and interpretation generally—Thomas was predictably unhappy with her treatment of the solos—by saying that Jenny Lind herself had inserted the breathing marks in the part, which, alas, she had been unable to use because Thomas took everything so fast. Patti complained that "Mr. Thomas is not a musician. He can hardly play a piano accompaniment," although she conceded later that he was a "really good performer on the violin." The interview ended with a final slap at Thomas: "Last night he was drinking brandy and had the audacity to offer a brandy bottle to me."[22]

It appeared that, initially, Thomas had angered Patti by failing to accompany her to her seat on the platform—the prevailing custom with prima donnas—at the start of the oratorio. Then, to her mortification, she found Annie Louise Cary occupying the seat next to the conductor, something that Patti said was never done. The press showed its appreciation of the material she provided with creative headlines: "Pretty Patti Piqued" and "After the Messiah Comes the Day of Wrath."[23] Thomas had only himself to blame. He had wanted to make Nichols unhappy and in doing so had suffered a serious lapse in judgment, if not professional integrity. Patti was not interested in the *Messiah*, had not wanted to rehearse, had followed him badly, and was primarily responsible for an undisciplined and erratic performance of a great work. Ironically, the box office was quite good, and the CMFA's substantial profits alleviated losses that the Thomas Orchestra had incurred from two poorly attended concerts prior to the *Messiah*.

Nichols had far more trouble with Patti in February, when she pleaded a sore throat and did not sing until the opera festival's closing night. This and other difficulties resulted in makeshift performances, although, overall, the season was another huge financial success. James Mapleson and his opera company cleared $34,000, Nichols $16,000, and Patti $14,000, despite her illness. Nichols's triumph was short-lived, however. Max Maretzek, the guiding artistic force behind the festivals, resigned from the college on March 10 for the same reason Thomas had—he could not get along with Nichols. On hearing the news, the *New York Times* first chided the college and then interviewed Maretzek and Thomas, who had gotten together in New York to share a laugh at Nichols's expense.[24] During the interview, a wire arrived from the Cincinnati "Circus of Music," as the two men had dubbed it, asking Maretzek to return at any price. He said no.

Thomas had become as susceptible as the public to the magic word "festival." His successes at Cincinnati, the 1880 trip to the mammoth Handel Festival in England, and the joy and power he felt in conducting large choral-orchestral groups, as well as his growing skill with them, had convinced him of their worth. They brought great music to the people, kept his orchestra working, and made money for him and/or the sponsors. Thomas felt he was now ready to direct festivals on a massive scale and proposed a tri-city music festival—three consecutive one-week festivals in New York, Cincinnati, and Chicago in May 1882. The New York and Chicago festivals would be held in halls that could seat 10,000 people—the Seventh Regiment Armory in New York and the Exposition Building in Chicago—and each festival would prepare its own chorus of local and regional choirs, as in Cincinnati. The orchestra and soloists would be the same for all three festivals. It would be Thomas's most challenging project to date, and he looked forward to every minute of it.

Boards were formed in New York and Chicago and, together with the CMFA, worked out mutually satisfactory aggregate fees for the orchestra and soloists. Thomas made all the artistic decisions—soloists, programs, hall arrangements. He worked agreeably and harmoniously with all three boards, belying the rumors in some quarters that he had become an irascible, crusty autocrat. On the contrary, he was now more patient, more temperate, perhaps even mellow. He could not take on the world single-handedly, and he had licked enough wounds from earlier defeats to appreciate the benefits gained from cooperating with others to achieve his goals.

Although Thomas had called his 1873 series of April concerts in New York a "festival," this 1882 festival would be his first truly grand one in the Empire City. Leopold Damrosch had directed a much-appreciated five-day festival in the spring of 1881 at the then-new Seventh Regiment Armory, attracting capacity audiences.[25] Damrosch, another victim of festival fever, had used an orchestra of 250 and a chorus of 1,200, the nucleus coming from his New York Symphony, now a firmly established group, and his Oratorio Society. Thomas's tri-city festival plans called for an orchestra of 300 and a chorus of 3,000. The press made much of the fact that Thomas's announcement had come but a few days after Damrosch's festival had concluded (although Thomas earlier had outlined his dates and other festival details) and attempted to play up the antagonism between the conductors. Both men wisely refrained from comment, and one might suspect that the real "feud" was between their respective supporters, who went to great lengths to champion and promote their heroes. The arena even extended to academe: no sooner had Columbia College awarded Damrosch an honorary doctorate to match Yale's degree to Thomas than Hamilton College gave Thomas a second honorary degree.

The Music Festival Association of New York guaranteed up to $100,000 at the outset to cover deficits incurred and then moved ahead swiftly to put Thomas's plans to the test. The group's president was the articulate George W. Curtis, editor of the popular *Harper's Weekly* and an avid admirer of Thomas; the board was made up of New York's leading and moneyed citizens, a more influential group than Damrosch's festival association. (Damrosch was still considered something of a parvenu; and anti-Semitism, which was beginning to rear its ugly head among the rich as well as the poor, was also a factor.) Just one month before the festival began, Thomas, exuding confidence from every pore, explained to a *Herald* reporter that the programming would be "grand and uncompromising. . . . 'You see,' said Mr. Thomas impressively, leaning forward and speaking quietly and earnestly, as one deeply impressed with his own convictions, 'we must place the great masters before the people at these festivals in the best way, or our work goes for naught.'" He went on to say, provocatively, that American performances were better than European ones since "everything is bigger here, immense, the Philharmonic is the *largest* orchestra anywhere. Europe lacks America's musical vitality." Each new concert in the United States must be "bigger, greater, more impressive than its predecessors," for Americans have an "ambitious driving purpose which compels us to extend our efforts."[26]

Field marshal of the largest and most impressive musical forces assembled since the Gilmore extravaganzas of a decade earlier, Thomas could not have been better placed. For those who cared, what occurred matched Britain's gargantuan Victorian festivals in size and scope. The festival chorus was composed of Thomas's New York and Brooklyn choruses (1,200), the Handel and Haydn Society (550), the Caecilian Society of Philadelphia (350), the Worcester County Musical Association (450), the Baltimore Oratorio Association (550), and the Reading Choral Society (100). The festival orchestra consisted of the Philharmonic, 150 other New York instrumentalists, and 45 players from various cities, including 18 from Chicago and 17 from Cincinnati, most of whom would play again at their own city's festival in the coming weeks. There were 100 violins, 36 violas, 36 cellos, and 40 double basses, 6 or 8 players on nearly all of the woodwind and brass instruments, and an enlarged percussion section. Thomas was thrilled with this "orchestra of orchestras," as were the players, many of whom were his favorite musicians from

Thomas orchestras past and present and with whom he had weathered a number of storms. Rare good cheer and camaraderie prevailed at the rehearsals and performances.[27]

The festival soloists were the best that Thomas could find on two continents: Annie Louise Cary (her final engagement); Myron Whitney; Georg Henschel, conductor of the Boston Symphony; Italo Campanini, the Italian tenor who was to stay on in the United States after the festival; Etelka Gerster, the brilliant young Hungarian coloratura whom James Mapleson had introduced to Americans a few years earlier; and Amalie Materna, the German dramatic soprano and the frosting on the cake. A leading singer at the Vienna Opera, Materna had premiered the role of Brünnhilde at Bayreuth when the Festspielhaus had opened in 1876. Wagner's favorite, she would perform Kundry at the premiere of *Parsifal* at Bayreuth later in the summer of 1882. Despite a wide vibrato and a tendency to sing flat, Materna was one of the great voices of the era. For Thomas, having her was almost like having Wagner, and this was reflected in the royal treatment accorded her.

The festival began with a barrage of publicity heralding the German soprano's arrival in April. Met at Ellis Island in New York Bay at dawn by members of the festival's board and the press, Materna was pleasant, companionable, and unpretentious; indeed, she seemed more like a central European hausfrau than a prima donna. (Of course, New York's Germanically oriented musical press would have been more than disappointed to have Wagner's soprano look and behave like a diva.) Later in the day, Materna attended a concert of *Ring* excerpts in Brooklyn, with Thomas conducting, and, like other European artists, she was overwhelmed by the Thomas Orchestra. Thomas's Wagner—she had "studied every little note of this music with the master himself"—was "just glorious." After hearing Beethoven's Fifth, she exclaimed, "What magnificent musicians you have."[28]

Materna intrigued Wagnerites with her comments about the Kundry role: "It is a splendid acting part; I don't have to sing much except in the second act, and there are some real deep alto notes in it that distress me a little. But the master says they can be overcome." Her attentive husband, the actor Karl Friedrich, said that Verdi liked her Aida so much that he was writing the role of Desdemona in his next opera, *Otello*, expressly for her.[29] To end Materna's first day in New York, a festival-sponsored military band serenaded her below her hotel window, and then Thomas led her proudly and ceremoniously downstairs to meet the musicians.

Press and public alike had admired the space but not the acoustics of the Seventh Regiment Armory Drill Hall used for Damrosch's festival. Thomas, however, was confident that if the performers were appropriately placed, they would be heard to advantage in the armory's furthest reaches. Two platforms were built, one for the chorus and a second, smaller one, one level lower, for the huge orchestra. Thomas had the players seated in a square configuration (if they were spread out too much to his right and left he might lose contact with them), which, along with large wooden backdrops behind both platforms, helped make the sound full and homogeneous.[30] Drapes, plants, and flowers lessened the hall's bleakness and cane-bottom chairs were used instead of Damrosch's wooden benches. In the end, the armory's vastness created an air of anticipation that was compelling.

Scheduling rehearsals effectively for 3,000 choristers from seven cities called for administrative virtuosity, but it came off with barely a slip. Thomas wanted the chorus to begin working in New York one week before the festival opening, and so it did. New England choristers used the boat they came in as a dormitory while they were in New York; others chartered trains and requisitioned hotels. An auction for choice seats was held at Chickering Hall, with New York's mayor in attendance.[31] Press coverage was abundant, and advertisements, posters, and handbills were everywhere. There was a feeling of excitement in the air, yet ticket sales moved slowly. Although 10,000 seats were available for each of seven concerts, attendance fluctuated between 5,000 and 8,000. All choristers received a guest ticket for each concert, but still there were more empty seats than one cared to mention.

Henry Krehbiel, *New York Daily Tribune* critic, edited a 143-page program that not only listed every festival participant from board member to chorister but included extensive annotated program notes. The introduction stated the event's raison d'être: the festival was not "mere sensationalism" but necessary if one were to hear the "monumental creations in . . . choral music" that would be brought out in "their full potency, with solo and instrumental forces commensurate in all respects with the magnitude and magnificence of the choir."[32] However, if this was what late nineteenth-century American musical audiences wanted, then the festival was probably held in the wrong building. Materna was unhappy because, despite her huge voice, she had to force herself to be heard in the vast hall. At least two singers—Aline Osgoode, the soprano, and Annie Louise Cary—were ill for the *Missa solemnis*, and Italo Campanini had not bothered to learn his part. The female replacements did their best, but Thomas hovered on the brink of disaster several times during the performance. *Israel in Egypt*, the best-performed choral work, was the most poorly attended.

Symphonic music drew more plaudits than choral music. Thomas, praised by critics for his reading of Mozart's "Jupiter" with a 300-piece orchestra, delightedly told the *Herald* that the ensemble "was so well balanced as to perfectly reproduce the relative proportions, the coloring, the exact sentiment of a symphony written for thirty or forty instruments. . . . The orchestral tone [had] a purity and sonority that is only obtained by immense musical forces.

. . . All the delicacy of shading, the effect of contrasts . . . were preserved and emphasized. An adroit precision and excellence of phrasing were as noticeable in the festival orchestra as in a small body of instrumentalists."[33] Looking for equal praise for his massed chorus, Thomas claimed that he controlled it as well as a group one quarter the size. One wonders whether he was so mesmerized by his "immense" forces that he had lost his judgment. Was this what the fine and delicate art of music was all about?

George Curtis of *Harper's*, cultured and sophisticated, was as carried away as Thomas. He gave eloquent testimony to the artistic aspirations of his age: the music was done "incomparably." Of American festivals to date, this one had "legitimate grandeur [and] symmetrical precision. [It was] the highwater mark in the musical annals of the country." Curtis panegyrized Thomas —"Without Napoleon there had been no Austerlitz; without Thomas, no Festival"—and attributed his success to his "courageous confidence" in public taste and the fact that he aimed "higher and higher," toward a "broader and grander horizon."[34] Praise like that held Thomas back from questioning the validity and purpose of such grand festivals and whether they really helped the cause of great music.

There were no questions about artistic validity, however, when it came to the Cincinnati festival. There Thomas had a proper hall, a chorus that had rehearsed its repertoire for almost two years, and a more reasonably sized orchestra. The attention that New York's festival had received in the Cincinnati press helped ticket sales and cheered the CMFA, which had feared all spring that the local public had drained its purses of theater-going money at Nichols's opera festival and would have nothing left for the May Festival. An additional concern was that Thomas's programs were heavier than in the past, particularly with Bach's *St. Matthew's Passion*, which would be done for the first time in America in its entirety (and would draw a capacity house).

To the city's credit, the audiences at the festival were at least as enthusiastic as earlier ones. Thomas was right again: do not underestimate the public's musical taste, given that it is developed gradually through first-class performances, from the light to the serious. Camille Saint-Saëns and Carl Reinecke, the composer and head of the Leipzig Conservatory, were the judges, along with Thomas, for the second composers' competition. The winning work was William Wallace Gilchrist's *A Setting of the Forty-sixth Psalm* for organ, orchestra, and chorus; it was the festival's only letdown and finally soured Thomas on competitions. On reflection, he realized that he could do without their many problems: selecting the best from a raft of mediocre works, preparing the full score and having the parts copied, coping with last-minute changes, dealing with the judges—Saint-Saëns, for one, complained about his expenses—and, in the end, sharing bad reviews with the composer.

The festival lost money—about $8,000—for the first time, but thanks to Christmas *Messiah* profits, the CMFA treasurer reported that the surplus was still intact. President Pendleton wrote in his annual report that, so long as festivals did not lose money, "save from unavoidable causes"—he was alluding to the opera festival and the costly soloists Cincinnati had to share with New York and Chicago—he considered them "financially successful." And even if the festival did lose money, "artistic merit should be the only standard so long as there is prudence in the management." Then Pendleton harked back to the *Messiah* with Adelina Patti and, full of pride, called it "the greatest American rendering of this work. Outside of our city it is made the standard of comparison for all such performances. The financial success of this concert was unprecedented." [35]

Chicago eagerly awaited its turn. The last of the three festivals was planned on a grand scale, like New York's, and the local press puffed tirelessly with superlatives about the festival's virtues, that "the greatest railroad center in the world" would now host "the greatest musical event in the history of America." The huge Industrial Exposition Building had a "grand look": eighty Brush electric lamps, each with 200 candle power, filled the hall with a radiating light of such intensity that observers claimed it was unequaled in any other hall in the United States. [36] The ballyhoo worked: three days before the festival began, it had taken in an impressive $35,000, well past the break-even point.

Chicago's spring weather, unpredictable at best, was intolerable that year. The Exposition Building, in the face of Lake Michigan's storms, was scant protection for the chilly, rain-soaked festival-goers, yet several of the evening concerts attracted 10,000 people—and this in spite of uncompromising, long programs. The music was played as well as one could hope by the mammoth orchestra, the same numbers as in New York. The Apollo Musical Club and its director, William Tomlins, worked particularly well with Thomas and were the equals of their counterparts in Cincinnati. While the ensembles outdid themselves, the soloists, faced with another monster setting, did not. Annie Louise Cary, primed to end her career with a flourish, was again plagued with a sore throat, and Amalie Materna let down the audience with her "Immolation" scene from *Die Götterdämmerung*. The acidulous Oscar Wilde, visiting Chicago at the time, told the press that he fully expected her to sing badly. [37]

Yet, all in all, Thomas was delighted with the Chicago festival and foolishly irritated New Yorkers by stating that there had never been a festival of "such a high artistic standard of excellence." (It was the first of several such comparisons of music in the two cities, with Chicago coming out on top.) The *InterOcean*, one of Chicago's leading dailies, wrote with tongue in cheek that it was relieved when the festival was over—some people had actually worked themselves into a frenzy over it. Frenzy or not, the newspaper applauded what the festival had done for "public knowledge and, indirectly, public morals." Thomas, with his heavy programs, "continues to discipline Chicago successfully in the growth of its taste."[38]

7

Undisputed Ruler

In the spring of 1882, the Philharmonic Society of New York, for the first time, unanimously elected its conductor—Theodore Thomas—an unprecedented, yet well deserved, vote of confidence. Subscription sales had continued to rise, with correspondingly high dividends, and differences between the conductor and the society appeared to be in the past. To show his good will, Thomas arranged for his festival soloists to perform with the Philharmonic at little or no fee; in return, the society loaned him music for non-Philharmonic activities. In addition, most of the Philharmonic players earned extra money at his festivals and summer concerts.[1]

Thomas's popularity had grown steadily since his return to New York in 1880. His income was substantial; he had, to his great relief, paid off his debts; his family was comfortably ensconced in Europe; and he had temporarily put aside his wish for a permanent orchestra, so absorbing was his work with the Philharmonic and his own orchestra. With the time and inclination to concentrate on artistic concerns, he threw his energy into making the Philharmonic as responsive and precise an instrument as the Thomas Orchestra had been ten years earlier. Unfortunately, he also chose to take issue with Philharmonic players who worked for Leopold Damrosch, letting them know that he preferred that they do otherwise. The unfriendly *New York Times* heard of Thomas's high-handedness and warned that he was out to "cripple" other musical organizations and "drive out all competition from the field." It named the New York Symphony Society, with its "progressive spirit," as Thomas's principal target and reported that Damrosch's tour of the West that year was a success despite the "one man power" of Thomas in large cities. The paper hammered home the message that there were other conductors and other orchestras.[2]

One wonders why Thomas, happier on all counts than he had been for a decade, could not let things rest. Perhaps he believed that he functioned best when he was either on the attack or under siege. He saw Damrosch, the organizer and conductor, as a roadblock, preventing him from developing the finest orchestra(s) in the world. Further, his personal dislike of Damrosch had grown, as had his dislike for Damrosch's overly demonstrative conducting—a style that was gaining popularity in Europe—which he thought was superficial and benefited the gallery, not the music. It was common knowledge that Damrosch talked too much at rehearsals, while Thomas, a man of few words, let his baton do the talking. Damrosch's advocates said that Thomas was stodgy and merely a time-beater, and they doubted that his straightforward and unobtrusive efforts brought out the composer's intention with sufficient interest and fidelity. Yet no one doubted that Thomas was the stronger conductor.

Having two competitive conductors in New York did make musical life there more interesting. *Freund's*, a leading music journal edited by John C. Freund (later co-founder of the popular journal *Musical America*), said metaphorically that Thomas "offers a good sound menu, well prepared and put on the table, though expensive, as he is fond of the best and most renowned dishes, and [Damrosch] chooses daintily here and there, does not take the foremost or grandest, but often out-of-the-way peculiar dishes for his menu, which he prepares in a peculiar though able manner."[3] There were stories about how each conductor tried to beat the other in giving first performances of works by important European composers. In the end, it was a draw.

In April 1882, a new opportunity came Thomas's way: William Steinway invited him to direct the Liederkranz Society along with the semiretired Agriol Paur, its conductor for nearly thirty years. Wealthy German Americans supported their choral societies handsomely, and the Liederkranz was no exception. Its members had raised an astonishing $105,000 in two days to fund the construction of a new clubhouse at 11 East Fifty-eighth Street, and its women's committee raised an additional $25,263 to furnish the interior. Enormous sums for the time, they were an indication of the importance the German community attached to preserving its traditions.[4]

Thomas happily accepted the invitation, perhaps because Damrosch had been conducting the Liederkranz's friendly rival and sister organization, the Arion Society, for over ten years, but also because he wanted to maintain contact with German-oriented groups. The Thomas Orchestra and the Liederkranz Choir performed together at the opening of the new clubhouse on November 26, 1882. Nineteen-year-old Emma Juch, born in Vienna of American parents and a Thomas favorite, was the soloist; Rafael Joseffy also played. The concert was given in the society's new 1,200-seat concert hall.[5] The Liederkranz joined the Thomas Orchestra on other occasions, attracting wide public attention, and began to compete with the Arion for audiences.

The rivalry continued until 1884, when both Damrosch and Thomas resigned from their posts because of other, more demanding activities.

During this happy and productive period in the first half of the 1880s, Thomas involved himself in several other important musical issues and activities. One concerned the pitch to which orchestras tuned, a controversial subject in continental Europe for many years. Pitch had gradually crept up as wind instrument construction was refined to improve tone, putting more and more strain on keyboard and stringed instruments and on voices. In 1859, France decreed a low concert A of 435 cycles per second (c.p.s.). Other European countries followed suit, but not Britain or North America, where the higher A of 459 c.p.s. prevailed. The disparity presented problems for soloists, particularly singers, who performed in different countries.

Thomas had, for some years, wanted to adjust American pitch to the prevalent European diapason normal. He believed that the higher pitch, in addition to creating problems for soloists, unfavorably affected orchestral sonority, although changing to a lower A meant that wind players would have to have their instruments adjusted, rebuilt, or, more likely, replaced. Despite the inconvenience and expense involved in such a changeover, its benefits would, according to its adherents, be worth the trouble. Thus, in September 1882, at Thomas's instigation, the New York Philharmonic delegated a committee to introduce a lower pitch by February 1883. Seeing the need, the orchestra quickly adopted A435 without trauma and on schedule, and wind players switched to new instruments. Soon, other orchestras across the country followed suit.[6]

Another issue that interested Thomas was copyright and the need for clarification of prevailing laws. He had acquired exclusive North American performing rights from the French composer Charles Gounod for his recently composed sacred trilogy, *The Redemption*. Although it had had a mixed reception at the Birmingham Festival, Thomas was eager to add it to his festival repertoire before it reached Damrosch and other conductors. Thomas's rights, however, meant little to J. G. Lennon of Boston, who planned to do the work with his own orchestration. The only authorized orchestration was, of course, Gounod's, and Lennon was clearly violating the law. At Thomas's instigation, Lennon was served an injunction on January 23, 1883, preventing him from performing the work. The action, authorized by the United States Circuit Court of Appeals, set a precedent: in the future, only the composer or his designate could make an orchestration from a vocal score. "An opera [or oratorio] is more like a patented invention than like a common book," the ruling declared.[7] Dudley Buck drew a most apt analogy: "A composer's instrumentation is part and parcel of his world. . . . The piano score corresponds to a *pencil* drawing of an oil painting. . . . The original colouring is *more than half the work*."[8] No one seemed inclined to dispute this.

On February 13, 1883, Richard Wagner died, and musicians everywhere paid tribute to him with eulogies and memorial concerts. Thomas, America's leading Wagnerian, recorded his thoughts in the Boston-based *Musical Record* by comparing Wagner, rather simplistically, to Gluck: ". . . both men had the same aim, although Wagner was the greater musician. Music to both was only a means to an end, not the end in itself as it was with Mozart, Beethoven and Weber, and this is the reason why both . . . were not understood by conservative musicians." Thomas believed that Wagner's importance in musical history could not have been determined while he was alive, for Wagner was "underrated by his opponents" and "overrated by his supporters." He added: "If anyone has doubts as to his real greatness let him look at the present repertoire of the opera houses of the world, and at the void he leaves behind him." Wagner's greatest accomplishment was the *Ring*; *Parsifal*, his final work, was a letdown, according to Thomas. However, he was confident that Wagner's achievements as a musical dramatist would have a beneficial influence on Italian operatic composers who, Thomas felt, concentrated unduly on the music at the expense of the drama[9]—and to a considerable degree, he was right. Through music, Thomas paid Wagner a still sounder tribute by conducting special concerts of his work in New York and Brooklyn.[10]

In 1883, Thomas also played a role in the ongoing fight by women for equal rights. James Mapleson, who directed Italian opera at the Academy of Music, planned a benefit concert for the New York Exchange for Woman's Work, a placement service run by well-to-do, "educated" women for "unfortunate gentlewomen, who, owing to pecuniary losses, are obliged to support themselves by doing any kind of work for which they have a taste and talent."[11] Thomas volunteered his services both because he believed in the cause and to build up his credit with his women supporters. Adelina Patti, the Canadian soprano Emma Albani (Louise Cecelia Emma Lajeunesse), the Italian contralto Sofia Scalchi, and other greats performed for this gala with the Thomas Orchestra on April 12, 1883.

Another highlight of 1883 was the opening at Thirty-ninth Street and Broadway of the Metropolitan Opera House, which was to have a monumental influence on New York's operatic life for eight decades. It had been financed primarily by a group of nouveau riche tycoons who had been unable to purchase boxes at the Academy of Music because they were all owned by a small, exclusive group of New York's 400. These frustrated and deprived opera lovers, if we may call them that, had no recourse but to build a new opera house, where they could have their own boxes. The Met (as it became known) boasted a striking interior, a large stage, good acoustics, and better sightlines than at the Academy of Music, but it had inadequate backstage space and storage facilities for scenery and properties, which ultimately led to its undoing.

The Brooklyn Bridge was also completed in 1883. Justifiably referred to as the engineering marvel of the age, it linked Manhattan and Brooklyn, thus enabling the city's burgeoning population to fan out to the boroughs. There were more and more new buildings, improved rapid transit, and other services, and some people thought the great city would begin to support performing arts organizations not only in word but in deed. However, laissez faire ruled supreme in Gotham's theaters, opera houses, and concert halls, with civic, state, and federal subsidies still almost a century away. Opera in the Met, as in the Academy of Music, was entrusted to profit-seeking impresarios. The Philharmonic Society, now over forty years old, continued to give but a handful of concerts annually. Civic leaders spoke eloquently of Thomas's achievements but refused to sponsor a civic orchestra, as in Boston.

Once again, Thomas had to look elsewhere to earn enough money to meet his personal needs and to keep his orchestra together. The answer, of course, lay in touring, but with a new twist—a festival tour, involving perhaps twenty cities across the land. As in the tri-city festival, each center would prepare its own chorus and then, together with the Thomas Orchestra, and depending upon the city's size, hall, and potential box office, would present an impressive music festival. Where this was not feasible, concerts only would be given.

The entire scheme was entrusted to two entrepreneurial brothers from California, Charles and Seymour Locke. Their optimism knew no bounds: before Thomas even began the tour, they claimed that they had received guarantees from tour cities that ranged from $1,250 to $25,000, that some of the festivals and/or concerts were already sold out, and that twice as many engagements could have been booked. The *New York Daily Tribune*, infected with enthusiasm for what looked to be Thomas's greatest triumph to date, reported that "the aggregate of all the funds is $198,000. . . . In San Francisco, where the most elaborate festival is to be given, Mr. Locke declined to accept any price for the series, preferring to give the performances as a personal speculation. It is estimated that the subscription there will reach $50,000. Over $22,000 had been subscribed by March 25." [12]

The United States, in a period of unprecedented prosperity, was ready for this "Ocean to Ocean" tour, or, as George Upton called it, Thomas's "March to the Sea." American railroads had expanded across the land, creating new cities in their wake; now, almost fifty million people lived in urban centers. The country seemed less spread out than ever before. One could travel from the Atlantic to the Pacific in under a week, and New York's news could reach San Francisco in minutes, thanks to effective wire services. Many cities, however, had not heard good music and, especially, Theodore Thomas. He intended to remedy that.

Thomas was cautious enough to get the enterprising Lockes to give him a cash guarantee of $50,000 at the outset, for he did not want to be abandoned, along with his orchestra, in some remote corner of the Wild West. The two brothers turned to the Decker Piano Company, which provided the money and sponsored the tour; Steinway was asked first—the company had backed other Thomas tours—but declined. Julia Rivé-King, an excellent young American pianist, would be the tour soloist and would, of course, play a Decker piano. Her husband, Frank King, would be the tour's business manager.[13]

The agreement called for twelve festivals, ranging in length from three to seven days, from Baltimore to San Francisco and Memphis to Minneapolis; in addition, the orchestra would play in twenty other cities for one or two nights. The tour would begin on April 26 in Baltimore and conclude in Burlington, Iowa, on July 7—seventy-three concerts (sometimes two a day) in seventy-three days. The 3,000-voice Mormon Choir of Salt Lake City would be the largest group the orchestra performed with, and the Minneapolis Choir, with 380, the smallest. Once the tour was under way, dispatches to New York papers raved about the public response, the huge audiences, and the money earned. Thomas followed his usual pattern of short pieces and soloists at matinees, with longer pieces, including symphonies, at evening concerts; and in festival cities, he frequently added oratorios. A city's size and Thomas's appraisal of its musical sophistication determined program content. He was rarely wrong.

Each festival center printed its own program, which usually included notes on the music, the conductor, and the soloists and, occasionally, some revealing information on the musical activities of the city.[14] Leaders in Columbus, Ohio, for example, had had difficulty in funding the city's three concerts and wrote enviously of its more successful neighbor to the south: "Cincinnati owes its reputation, standing and progress to no one thing more than to its enterprise in matters of music." In other words, they believed that a thriving musical life reflected in good part a city's economic and social outlook and position and its quality of life—a cogent argument that would be used frequently in the future.

The tour made America a land of May and June festivals with Theodore Thomas as the director. He raised the level of music across the country and encouraged the organization of orchestras and choirs, the building of new halls, and the renovating of old ones. The program for Kansas City, Missouri, reveled in the city's maturing musical taste and lauded its citizenry in vintage prose. Where "OFFENBACH, STRAUSS and SULLIVAN have been classed as the limit to the tastes and wishes of the west [there is now] a greater order of masters, whom the coming of THEODORE THOMAS has brought to our theatre and made familiar to our households." George W. Warder, an inspired local poet, floridly concluded his contribution to the program:

> We drink in song, and thirst for more,
> Our hearts beat to a mystic rhyme
> That silence utters o'er and o'er,

Like echoes from a far-off clime.
Perhaps it is angelic song
Vibrating from the heavenly shore,
That listening souls have heard so long;
They can but answer, sing and soar.[15]

No city heralded Thomas's arrival more than San Francisco, its thorough preparation for the festival reflected in a 110-page program that rivaled the New York festival's in scope and content. Included were: the seven concert programs; annotated program notes with musical examples; full texts for choral compositions; biographies of Thomas and the soloists; lists of members of the local advisory committee, subscribers to the guarantee fund, and members of the 500-voice chorus and orchestra; a history of American music festivals, beginning with the Cincinnati *Sängerfest* of 1849; and "A Local Retrospect," which gave accounts of instrumental music in San Francisco from its beginnings thirty years earlier and of the work of Rudolph Herold, the city's first serious musician. The leading urban center of the Far West proclaimed that it needed "endowments" to establish a permanent orchestra like Thomas's and build a symphony hall like Cincinnati's.

Location notwithstanding, the level of San Francisco's cultural life was not much below that of leading Eastern centers, and the city's intelligentsia was more concerned about raising the standards of musical taste than its counterparts west of the Mississippi. Thomas, aware of this, programmed carefully and judiciously. If the San Francisco concerts were not quite up to New York or Cincinnati levels, they were more ambitious than those he gave at Kansas City and other large western centers new to the "Thomas Highway." Among the festival's highlights were an all-Wagner concert and Schubert's Unfinished Symphony.

With the orchestra in San Francisco for a full week, the local newspapers devoted considerable space to Thomas. The *Chronicle* described him as "a military looking man of medium stature, cast in a solid mold, showing his forty eight years in a slight silvering of the temporal locks, with a pair of keen eyes rather dimmed by travel, a broad high forehead, a solid nose flanked by heavy lines, a mouth hidden under a full moustache and a massive chin running into a thick neck, which in turn spread in a pair of broad shoulders." It referred to him with respect bordering on affection and concluded by likening him to a "Prussian General" whose "word is law."[16]

Alas, to the dismay of the pretty American soprano Emma Thursby, who had joined the tour in San Francisco, Thomas's word was law. Thursby, at twenty-nine, was a local favorite. Just in case the Thomas Orchestra was unable to attract crowds, she was Charles Locke's "insurance policy," for she sang acrobatic arias guaranteed to bring the house down. Thomas had no objection to Thursby's popularity or even what she sang—he had gotten used to doing light and even "poor" light music years before—but he did object to the fact that no matter what she sang or how she sang it, the audience would indiscriminately, if not naively, shout "encore." A forbidding program notice duly warned concertgoers that "such encores only will be permitted as do not break the continuity of the programmes or seriously increase their length."[17] In the face of what, in Thomas's view, were unruly responses to Thursby's singing, the conductor overreacted and stubbornly refused her any encores whatsoever, from the first concert to the last. Such intransigence fostered much hostility from Thursby and her adoring public.

The San Francisco press, grabbing hold of the dispute, took up Thursby's cause and suggested to Thomas, first politely and then firmly, that he relent. Thursby's supporters wanted to hear her, not the orchestra, and the orchestra (and its conductor) should therefore please them.[18] Thomas's adherents defended him and his policy, insisting that the overall plan of the concert was more important than giving in to tasteless audiences and spoiled sopranos. The "battle" raged through the closing concert of the festival, with the audience hissing and stamping when Thomas refused to allow Thursby to encore even her final piece.

Following the concerts, Thursby issued a public statement pointing out that she had wanted to give encores and that she would have sung more works if Thomas had let her: "I feel that in my limited performances I have not reached the hearts of the public as I would wish."[19] Thomas did not comment publicly, but privately he was furious with Thursby, for she had agreed to the no-encore policy prior to the festival; and, once the festival got under way, she had not confronted him with her displeasure. Now, her statement made Thomas seem the villain of the piece—which, in a sense, he was, for in retrospect he knew that he could have avoided the problem if he had permitted an occasional encore. His spirit of compromise, developed since leaving the Cincinnati College of Music in 1880, seems to have lapsed temporarily.

Thursby lived up to her contract, sharing the concert platform with Thomas in Salt Lake City and Denver, the next two tour stops. She continued to receive the same treatment and later, in New York, talked widely about Thomas's conduct. It did little to help his reputation (which was already none too good) with other singers and operatic managers. Yet Thomas was now contemplating a career as an operatic conductor.

Exhausted from the "Ocean to Ocean" tour, Thomas arrived in Chicago on July 13 and met with Charles Locke and members of the Cincinnati and Chicago music festival associations to discuss plans for still another joint festival in 1884 (New York was evidently not interested).[20] They chose dates and soloists and arranged to dovetail the two festivals, along with another national tour. The commanding general of music in the United States, weary as he was of poor hotels, bad food, dirty trains, and temperamental sopranos, was prepared to march across the continent once again. There were cities in which he had not conducted and others that wanted him back, which made it all bearable.

While in Chicago, Thomas stayed with the philosopher Charles Pierce, whose wife, Melusina, was a member of the Fay family, with whom Thomas had struck up a friendship. Charles Norman Fay was a Chicago businessman with a keen interest in music; his sister Amy was a well-known pianist and the author of the popular *Music Study in Germany*; another sister, Rose, was an active participant in the Ladies Amateur Musical Clubs of America. Thomas had spent many happy hours with the family since meeting Charles Norman Fay in 1881, and he and Rose Fay had begun a correspondence which, as the years went by, revealed many of his personal and professional views. After the death of his wife, Minna, his friendship with Rose, always proper, led to love and marriage.

After leaving Chicago, Thomas wrote to Rose Fay from Milwaukee: "The weather is very cold here. [It] affects the pitch of the orchestra, and the light was very poor at the concert last night, so I was thoroughly MAD by the time we got to the second piece on the programme. The third piece was the Allegretto from the Seventh Beethoven symphony, which of course suffered under the circumstances, but the fourth and close of the first part was the Liszt Rhapsody, which gained under the influence of temper and angry feeling." A more personal letter from Atlanta some months later complained—typically —of overwork and of his dislike of Europe, which he had visited in late August on festival business and to see his wife and children. Thomas also struck a lonely note: "To me the future does not look dark, but only like an idle dream. I have not had the good fortune of a Christian education to sweeten my life." [21] Feeling sorry for himself was one of Thomas's less endearing qualities, and Rose Fay's shoulder would be convenient to cry upon in the coming years.

By November, Thomas had changed his plans for the following spring: instead of a festival tour, he would do a Wagner tour in 1884: seventy consecutive concerts in nineteen cities;[22] and he would not return to the Far West until 1885. Unstaged Wagner excerpts would be the principal fare; some works by other composers would also be included. The three German soloists who had created the principal roles in the premiere of *Parsifal* at Bayreuth the year before had been booked: Amalie Materna, again; Hermann Winkelmann, a tenor; and Emil Scaria, a baritone. Thomas also named four other soloists, including the Swedish prima donna Christine Nilsson, whose popular repertoire—she was famous for the "Jewel Song" from *Faust*—would, he hoped, placate (if not attract) anti-Wagnerites.

The tour was still another way for Thomas to identify himself with Wagner and maintain his position as the composer's number one American advocate. He had introduced most of Wagner's works in New York, from the Overture to *The Flying Dutchman* at his debut concert in 1862 to the "Good Friday Spell" from *Parsifal* twenty years later. But an increasingly enterprising and resourceful Leopold Damrosch now threatened Thomas's supremacy as Wagner's interpreter. Two years earlier, both he and Damrosch had done first performances of "The Transformation" from *Parsifal* on the very same night, Thomas in Brooklyn and Damrosch at the New York Academy of Music. With Wagner's popularity growing steadily, there were rumors that the new Metropolitan Opera House would stage his operas in the near future. Thomas hoped to conduct them, and he wanted this Wagner tour to prove that he should.

Intensive preparations for the tour did not prevent the indefatigable Thomas from adding two new local concert series to his 1883–84 schedule. One involved three Saturday afternoon orchestral concerts for young people between the ages of ten and sixteen. Thomas, who realized the importance of exposing children to great music, had been considering such concerts for ten years, but now there was real support for them, sparked mainly by a vivacious and wealthy New Yorker, Jeannette Thurber (who would play a significant role in Thomas's life in the next few years), and several other prominent socialites. The concerts would be short and of a "lighter character, with a view to instructing the children in the formation of a correct musical taste as well as to entertaining them."[23]

Subscriptions for the young people's concerts were $2.50, single admissions $1.00; advance sales were good. The concerts were the first of their kind anywhere, but their success was debatable. Thomas, who lacked the perspective of present-day educators, saw children simply as young adults and therefore used the Central Park Garden approach, starting with short, light pieces and then working up to complete symphonies. Keep the children quiet, make them listen, and love for good music would soon develop, he maintained. It did not happen quite that way.

Press reaction was mixed, and Thomas was applauded more for his efforts than for his results. *Freund's* thought *The Beautiful Blue Danube* too heavy for children. The *New York Times* observed that the "children listened attentively to the music and held their tongues in a manner full of suggestion to many older concertgoers," but it noted that more adults than young people attended the final concert.[24] Nevertheless, Thomas was sufficiently encouraged to plan six young people's concerts for the following year.

The other new 1883–84 venture that prompted *Freund's* praise of Thomas as the "national music teacher in the widest and broadest sense" was his working people's concert series. In contrast to the relatively high-priced children's concerts, these had no admission charge, yet the working people who attended were, according to the *Herald*, representative of "the better class—the poor but genteel." The *Evening Post* said that they were "a respectable class of people whose income and engagements do not allow them to attend high class entertainment," whereas the *Evening Sun* called them "superior working people." The *Times* complained about the "dressy" people and noted that the "non-genteel" poor were conspicuous by their absence.[25] As for the concerts, which mixed the serious with the light, the *Herald* observed that they were received with "demonstrative gratitude and evident gratification and, strange to say, the Beethoven Symphony [No. 5] and Wagner's Overture [to *Rienzi*] seemed to hit the taste of the audience more than the lighter selections," which included Weber's *Invitation to the Dance*, Mendelssohn's Overture to *A Midsummer Night's Dream*, and some songs of Schubert and Schumann.

Were the concerts charity? The social critic Felix Adler, founder of the Society for Ethical Culture, said emphatically that they were not. An advocate of free concerts for all, Adler believed that they served the community much like public schools, public galleries, and public libraries. He expected the programs to be serious, for the poor deserved the great masterpieces as much as the rich: "When art galleries are thrown open to people they are not invited to look at cheap chromes." He predicted, almost contradictorily, that "the time will come when the bigoted people will recognize . . . that there is more true religion in a good waltz or polka than in a wretched hymn."[26]

In truth, the series was patronizing; it was artistic charity, symptomatic of the hypocrisy of the Gilded Age and the pervasive Victorian morality and artificial gentility at its roots. But could it have been otherwise? *Freund's* declared, penetratingly (or patronizingly?), that the concerts were "make believe. . . . To find music for which the masses have affinity we must first understand the masses."[27] Prophetically, it was this lack of understanding of the masses and the music they wanted that was the series' undoing. Good music need not be shrouded in mystery to be enjoyed, nor is it any less meaningful to the uneducated than to the educated, to the rough and ready than to the genteel, if played well in a satisfactory setting. But it takes time to understand and appreciate music well, for personal sensitivity to music to flower. No one knew this better than Thomas.

By March 1884, Thomas was totally caught up in the Wagner tour. He was supervising six copyists preparing orchestral parts for Wagner excerpts and organizing choirs and solo singers, and he still conducted several concerts weekly. Although the workaholic conductor/entrepreneur loved the enormous project on which he had embarked, he wrote to Rose Fay for sympathy: "Every twenty-four hours I have enough work to do to kill the average man."[28] It all seemed worthwhile, however, when he received the news that advance sales in Boston, the tour's first stop, had exceeded expectations.

The Boston festival, which began on April 14, had six concerts in four days, all given at the Mechanics Institute. Several of the programs attracted up to 8,000 people and were all Wagner, with two exceptions: Beethoven's "Eroica" at the second evening's concert and his Fifth Symphony on the fourth and final evening. Bostonians, it seemed, loved Wagner as much as New Yorkers did, and Thomas obligingly put his three uncomplaining German singers through their paces. Materna, whose wide vibrato was less irritating than before, sang Isolde, Brünnhilde, and Kundry; Scaria sang Wotan, Sachs, Pogner, and Gurnemanz; and Winkelmann sang Tannhäuser, Siegfried, Walther, Tristan, and Parsifal. Among the American singers, Emma Juch did a noteworthy Eva.

For this first engagement, Thomas had augmented his orchestra to 150 players and used 600 local voices along with his own Liederkranz Chorus. William Steinway had shepherded the latter from New York, but not without difficulty. Because of a mix-up in railway scheduling, they arrived only minutes before their appearance in Act 3 of *Die Meistersinger* and performed without rehearsal. Despite such difficulties—the choruses were generally under-rehearsed—nearly all of the informed who heard the programs felt that Wagner had never been done better in North America.[29] Thomas's grasp of the music and his superb control of the huge forces onstage brought him kudos from all sides. The program notes were lengthy and informative, and libretto translations were available, since few Bostonians knew German. Henry T. Finck, music critic of the *Nation* and the *New York Evening Post,* prepared a Wagner handbook that included essays on different aspects of the composer's life. Nothing was said about a chorus that occasionally sang in English while soloists sang in German, nor about whether an outsize orchestra of 150 was appropriate.

What explained Wagner's extraordinary popularity with American concertgoers? Was it the music's rich harmonies and the tension they aroused in listeners, its textures, its orchestrations, and its motives, which unified music and stage action? Or was it the romantic, unreal librettos and their almost fairy-tale quality? (Only the pre-*Tristan* operas had been staged in the United States before 1884.) Charles Dudley Warner, who, with Mark Twain, had written *The Gilded Age,* may have spoken for many when he wrote in the excessive prose style of the day that *Parsifal*

> had a supernatural note—an unworldly, not to say a spiritual suggestion. It rose and fell, more importunate than strident, in pleading, in warning, in entreaty . . . like the wind in a vast forest of pines in a summer day. It appealed to the imagination, it excited expectation, it begot an indefinable longing; and now and then a minor strain, full of sadness or of passion, suggested a theme like the opening of a window into another world—a theme which was to be renewed again and again in the drama, when it came to us like a reminiscence of some former life.[30]

The soloists and orchestra went on to New York and then to Philadel-phia. According to the *Musical Courier* correspondent, who had also covered the Boston and New York concerts, the Philadelphia performances were the best yet, even though audiences were small—less than a thousand at some concerts. The Quaker City's musical press wrote in detail about Thomas's interpretation of the "Bacchanale" from *Tannhäuser.* Unfortunately, Thomas failed to inform the press that he had made a substitution on the program. It was a critic's nightmare.[31]

Without a break, the company went on to Richmond, Virginia, followed by Washington, D.C., Baltimore, and Portland, Maine; then came Boston, New York, and Philadelphia, for a second round. (Locke was confident that Philadelphia would have larger houses this time, and he was right.) Christine Nilsson had now joined the company, and sales increased. Her first appear-ance was as Elsa in the "Euch Euften" duo from Act 2 of *Lohengrin;* Materna sang Ortrud. Nilsson, a mainstream prima donna, brought on hurrahs and frenzied cries for more, even though some thought Materna outsang her.[32] The two sopranos got on well on the tour, although they rarely sang together after that.

Cincinnati's May Festival, its sixth since 1873, neatly dovetailed into the Wagner tour, but Thomas approached the city with some foreboding. Cincinnati had suffered through near-catastrophic floods in February. And at the end of March, a Cincinnati court had sentenced a convicted murderer to twenty years in prison, amid feelings that the jury had been directed to invoke a too-light sentence. Riots ensued, protesters burned down the courthouse, and the state militia, called in to control the disturbances, mercilessly killed and wounded scores of people. Terror and depression had settled over the city.[33] Thus, it was no small challenge for the redoubtable Cincinnati Music Festival Association to create a festive "mood."

Rumors persisted that the May Festival was "pre-destined to failure"—and a failure it was, financially speaking. There was far less income than in 1882, and less than half that of the first festival at Music Hall in 1878, in spite of such star attractions as the Wagner trio and Nilsson. The board's statements of income and expenses tell the story:[34]

	1878	1880	1882	1884
Director	$5,000.00	$5,000.00	$5,000.00	$5,000.00
Assistant director	—	1,600.00	1,830.00	2,000.00
Orchestra and transportation	9,871.90	14,891.82	14,717.57	13,782.46
Soloists	7,466.75	7,896.00	8,927.00	14,785.00
Music Hall	918.50	1,064.50	1,386.08	788.16
Prize	—	1,000.00	1,000.00	—

Music	—	951.50	2,067.40	3,404.94
Advertising	1,960.78	1,481.00	2,399.42	2,456.03
Printing	—	1,350.21	3,059.36	2,150.41
Various	—	10,643.75	13,673.34	6,643.69
TOTAL EXPENSES	$37,103.01	45,878.78	52,536.52	51,010.69
RECEIPTS	$69,631.87	53,387.72	44,415.85	32,053.50
SURPLUS (DEFICIT)	$32,518.86	7,508.94	(8,120.67)	(18,957.19)

Obviously, the CMFA would have to subsidize future festivals. The civic-minded president of the association stated at the annual meeting in June: "We can not afford to swerve one iota from our devotion to the highest order of music. The financial result must be a secondary one to this or our festivals will come to a lamentable end, instead of being continued as a matter of honor and pride."[35]

Artistically, the 1884 festival was not a resounding success. Cincinnati audiences found Gounod's *Redemption* "tedious and monotonous with too many recitatives and an ubiquitous organ," although, thanks to soprano soloist Nilsson, the hall was almost full. Handel's *Israel in Egypt*, another first for the Queen City, attracted a poor house because its soloists were relatively unknown. The *Cincinnati Enquirer*, which viewed the festival as more than mere "showbusiness," castigated the public both for its failure to appreciate *Israel* and for its vociferous response to what the paper thought was Nilsson's poor singing in *The Redemption*.[36]

The chorus was praised, even though it had three times as many women as men. Thomas had finally found a good resident chorusmaster in Arthur Mees, who, like Thomas, stopped at nothing to achieve excellence. Mees kept Thomas informed of the chorus's progress between festivals and told him occasionally about other local happenings of interest. (Although he was born in Columbus, Ohio, he corresponded with Thomas in fluent German, thanks to having studied music in Berlin.) Mees had enticed many of the better local choristers away from their own choirs to join his group, and the result was hard feelings among local choirmasters toward him and Thomas, which persisted for years.[37]

Back in March, Henry Krehbiel, who had begun his writing career in Cincinnati, had noted that "the influence of the Cincinnati Festival goes out like leaven through the whole lump of musical activity in the country. . . . [Cincinnati's] motive has always been something higher than the sensationalism which is the too frequent product of the tendency to combination which now pervades almost all social, commercial, artistic and political activities."[38] Krehbiel was speaking out against festivals that put bigness for its own sake ahead of art by merging several groups into one large group, by cramming several events into one, by seeking more people to perform in still bigger and less musically attractive halls, and by allowing volume to take precedence over quality of sound. But was all of this Thomas's doing? Krehbiel's piece was clearly the beginning of a backlash that would ultimately rein in the festival movement in the United States.

The Wagner tour moved on to Chicago, where, alas, the reception was not as warm as it had been two years earlier, despite acoustical improvements in the Exposition Building. Both Thomas and the public noted the crowded seating, which made latecomers and "early leavers" more irritating than usual. Toward the end of the opening-night concert, the last part of Haydn's *Creation* —only one of the six concerts was all Wagner—was drowned out as much of the huge audience hurried toward the exits to secure places on the few streetcars and trains that would take them home. Thomas, thoroughly vexed, stopped the music abruptly. The *Chicago Tribune*, for one, thought Thomas's action was justified: "A well-bred audience sits still until the performance is through."[39] Not everyone reacted as sympathetically, however, and the incident cast a pall over the festival.

Another negative element was the local chorus. Most successful in 1882, it was used more sparingly in 1884 because it was not needed in many of the Wagner excerpts. The Chicago press took Thomas to task for minimizing the city's role in the proceedings; further, the public clearly wanted more choral music. The press also noted that ticket prices were higher than in Cincinnati, whose Music Hall was smaller and more desirable—that is, a *real* concert hall—which the Chicago Exposition Building decidedly was not.[40] One newspaper made capital of the high fees for the orchestra and soloists (which the brash Charles Locke had divulged), and there were insinuations that Thomas and Locke were making a financial killing on the festival at the expense of trusting Chicagoans. As in 1882, the weather was poor; unfortunately Thomas's other tour dates made it impossible to hold the festival in June rather than May.

In a fit of pique, the *Tribune* described the Exposition Building, with "its great sounding boards of bare pine, its hideous red-ochre sides, its dirty blue roof, its flaring gas jets and its bare girdings, [as] neither more nor less than an old ugly barn." But then it rhapsodized: "When 5,000 or 10,000 enthusiastic people get beneath its roof, when a thousand brilliant costumes hide its deformity, and a thousand attuned voices make its rafters ring, it becomes a temple in which the divinities of music and of beauty are worshipped with absorbing reverence. The stage was a perfect conservatory of wondrous hued flowers, sea green, emerald green, ultra-marine blue . . . every colour of the rainbow." A thoroughly sexist description of the female choristers followed: "To see this great body of beauteously-dressed femininity rise in a solid mass, as though moved by clockwork, displaying 600 animated faces, 600 heaving bosoms, 600 pairs of flashing eyes, and 600 elegant and variegated costumes is enough in itself to repay the most non-musical in the audience, that is if he has an opera glass."[41]

Almost 10,000 people attended the festival's first matinee and, as in Philadelphia, heard Nilsson and Materna sing *Lohengrin* excerpts. Of the two, Nilsson was the more popular. The *Tribune* declared: "Mme. Materna is without doubt a great singer, but in the hearts of the people Mme. Nilsson is greater in every respect except the one of physical strength." In blissful ignorance, the *Morning News* observed, "Nilsson's great impersonation of Elsa loses much when it has to give up its customary [sic] Italian."[42]

Thomas closed the festival in Chicago with Gounod's *Redemption*, determined to get his money's worth out of the work. The solo "From Thy Love as a Father" went badly for Nilsson, who ended the section singing almost a half tone flat. Nevertheless, the audience pressed for an encore, which Thomas refused, fearing that her second try might yield even worse results. Twice he tried to start the next number, only to have the crowd drown him out. Then, "signaling to the chorus to rise, he called out 'Trumpets!' and started in on the chorus 'Unfold ye portals everlasting' with such a crash as silenced every other sound in the house. After this episode everything went off beautifully." Even Nilsson sang better.[43]

Some days after the festival, the *News* warned Thomas that a "musical festival is not a circus." The *Saturday Evening Herald* called festivals jumbo entertainment and declared, "Such monster affairs are of [no] benefit to the cause of musical culture." It preferred a small, well-drilled chorus in an appropriate concert hall. Chicago audiences "have done their duty, nobly. Fashion is appeased. They have eaten the leek, not because they like it but for the simple reason that leeks are fashionable. If Musical Festivals were not fashionable the audiences would not be as large as they are."[44] It was a variation on Krehbiel's theme in the *Musical Courier* two months earlier and ushered out Thomas's last festival in Chicago.

Thomas wound up the Wagner tour with five concerts in Montreal, his first visit to Canada's largest city. The programs were given at the Victoria Skating Rink, which, like the Seventh Regiment Armory and the Exposition Building, had been attractively dressed up for the viewer but did little for the listener. There was no local chorus, and the opening all-Wagner concert exhausted an audience ill prepared for it. Nilsson was torn to shreds by conductor-composer Guillaume Couture in the French-language daily *La Patrie*, while Materna thrilled him. The informed Couture particularly liked the orchestra in the German works and urged Thomas to return another year to Montreal's Queen's Hall, where the orchestra could be heard properly.[45]

Generally disappointed with the tour's results, Thomas lost his zeal for traveling festivals and shifted his attention to opera. After finishing his summer season in Chicago, he left for Europe to see his family and visit opera houses. He was away for over four months, too long in view of the events that occurred in his absence and that seriously affected his future.

The Metropolitan Opera House's first season, in 1883–84, was given over to Henry Abbey's Italian Opera Company, with disastrous financial results. Undeterred, the board of directors of the Met asked Ernest Gye, managing director of the Royal Italian Opera Company at Covent Garden, London, to run its second season.[46] The Met, which had lost over $300,000 because of Abbey, wanted Gye not only because of his considerable reputation but also because his company was wealthy—reputedly, it had £125,000 in funds and costumes worth another £80,000. Gye was interested; however, after protracted negotiations that filled many a column in New York's daily newspapers between February and early August 1884, he ultimately refused the offer because the singers he wanted would not agree to stay in New York for an extended period. In the meantime, the city was rife with rumors that a new company might be formed to serve both the old Academy of Music and the Met. The plan made sense, but since the boards of the two theaters would have to agree on policy and other details, it seemed unlikely that it would be implemented.

In July 1884, James Roosevelt, the Met's president, asked James Mapleson, general manager of the Italian Opera Company at the New York Academy of Music, to manage a new Italian company. Mapleson had had a particularly difficult time with the academy board that spring over a loan it had granted him. His contract with them was too tightly drawn, however, and Roosevelt discreetly withdrew. Then Hilborn Roosevelt, James's nephew and the president of the New York Symphony Society, proposed that the Met abandon Italian opera and have a season in German under Leopold Damrosch, his close friend.[47] The city's German-speaking population, estimated at 250,000, was clamoring for opera in German, and Thomas had proved that there was a large public for Wagner, whose operas would obviously be a major attraction in a German season. Damrosch advised Hilborn Roosevelt to tell the Met board that ticket prices would be lower than in the past, with resultant increases in sales, because German singers charged less than their Italian counterparts. There was also a pervasive feeling in New York that Italian opera had seen better days and that it was time for a change.

The Met's directors, as much out of desperation as confidence, accepted the Roosevelt-Damrosch proposal, taking financial responsibility for the season and appointing Damrosch musical director. He was to select the operas to be done, engage the singers, conduct the performances, and abide by the board's fiscal controls—an awesome task for anyone.[48] Damrosch's chances for success were probably better than most, as he had an impressive operatic background and was easy to work with. (Thomas lacked experience in opera per se and, as all knew, had a bad reputation with singers because of his stubbornness and intractability.) Damrosch had been in the right place at the right time, and he certainly knew the right people.

Thomas was clearly disappointed. He had expected to be asked to do German opera at the Met and had even discussed terms with Henry Abbey early in 1884. But Abbey was already in financial difficulties, and nothing was resolved.[49] Twenty years later, Thomas wrote in his autobiography about refusing an offer to conduct at the Met because he first wanted to visit opera houses in Germany and Austria and study their work. The offer, however, had come from Abbey, not from the Met's directors, who may not have known about it. When the directorship was offered to Damrosch, Thomas was in Chicago, then Europe.

The Met's new venture was a success from the start, with good advance sales and a supportive press. On November 18, the season opened in fine style with *Tannhäuser*. Audiences, however, were warned by the *Daily Tribune* not to approach Wagner's operas frivolously, for they were not Italian operas: "Old standards of criticism will have to be abandoned, tastes . . . will have to be reformed, the prevailing opinion concerning the mission of the operatic artist will have to give way to one much nobler, and even the esthetic canons which have heretofore been applied to the estimation of performances will have to undergo a modification."[50] This was the same quasi-religious approach that was thought to be appropriate for Beethoven's symphonies or Handel's oratorios.

Thus, the Metropolitan Opera House became Wagner's shrine in the New World, and his operas were probably done as well there in the next seven years as in Europe's leading houses. To Thomas's annoyance, Amalie Materna made her stage debut in *Tannhäuser* in January 1885. (He felt that, ethically, he had an "exclusive" on her North American appearances, having introduced her to the continent in 1882.) Two nights later, she sang Valentine in *Les Huguenots*, in German. The Met, flushed with the success of a season not even dreamed of eight months earlier, resumed talks with Academy of Music representatives to buy out its Italian company and gain a monopoly on grand opera in New York City.[51] Mapleson's season had been short and undistinguished, while houses were full uptown. Clearly, the Germanization of New York's operatic life was well under way—without Theodore Thomas.

Everything came to a halt when Leopold Damrosch died unexpectedly of pneumonia on February 15, 1885, after a brief illness. His exhausting work schedule undoubtedly had contributed to his sudden demise at age fifty-three. Every seat was taken at the memorial service at the Met, where Henry Ward Beecher pointed out, in his eulogy, that the large turnout was "more usual for war heroes and statesmen" than for an artist. Then, he took the opportunity to emphasize what the musical world already knew: "America can not be too grateful to her immigrant population. She owes much to Italy, much to France, but more to Germany than all the others. I thank God for the inspiration that we have gained from German leaders of music."[52]

Thomas did not attend the memorial service, and his absence was noted and condemned. The Philharmonic Society claimed that he had not been invited. The Symphony Society, in charge of details, disagreed. *Freund's* said that Damrosch "was the object of the remorseless hatred and persistent persecution of the clique which has Theodore Thomas for its ostensible head and Steinway Hall for its headquarters." One month later, the journal quoted Bernard Ullman, the opera manager for whom Thomas worked in the late 1850s, who called Thomas "an impertinent and arrogant fellow—no artist, but smart—ungrateful and no gentleman."[53]

Damrosch's death should have allowed Thomas to break through at the Met, but it was not to be. Walter Damrosch, just turned twenty-three, temporarily assumed his late father's position until Anton Seidl, a well-known European conductor with much experience in conducting Wagner's operas in Germany and Italy, was engaged as the Met's new musical director. Thomas had been passed over for a second time in less than a year.

The 1884–85 New York season went well for Thomas, despite the competition from the Met. Both the Philharmonic and the Thomas Orchestra had enough work to keep them busy, making an extensive winter tour unnecessary. The Philharmonic's box-office receipts for its series of six pairs of concerts amounted to almost $18,000, or $2,000 more than the previous year and $16,500 more than when Thomas had taken over eight years earlier.[54] Thomas's twenty shares came to approximately $4,000, but he took only the guaranteed fee of $2,500, a policy he maintained for his remaining years with the Philharmonic. In all likelihood, he could have given weekly, not monthly, concerts in 1884–85 and still filled the hall. Subscriptions were sold out in two days, and it was virtually impossible to get seats for single concerts.

The Philharmonic's improved attendance was all the more impressive because of the formidable competition from Damrosch's symphony and oratorio societies and from a newcomer to New York, the young American conductor Frank Van der Stucken, who had, in the spring of 1884, succeeded Leopold Damrosch as conductor of the Arion Society. Born in Texas in 1858, Van der Stucken was educated in Belgium and Germany, had studied composition with Reinecke and Grieg at Leipzig, and had been kapellmeister at Breslau in 1881–82. During his first year in New York, he led a series of four novelty concerts at which he did only new music, with one concert devoted entirely to new American music. His excellent orchestra of sixty consisted mainly of

Thomas players,[55] and although the programs attracted small houses, they made New York audiences more conscious of and hospitable to contemporary music, American and otherwise.

When it came to new music, Thomas's taste followed no particular pattern. He was, in the best sense of the term, an eclectic who conducted all styles, who admired the works of established composers like Brahms but fearlessly did works by young and unknown composers like Richard Strauss. Thomas premiered Strauss's Symphony in F Minor—now almost forgotten —with the Philharmonic in December 1884; it was received well. Another major contemporary work, Alexander MacKenzie's *Rose of Sharon* oratorio, performed a few months later at one of Thomas's own concerts, was condemned by New York's music critics, who attacked Thomas for doing such a dull piece by an admittedly competent but singularly unimaginative British composer. It was suggested that if Thomas insisted on doing dull oratorios in English, he at least do works by Americans.[56] The criticism, however veiled, was not unjustified, for Thomas was paying insufficient attention to American music during this period. At Philharmonic concerts that same season, he had, for example, done compositions by minor European composers like Frederic Cowen, Jean-Louis Nicodé, Hugo Reinhold, and Josef Rheinberger, as well as Dvořák's dramatic overture *Husitská*', but no works by Americans. Worse, he would not include a single American piece at the Philharmonic from 1883 to 1886.

The *Rose of Sharon*'s failure in New York aroused the ire of Joseph Bennett, music critic of the *London Daily Telegraph*, who had written the text of the oratorio. He claimed in an article in London's *Musical Times* that New York's German-American critics—many of them had German names, but nearly all were born or reared in the United States—dominated the musical press and suffered from "Anglophobia." Bennett yearned for more critics "of Anglo-Saxon blood and sympathies [to counteract] the influence of Germans and men of German origin. Music with them means the works of Wagner, Liszt and their imitators who, without the genius of one and the cleverness of the other, act as though the art appealed only to nerve centres, like the sharpening of a saw."[57]

Bennett was showing rancor, not good judgment, for Wagner and Liszt were just as popular in London. He was more observant of other aspects of American musical life, thanks to a visit he made to the New World in 1884–85, during which he wrote an excellent account about Thomas, his orchestra, and his rehearsal techniques for the *Musical Times*. Bennett stated that Thomas was "head and shoulders above all his fellows," as conductor, educator, and tastemaker; indeed, only Charles Hallé, the Manchester conductor, was comparable, and then "on a much smaller scale":

Thomas exercises absolute control, making [his players] the creatures of his will in all that concerns their artistic labours. His *baton* rules an orchestra of which the best conductor in the world might be proud. The orchestra is not faultless. . . . The violins' sound is poor by comparison with the fine, sonorous strings of our best orchestras. Defects, such as these, however, are dwarfed when placed in the field of view with an admirable ensemble. Mr. Thomas' orchestra plays with one mind and one soul. This invaluable quality of oneness is, as every amateur knows, the proof of a perfect orchestra, and to secure it every good conductor tries his best as far as opportunities allow.

He described a Thomas rehearsal of Beethoven's Seventh Symphony, a work that was "perfectly familiar to the executants, who could have played no small part of it with closed eyes. [Thomas] rehearsed the well-known movements as carefully as though none of them had ever been heard before; devoting attention to the faintest shade of nuance and the execution of the most trifling *appoggiatura*, not less than to those broader features which an audience would be likely to note."

Praise was bestowed on the orchestra for its discipline, Bennett noting that "every man gave patient attention to his work, permitting no distraction, and showing no restiveness as passages were tried again and again." He attributed this discipline to the players' predominantly German origin:

When a nation is carefully policed by a paternal government for generations, its habits of obedience ripen almost into an instinct. The Englishman, on the other hand, not having a paternal government and not being forced to attend a national disciplinary school [Germany's compulsory three-year military service], is apt to assert his personal liberty at inconvenient moments, and to show a want of respect for the office of his superiors. Readers of musical literature are familiar with stories about unruliness of English orchestras— how they saddened Spohr, and brought tears of vexation into Mendelssohn's eyes.

Thomas's technique reminded Bennett of Sir Michael Costa, one of England's first disciplinarian-conductors whom Thomas had observed in 1880: "There was the same quiet firmness, and the same impression of devotion to the work in hand. Hence the rehearsal—a long one—proceeded in the most orderly fashion to its close. But when the word of dismissal had been uttered, Mr. Thomas's well disciplined men resembled a lot of boys let loose from school. The noise of their tongues, and the quickness of their dispersal showed how great had been the demand upon time and patience." The concert that followed, Bennett wrote, "ranked as high as anything we have in Europe." But he wondered whether the works of Wagner and Liszt "represent the eminent conductor's personal taste. . . . He has probably drilled himself into the position of an eclectic, and is equally happy whether on the side of Paul, pleading with the Gentiles, or on the side of Peter, arguing with the Jews. One fact is pretty clear—Mr. Thomas would not devote so much attention to modern works if his public had not a special ear for them. The supply is so profuse that I am bound to believe in demand."

Both Thomas and his orchestras received similar praise from a number of other musicians during the 1880s. James Mapleson, after retiring to his native England, observed that London needed an orchestra like Thomas's: "Orchestras in London are nearly always 'scratch' affairs where players are allowed to miss rehearsals if more lucrative engagements come up." This would not be so in the Thomas Orchestra, which Mapleson, a trained singer and violist as well as an opera manager, believed surpassed even the Hallé and the Lamoureux and Colonne orchestras of Paris, because of its "fineness and fullness of tone [and] force and delicacy of expression." He declared that Thomas's orchestra was so successful because "its members work together habitually and constantly; they take rehearsals as part of their regular work; and they look to their occupation as players in the Theodore Thomas orchestra as their sole source of income. As for substitutes, Mr. Thomas would no more accept one than a military commander would accept substitutes among his officers." Mapleson hoped that Thomas and his men would soon make a trip to England, to "show our public what a good orchestra is, and our musical societies how a good orchestra ought to be formed and maintained." [58]

Lilli Lehmann was another Thomas admirer. A German soprano at the Metropolitan Opera House, she created nearly all of the leading Wagnerian roles there and also sang *Norma*, Donna Anna in *Don Giovanni*, *Aida*, Leonora in *Fidelio*, and Valentine in *Les Huguenots*, all in German. Lehmann recalled the first time she heard the Philharmonic under Thomas:

> I noticed something in the tone of the orchestra that had never struck me elsewhere. What might it be? I gave myself up to the enchantment of it over and over again, until, after much speculating, I was able to explain the wonder to myself. The violins used their bows in unison so that eye and ear were soothed; the woodwinds, who suited their tone and sound colour exactly on their entrances to the instruments that had preceded them, were not shrill or inharmonious as we are accustomed to hear them, but mingled with soft unobtrusiveness and melodiously in the volume of tone, without once perceiving where they or the other instruments came in and dropped out. That was the solution of the riddle, and was the spell that had charmed me. Why do nearly all instrumentalists suffer such an effect to escape them, and why are not the conductors alive to it? [59]

Lehmann admired how Thomas blended orchestral sound and made each player conscious of his role in the process. She wrote in her autobiography: "Once when Thomas resumed a rehearsal after a pause, he rapped again to stop his men, and, turning to the orchestra, said, 'But, children, tune your instruments; it is quite unbearable!' I must admit that I had not perceived anything especially impure, in spite of my keen ear." The great singer then hit upon the very essence of Thomas, "a man, take him all in all, to whom I would like to erect a monument, for he was a sound kernel in a rough shell, and music, that is his ideal art, was as exalted to him as mine is to me. I cannot say that he was a graceful conductor, but his orchestra understood him, and he made no concessions to the American public when he wished to instruct it, by sparing it anything he proposed to carry through."

Thomas was, most assuredly, one of the first conductors to exact the best from his players through disciplined and demanding rehearsal procedures, similar to those used in more recent times by Toscanini, Reiner, and Szell. He may have lacked the magic touch of Nikisch and Furtwängler, but he strove constantly to interpret a composer's wishes. The results were at once sound, predictable, and, in the best sense of the term, controlled.

The outside world believed that Thomas had a "permanent" orchestra, but he knew otherwise. His view of a permanent orchestra was a year-round group that did nothing else but play good music under his direction or under deputies assigned by him. Thus, his hopes soared when William R. Grace, the mayor of New York, and "3,000 others" sent him a letter on New Year's Day 1885 that proposed an 1885–86 series of weekly concerts and matinees by the Thomas Orchestra, for which they promised to find the necessary funds. Would he discuss this with them as soon as possible? Of course he would, wrote Thomas, who was already planning his biggest local season in many years. Nothing came of the proposal, however, just as nothing had come of similar ones in the past; the letter was simply the mayor's way of sending his best wishes, encouraged as he was by "rich and musically inclined society ladies."[60] Thomas never again thought seriously of a permanent orchestra quartered in New York.

A dispute with the Philharmonic in the spring of 1885 made Thomas aware of how much was still wanting in his conducting career and how far he was from creating, according to his own standards, a great orchestra. Rumor had it that he would resign at the end of the season and form a new orchestra in Europe.[61] After eight years with the Philharmonic, he was still unable to come to terms with those musicians who were simply not up to the task; and now, the orchestra's younger and better players were also unhappy and discontented. Although Thomas was the conductor, he was not, in the contemporary sense, the Philharmonic's musical director, and he needed the support of the board to dismiss players.

This was the setting for an unhappy confrontation in the spring of 1885 with the Philharmonic's principal oboist, Joseph Eller. Thomas, who was displeased with Eller's playing, had already dismissed him from the Thomas Orchestra, permitting him to assume the same post in Damrosch's orchestra. Then he tried to remove him from the Philharmonic. Eller missed two spring concerts but was back at his place in the fall. The conductor had been over-ruled by the society, a reminder that his association with the Philharmonic would always be subject to certain limitations.

Convinced that there was no other oboist in New York up to the post, Thomas decided to import a Belgian, Felix Bour, to replace Eller in the Thomas Orchestra. But this violated the regulations of the Musicians Mutual Protective Union (MMPU) of New York, which decreed that six months' residence in that city was required to gain membership in the union and that members were forbidden to play with nonmembers.[62] Thomas found himself in his first—but not his last—dispute with a musicians' union. Ironically, he had but a short time earlier encouraged the MMPU to set the six-month residence regulation to prevent a German orchestra from playing at Long Beach, a New York City summer resort, at fees substantially less than a local orchestra would ask. The implications were obvious: foreign musicians must not be allowed to flood New York and take work away from local musicians.

The "illegally" imported Bour toured with the Thomas Orchestra in the fall, as the New York union regulations did not apply outside the city. Thomas knew, however, that when he returned he would have to "face the union." Consequently, he asked the MMPU to call a special meeting to waive the residence requirement for Bour. It made sense in that oboists were in short supply in the United States and importing them could be a start in developing American oboists for the future. The union, however, had no intention of relaxing its new regulation and used a technicality to say so: three months' notice was needed for a special meeting.[63]

The Bour incident was one of the first disputes in which a conductor's artistic imperatives clashed with a union's protective policies. The MMPU believed such curbs were necessary; similar ones were enforced in other crafts. But did they have a place in the arts? Should a country's gates ever be closed to gifted practitioners? The U.S. Congress had, on February 26, 1885, passed an act that prohibited importing by prearranged agreement or contract "any alien or aliens, any foreigner or foreigners into the United States . . . to perform labor or service of any kind. . . . The provisions of this act [shall not] apply to professional actors, artists, lecturers or singers."[64] But what of orchestral musicians? They had slipped between the cracks, halfway between artists and craftsmen (where some say they still are).

A situation similar to Bour's had already been resolved in Boston, where the musicians' union had no influence. Wilhelm Gericke, the new conductor of the Boston Symphony, had imported a Rumanian-born German concertmaster, Franz Kneisel, to replace the retiring Bernhard Listemann, who had also been Thomas's concertmaster in the 1870s. The appointment led to hard feelings in the orchestra, and the press took up the players' cause. However, since Boston Symphony members were forbidden by sponsor Henry Lee Higginson to belong to the union or even to speak on the matter, the appointment stood.

In early November 1885, immediately prior to an Academy of Music concert, the MMPU served Thomas notice that a fine of $10 would be levied on him and on any member of his orchestra who played with a nonunion musician.[65] Thomas, caught up in the principle of the dispute as much as in the artistic reasons behind it, had no intention of performing without Bour and personally offered to pay his orchestra's fines, in toto some $750. But the union threatened additional punishment: if the orchestra played with Bour a second night, the fine would be raised to $20 per member; and a third violation would mean expulsion from the union.

Thomas retaliated by obtaining an injunction restraining the MMPU from enforcing its penalties until their legality was established. Each side accused the other of improper action, and on December 2, Judge Andrews of the New York State Supreme Court heard the arguments.[66] Thomas claimed that the restrictive bylaws were "unreasonable, vexatious, oppressive, manifestly detrimental to the interest of the Thomas Orchestra and its members, and against public policy, being in restraint of trade." If such a "disciplinary starvation" continued, he threatened to give up his orchestra. Unmoved by Thomas's threat, the MMPU maintained that members who chose not to abide by its regulations could leave the union; thus there was no restraint. It argued speciously that six months were needed to determine whether immigrant musicians were of sufficiently good character to be admitted to the union, since usually nothing was known of their personal background. The MMPU declared that there was a union oboist who was as good as Bour, adding bitterly, "Mr. Thomas was not so much concerned for the advancement of music as for the success of himself individually."

Judge Andrews upheld the injunction in January 1886,[67] and in June 1888, the New York State Supreme Court ruled that the MMPU did not have the right to expel Thomas or members of his orchestra because they played with Bour and that the six-month waiting period was illegal and unconstitutional. The union restriction "strikes at talent, distinction, usefulness and the enjoyment of a meritorious performance. . . . It is not only against public policy but antagonistic to the right of every man to earn by his labor, lawful in itself, whatever it may be worth, whether the laborer or artist be native or foreign born."[68] The one dissenting opinion pointed out that since Thomas had continued to be a member of the MMPU, he must abide by its regulations and not engage Bour. In April 1890, the pendulum swung the other way when the New York State Court of Appeals reversed the supreme court's decision and ruled in favor of the MMPU. And there the matter rested.

In the spring of 1885, after completing his winter season, Thomas did a second cross-country tour, which enabled him to consolidate the gains he had made in building western audiences and to keep his orchestra together until its summer engagement in Chicago. Now fifty years old, he had not lost his pioneering spirit, his wish to elevate America's musical taste, or his desire to see audiences clamoring for Beethoven and other great masters as for its daily bread.

Charles Locke was again the tour manager. The route and scheduling were similar to two years earlier but without festivals. Principal soloists were Amalie Materna (she and Thomas had patched up their differences), Emmy Fursch-Madi, a French soprano who had settled in the United States, and Emma Juch. Thomas conducted in Boston for the second time since the founding of the Boston Symphony in 1880. The highlight was a matinee for young people, including Moszkowski's *The Nations*, a suite in six sections, each portraying a different European country.[69] The program elicited a warm response from Boston's public and reminded it how much it missed Thomas.

All in all, the tour was relatively uneventful. The three concerts in Cincinnati were particularly well received, but San Francisco's seven concerts lost $9,000, which Locke attributed to the high cost of travel to the Pacific city and the soloists' fees. His financial difficulties had no effect on Thomas, however, who, with his orchestra, worked for a guaranteed fee.[70] The last stop was Chicago, where Thomas had his best summer to date. Then he joined his family, which had returned from Europe, for several weeks of rest at Fairhaven, a large, comfortable house on the seashore near Boston which he had recently purchased. There he would spend much time with his wife and children, enjoying a respite from his active professional life.

By September 1885, Thomas was back to the nomadic musician's life, giving concerts in town after town, directing a four-day festival in St. Louis, keeping his orchestra working. He was also preparing for his biggest season yet in New York. The leader of the orchestral world was priming himself to assume a similar role in opera.

Theodore Thomas in his middle years. (Author's collection)

Cincinnati's Music Hall flanked by the exposition buildings, 1880. (Courtesy of the Cincinnati Historical Society)

A troubador, Victorian style, highlights a poster announcing the 1880 May Festival. (Courtesy of the Cincinnati Historical Society)

George Ward Nichols, adversary of Theodore Thomas. (Courtesy of the Cincinnati Historical Society)

Daniel Burnham, architect, town planner, and close friend of Theodore Thomas. (Courtesy of the Newberry Library)

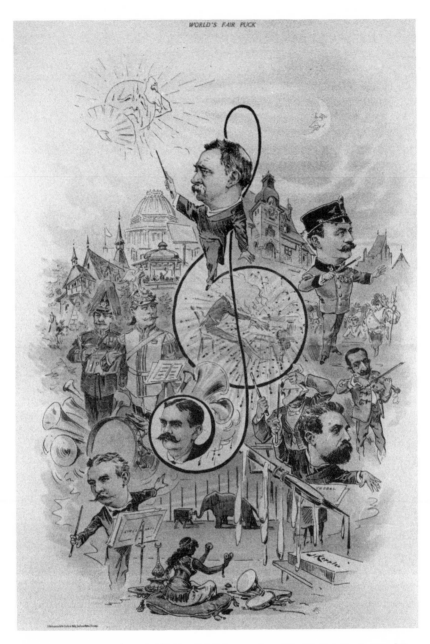

"Harmony Reigns at the World's Fair." A July 10, 1893, *World's Fair Puck* cartoon by Joseph Keppler. (Courtesy of Richard S. West)

The interior of the Manufacturers' Building at the World's Columbian Exposition on Dedication Day, October 22, 1892. (Courtesy of the Chicago Historical Society, ICHi-02204; photograph by C. D. Arnold)

8

From Boastful Dream to Catastrophe

By 1885, two years after completion of the Metropolitan Opera House, the German Opera Company had successfully consolidated its position there. Leopold Damrosch's death had not been the catastrophe feared at first. The Met's board had resisted the entreaties of Damrosch's talented and engaging son Walter, who wanted his father's job for himself, and had instead resolved to use its considerable monetary resources to engage the finest European conductor available, Anton Seidl. There was little doubt that the Met was putting New York opera on a much sounder footing than ever before. Unfortunately for Theodore Thomas, its plans did not include him.

With the Wagner tour and its mixed results behind him, and reconciled to not being asked to work at the Met, Thomas looked hard for his own operatic outlet. He found one in a company committed to staging operas in English. This was, in itself, not a new idea. Fifty years earlier, nearly all operas performed in the United States, such as they were, had been sung in English; by the end of the 1860s, however, operas in New York were sung almost completely in Italian and German. Enter Jeannette Thurber, wife of the antimonopolist Francis B. Thurber, whom Thomas had first met when planning the young people's concerts in 1883 (she donated money to the concerts, as she did for the Wagner tour the next year).

Thurber, a wealthy patron of the arts, published in March 1885 a "manifesto" announcing the formation of the American Opera Company (AOC), which would produce operas in English only, would encourage American composers and librettists to write for it, and—most important for the future—would form an opera school where promising singers from all parts of the United States could study without fee.[1] (Later, branches of the company and school would be established in other parts of the country.) The company's singers would be Americans only, and Theodore Thomas, who was "heartily in sympathy" with the scheme, would be its musical director and would, it was erroneously stated, work without remuneration. According to the manifesto, the United States was ripe for operatic development and could count on the support of some of the country's richest and most powerful people. Among those Thurber had enticed to be on the AOC board were George Pullman, August Belmont, Parke Godwin, Henry Seligman, N. K. Fairbank, and Chauncey Depew, with Andrew Carnegie serving as president. It was all very exciting, if not downright incredible.

The opera company's prospectus was issued in September 1885, a puffed-up piece in doubtful taste, even for the Gilded Age. The company's leading singers would be front-rank Americans, many of whom were putting aside European careers to join the group. They would be supported by "the largest chorus ever employed in grand opera in America and composed entirely of fresh young voices," as well as the "largest ballet corps." Three hundred costumes would be used for *Lohengrin*, many brought especially from Europe, and there would be 4,000 new costumes in all, as well as "the best scenery painted by the most eminent scenic artists of America."[2] Such Barnum-like ballyhoo was frowned upon by the music critics of the city's leading papers, as it was by Thomas, who had always resisted such publicity about his own activities.

In November 1885, the German Opera Company had begun its second season at the Met with the newly installed Anton Seidl on the podium. Born in 1850, Seidl had studied in Leipzig and been Hans Richter's chorusmaster at the Vienna Opera before going to Bayreuth, where he had worked with Wagner. He was infinitely more competent than Leopold Damrosch, and his Wagner connection, for Wagnerians, was tantamount to his having communed with God himself. Seidl's conducting received extravagant praise, and it was clear that he was a threat to Thomas's supremacy. Thomas was jealous of both Seidl's ability and his pleasant and suave demeanor, which won him friends everywhere.

The American School of Opera, housed at the Academy of Music, held its formal opening ceremonies on December 17, 1885, at which Thomas spoke briefly and prophetically about the need to import good teachers rather than to export young talent.[3] By the new year, there were enough press clippings about the company and the school to fill several scrapbooks. A fifteen-week season with forty evening performances and sixteen matinees had been planned, and when the box office opened on December 28, just a week before the much-heralded season was to begin, the demand was such that sales were limited to ten tickets per person, with first-day receipts totaling $3,000.[4] Thomas had chosen *The Taming of the Shrew* by the Prussian composer Hermann Goetz for the company's grand opening on January 4. Goetz, who died in 1875 at the age of thirty-five, had been a prolific composer. This opera, one of his last works, had been premiered in Mannheim and then staged successfully throughout Germany. The Carl Rosa Company in England subsequently adapted the work in an English translation and performed it at the Drury Lane and His Majesty's theaters in London.

As luck would have it, the German Opera Company gave the American premiere of Wagner's *Die Meistersinger* at the Met on the same night. Obviously unable to attend both openings, some critics went to the AOC dress rehearsal; others attended the Philadelphia preview of *Die Meistersinger*. The clash in first nights notwithstanding, both houses were full and the audiences resplendent. The English-language company was out to prove "that there is no lack of American singers who require but encouragement of opportunity to do honor to the musical reputation of their native land," and this it did, if only in part. Commendably, the conductor, the directors, and the designers got the same program billing as the principals. The orchestra was the "unrivaled" Thomas orchestra; the corps de ballet had eighty dancers.

The music in *The Taming of the Shrew* was ordinary and its libretto suffered in the translation from English to German and then back to English —it simply did not fit the music. The end result was grist for the mill of those skeptics who said that opera in English would not work, although most of the New York daily press worded its negative criticism in a delicate, tentative manner. The *Times* praised the company for its commitment to opera as an "organization" rather than a "star" attraction, and the *Tribune* suggested that "less severity of judgment must be exercised regarding the singing of the principals because they are Americans, must sing in the vernacular and are mostly inexperienced." Here was both a "nursery and an arena for American singers and a most attractive field for American composers."[5]

The music weeklies were either unenthusiastic or, like the *Keynote* (edited by the English-born organist Frederic Archer, who likely had a grudge against Thomas), positively vitriolic. According to the *Keynote*, the production was "vocally and histrionically an amateur entertainment" and inferior to average foreign groups; furthermore, Thomas let the orchestra dominate, buried his nose in the score, and committed some inexcusable gaffes. The *American Art Journal* could not understand the words and blamed the singers' European training—they had not been taught to sing in their native tongue—noting that "five or six hundred of the audience left after the third act." According to *Freund's*, the faculties of the daily press were "clouded with patriotism."[6] The opera was soon dropped from the company's repertoire and consigned to history.

Thomas was luckier with Gluck's *Orpheus and Euridice* (the Italian version translated into English) because of the work's intrinsic merit and because he was more at home with its straightforward recitatives, arias, choruses, and ballets. The production was typically static but had two fine American principals, Emma Juch as Euridice and an AOC "discovery," Helene Hastreiter, as Orpheus. Hastreiter, daughter of a Chicago tavern keeper, had been lured home from Italy. She was a contralto with imposing stage presence, said to have "phenomenal gifts" and the ability to sing "with feeling and taste[;] her enunciation is extremely distinct. . . . She possesses experience as well as tones, looks and temperament."[7] *Orpheus*, a succès d'estime rather than a crowd-pleaser, elicited many favorable comments from the New York dailies, which were reprinted in subsequent AOC programs.

During the first week in January, Thomas conducted four opera performances—on Monday, Wednesday, and Friday evenings and on Saturday afternoon—and led his orchestra twice on Tuesday at a popular matinee in Brooklyn and a popular request program that evening at the Academy of Music. On Thursday, he conducted an open Philharmonic rehearsal of Dvořák's Symphony no. 2 in D Minor (now no. 7) in its American premiere; the actual concert was on Saturday night. The grueling schedule also included rehearsals for all of these events, and there was some question of Thomas's and his players' ability to cope.

That same Saturday night, New York's music critics gave a dinner at the Hoffman House to honor Anton Seidl for conducting the premiere of the long-awaited *Die Meistersinger*. (They had honored Adelina Patti in a similar fashion two years earlier.) Thomas was invited to the dinner—some supporters said the critics chose Saturday night because they knew he was busy conducting—but pleaded fatigue. The editor of the *Musical Courier*, who had made the arrangements, said: "The critics have agreed to confer the honor of their invitation only upon such artists as are absolutely above criticism. . . . Such an artist is Adelina Patti and such an artist is Herr Anton Seidl" (Seidl was Hungarian, but New York's Germanophile critics called him "Herr" anyway).[8] Seidl's first New York season had, in fact, moved from strength to strength. By April, Philharmonic members who also played under Seidl at the Met pressed him to become the Philharmonic's conductor. When the society's annual elections were held and the votes were counted, he received an impressive twenty-one votes to Thomas's fifty-two.[9] Seidl was Thomas's first real competitor, and many now thought he was better.

Henry Krehbiel of the *Daily Tribune* was an avid supporter of the Met conductor, preferring his free-wheeling interpretations. When Seidl included Beethoven's Seventh Symphony in his 1886–87 orchestra series, Krehbiel went to the trouble of timing the tempos used by both Seidl and Thomas (the Philharmonic did the piece a few months later) and comparing them to Beethoven's own controversial metronome markings. Thomas's tempos proved to be somewhat slower than Seidl's, yet both conductors' tempos would be typical a century later.[10]

	Beethoven	Seidl	Thomas
Poco sostenuto, quarter notes	69	60	60
Vivace, quarter notes (*sic*)	104	110	104
Allegretto, quarter notes	76	64	60
Presto, dotted half notes	132	128	100
Assai meno: presto, dotted half notes	84	60	60
Allegro con brio, half notes	72	92	82

The American Opera Company played in New York and Brooklyn from January to April. An extravagant *Lohengrin* opened on January 20, its cost a prodigious $30,000. There was an "abundance of gorgeous and historically accurate costumes," observed the *Evening Post's* Henry T. Finck. He was "electrified" by Thomas's "grandiose and soul-stirring climax" at the end of the first act, which was all the more astonishing because Thomas "had not received the Wagnerian traditions at first hand."[11] Yet the music journals again were negative, and it was implied that Schwab of the *Times* and Krehbiel of the *Tribune* were being excessively kind because they had done English translations for AOC productions.[12] The *Musical Courier*, however, unreservedly praised William Candidus—brother-in-law of William Steinway, one of the journal's biggest advertisers—as Lohengrin, even though he was a modest tenor at best.

The company's production of *The Magic Flute* had a mixed reception, with Pauline l'Allemand being castigated for failing to negotiate the fiendishly difficult solos of the Queen of the Night. Some critics objected to the spoken dialogue, unaware that the opera was being done in authentic singspiel style.[13] The critical consensus about Otto Nicolai's *The Merry Wives of Windsor* was that the staging was good, the singing bad. The American premiere of Delibes's *Lakmé* was received more favorably: l'Allemand did well in the title role, and the lavish sets, costumes, and skillful dancing were a visual treat. The unusual scenic effects of *The Flying Dutchman* especially intrigued audiences. A double bill of Victor Massé's *The Marriage of Jeannette* and Delibes's ballet *Sylvia* ended the season, with some observers claiming that men attended the ballet performances in disproportionately large numbers because of the scantily clad dancers.[14]

Judging by this first season, Thomas was not at his best in opera. He had not prepared his scores meticulously, had not rehearsed sufficiently, and had little empathy with the singers. The press upbraided him for giving undue attention to the orchestra and suggested that he was a better symphonic conductor, which was true. Some people objected to his ubiquitousness: he was at the American Opera Company, at the Philharmonic, in Brooklyn, at the popular concerts, at the people's concerts. He was constantly in the public eye, which may have made him more vulnerable to criticism. The *Musical Courier*, in reviewing Thomas's plans for the next year, wondered how he could honor all of his commitments. Indeed, the published schedules of the Brooklyn and New York Philharmonic orchestras, his tours, and the opera company revealed conflicts in dates. Something would have to give.[15]

By April, there were rumors that the AOC would not have a second season; that because of only fair houses and its visibly lavish ways, it would soon run out of money, as had many opera companies through the years. The New York Academy of Music warily demanded an unreasonably large deposit before it would give the company 1886–87 reservations. Angrily, the AOC turned to the Metropolitan Opera House and booked dates there, which comfortably dovetailed with the German Opera Company. The Met bookings effectively sealed the fate of the Academy of Music as an opera house.

Financial troubles or not, the AOC planned an ambitious tour for the spring of 1886, with stops in major cities along the "Thomas Highway," ranging from one day to two weeks. Both Thomas and Thurber were convinced that an audience for opera in English could be developed. Accordingly, they mounted full productions wherever theaters could accommodate them, and there was no skimping on costumes, scenery, orchestra, chorus, or ballet. An enormous enterprise, the traveling company numbered 300 in all, including 25 principal singers and 35 technicians.

Boston, the tour's first stop, was encouraging. Both the audiences and the press were receptive to opera in English and sympathetic to the American Opera Company's aims—and both were long-standing admirers of Thomas. The influential *Evening Transcript* favorably compared the AOC to the Carl Rosa Company and also praised the group's uncommon attention to staging details. The *Traveler* predicted that "the day of the diva is over. The $5,000 a night prima donna is merely a tradition of the past, and in no sense a necessity of the present."[16] On a chauvinistic note, the *Advertiser* said that Pauline l'Allemand, as Jeannette, "was as plump as a quail" and that most of the eligible bachelors in the audience must have wished that "a similarly enticing capable and well-endowed damsel in their own situation might wait upon them in the morning with a blank wedding certificate in her pocket."[17]

The city's enthusiasm generated a local AOC chapter and plans for an opera school branch, as Jeannette Thurber had hoped. The company's manager, Charles Locke, feeling that the Boston success had truly established the AOC, fantasized that the "first epoch in the history of music in America began with the organization of the Thomas Orchestra. The second was with the [opening] performance of the American Opera Company last January 4th."[18]

The week in Philadelphia was not as successful. Philadelphians had conservative operatic tastes and were unprepared for "new" operas like *Orpheus*,

Lakmé, and *The Merry Wives*. The company's advance publicity stressed its educational rather than entertainment value and thus discouraged attendance. One can surmise that the public saw opera as a vehicle for vocal display, not as an art of lofty purpose, and the opera house as a palace where one went to admire and be admired, not as a place for profound artistic experience. Also, the top seats cost three dollars, too much, it was felt, without Adelina Patti or someone like her in leading roles. Besides, should opera in English be as expensive as opera in Italian?[19] When it came to opera, Philadelphians valued the language of Dante more than that of Shakespeare.

From Philadelphia, the AOC moved on to Washington, D.C., and then Baltimore, where it was shunned. The *Baltimore Sun's* police reporter was also its music critic, and he hurt sales with his uninformed comments about the productions.[20] After Baltimore, the company boarded an enormous train— eleven baggage cars, two day coaches and seven sleeping cars—for the twenty-four-hour journey to St. Louis. The "Gateway to the West" was still reveling in the success of the 1885 Thomas festival. It had a resident symphony of sorts and was well disposed to good music. Advertised as a "festival of grand opera in English," the AOC's visit was St. Louis's answer to the Cincinnati May festivals. Philadelphia and Baltimore aside, the tour was going well, and Locke effusively told the press that if ticket sales continued as they had, the company would return to New York with a handsome profit.[21]

An unexpected problem arose, however, that illustrated how women's sexuality was misunderstood in the Gilded Age and was a foretaste of the feminist revolution to come. Florence Wyman Richardson, a prominent St. Louis socialite, had a distorted view of French ballet, its dancers, and, especially, the costumes they wore, as did many other puritanical Americans. She complained to Jeannette Thurber that the ballet costumes were "suggestive of the nude" and that *Sylvia* portrayed "lewdness in both costumes and gesture." To be sure, the dancers were not as yet assigned to perdition, for some had "pure and even fine faces, confirming my opinion that it is possible for literally moral women to appear under such circumstances. But there must be some distortion or blunting of the moral sense when sensual nature is brought ostentatiously to the fore." She felt it a pity that women's "intellectual nature" was thus ignored at a time when "the elevation of women is one of the most popular ideas in the civilized world."[22]

Richardson's appeal that women leave behind such sensual pursuits as ballet dancing reached the newspapers and was widely publicized. There was much sympathy for her views, particularly among the clergy and churchgoers, but eventually the matter was put to rest after a grateful local press had milked the subject for all it was worth during the opera company's visit. Thomas managed to stay out of the dispute, but it was commonly known that, in keeping with his approach to music and morality, he neither understood nor was a fan of French ballet. Following St. Louis, the company broke its tour to allow Thomas to go to Cincinnati for the 1886 May Festival.

The next troublesome AOC episode—the doings of opera companies offstage as well as onstage have always made good press copy—occurred in Chicago, where the local newspapers publicized a contractual dispute between the beautiful and spirited Helene Hastreiter and the AOC.[23] The trouble had started, so Hastreiter said, when she had snubbed one of Thurber's friends. Then she accused Thomas of favoritism, pointing out that he gave Emma Juch better billing than her. Hastreiter's grievances were finally put to rest, but not to her advantage: an angry AOC—and Thomas—paid little attention to her for the remainder of the tour and did not renew her contract. Thomas valued Victorian gentility in women, not independent spirit, and he lost a fine young American singer because of it.

The two-and-a-half-month tour concluded at the end of June. Thomas was weary, having conducted nearly every performance. After a week at home, it was on to Chicago for his summer series. He kept in close touch with the AOC, however, which announced happily in August that it had guarantees of $100,000 each to start company chapters in Chicago and Boston, $50,000 each in Philadelphia, Washington, D.C., St. Louis, and Cleveland, and $25,000 in Louisville. The New York–based opera school had sixty students, who had been chosen competitively from across the nation.[24] According to the AOC, they had all agreed that, in return for free instruction, they would, after graduation, "contribute one-quarter of their earnings over one thousand dollars per annum, for a period of five years to carry on the educational work of the conservatory."[25]

Although the news release bragged ad nauseam about the AOC's work and the fact that 90 percent of the singers were of American birth, it suggested that the company would move away from an "Americans only" policy: foreigners—qualified ones, of course—would be brought in as needed. Clearly, the AOC saw a need for more good solo singers and realized that it would have to open the gates to "non-Americans." To make its new policy acceptable to the public, the company included a gratuitous tribute: "Whatever measure of success we have attained is largely due to the genius, energy and patriotic feeling of a citizen of foreign birth—Theodore Thomas—a name now inseparably connected with the musical history of our country."

Regrettably, it was not a peaceful summer for either Thomas or the company management, thanks to *McVicker's Theater* v. *The American Opera Company*, a case that found its way onto the front pages of New York and Chicago papers on July 19, 1886.[26] The AOC had played at the Chicago theater on its spring tour, and while there Locke had booked it for November 1886 and May 1887. Later, Thurber, with Thomas's agreement, had booked the

Columbia Theater for the same dates, thus nullifying the McVicker booking —a flagrant breach of contract, if McVicker's allegations were true. Locke prudently remained silent; theater-owner McVicker threatened to (and eventually did) sue.

In addition to the impending McVicker imbroglio, an eager press boldly asserted that the Chicago AOC chapter about which Thurber had spoken so enthusiastically was pure fiction and that the company's New York office was greedily gobbling up funds raised by satellite chapters.[27] Charles Norman Fay, who had helped organize the Chicago group, rose to its defense and added that it would soon reach its $50,000 target. But the seeds of doubt had now taken root there and in other cities.

On August 8, the same day that Thurber announced the AOC's plans for the coming year, McVicker upbraided Thomas in the press: "You have achieved a certain fame under the banner of art, aided by beer, tobacco and lemonade, to which you furnish a pleasing accompaniment and should be content with being acknowledged master of a field you have cultivated to a high degree, and not seek to encroach on a domain where your selfish nature cannot have full swing and must prove a bar to success." He told Thomas not to succeed at the expense of the human voice, which is "God's gift and cannot be made secondary to catgut and brass."[28] It would not be the last time that Chicago's newspapers printed scurrilous material about Thomas.

The AOC's music director assailed and the company's reputation blemished, it next reeled from a lawsuit by Emma Berger, an American soprano who had been working in Europe in the spring of 1885 when William Hoch, the AOC's stage director, had contracted her—without proper authority, apparently—for the first season. When Berger returned to the United States, there was already a full complement of principals in the company and thus no place for her. She filed suit against the AOC, seeking $5,000 in damages, but the courts ruled that since Hoch was not the AOC's legal designate, the company was not liable and the hapless Berger would receive nothing.[29] The suit did serve, however, to put the AOC in a poor light.

In September, amid rumors that Thurber was withdrawing her financial support, it was announced that a change of name and incorporation was imminent: the American Opera Company was to become the National Opera Company (NOC) and would be the blanket organization for the chapters being formed across the country; the AOC would be the New York chapter of the NOC and the national headquarters that first year, after which the NOC headquarters would rotate annually among the other chapters. The plan looked good on paper, but the feisty *Musical Courier*, which was watching the AOC very carefully at this juncture, gave little credence to the pronouncements and asked for proof that there were other chapters and funds to support them. Speaking for New York's musical insiders, who were wondering whether the company would have a second year, much less expand, the journal cried out for "facts and no fictions!"[30]

America's musical educator was, of course, in the thick of things. Thomas should have left the company at the end of the spring tour, but he believed in the AOC's mission, needed badly to prove that he was a good operatic conductor, had to keep his orchestra working, and liked the substantial fees he earned as the AOC's music director. Enthusiastic responses from abroad also encouraged him to stay with the project. On July 1, 1886, Henry Krehbiel wrote from London that British composers were delighted with the AOC and hoped that it would soon be doing operas by them. Carl Rosa, who had done pioneering work with opera in English in Britain and had already mounted six operas by British composers, urged the AOC to ferret out competent American composers to write works for the company.[31] There was recognition from the other side of the English Channel, including reports that the AOC would soon play in Paris. Whether these were true or not, the writer was confident that the American company's scenery and dresses would "command praise" anywhere in Europe. "As for the vocalists, if the company is but strengthened in certain directions there need be no hesitation in pitting the principals against the regular forces of the Grand Opera."[32]

With Thomas at the helm, then, the AOC (it was not yet officially the NOC) published an impressive 1886–87 schedule at the beginning of October, confirming appearances in major American cities as far west as the Mississippi, thus allaying fears for the future of the controversial company. But how would Thomas honor his New York concert commitments if he traveled with the opera company? Neither he nor his orchestra had been in top form at the popular concerts the previous year, and it became clear that he would do fewer concerts and cancel others already scheduled because of preseason operatic rehearsals—which, unlike the previous year, he was now demanding —as well as tours. His relations with his long-standing friends, his orchestral public, might well be in jeopardy.

Thomas's schedule had already been the target of criticism in Cincinnati the previous spring, during the 1886 May Festival, which he had sandwiched so neatly into the AOC tour. The festival program had been rich in great music—Bach's Mass in B Minor, Haydn's *Creation*, Berlioz's *Damnation of Faust* and *Symphonie fantastique*, Beethoven's Symphonies no. 3 and 7, and Schumann's Symphony no. 2—yet the local critics carped away.[33] Thomas, they reported, had been testy, impatient, and quick to anger at chorus rehearsals, which contributed to a general lack of enthusiasm and resultant poor attendance at the festival—500 empty seats on opening night for *Creation* and 1,500 the second night for the mass. Had he chosen programs that were too difficult? Were there enough rehearsals? Was he too rushed because of the AOC's tour? Was he too uncompromising, especially with the chorus? It was noted that Thomas had selfishly made all kinds of compromises with his own time at the expense of the festival. He had been conducting five or six times weekly since the previous October, had started an opera company, and had had emotionally draining disputes with both the musicians' union and the New York Philharmonic. Was he wearing himself out? He was in his fifty-first year and had already done enough for a lifetime.

The Philharmonic was now also a sore point. It rankled Thomas that at the most recent election, twenty-one of the players had actually voted for Seidl after all the fine work that he (Thomas) had done for the group. He failed to see that he was not above criticism himself, that he had not given the Philharmonic the attention it deserved in the past year. He was, inevitably, blamed for any problems the society had, such as its move from the Academy of Music to the Met, with its less-satisfactory acoustics—it was, after all, an opera house—and a stage that was too far from the audience. He also had showed doubtful judgment in opening the Philharmonic's 1886–87 season with Anton Bruckner's Seventh Symphony, despite its poor reception the previous summer in Chicago at the Exposition Building. In the words of one New York critic, "It fell like lead upon the listeners, fully one third of whom left the hall after the second movement"; in those of another, "Herr Bruckner belongs to the very large class of German composers that know exactly how ideas should be expressed but to whom Providence has denied one spark of creative power."[34] When the Boston Symphony performed the same work a few months later, it got a similar response; clearly, the composer's lengthy conceptions simply did not appeal to American audiences of the late nineteenth century. Chastised, Thomas did conventional works for the rest of the season and more or less recovered some of the ground he had lost.

In the fall of 1886, a determined Thomas began rehearsals with a reconstituted American Opera Company. New singers had joined the group, along with two fine vocal coaches—Arthur Mees and Jacques Bouhy, director of the AOC's National Conservatory. Productions for the 1886–87 season included *Faust*, *Aida*, and Meyerbeer's *Les Huguenots*. Victor Massé's one-act opera *Galatea* was paired with Rubinstein's ballet *Bal costumé*, an orchestral version of his piano fantasy *The Ball*. Aware of casting problems, Thomas chose his repertoire more carefully (or so he believed) than the previous year. The perennially popular *Faust* opened the AOC's season at the Philadelphia Academy of Music on November 15, 1886. In contrast to the company's first visit there six months earlier, the city took the AOC to its heart and filled the hall for the entire week.

Henry Krehbiel was there from New York, hoping for great things, but he was disappointed. The music critic found William Ludwig an outstanding Mephistopheles and Emma Juch a potentially engaging Marguerite, but

Charles Bassett as Faust was "not even a voice in costume." Still, Krehbiel urged readers to support the AOC.[35] The *Philadelphia Times* reported in the same vein, giving a thoughtful summary of the week's presentations and lauding the AOC's production skills but dealing harshly with its leading singers.[36] Reviews notwithstanding, the company's Philadelphia gross was $30,000, double the year before. Encouraged by "the most successful opera season in the history of Philadelphia," the AOC promptly booked a second week there for January 1887.

Cincinnati greeted the AOC with much excitement, its press recalling nostalgically George Ward Nichols's opera festivals, now defunct for almost three years: "The old time opera spirit is once more manifest in our midst," noted the *Enquirer*.[37] Philanthropy was also in the picture: all AOC profits were to be turned over to the opera department of the Cincinnati College of Music, which would, in the future, cooperate with the AOC's National Conservatory (Thomas's grievances with the college apparently forgotten for the sake of opera). Advance sales were good, the Music Hall, which showed signs of wear, was refurbished at AOC expense, and formal steps were taken to launch a Cincinnati opera chapter. Everything looked rosy. By the end of the run, however, it was clear that there would be no profits because sales had not been up to expectations and the renovations had been too costly. The music college got nothing, no local chapter was established, and the AOC was soon forgotten in the Queen City.

St. Louis was next, still a Thomas bastion, albeit less secure since the company's first, controversial visit. Trouble was brewing there in the form of the Evangelical Alliance and the Women's Christian Temperance Union, ever-watchful guardians of morality, whose members led an organized attack against the AOC's corps de ballet for its "corrupting tendency." "Christian people" were counseled not to patronize the opera company, whose "spectacular representations of sensuality are manifestly immoral in their influence and destructive of spiritual light."[38] Mamet Bibeyan, the AOC's dance director, could not accept this mean-spirited attack on his life's work and fought back in kind, explaining that he was a good Roman Catholic, his cousin was a priest who supported his activities, his dancers worked hard, and his own work was honest labor.[39] The St. Louis papers once again played up the dispute during the visit. After much editorial discussion of ballet and its morality, the press concluded that ballet was welcome, and moral to boot.

During this same week, St. Louis was absorbed in a fracas between the soprano Emmy Fursch-Madi and Theodore Thomas. Fursch-Madi had joined the company, her French nationality notwithstanding, to sing Valentine in Meyerbeer's *Les Huguenots* and also Aida. She disliked William Hoch's production of the Meyerbeer opera, scheduled for the AOC's second night in St. Louis, and showed little inclination to take Hoch's direction—she had, after all, sung under the composer himself and had no intention of letting anyone forget this. Rehearsals went badly, and, as fate would have it, Fursch-Madi tripped over a table at the dress rehearsal and blamed Hoch's set for the accident. Hoch's rejoinder was unsympathetic, and the soprano indignantly walked off the stage.[40]

After due reflection, a contrite Fursch-Madi apologized to Thomas and offered to re-rehearse the opera on the day of the performance. Thomas refused, telling her: "You insulted the Company which I direct, and while I overlook the insult to myself, I cannot overlook an insult to the 250 persons who compose the Company."[41] He insisted that she apologize to Hoch and her colleagues, but she refused. Thomas thereupon suspended her until she would do as he asked. Meanwhile, the performance proceeded with an unprepared understudy and, as one might expect, went badly.

Urged on by Signor DeVivo, a "confidante" and "protector" who supposedly "represented" her husband during the tour,[42] Fursch-Madi wired Jeannette Thurber for help. Thurber promptly fanned the flames by informing the New York press that the singer "is a friend of mine," that only the board had the power to suspend her, and that Thomas and Hoch had overstepped their authority and acted unwisely.[43] Worse, she said that Thomas was head of the New York company only and lacked directorial power when the company was in St. Louis (possibly a misquote). The loquacious Charles Locke supported his patron and said publicly that Fursch-Madi's punishment was excessive.

An affronted Thomas was losing his patience. Why this assault on him by Thurber and Locke? To resolve the affair firsthand, he left St. Louis for concerts in New York one day earlier than planned. St. Louisans were unhappy on two counts: Thomas had conducted only three nights instead of four, and he apparently had deprived them of hearing Fursch-Madi. Opera lovers tend to forgive errant sopranos more readily than strong-willed conductors. Many felt that Thomas had overreacted, that he had been too hard-nosed in not accepting Fursch-Madi's apology, and that, in the end, he should have relented. When he arrived in New York, he was described as being in a "bearish" mood[44] and refused all interviews. He had told midwestern reporters earlier in the week: "If any institution like the AOC depends on the caprices of any one man or woman it is better to stop now than submit. I think I have a right to speak about proper organization and discipline for I only ask of others that which I rigidly observe myself. No one has ever known me one minute late for a rehearsal or for a performance or to take the least liberty that I have not allowed others under my direction."[45]

Thomas was right, of course, but he had not banked on the reactions of Thurber, who usurped his authority with impunity, or Locke, who knew little about managing an operatic organization or how to deal with an operatic public. Thomas had to learn that directing an opera company was not as straightforward as directing a symphony orchestra, that the operatic world was infinitely more volatile than the symphonic world, and, as the *St. Louis Post-Dispatch* declared, that "the American heart always goes out to a woman in distress."[46] Compromise was a must. So that both Thomas and Fursch-Madi could save face, DeVivo, who had insisted on being present at all rehearsals and had irritated the entire company, became the sacrificial lamb: he agreed to absent himself from all future rehearsals. Fursch-Madi thus resumed her place in the company and sang Aida before a cheering St. Louis audience at the end of the week.

The AOC, hoping for quieter times, moved on to Chicago. *Faust* was never done with "greater magnificence,"[47] and Fursch-Madi scored again in *Aida*. But the roof fell in with *Lakmé*, as once again morality was the issue. The company had modified its Indian costumes, and, according to an irate *Chicago Tribune*, the results were grotesque: "The management, moved by clerical denunciations or Philistine ignorance, has changed the whole picture. The coryphées have been thrust into striped trousers, stretched from the waist to the ankle, and the effect is laughable. Before, the ballet was a glimpse of the poet's world, now it is but the posturing of women, whose lack of clothes is heightened by a ridiculous device."[48]

Had whimsy led the AOC to invite a number of leading Chicago clergymen to a performance of *Lakmé* so that they could judge for themselves if the company's dancing was immoral? The *New York Times* printed a gleeful front-page description of the event: "The clergymen had come to sit in judgement upon the ballet and the audience upon the conduct of the clergymen. The clergymen behaved very nicely. They did not wear high bonnets to obstruct the view of those sitting behind them; they did not hum the music of the operas; they did not whisper and annoy other people, nor did they go out between the acts and come in accompanied by the odor of mixed wines."[49] St. Louis ministers denounced their Chicago brethren; they were "shocked at their worldliness" in accepting the invitation.[50] Yet there was a happy outcome to this nonsense: the Chicago men of the cloth saw nothing immoral or distasteful in the happenings onstage, which satisfied Chicago and St. Louis and amused New York. Undoubtedly, their reaction helped to sell more newspapers and more opera tickets.

Ticket sales were not up to expectations, however, and to save money, the AOC discharged some of its dancers, chorus singers, and orchestral players. This, too, backfired. The young, pretty, unhappy, mostly Italian dancers received only half a week's salary and rail fare as far as New York, where their tales of woe were lapped up by the press. (The Fourth Estate did not seem to be as interested in out-of-work choristers and musicians.) How would the dancers get home? And was Thomas at the bottom of it all?[51]

The *McVicker* case of the previous summer was finally heard in court. Having demanded $3,840 for the breach of contract with his theater, McVicker succeeded in attaching AOC scenery to assure payment, thus forcing a settlement. DeVivo, tired of cooling his heels in New York, vindictively told reporters that the company's weaknesses were due to the "superfinite personal vanity of Mr. Theodore Thomas and his enormous salary," which, he revealed, was $1,000 per week. (William Candidus, one of the leading tenors, received the same, and Emma Juch got $800. Apparently, conductors were not expected to earn as much as singers.) He also claimed that Juch was the real power behind the throne—hence her pretentions and privileges—and that she was behind the AOC's difficulty with Emmy Fursch-Madi, as she had been with Helene Hastreiter the year before. According to DeVivo, Thomas knew nothing about managing an opera company: "His weaknesses will always be a bar to the popularity of the National Opera scheme. . . . He doesn't want to please the public."[52]

Battered by such accusations, Thomas next read in the usually friendly *Chicago Tribune* that the AOC would soon break up because of bad management, exorbitant principals' fees, too many dancers, mediocre soloists, and extravagant sets and costumes.[53] There were other rumors that Thomas and Juch would soon resign from the company. Juch, a resourceful and independent twenty-four year old, denied this publicly and produced a letter signed by her colleagues refuting DeVivo's charges concerning her place in the company and her influence on other singers and the musical director himself.[54]

In spite of these troubles, the National Opera Company was registered, finally, on New Year's Day 1887, with Theodore Thomas as its president.[55] Under the terms of incorporation, the NOC could relieve the AOC of its financial obligations and rewrite contracts with singers and other employees for shorter periods than those set initially. As a result of these new contracts, a number of lawsuits were initiated by singers, directors, dancers, and stage managers against the AOC, the NOC, or both, and unpaid fees and other bad debts came into the open. Locke was clearly the villain, but Thomas was judged guilty by association. The press was merciless, and Thomas, too proud to fight back, questioned whether this obvious device to get rid of past sins and limit financial commitments for the future was worth it. The lawsuits dragged on for years.

The NOC's Boston visit in early January met with full houses and critical approval. The city had raised $37,000 for its NOC chapter but needed another $63,000 to reach the designated target of $100,000. Fifty wealthy Bostonians gathered to raise money and to launch a new campaign, but it came to naught.[56] Jeannette Thurber had tried to get Henry Lee Higginson, the patron of the Boston Symphony, to head the drive, but he had lost interest in the project because of the NOC's financial difficulties.[57] In March, she tried to curry favor with Boston by identifying it as "the most patriotic city in the U.S. There is less mixture of blood there. They are more American than New Yorkers."[58] Still no money was forthcoming.

Washington, D.C., was a triumph, so much so that Thomas and his troupe felt reassured that they were on the right track after all. The *Washington Post* compared the national company's eager young singers to Mapleson's chorus of "village maidens . . . eleven women not one of them under forty and most of them over sixty." It rejoiced in the "magnificent ensemble," which made up for the lack of great stars, and hoped that "the star system of opera is gone never to return."[59] For the rest of the winter, a reconstituted NOC played with considerable success for up to a week in each of eight large eastern cities, followed by a five-week engagement in New York. It seemed finally on its way to becoming a stable opera company.

In the spring of 1887, the New York music critics gave Anton Seidl another dinner, this time to honor him for bringing *Tristan und Isolde* to the Met. Of the thirteen works presented by the German Opera Company that season, it had drawn the largest houses; Max Alvary and Lilli Lehmann, especially, had been memorable in the title roles. Thomas's supporters mumbled that the critics were showing favoritism toward Seidl and had been taken in by the conductor's charm. A week after the dinner, it was announced that Seidl would be leaving New York to take up the post of director of the Berlin Opera.[60] Thomas breathed a sigh of relief. Once again, he had a clear field in New York.

Just prior to the NOC's New York opening in March, the *Herald* published a lengthy interview with the usually taciturn Thomas, conducted in the "cheerful library" of his home on East Seventeenth Street: "On the desk . . . over a miniature easel stood a photograph of Wagner . . . taking a pinch of snuff prior to beginning the first rehearsal of *Tristan and Isolde*. . . . The sun illumined an oil portrait of Beethoven, and about Mr. Thomas' library, with its rich store of musical works, were many other portraits of distinguished musicians." The reporter suggested that Thomas's life at present was not "a perpetual holiday, to which Thomas replied in a good humored, off-hand way that he was having a rather lighter week's work than usual . . . two trips to Boston, [where he] conducted two operas [and] held a five hour rehearsal of Rubinstein's *Nero*, led private and public rehearsals of the New York Philharmonic Society and had the Philharmonic concert in prospect for the evening."[61]

Thomas proceeded to expound on his ideas for the betterment of music in the city and to argue that it was being held back by the "present epidemic . . . for bringing the sensational and realistic from the stage to the concert hall"—he meant Wagner—and the lack of a good concert hall for orchestral and choral programs. Expanding on the first point, he declared: "Masters . . . show their power more in the sense of suggestion, in the beautiful and thrilling ideas that are expressed in musical form, than in the sense of vivid realism which is necessary for the operatic stage. . . . To preserve the dignity and chastity of the concert hall we must separate it absolutely from the stage."

When Thomas rashly stated that "the strongest Wagnerites are unmusical people," the reporter asked, "But are not you a Wagnerite?" Thomas replied: "Well, for 20 years I drove people out of the concert room by dosing them with Wagner, and I finally forced Wagner down their throats. . . . The . . . merits of Wagner . . . are not understood by . . . most Wagnerites. They dwell upon what they call his dramatic power and leave out the musical part. . . . Give me a proper concert hall . . . and I will banish opera and music drama excerpts from my performances."

Next, Thomas turned to the NOC. Yes, it was progressing, and its spirit and enthusiasm were admirable. Operas were being chosen with casting in mind, a fundamental rule in directing an opera company. Rubinstein's *Nero* was to be one of the grand premieres of the New York season, and, Thomas hinted, it could be *the* opera of the year, *Tristan* notwithstanding. That said, the physically fit conductor set out on his daily ten-mile walk.

It should be noted that Thomas's comments about concert music had been sparked by Seidl's triumphs and by the success of the Boston Symphony, which had given its first New York concert one week earlier, with Wilhelm Gericke conducting. Many thought Boston's a better orchestra than the New York Philharmonic, proof that only a permanent orchestra could achieve real excellence. The Boston Symphony had regular rehearsals, played only serious repertoire, and kept its touring within bounds; also, its players were on exclusive contracts and worked reasonable hours.

New Yorkers had now heard two other conductors, Seidl and Gericke, perform as well as Thomas had when at his best, and Thomas surely was not at his best in the spring of 1887.[62] His popular concerts were even less well prepared than in the previous year. He conducted listlessly, and the Thomas Orchestra showed the ill effects of overwork. The Philharmonic had few rehearsals, and its best musicians were often absent because they were touring with the NOC.[63] Thomas himself was going through much soul-searching as to where his career was headed.

To everyone's surprise, news came from Germany that Seidl's arrangements with the Berlin Opera had fallen through. Edmund Stanton, manager of the Met, rushed to Europe to re-engage Seidl for 1887–88.[64] Now Seidl could also stand for election as the Philharmonic's conductor. Fortunately, Thomas's relations with his players were good; their Philharmonic earnings were substantial, and Thomas had personally paid some of their NOC salaries when the company had cash-flow problems. He would blunder badly on several occasions in the coming spring, but he would not lose their support. Thus, there was no palace coup, as some had expected, when Seidl's candidacy was announced: Thomas got fifty-one of the seventy-three votes cast, Seidl, nearly all the rest.[65] Some said that Seidl was not really interested in the post, but it is more likely that the vote went to Thomas because his leadership stood for good programming, sound direction, good houses, good money, and generally high quality, in spite of his preoccupation with opera—which, many suspected, would not last much longer.

Rubinstein's *Nero*, scheduled to launch the NOC's five-week season at the Met on February 28, 1887, was postponed until March 14 because Thomas needed more rehearsal time. He was taking no chances—the work had to succeed. Joseph Pulitzer's *New York World*, whose circulation outdistanced all other New York dailies, had taken an interest in the NOC and, by publicizing *Nero* relentlessly for several weeks prior to its opening, drummed up more local interest than usual in a new opera. Rubinstein himself had no pretensions about the work's quality: it had received a mixed reception in Europe, and he authorized Thomas to make cuts at his discretion.[66] But Thomas foolishly did the work almost in its entirety—four hours of routine music without drama. Were it not for the lavish scenery and costumes, much of the audience would have departed well before the final curtain.

As a composer, Rubinstein was no Wagner, but this bothered neither the *World* nor Thomas. Confident that he had a winner, Thomas told the newspaper in an interview after the first performance: "I feel proud and consider it the greatest triumph of my life that I should have been the first to bring out in English the great work of Rubinstein and that its initial representation should have gone so well."[67] The *World* declared that *Nero* achieved "a scale of splendour never before given to opera in this country, extraordinary magnificence, culminating with the burning of Rome."[68] This "splendour" attracted large audiences, but it was a costly production and put the national company into an even more insolvent position.

At the last minute, the NOC's management decided on a spring tour even though its financial backing was fast disappearing. Fursch-Madi had had the box-office receipts from the final performance of *Nero* attached in order to collect back fees owed her. The *New York Graphic* wrote about the company's "woeful waste" of funds and claimed that Thomas "was spoon-fed on the molasses of unqualified adulation." Thurber and her friends "have been dragged deeply into this quagmire."[69] The *Times* claimed that Thomas greedily took his own salary (untrue) despite the NOC's weakened financial state and cared only for his orchestra (closer to the truth). Thomas should have refused to go on tour—he had not been paid since December—but when Locke came up with a $10,000 cash advance for the orchestra, he agreed.[70]

The NOC left New York on April 2, "in hopes and with prayers [that] they won't have to walk back."[71]

This tour was like the earlier ones: the ballet was adored, spectacles like *Nero* were admired, the orchestra and chorus were congratulated, and the solo singing was roundly criticized. On April 13, ten days into the tour, the Union Pacific Railroad, concerned with the NOC's financial state, demanded payment in advance before conveying the company train from Omaha to San Francisco.[72] Departure was delayed until the cash could be obtained. Then, the Central Pacific refused to cooperate for the Ogden to San Francisco portion of the journey, causing further delays. The NOC finally made it to the Pacific, but not until the evening of its first performance there, and a half-filled house greeted the tired and disheartened company. San Francisco houses did improve, however, and thought was given to extending the ten-day run an additional week, but money problems persisted. There was a union dispute over the use of a few local nonunion instrumentalists and rumors that the members of the chorus would strike if they did not get their back wages. Travel expenses were, as usual, greater than anticipated. Locke's inept management made disaster imminent.

Returning eastward, the harassed company heard that Thurber had withdrawn her support. Disgusted, Thomas wired the NOC board from St. Louis on June 7: "Troupe completely wrecked. Workingmen have gone without meals to the shame of the Directory. I have nothing to do with the business management, but I did not dare to leave the troupe in San Francisco, and only stay now until everyone can reach New York. We have been deserted and sold by everybody, and if you will get us home after the Louisville engagement you will save money."[73] The board ignored his entreaties, and the company continued on its way. On June 16, at Buffalo, the money for the orchestra ran out. Thomas and his players left the group and returned to New York City. Locke also fled, abandoning scenery and wardrobes in a Buffalo railway yard. Members of the chorus and the ballet slept on the stage, as there was no money for hotel rooms.[74] What remained of the company went on to play in Toronto and then disbanded.

It later came to light that the National Opera Company owed Thomas more than $18,000 in back fees.[75] Unable to attend an employees' meeting called to deal with unpaid salaries and other grievances, he wrote instead how sorry he was that the troupe had been broken up: "We have had in ourselves all the elements of good work and prosperity, if only the first and vital condition of success in an undertaking had been observed by the directors and management of the NOC—viz. prompt payment of all employees." This laconic note did not help. It was felt that he could have said more, that he could have shown more sympathy, that he could have even suggested helping. Thomas might have assessed the company's administrative tactics accurately, but he, as music director, was also to blame. In his own mind, he absolved himself when he wrote later that he had accepted the leadership of the NOC because it provided his orchestra with permanent employment and relieved him of paying salaries.[76]

Was this a good enough reason to found an opera company? There were, Thomas noted in his autobiography,

> peculiarities of management which neither art nor business could endure. Financially the case was soon hopeless, and the only question left for me was how to get out of the toils in which I had been so completely ensnared. The management refused to allow the much-abused and at last fatally stricken organization to die a natural death or have a decent burial, and so it came about that toward the close it was either a disgrace or a calamity to everyone connected with it. Even after it was finally dead its apparition haunted different cities all over the country for a time. My official connection with it had been limited to that of musical director. I had no business interest in it whatever, but I was for years afterwards involved in lawsuits brought against me by its victims.

Still, Thomas *was* responsible in great part for the company's demise. He had, in selecting, casting, and preparing the repertoire, made too many wrong decisions. Rather than using up funds in lavish productions, Thomas should have engaged better, albeit more expensive, principal singers. He overdid his abhorrence of the star system; his principal singers had been weak, and he had dealt insensitively with them. Singing is the most personal form of musical communication, and most singers are usually in emotional turmoil of one kind or another, especially prior to the curtain going up; at such times, they need understanding and musical empathy from the conductor, which Thomas did not provide. Further, he rarely allowed singers vocal liberties on stage in an age when it was still de rigueur to take them, and he seldom adjusted tempos and nuance to their satisfaction. He was not a pianist and therefore could not play through operatic scores at the keyboard and prepare his casts personally. Lack of pianistic skill is not an insurmountable handicap for an operatic conductor, but it must be compensated for by an inside-out knowledge of the score from the singer's viewpoint, and this is something Thomas did not have. Worse still, he did not see the need for it.

Thomas had been unconcerned with the NOC's poor librettos and translations, and his performances showed a singular lack of dramatic understanding, if we are to believe the more responsible critics of New York and Boston. He often conducted the orchestra with little attention to events onstage, making it apparent that he did not understand that opera is, ideally, a blending of all the performing arts. Its composite magic eluded his sober and earthbound mentality, but in this he was not alone. Few conductors in the 1880s saw opera as an art form in its own right, something more than the sum of its parts.

The development of American opera was set back with the denouement of the National Opera Company. If it had been operated on a more modest scale and had had sounder artistic goals and less hyperbole and chauvinism, the NOC might still be with us today. But Thomas, jealous of Leopold Damrosch and Anton Seidl, had resolved to steal their thunder at all costs, even if art and his personal ideals would be the losers. Angry with the Met for ignoring him, he aimed to show the new opera house the error of its ways. It would take time before Thomas lived down his own errors in judgment and the sorry memories he and his opera company left behind.

9

More Catastrophe and Picking Up
the Pieces

Thomas had a difficult summer in 1887. He felt sorry for himself but got
little sympathy from others, who said that he should never have been
connected with the American (later National) Opera Company. Luckily, he
could cry on Rose Fay's shoulder.[1] His tiresome lamentations to her about
money—"Although I have not received a penny of salary from the National
Opera Company, I am still 'flush' enough to pay my expenses"—did not
disturb their growing friendship. She revered him and salved his damaged
ego. His frequent letters to her were personal and revealing—unusual, since
Thomas was not a good letter writer—and help to explain this discouraging
period in his life.

Wisely, Thomas turned away from opera and vigorously resumed his
orchestral career. The Chicago summer concerts went well, and by September
he had some eighty events set for New York: twelve popular concerts, each
with a public rehearsal; twelve young people's concerts at Steinway Hall; and
full seasons for the Brooklyn and New York Philharmonic orchestras. He was
back where he belonged, in front of his orchestra, doing what he knew best.

Times had changed, however, and Thomas seemed to have lost his faithful followers; his concerts did not sell as well as they had in the past. Anton
Seidl, Walter Damrosch, and Frank Van der Stucken had made substantial
gains while he had been absorbed in NOC activities; the Boston Symphony
had also begun giving regular, well-received programs in New York. Thomas
had measured up favorably to competition in the past, but now the public was
no longer so sure. Unflattering newspaper stories about his NOC activities
persisted.

There was unexpected new competition in an eleven-year-old Polish
piano prodigy, Josef Hofmann, who filled the Metropolitan Opera House for

eighteen concerts between mid-November 1887 and mid-February 1888. He always played with an orchestra, and when the dates clashed with Thomas's concerts, as they frequently did, Thomas could not attract enough people to fill the much smaller Steinway Hall. The boy, who was being ruthlessly exploited by both his father and his manager, Henry Abbey, fortunately was saved by an anonymous philanthropist, who gave the family enough money to allow young Hofmann to grow up away from the concert platform.

What else could Thomas do but look to touring again. Although he had traveled enough for ten lifetimes, he considered yet another spring trip, only to be thwarted by a new federal interstate regulation that forbade special fares for preferred groups like his orchestra. Without travel discounts, he could no longer turn a profit. The "Thomas Highway" was now history.

On May 1, 1888, Thomas complained to Rose Fay that Gotham audiences wanted too much Wagner and Liszt and not enough of the classics and that there was a widening "breach" between him and his public. He also bemoaned his financial situation: "I lost heavily this winter again, and I am too poor to allow myself anything beyond reasonable comfort. I shall take one room in a hotel, be saving during the five weeks in Chicago, and bring home all I can." These references to his poverty were unconvincing. He maintained a substantial house in New York City and owned a second one, Fairhaven, which, according to Fay,

> was very large and a fine specimen of the "Old Colonial" style of architecture. . . . The rooms were furnished with appropriate mahogany furniture. . . . Everything about the house was genuine. . . . The things that looked old *were* old, and those that were modern were not imitations, but only selected so as to be in keeping with the rest. Each room had a big, generous fireplace for wood, with polished brass andirons and fender, and the house was surrounded outside with large grounds, laid out in lawns and gardens and shaded with fine old trees.[2]

Fay thought his income "ample" and wrote admiringly that he was "a connoisseur . . . not satisfied with anything but the best." His "simple life" included "rare wines, fine cigars, clothing of the best material and make, horses and carriages, delicate cooking, large and handsomely furnished city and country houses, books, scores and expert service of all kinds. The only simplicity in his home was its kindly and unconventional atmosphere, and the absence of all ostentation." His approach to personal finances, however, was naive:

> He knew very little about the actual cost of anything, and really imagined that he only lived in reasonable comfort. He did not wish to have anything to do with money matters, and would not even cash his checks, as they came

in, but merely signed them over to his wife to spend or invest as she thought best. All he wanted was to have two new fifty dollar bills in his pocket. He would keep them unbroken as long as possible, partly because he enjoyed the feeling of having the two nice bills in reserve, and partly because he did not like to carry the dirty money he got in exchange. When he handled the latter, he would either put on gloves or carefully wash his hands afterwards! Indeed it would be difficult to find a man of more fastidious tastes and habits than Thomas.[3]

How full of paradoxes was this former work-a-day violinist from a poor immigrant family! Is it possible that he had changed that much from his earlier days when he handled all of his orchestra's finances personally? Perhaps his losses in the Chicago Fire, the Centennial, and the National Opera Company made him this way. Or was Rose Fay exaggerating Thomas's affectations?

In the summer of 1888, Thomas's life seemed to crumble. His wife, Minna, was seriously ill. And he had gone ahead with plans for an 1888–89 New York season on the premise that a new music hall would be built— more commodious and attractive than Steinway Hall and with 1,000 more seats—and that rich friends would establish a guarantee fund for his concerts. By August, it was clear that neither the hall nor the fund would materialize; Thomas shared the bad news with his players a few days before the end of the Chicago season.[4] Although there was still hope, he said that he could not promise his players sufficient employment to put a hold on their services for the coming season. In effect, the Thomas Orchestra, which had played to hundreds of thousands of people over two decades was no more.

As expected, the press proclaimed the orchestra's demise a "public calamity" and attributed it to a lack of public support, growing competition, the high cost of travel, and Thomas's loss of prestige and changing tastes.[5] The simplest explanation was that a symphony orchestra could not be self-supporting on a continuing basis, that it needed a benefactor, as in Boston, or a citizen's board, as in St. Louis (where an orchestra of sorts was gradually taking shape). Other large cities—Cincinnati, Pittsburgh, Philadelphia, Minneapolis—were developing their own orchestras because of the impetus of the Thomas Orchestra. Although it would be some years before the orchestras were in place, there were signs that these cities increasingly resented Thomas's visits, which they felt hurt attendance at the concerts of their own groups.

During the fall, Thomas led several Philharmonic concerts in New York, Brooklyn, and Orange, New Jersey, as well as a three-concert festival in Rochester, but nothing more. His least-active season in twenty-five years caused him to wonder whether his work was over. He had brought great music to all corners of the country, had inspired the growth of local orchestras, and had developed a taste for the classics among the people, but now he no longer appeared to be needed. He considered a part-time position as head of the orchestral department at the Cincinnati College of Music, which he had left so unhappily nine years before,[6] but in the end, he put his time into preparing several orchestral transcriptions, finishing a short "Festival" March, and attending to his wife, whose health was failing rapidly. His life was hardly one of a recluse, but it seemed so to Thomas after his years of almost daily exposure to the public. It did not help his morale to observe Seidl completing New York's first *Ring* cycle at the Met, something he had hoped to do himself.

To stay active, Thomas fixed a three-month spring series of twelve concerts. Steinway Hall was solidly booked, but the smaller Chickering Hall was available, and the Chickering Piano Company cooperated by charging him an unusually low rent. A Committee of Patronesses, wealthy women from New York's 400, promised to underwrite the concerts. Thomas's programs were as interesting as any he had ever put together, thanks to the preparation time he had. One highlight was the first North American performance of Brahms's Double Concerto, with Max Bendix and Victor Herbert as the violin and cello soloists. Bendix, only twenty-two, would be Thomas's concertmaster for the next ten years and later a prominent conductor. Herbert had come from Ireland in 1886 and joined Thomas the next year; his career as bandmaster, conductor of the Pittsburgh Symphony, and composer of American light opera was still a few years in the future. The wonderful Double Concerto got mixed reviews, and Thomas's Festival March elicited the word "rot" from the *Musical Courier*.[7]

Thomas was showing a renewed interest in early music. At a February concert, he conducted a long-lost flute concerto by Baroque composer Johann Joachim Quantz, who was virtually unknown to the American musical public. In the same concert, Thomas earned a warm reception for his reading of Arthur Foote's Suite in E Minor for strings. Foote, who had studied with Paine at Harvard, was a pianist, an organist, and a composer; he would later help found the American Guild of Organists.[8]

The most significant American "novelty" was provided by a young American pianist and composer, Edward MacDowell, who premiered his Concerto no. 2 for piano and orchestra with Thomas on March 5, 1889. Born in New York in 1861, MacDowell entered the National Conservatory in Paris at age seventeen and one year later moved to Germany, where he worked with Raff at Frankfurt and, for a short period, with Liszt at Weimar. His gifts recognized, ten of his works were published in Germany by such prestigious houses as Breitkopf & Härtel before he returned to the United States in 1888.

Thomas, one of the first American musicians to note MacDowell's talent, had done his First Concerto the previous summer in Chicago with the young artist's former teacher, Teresa Carreño, as soloist. The Chicago event had been a happy reunion for Thomas and Carreño for they had played together thirty years earlier, when she was eight. Carreño wrote Thomas a touching note after the Chicago concert: "Thank you from all my heart once more for the kindness and consideration with which you treated me yesterday, and to tell you how proud and happy I feel that once again I have been allowed the pleasure and privilege of playing under your baton. . . . If I may, I will come and knock at your door when you are in New York, and hope that you will always look upon me as the same little girl whose tottering footsteps in her profession you, with your powerful hand, were the first to guide and support."[9]

So impressed was Thomas with MacDowell's work, that he had written to him before the March 1889 concert: "I do not need to see the score before the rehearsal. . . . Let me know the time the Concerto takes to play and the general character of the music . . . that I can arrange the programme accordingly." How extraordinary for a conductor to sight-read a concerto at a rehearsal just prior to a concert! Henry Krehbiel, the *Daily Tribune* critic, praised the performance: "MacDowell . . . had the good fortune of an accompaniment which put no fetters on him, but aided him in giving a spirited and eloquent exposition."[10] He enjoyed the concerto more than Tchaikovsky's Fifth Symphony, done on the same program.

Andrew Carnegie, who would figure significantly if indirectly in Thomas's life, had arrived in the United States as a youth, and now, at age fifty (the same as Thomas), was one of the richest men in the country. He was greatly interested in the arts and education and spent much of his enormous fortune on them. On board ship to Europe in 1887, Carnegie had met Walter Damrosch, who charmed him with his personality and his brilliant impromptu piano playing. By voyage's end, Damrosch had broken ground toward convincing Carnegie to accept the presidencies of his New York Symphony and Oratorio societies. On March 15, 1889, the New York newspapers reported that the city "will probably soon rejoice in the possession of a music hall" on the corner of Fifty-seventh Street and Seventh Avenue. There would be one main hall seating 3,000, plus smaller rooms for chamber music, lectures, and meetings. Carnegie was identified as "the moving spirit in this scheme," whose total cost was estimated at $800,000. "The new hall shall be a home for the musical societies of the city—the Symphony, Oratorio, Choral, Orpheus and Musurgia, and all others that may need quarters."[11]

Within a week came another announcement: a second new concert hall was "being perfected" in the Monitor and Merrimac Building at Fifty-ninth Street and Madison Avenue, where a revived Thomas Orchestra would give nightly concerts by the end of the summer. However, the Lenox Lyceum, as the Thomas hall was to be called, was a poor substitute for the music hall planned for Fifty-seventh Street, the hall of Thomas's dreams. Since the city was behind the scheme, Parks Commissioner John D. Crimmins had consulted Thomas on renovations that would make the new venue an updated Central Park Garden, but with one major exception: "No intoxicating drinks will be sold in the boxes or anywhere else." Crimmins declared, "I shall not even have a bar in the place." [12] That decision, in Thomas's opinion, could well doom popular concerts.

Still a third concert hall in the Empire City was proposed, this one to be in a "rehabilitated" Madison Square Garden. The *Musical Courier* ran interviews with William Steinway, Thomas, and Walter Damrosch as to the project's feasibility. Steinway, practical businessman that he was, warned that "three new halls are apt to prove three white elephants." Thomas was confident that, "when we can give our people the best orchestral music under the best conditions there will be an immense popular appetite created for it." According to him, good halls would create new and larger audiences, and he urged that the venues be attractive, comfortable, even luxurious, with spacious foyers and anterooms. Thomas thought that Madison Square Garden and the Lyceum could each pay for itself. Damrosch, speaking from strength, saw no need for a third hall. The Fifty-seventh Street hall was to be "a veritable temple of music, where all may be heard who wish to be heard, whether they use the piano of Chickering or that of Steinway. . . . It is designed to wholly exclude the mercantile spirit from its management. . . . The Philharmonic Society will give its concerts in our hall and in short there will be enough room for all." [13] (Despite this pronouncement, Thomas and the Philharmonic's board had a gnawing suspicion that the ambitious and opportunistic Damrosch would trick them in the end and keep them out of the new hall.)

Thomas put on thirty-six concerts from January to April 1889—no small feat—and while they were artistic successes, the audiences were small. His patronesses had not come up with a sustaining fund, and Thomas personally lost money. Other conductors were doing better, especially Seidl, who had been invited to direct a five-day festival in Pittsburgh in May. Hans von Bülow also provided unneeded competition, having returned to the United States after a fifteen-year absence, this time to conduct rather than play the piano. For his debut, the normally feisty von Bülow conducted a charity concert at the Met on March 27, with an orchestra composed of the best players from both the Philharmonic and the Symphony Society. The concert drew unqualified praise from the critics, who felt that von Bülow was unsurpassed on the podium. They also noted something most exceptional for the time: von Bülow conducted without a score. [14]

On April 7, 1889, Minna Thomas died after a long and painful illness. The *Daily Tribune* reported: "About five months ago Mrs. Thomas was taken ill with a form of nervous prostration which soon brought her to her bed. Her trouble puzzled the physicians, although hope of recovery was not abandoned until a few weeks ago. Mrs. Thomas was known as a woman of fine intellectual attainments and strong character." [15] When he heard of her death, Thomas was in the midst of rehearsing a concert for Mrs. Gillespie's series at the Academy of Music in Philadelphia. He continued the rehearsal and even conducted as scheduled the next night, feeling it his duty to honor his professional commitments. Coincidentally, he had programmed his arrangement of Chopin's *Marche funèbre*, and, according to one cellist in the orchestra, during its performance, "tears ran down his cheeks. The latter part of the score was played practically without direction." [16]

His wife's death did not prevent Thomas from filling other conducting assignments in April, including a "monster concert" with huge instrumental and vocal forces at Madison Square Garden, part of a three-day celebration of the 100th anniversary of the inauguration of George Washington. (He must have needed money badly to take part in such an event.) Then Thomas fled to Fairhaven to grieve, for he had loved Minna deeply. He turned to Rose Fay for solace: "I have had no sense for music or anything else since my loss, except to be with my children. . . . I need rest and I am glad I am at home." He wrote about his three sons, about refurnishing his study "very inexpensively," about bringing busts of Shakespeare and Bach from New York, about pictures he hung of Mozart and Beethoven and one of Goethe that he had bought in Weimar: "It represents him as an old man, but strong. I have never seen one like it before or since. Opposite hangs a picture of Schiller's house and garden, as I saw it in Weimar. . . . Next week [I] will hang a picture of Schubert, and opposite to him one of Schumann. These I purchased to-day in Boston. Here you have my *Glaubens Bekenntniss* [my credo]." [17]

Toward summer, Thomas had recovered sufficiently to write: "As a little by-play last week I arranged Siegmund's Love Song for orchestra and yesterday I began on Schubert's 'Erlkoenig,' which is already half finished. . . . To-day I tried to make the first week's programmes for Chicago. Work for a living begins again—Brrrrr!" Just before his departure for Chicago, he commented that scoring the "Erlkoenig" is "so easy for me that the writing down of it is doubly tedious. . . . But I find it very hard to live as other people do in summer —doing nothing." Thomas continued: "If I cannot do a certain amount of work every day I feel very *mean*, which is the lowest depth I can conceive. But when I can work I am satisfied."

Even though he was at the height of his powers, Thomas, at age fifty-three, was fast becoming part of American musical history. In a sense, he suffered from overexposure, having been a public figure for too long with more than his share of ups and downs. He had loyal friends and formidable enemies; and there were many, especially in New York, who had tired of his constant complaints about the lack of support for a permanent orchestra and his incessant fuming at this and that. It therefore came as a pleasant surprise when a Minneapolis group, identifying themselves only as "Many Music Lovers," wrote to the *New York Daily Tribune* on April 22, 1889, to suggest a "testimonial tour" by the Thomas Orchestra: "a grand triumphal march for the great conductor. . . . There is a deep feeling of regard amongst the musicians and people of America, and, whatever may be said of the sharp points of his character, they are ready to testify to it." [18]

The letter received immediate support from the *Tribune* and other newspapers. Arrangements were made without delay, and the press, as one, took up the cudgels for Thomas, America's elder statesman of music, and warned that this might be the last opportunity to see and hear a Thomas concert. George W. Curtis wrote to Thomas in June on behalf of a group of illustrious citizens—Vice President Levi P. Morton, former President Grover Cleveland, Carl Schurz, Theodore Roosevelt, William Dean Howells, Charles Dana, Chauncey Depew, Andrew Carnegie, Cornelius Vanderbilt, J. P. Morgan, and others—that the tour was cause for "national pride and joy." He considered "the growth and development of a taste for the higher forms of art . . . one of the most powerful forces to which we must look for the necessary chastening of the material and commercial spirit," and in music no one had done more in this respect than Thomas.[19] The conductor responded gratefully and awkwardly: "To one who has endeavored to do his duty, the knowledge that his work is appreciated is peculiarly encouraging. . . . I will not refuse to believe that this movement represents the popular feeling." [20]

The *Chicago Tribune*, which showed a special interest in the tour, leaked the news that the Windy City wanted Thomas to put it "on a secure and prosperous musical footing," that Thomas and New York had wearied of one another, and that Thomas, given that there would be an orchestra for him to conduct, had been thinking of settling in the West.[21] As proof, the paper noted that he had engaged a large contingent of Chicago players for the 1889 summer series in the Exposition Building to see whether they would measure up to his standards. Unfortunately, most of them did not. If there were to be a Thomas Orchestra in Chicago at some time in the future, most of its players would have to be imported.

Meanwhile, plans for the testimonial tour went forward. There would be twenty-five concerts in twenty-two cities, beginning in Brooklyn on October 9, then following a northern route (Minneapolis, the home base for the initiators of the tour, was not, in the end, part of it). In late September, Thomas brought together in New York his old orchestra of fifty-two players and began rehearsals. He wrote to Rose Fay of his anxiety about the task ahead and then reassured her that he had "all the old power. . . . I am growing all the time and feel my strength, if I could only use it to better purpose. . . . We start for the fall tour in a few days, and are in Albany on October 11. Will you let me have a letter on that day? It is my fifty-fourth birthday." [22]

Two of Thomas's favorite soloists, Rafael Joseffy and Victor Herbert, were booked for the tour with Sam Franko as concertmaster. The repertoire was for everyone, a compendium of American popular taste in orchestral music in 1889. Thomas gave each city a choice of three programs:

> Program 1: Overture to *Coriolanus* and "Adagio" from *Prometheus* for cello solo (Beethoven); *Invitation to the Dance* (Weber); *Les Préludes* (Liszt); Piano Concerto in E Minor (Chopin); two string pieces (Grieg); "Waldweben" and the "Ride of the Valkyries" (Wagner)

> Program 2: Overture to *Tannhäuser* (Wagner); Andante from the Fifth Symphony (Beethoven); *Fantasie on Hungarian Airs* for solo piano (Liszt); selections from the *Damnation of Faust* (Berlioz); Overture to *William Tell* (Rossini); *Träumerai* (Schumann); three short pieces for solo piano; "Hochzeitsklänge" Waltz (Strauss); "Torchlight" March (Meyerbeer)

> Program 3: Overture to *The Flying Dutchman* (Wagner); Allegretto from the Eighth Symphony (Beethoven); Piano Concerto (Schumann); *Marche funèbre* (Chopin); *Serenade* for cello and strings (Volkmann); Hungarian Rhapsodie no. 2 or no. 12 (Liszt); two selections from Goldmark

Program 2 was the most popular, probably because it included the perennial Thomas favorite, *Träumerai*. Some cities had formal voting procedures— Pittsburgh, for example, cast 740 ballots for #2, 146 for #3, and 54 for #1. Thomas even complied with requests for works from more than one program.

Once the tour began, Thomas was in his element, in total command of orchestra and public, weaving his spell over all. After the first concert (Program 2) at the Brooklyn Academy, the *New York Times* praised his "great magnetism and control."[23] Later, it added:

> How Mr. Thomas's programme carried one back into the past. It was redolent of the perfumed warmth and harmonious laziness of the old days in Central Park Garden, before ever Seidl was, or the Nibelung Trilogy was brought forth. The delicious "Träumerai," with its delicate interweaving of sweet and subtle imitations, dreams within a dream, was certainly a memory of good old times. And there was the Strauss waltz, the "Hochzeitsklange," with its languorous alternation of piano and forte, and its rhythmic suggestion of wedding guests tripping the merry dance, played as only Thomas can play a waltz, transformed into a terpsichorean poem, as though it might have been a musical translation of old Horace's "Nec sperne puer."[24]

American audiences nostalgically poured out their affection for their nation's leading warrior of the symphonic battlefield, and the tour went well indeed. New York was the final stop. There, Thomas led an orchestra of 150, which made it much more an "event" than an evening of memorable music-making. Thomas wrote, "For once every musician has thrown off personal feelings and I will have an orchestra the best the country can afford. The whole profession have offered their services, and I could have an orchestra of a thousand." [25]

Rose Fay had written a birthday greeting to Thomas in Albany, as requested, and had enclosed a volume of Emerson prose, for which he thanked her at length. A week later, from Cleveland, he was complaining again about touring:

> I do need a decent glass of wine, and I do need a cup of strong coffee when I work as I must—both are impossible to get. The traveling public drinks beer or whisky, and I am forbidden to drink either. . . . Last night after the concert I was so tired that I refused to speak. . . . This kind of life is impossible. . . . I shall continue this year in order not to run behind, but next year if I cannot make twenty thousand dollars, I will have to learn to live on ten, or even less if necessary. Other people do, and so can I, and if I want to help my boys for a few years yet [Thomas seemed unconcerned about educating his daughters, Minna and Marion], until they are established in life, I must economize.

He added, quoting Emerson: " 'Nothing can bring you peace but the triumph of principles.' This I have known myself for years, and very clearly from experience." Then he was back to self-pity: "while I have become clearer in my mind . . . I have been so unmercifully tossed about on the waves of the ordinary world that I have not been able to anchor anywhere." [26]

One wonders how his future wife reacted when Thomas wailed that his income might be cut? Twenty thousand dollars annually was, after all, a great deal in late nineteenth-century America; even $10,000 was substantial. Some might contest his claim of being "tossed about," in view of his income and considering that he continued to hold three conducting positions—with the New York Philharmonic, the Cincinnati Festival, and the Chicago Summer Night Concerts.

Following the testimonial tour, Thomas gave but a few concerts in New York, Brooklyn, and Philadelphia prior to the New Year. He led one special all-Beethoven program at Steinway Hall on December 15; the proceeds would help preserve the master's birthplace in Bonn. A mammoth orchestra of some 150 was again assembled, with soloists Lilli Lehmann, her husband, tenor Paul Kalisch, and Victor Herbert, assisted by the Liederkranz Chorus.

Thomas's letters to Rose Fay grew more frequent and personal. He wrote of his dissatisfaction with his work and worried that he would no longer be asked to do musical things of importance in the United States—"This we have to thank Wagner for; how long it will last no one can tell." Quite simplistically, he blamed Wagner for what he saw as a diminishing interest in classical composers—Mozart, Beethoven, Schubert, Mendelssohn, and other symphonists. What he really meant was that New York was taking Seidl and Seidl's Wagner to its heart, at least as much as it had Thomas and Thomas's Wagner in the past. "Meantime," he wrote, "I will learn to do something else for a living—but it is rather late, and tough for me." [27]

After the New Year, Thomas began a series of concerts at the now-completed Lenox Lyceum, sharing the podium with Victor Herbert. The Lyceum had 1,800 seats, acceptable acoustics, and was physically attractive. The programs were mainly popular and well received; and Thomas, true to form, sporadically slipped in movements of symphonies and other serious music. But the concerts' popularity left him unmoved and even demeaned. He wrote bitterly that "if the people see or can read in my back that I now play for money, let them—I cannot help it, and they deserve nothing better." [28]

In these dark days, Thomas gave little weight to his role as conductor of the Philharmonic, whose performances still attracted New York's most mature audiences. Nor was he particularly pleased that his lighter and less-demanding work schedule gave him more time for score study and concert preparation. Its benefits, however, did show: the 1889–90 Philharmonic season was altogether superb, its highlight being Beethoven's Ninth, about which the usually restrained Thomas wrote: "Last night's performance was great in every sense of the word, and the ripest and greatest I ever gave at any time and of anything. The audience knew what was going on and stood on their chairs, and waved hats and handkerchiefs when they got me out on the stage again, and the members of the orchestra congratulated not only me but each other." [29] Evidently, his confidante had questioned him about the work, and he replied with feeling: "I think the first movement the greatest, and nothing about it is more remarkable than its opening sixteen measures. Beethoven apparently wished to produce here the effect of a mysterious foreshadowing of something great and portentous to come." He then referred to the ambiguity of the key and its resolution at bar 17 into the principal theme, at once "somber, grandiose, and fraught with a restless energy which knows no peace or satisfaction." [30]

Rose Fay hoped that this performance would close Thomas's period of "spiritual convalescence," but his letters got worse: "The world pull[s] everyone down to its level, and one must fight for a respectable standard. I cannot fight any more, so I have renounced, for I would rather take my fiddle and play on the streets for a living than sell my honor as a man or an artist." [31] Thomas threatened to leave the concert stage and seek a teaching post in a college or school of music, but could he be taken seriously? His friends suspected that all he needed to brighten his professional life was more prestigious conducting opportunities and more recognition and praise to feed his ego. Thomas's "limited" activity was still more than enough for most conductors, and he still earned far more as a conductor than he could ever earn as a teacher.

On May 7, 1890, Rose Fay and Theodore Thomas were married in Chicago; she was thirty-seven, Thomas fifty-four. The marriage was not un-expected. As early as February, Chicagoans had read that "wedding bells are soon to ring again for Theodore Thomas, the great orchestral leader. . . . His fiancee is a Chicago lady of high social position." [32] When the couple obtained their marriage license in Chicago on April 25, it was duly noted in the New York press. [33]

The wedding itself was widely publicized. The *Chicago Tribune*, under a headline reading "MARRIAGE OF THE FAMOUS MUSICIAN TO MISS ROSE FAY," described the Episcopalian ceremony as restrained and in good taste:

> Roses, calla lilies, and ferns . . . adorned the center and ends of the altar, filling, too, several arched niches below. Among them gleamed the altar lights, making a beautiful effect. To the right stood a large floral lyre formed of white roses, carnations and smilax, while on the other side were bouquets of roses variously arranged. [Rose wore] a white satin brocade with plain satin train, over whose long folds floated a tulle veil fastened with a spray of orange blossoms. The bodice was high in back, but cut low and square in front, displaying to advantage a large string of Roman pearls worn about the neck. Half sleeves were met by white gloves, and she carried a cluster of bride's roses. [34]

Rose's sister, Amy, was the bridesmaid, and her brother, Charles Nor-man, gave her away. (Rose's late father, Charles Fay of Boston, had been a prominent Episcopalian clergyman, and her mother, Emily Hopkins Fay, was the daughter of the presiding bishop of the Episcopalian House of Bishops.) "At its conclusion the happy, handsome groom, with a smile on his face and a white rose in his buttonhole, led his blushing bride away from the chapel. Strains from Beethoven's fifth symphony slowly followed to take carriages to the reception." Other music played at the wedding by leading Chicago organist Clarence Eddy included a Toccata and "Wedding" March by Bach, excerpts from *Meistersinger* and *Walküre*, and the March from Weber's *Concertstück*. [35]

The happy couple received many gifts. The New York Philharmonic gave them an ornamented clock with two candelabras (first the membership voted on whether to give a gift; then it fixed the amount—$500); E. Francis Hyde, the society's president, made a personal gift of $150. [36] From a group of Cincinnati ladies involved in the May festivals came a bronze figure of an old black man "dreamily listening to the strains of a plantation melody as he played it on a banjo." Evidently, Thomas took umbrage over this gift, regarding it as an insult intended to recall his days as a "nigger minstrel performer," and never acknowledged it. He accepted no explanations. [37]

On May 13, 1890, less than a week after the wedding, the cornerstone was laid for the new music hall at West Fifty-seventh Street and Seventh Avenue in New York. At the ceremony, Andrew Carnegie prophesied a great future for the hall that would bear his name: "Who shall venture to paint its history or its end? It is built to stand for ages, and during these ages it is probable that this hall will intertwine itself with the history of our country."[38]

Thomas and his wife were, of course, invited but could not attend, since they were in Cincinnati preparing for the city's Ninth May Festival. The newlyweds returned to New York at the end of May for Thomas's Lenox Lyceum series, which did not go well. The audiences, smaller than in the winter, complained that the concerts were too formal for summer evenings and that beer was too hard to obtain. By mid-June, the orchestra was put on notice that its engagement would terminate two weeks early.

Just as the Thomas Orchestra was closing prematurely at the Lenox, the Eduard Strauss Orchestra of Vienna was opening at the newly renovated Madison Square Garden. Strauss, a cousin of Johann, Jr., had a somewhat bizarre conducting style—he would face the audience while conducting and keep time by swaying his body and tapping his foot. His appearance was "picturesque," to put it mildly, but became "monotonous" after one or two numbers. According to one critic, "He is an exceedingly effective answer to the demand of some idiosyncratic persons that conductors should be polite enough to face the audience."[39]

Naturally, Strauss was at his best with Strauss music; but, in the opinion of the most informed critics, he was no better than Thomas himself, the acknowledged master of the waltz in the United States. The *Times* reported: "In smoothness, sweetness, and purity of tone, in delicacy of gradation, and in dynamic effectiveness the American conductor is his superior."[40] Small consolation for Thomas, who had unexpectedly lost two weeks of work due, in part, to the Austrian attraction. He nevertheless did more Strauss than usual at his Chicago summer season, which followed the Lyceum engagement. The *Chicago Journal* declared that Thomas's music was lighter and more popular than in previous years, no doubt attributable to his marriage: "He would be a sorry bridegroom who would not prefer dance music to Wagnerian thunder."[41]

10

A Vote of Confidence

On November 7, 1890, newspapers across the land announced in bold headlines that Theodore Thomas would move to Chicago to head up a newly organized Chicago Orchestra, which would give its first season in 1891–92.[1] The Windy City promised him a first-class permanent orchestra, like the one in Boston: he would have no management or financial responsibilities, and he would be able to bring the best players from anywhere to Chicago to fill the orchestra's ranks. Thomas admitted that leaving New York would not be easy, but what Chicago had created for him was worth it. He would miss the New York Philharmonic, but, as he explained, it gave only twelve concerts a season, not enough to develop a really fine symphonic instrument, and it was not *his* orchestra. The new Chicago Orchestra would give at least two concerts weekly during an eight-month season, and it would play only for him during that period.

Still disappointed that New York had not rallied to his aid when he had disbanded his orchestra two years earlier, Thomas lamented that voters had again brought to power the corrupt Tammany Hall, which had ruled the city for most of the century and had done nothing for music. What future did the city have? According to Thomas, New Yorkers were slaves of fashion and supported any new fad regardless of its quality (an indirect reference to the continuing success of opera at the Met). In the end, he hid neither his bitterness toward New York nor his elation in moving from the city he had loved so much.

The success of the Chicago plan—the orchestra, Thomas as conductor —was due to the work of Charles Norman Fay, a prominent Chicago utilities executive and a man of competence and charm who mixed easily with the rich. As devoted to music as were his sisters, Fay had first heard the Thomas

Orchestra at the Chicago Summer Night Concerts during the Pullman strike of 1877, and the orchestra had made a profound impression on him. Two years later, he had written Thomas—they had not met personally—asking him to organize and lead a Philharmonic Society in Chicago. Anticipating a busy year at the Cincinnati College of Music, as well as monthly trips to New York and Brooklyn, Thomas had refused the offer. Fay let the idea rest because he wanted Thomas and no one else.

Fay and Thomas finally met in 1881 and became close friends—as much as anyone could become a close friend of Thomas—seeing each other whenever Thomas was in Chicago. One day in 1889, they met by chance on Fifth Avenue in New York and went on to dine together at Delmonico's. There, Thomas told Fay how discouraged he was that, with his orchestra disbanded, he had to conduct scratch orchestras: "My friends . . . do not care. They think I have always kept the body and soul together somehow, and that I always will—that I have nowhere else to go. They treat me as a music merchant, a commercial proposition, subject to the laws of supply and demand." Fay recalled that he asked Thomas, "Would you come to Chicago if we could give you a permanent orchestra? The answer, grim and sincere, and entirely destitute of intentional humor, came back like a flash. 'I would go to hell if they gave me a permanent orchestra.' Then and there the general principles of an agreement for the Chicago Orchestra were roughed out."[2]

These "principles," once translated into action, meant that Thomas would be resident in Chicago, have complete authority over the orchestra and its programs, be free of ties with any business organization, be authorized to contract players exclusively for twenty-eight weeks annually and to conduct twenty pairs of concerts on Fridays and Saturdays plus eight weeks of touring. Fifty guarantors had promised $1,000 each to the orchestra on an annual basis for its first three years, if needed. They met on December 17, 1890, formed the Orchestral Association, drew up its charter, and offered Thomas a contract.[3]

It all sounded too good to be true, but it was: what Fay and Thomas had sketched out at Delmonico's was now formalized in articles of incorporation. One important clause amazed Thomas: "The Musical Director is to determine the character and standard of all performances . . . make all programmes, select all soloists, and take the initiative in arranging for choral and festival performances. [He is to have] the power and responsibility for the attainment of the highest standard of artistic excellence in all performances given by the Association." A delighted Thomas told his wife: "I never expected to see the day when I would be told I would be 'held responsible' for maintaining the highest standard of artistic excellence in my musical work. All my life I have been told that my standard was too high, and urged to make it more popular. But now, I am not only to be given every facility to create the highest standard, but am even told that I will be *held responsible* for keeping it so! I have to shake myself to realize it."[4]

Thomas's contract with the Chicago Orchestra—later called the Theodore Thomas Orchestra and finally the Chicago Symphony Orchestra—was for three years, not a very long period in which to develop an orchestra, at an annual salary of $15,000. He agreed to put his music library, valued by him at $150,000, at the disposal of the orchestra. It included scores and parts for some 1,600 symphonic works, which were carefully stored in a fireproof building.

The contract allowed Thomas to hire up to eighty-six players "to rank with those of the New York Philharmonic and the Boston Symphony." (There was no mention of the third major orchestra in the United States, Damrosch's New York Symphony Society.) The orchestra's season, in addition to concerts and touring, could also include up to eight weeks of playing for the Italian Opera Company at the Chicago Auditorium, whether Thomas conducted or not. Thomas agreed not to take personal conducting engagements, other than with the Cincinnati May Festival, without the association's permission.

To be sure, Chicago was proud of its new venture and made much of it in the press. The city's appetite for orchestral music had been whetted since Thomas's first visit in 1869. Now America's second city was to have its own orchestra, and it would do Boston one better by having it supported by a substantial number of community leaders rather than only one. Support for the orchestra was thus ingrained in Chicago's citizenry from the outset.

As expected, New York's musical community was in a furor. Why was Thomas leaving? How *could* he leave? Might he still change his mind? According to his wife, three different New York groups approached Thomas with enticing offers when his Chicago appointment was announced; he would have considered them, she said, had he not already signed a contract with Chicago.[5] As for the effect of his departure on the New York Philharmonic, the president told a society meeting on January 6, 1891, that Thomas had properly declined an invitation to be a conducting candidate for 1891–92 "on account of his future engagements in Chicago."[6] Hyde named a committee to seek out appropriate candidates for the coming season, the society's fiftieth. Ironically, the conductor who had done the most for the group in its first half-century would not take part in the celebrations being planned.

The society's action should have quieted speculation that Thomas would continue to conduct Philharmonic concerts while based in Chicago, much as he had done when he was in Cincinnati, especially as it was doubtful that Chicago would let him do this. Yet Thomas's Philharmonic supporters persisted, and his candidacy was asked for again on January 27. Thomas, ambivalent and flattered, replied that he was "willing to serve if matters could be arranged with the Orchestral Association of Chicago, the organization to which he was bound by contract."

Why was Thomas so reluctant to give up the Philharmonic? Was it because he wanted to retain his New York ties or because he feared that Chicago would not work out, that it would be another Cincinnati? On February 6, it was disclosed that Walter Damrosch had been promised $50,000 annually to make his Symphony Society a permanent orchestra like Boston's and that his backers included the Vanderbilts, J. P. Morgan, and Andrew Carnegie.[7] Could Thomas dare hope for comparable support for a reconstituted New York–based Thomas Orchestra or for a permanent Philharmonic?

Certainly, Thomas's morale was never better—he felt as "wanted" as any conductor could hope for—but he knew Chicago's expectations and that he must come to terms with them. On February 14, the *Chicago Tribune* warned that the Orchestral Association would not share its musical lion with New York.[8] A few days later, the association made a "concession" and agreed to let Thomas conduct six Philharmonic concerts during Chicago's six-week opera season, an empty offer since the Philharmonic wanted him for six weeks spread over five or six months. At a society meeting on April 1, Hyde said that Chicago had definitely denied Thomas permission to conduct the Philharmonic in 1891–92. He also affirmed that the Philharmonic would give its concerts at Carnegie's new music hall, which would open in about a month—as Carnegie had promised, the hall would be used by both the Philharmonic and Damrosch's Symphony Society. Hyde closed by proposing to decorate Thomas's conductor's stand with flowers at his final Philharmonic concert and to present him with a floral wreath at its conclusion.[9] On April 29, 1891, the Philharmonic elected Anton Seidl its new conductor.

Thomas's conducting days in New York were over. With the popular Seidl at the Philharmonic, there was no turning back: Thomas had to be successful in Chicago. He would soon find that problems loomed large there, for Chicago in 1891 lacked the cultivation of Boston and New York and was only marginally ready for a resident orchestra, in spite of the generosity of Charles Norman Fay's rich friends. The city's population had doubled to one million between 1880 and 1890, yet in many ways Chicago resembled a wild-west boomtown, where life was rough-and-ready and laws were as much ignored as obeyed. The majority of its citizens were uneducated immigrants preoccupied with finding jobs in the stockyards and battling poverty. Although educational and cultural institutions were developing rapidly, only a disproportionately small group of cultivated Chicagoans attended events like formal and serious symphony concerts.

Another—and unexpected—problem was the new Chicago Auditorium, where Thomas's concerts would take place. At its opening a year and a half earlier, President Benjamin Harrison had promised that the great building would remove the people of Chicago "from the cares of business to those enjoyments and pursuits of entertainments which develop the souls of men." [10] Designed by Louis Sullivan, one of America's most brilliant and innovative architects, and Dankmar Adler, the 4,500-seat Auditorium was beautifully proportioned and, unlike European opera houses, almost without ornament. The huge stage had twenty-six hydraulic lifts and other technical equipment unequaled anywhere; the stage area alone, Chicagoans bragged, had cost nearly $200,000. Although the acoustics were excellent, Thomas still had to build a boxlike shell to blend the different sections of the orchestra and project its sound throughout the vast hall. And the number of seats available meant that nonsubscribers could buy single-performance tickets, thus discouraging season subscriptions; the public could choose popular concerts and avoid others. If we are to believe Rose Thomas, her husband worried about this even before he left New York, and his worries became a reality once the first season got under way.

As anticipated, Thomas had problems with the Chicago Musicians' Union. Although his appointment commenced in September 1891, he went to Chicago in the spring of 1891 to assemble his orchestra. He was determined to have the best players and to pay them well, but he feared that as few as one-third of them might be Chicagoans. To give local musicians every opportunity to prove themselves, and to show how fair he was, Thomas booked several concerts at the Auditorium for the end of March 1891, with a number of Chicago players in the orchestra. However, on March 10, these same musicians canceled their contracts because they objected to Thomas's ultimate authority to hire whomever he wanted, local or not. [11]

The dispute escalated, and on March 22, in an interview with the *Chicago Tribune*, Thomas stated bluntly his case for omniscience and omnipotence, calling the notion of his "refusal" to employ local musicians "absurd." After all, he was

> the friend of all good musicians, but he had to uphold standards. Chicago musicians must understand . . . that this undertaking . . . is in the interest of art, not of business. . . . I insist that I shall judge for myself in this matter and refuse to consult any one. I am responsible for the success or failure of these coming entertainments. . . . I shall come here with the nucleus of my orchestra and fill it out with capable musicians without respect to the locality from which they come. I am very sorry that this matter has been so much talked about. I do not wish to enter into any controversy. Such quibblings are not to the best interests of the art in which we are seeking to gain perfection. [12]

The local musicians yielded, and the first "experimental" concerts were presented. They were only moderately successful, and a second series, given in

April, fared even worse, mainly because Thomas used still more local players. Only then did the union surrender. Thomas hired the men he wanted, and the Chicago Orchestra was soon ready to begin its first season.

Returning to New York in mid-April, Thomas wound up his thirteenth season with the New York Philharmonic by conducting the "Eroica." For his final concert in Brooklyn, which he had served for almost three decades, he asked his loyal audience for "requests," and they selected Schubert's Unfinished, Beethoven's Seventh Symphony, Wagner's *Faust* Overture and Thomas's arrangement of Chopin's *Marche funèbre*. Brooklynites regretfully wished him "the greatest successes in his new field of duty" and bid him an affectionate farewell. The city then booked the Boston Symphony, conducted by the charismatic Arthur Nikisch, for its next season.

Thomas's New York friends—leading musicians, artists, civic officials, businessmen—gave him a testimonial dinner at Delmonico's on April 22. He spoke briefly, recalling his early years, especially the Mason-Thomas concerts (William Mason was at the dinner) and then, "with deep feeling," paid tribute to his predecessor at the Philharmonic, Carl Bergmann, from whom he had learned so much and who "went to pieces not because of the want of musical taste in the city, but because of its indifference."[13] Yes, Thomas implied, New York had let him down as it had Bergmann, but he, Thomas, had not turned to drink and a dissolute life, as Bergmann had; instead, he chose to leave for fairer climes to get what he wanted. Such acrimony at this happy time in his life was inappropriate at a dinner in his honor.

The speeches that followed were laudatory. William Steinway reminisced about Theodore Thomas the violinist, who, forty-one years before, had been "a young, rosy cheeked fellow [with] a tone as large as any three ordinary violinists together." He told the dinner guests how he had seen Thomas playing the violin with Lind and Sontag, how Thomas had stepped in to rehearse Bergmann's orchestra when the latter was ill in 1855, how the iron-willed conductor had refused to accept bankruptcy after the Centennial and had subsequently freed himself of debt in seven years. Master of ceremonies George W. Curtis eloquently added that "virtuosos of every kind have appeared, have charmed us, and have vanished. . . . But through all changes the one figure which has remained, the laureate of the past and the herald of the future, is Theodore Thomas."

Curtis, in his address, compared Thomas's interpretations of the great works of the German masters with those of the Gewandhaus Orchestra of Leipzig and the Conservatoire National Orchestra. He cited Amalie Materna, who said that Thomas played Wagner's music better than anyone, anywhere: "If he has revealed to us more fully the Beethoven we knew, it is he also who first showed us that there was a Wagner worth knowing." Then Curtis speculated: "New York only lends Theodore Thomas to Chicago. With metropolitan magnanimity she decorates with one of our own precious jewels her younger and successful competitor of the great fair. But presently she will reclaim it and restore it to her crown with a fresher luster gained from her sister's coronet." The "great fair" Curtis referred to was the World's Columbian Exposition, slated for 1893, which had been awarded to Chicago rather than New York. Thomas was expected to be its musical director, although no official announcement had been made.

Two weeks after the Thomas dinner, Carnegie's new hall opened its doors. The temperamental Peter Ilyich Tchaikovsky was there, both to dress up the occasion and to conduct the New York Symphony Society at the grand first concert. Getting Tchaikovsky was a coup for the young Damrosch, who shared the podium with the Russian composer. Episcopalian Bishop Henry C. Potter, the "orator" for the evening, praised the absent Thomas for his contribution to American musical life and Carnegie for making the hall possible. The next day, the newspapers told the world that New York had an impressive hall with excellent acoustics. They were not as kind to Damrosch, complaining that choir and orchestra were badly seated for Berlioz's *Te Deum* and that Damrosch's conducting was poor. (Tchaikovsky reportedly found the performance "wearisome.")[14]

The New York press was generally ill disposed to Damrosch, not only because of his shortcomings as a conductor, but because it was rumored —yet never confirmed—that James G. Blaine, his influential father-in-law, had engineered a government steel contract for Carnegie in exchange for Carnegie money for the Symphony Society and, by extension, the new music hall. Carnegie's devotion to Damrosch remained unshaken, and he not only continued to support his activities but, some ten years later, began giving Damrosch annual gifts of $5,000; Carnegie stipulated in his will that the gifts would continue until Damrosch's death.

Thomas missed the opening, as he had missed the laying of the cornerstone, because his orchestra was playing elsewhere. He returned to New York for the summer and gave forty-two concerts at Madison Square Garden; he was jovial, the programs were light, and the audiences were large and relaxed. He was feted, too, first by the Liederkranz and five days later, after his final concert at the Garden, by the Aschenbrödel Verein, where a large number of symphonic musicians who had played with him since the 1850s paid their respects. Then Thomas shook the dust from his boots and headed for Chicago to begin the final stage of his career.

So many things went wrong during the Chicago Orchestra's first year that, if Thomas and the Orchestral Association had not been so committed, the group would have broken up by the end of the season. The press attacked

Thomas's programming, his conducting, the orchestra's playing, the Auditorium, the season's subscription rates—$30 to $10 for evenings, $20 to $10 for matinees; boxes, which seated five, were $200 for evenings and $150 for matinees—the single-ticket prices, and even the days and times of concerts. An administrative misunderstanding resulted in awkward out-of-town bookings that demoralized both conductor and orchestra. And Chicago's musical public, which had enthusiastically attended Thomas's light summer concerts, was, in great part, reluctant to attend his serious winter programs.

Clearly, Thomas had overestimated his audience. He was eager to put the performance of great music before everything else, and the new orchestra's programs were more suitable for an already mature public than a developing one. Some concerts were too long, with overdoses of heavy and tiresome works by German or German-inspired composers, which might have been acceptable in New York but not Chicago. There were "popular" and "request" programs, but these, although welcome, did not appease those unhappy Chicagoans who felt that Thomas's music was over their heads. Conversely, the light programs annoyed serious listeners, who thought they were either not light enough or too light. The New York Philharmonic under Thomas's leadership had been a musical archive, a performing museum of the great repertoires—particularly German—of the past; this was what its membership and subscribers wanted. The Chicago Orchestra, as Thomas was to learn, was a civic orchestra that had to respond to the wishes of the city as a whole.

The Chicago Auditorium was full on October 17, 1891, for the orchestra's long-awaited first concert, and the applause was generous. Two Thomas staples, Wagner's *Faust* Overture and Beethoven's Fifth, were played before intermission; Tchaikovsky's Piano Concerto no. 1, with Rafael Joseffy as soloist, and Dvořák's dramatic overture *Husitská'* concluded the program. The Beethoven and the Tchaikovsky, both relatively long works, were too much for an opening-night audience that wanted to revel in its new orchestra. Further, local musicians and critics asked why Thomas had brought Joseffy from New York for such a special night rather than inviting one of several first-rank local pianists to be the soloist.[15]

The next week's concert was better received: Bach's Suite in D Major, Schumann's Second Symphony, and Tchaikovsky's Overture to *Hamlet*. Bass Antonio Galassi performed an aria from Gluck's *Paride ed Elena* and excerpts from *Die Walküre*. For the third concert, Thomas did three major works only: Schubert's Unfinished Symphony, Dvořák's Violin Concerto, with concertmaster Max Bendix as soloist, and Saint-Saëns's Third Symphony; many thought it too long and too heavy.

In November, the orchestra's only local concert was at the elegant Germania Club, where Thomas successfully programmed short pieces for the wellheeled German Americans, who then gave him an impressive ornamented baton said to be worth $1,000. In acknowledging the gift, Thomas used the occasion to thank Chicago for fulfilling his lifelong dream, for enabling him to establish an orchestra in which the players could devote themselves to orchestral music and nothing else and for which its leading citizens had committed their support. He also spoke with acumen of New York's active orchestral life: "There never will be any lack of orchestral bodies but quantity cannot be the proper criterion in music any more than in any other art, and quality cannot be obtained unless the means are offered to the artist to live for his art solely." [16]

By spring, whatever "honeymoon" Thomas had with Chicago's critical press and public was over. Attendance at most concerts had been spotty, but the worst was at an all-American program Thomas did for the eighteenth subscription concert on April 2, 1892. The composers represented were John Knowles Paine, George Chadwick, Frederick Grant Gleason, and Harry Rowe Shelley. Thomas learned that, simply put, he must program American compositions throughout the season, rather than bunch them into one special concert (no other American works had been scheduled that year). Later in April, he gave his final Request program, which included Brahms's Third Symphony and other representative works; he was subsequently accused of stuffing the ballot box to get the works he wanted. [17]

Not only Thomas's programs but his conducting came under fire. W. S. B. Mathews, a prominent piano teacher and editor of the Chicago monthly periodical *Music*, wrote that Thomas did not inspire his orchestra sufficiently, that he conducted with too much refinement and attention to detail. Consequently, the ensemble playing was excellent, but his interpretations were "conventional and safe, rather than sensational. His work is characterized by great repose, but also by great reserve." [18] Like most critics, Mathews had been hypnotized by Boston's Nikisch, who had set a new standard for conductors of the time. It was said that Nikisch's orchestras "sang like no others," that he "made the music visible, gave it substance, made it change before our very eyes . . . like someone throwing open a curtain." [19] Thomas was no Nikisch, but surely he was not as dull as Mathews implied. Indeed, six years later, Mathews wrote that when Thomas "conducts a tone poem by Richard Strauss or a symphony by Tschaikowsky, or even the later works of Wagner, . . . there is an impassioned swing in the conductor's beat, and a general air of having been thoroughly waked up, which the classical interpretations successfully conceal." [20]

Thomas had started the Chicago season sanguine, receptive, and cooperative, but when the press began to carp away at him and his new orchestra, he grew sullen and resentful. In March, at wits' end, he was alleged to have said: "In the art of music almost everything that is written for the daily press is rendered of no value on account of either the prejudices or the ignorance of the writers. Hence I rarely read newspaper cuttings about myself or my work, as I find in them nothing that either gives me assistance, knowledge, suggestion or encouragement in my art."[21] Needless to say, such comments were tantamount to waving a red flag in front of a bull, and the press made sure that he paid dearly for his indiscretion.

Thomas exacerbated the situation by refusing to talk about his plans for the 1893 Columbian Exposition. Shortly after his arrival in Chicago, as expected, he had been asked to be the fair's musical director. Once appointed, he was unnecessarily tight-lipped about his plans, which, of course, provoked the press still more. Many already saw him as an overbearing, independent, self-righteous conductor who had been given an orchestra and carte blanche to do as he pleased, yet he programmed concerts that were contrary to the wishes of the general public. Now, Chicago's increasingly notorious yellow press had additional grist for the mill. Had Thomas come to Chicago because of the fair, not the orchestra? Would he ignore Chicago's musicians when choosing fair performers? Would he rule music at the fair as he had ruled it in New York and now in Chicago? Although Thomas had weathered many a storm, it appeared that, contrary to his expectations, Chicago would provide him with the worst one yet.

The practical problem of what to do about the Chicago Auditorium did not go away. That it was too large and encouraged single-ticket sales instead of season subscriptions has already been mentioned. When popular artists were soloists, the hall overflowed; other concerts drew pitifully small audiences, and the city's millionaires, so generous in funding the orchestra, did not care to attend concerts in half-empty halls. The first season ended with a deficit of over $53,000, which the guarantors covered without a whimper.[22]

Thomas's resolve to give Chicagoans his kind of orchestra was supported by his wife in a letter to Frances Glessner, an excellent amateur pianist, who, with her husband, John, a prominent businessman and board member of the Orchestral Association, was to become a close friend of Rose and Theodore Thomas. The Glessners gave frequent musical evenings and post-concert parties at their magnificent house at 1800 Prairie Avenue, designed by the renowned Chicago architect H. H. Richardson. They also advised the Thomases on business matters and introduced them to the White Mountains in New Hampshire, where the Glessners had a handsome summer place. Rose Thomas's letter to Frances Glessner, dated May 3, 1892, is revealing.

> Mr. Thomas is here to establish a great art work, and to make Chicago one of the first musical centers of the world—and not to provide a series of cheap musical entertainments for the riff-raff of the public. The highest forms of art—whether it be in painting, sculpture, architecture, literature, music or any other branch—are not within the comprehension of the masses, they are the delicate blossoms which make the crown and glory of the shrub called

humanity, but which roots and branches and stems can only catch vague glimpses of through parted leaves, and never wholly see. So it is a useless task to attempt to produce the highest form in any art, in such a way that it can be appreciated by the ignorant. All that can be done is to *produce* it, and let it stand till the ignorant acquire a little education and begin to understand it.[23]

What Thomas had accomplished, which, in the end, would mean more to Chicago than first-year sales, was that most of the orchestra's eighty-six players were musicians he had wanted. Twenty-six were local men, the remainder from New York and Europe; from the Philharmonic, he had brought thirteen players, including Joseph Schreurs, the brilliant Belgian clarinetist, William Loewe, a tympanist who had played with Thomas for thirty years, and Henry Sachleben, a cellist and orchestra manager. The Philharmonic had expected a mass exodus of players to Chicago and was relieved when so few left.

Former Thomas Orchestra players who moved to Chicago included Max Bendix, the talented twenty-six-year-old concertmaster, Felix Bour, the Belgian oboist who had been the cause of Thomas's union dispute six years earlier, and Vigo Andersen, one of an eminent family of Danish flutists who had recently emigrated to the United States. Other fine European musicians in principal chairs had either been in the United States a short time or been brought directly from Europe by Thomas: Bruno Steindel, a cellist from the Berlin Philharmonic; Christian Rodenkircher, a trumpeter from Cologne; Hermann Dütsche, a French horn player from the Royal Opera House Orchestra in Munich; and Otto Gebhart, a trombonist from the Imperial Opera House Orchestra in St. Petersburg. Thomas was said to have wanted only "gentlemen" in his orchestra, and the appearance and general deportment of the players certainly drew favorable comments from the start.[24] Even board members, no doubt influenced by Thomas, treated the musicians with rare respect and entertained them lavishly on occasion.

Thomas's musicians were well paid compared to other orchestral players in the United States. A rank-and-file player earned thirty dollars a week for twenty-eight weeks, during which time he was expected to play a maximum of 108 concerts; for each additional concert, he would receive six dollars. Rehearsals were called at the discretion of the director, and players were not paid for them. The Orchestral Association could call a "dark" week during the season when the players would receive nothing, and there was no formal sick pay (that was left up to the director) or paid vacations. Players got board and travel expenses when on tour. Although many taught in Chicago music schools, Thomas ruled on other jobs his men might take during the season: ". . . he will play at no balls, and at no performances of any kind in which the orchestra does not take part, without permission of the director."[25]

The orchestra made slow progress as an ensemble in its first year, due, at least in part, to its schedule of "run-out" concerts in nearby cities. These were usually given early in the week, with the group returning to Chicago on Wednesday or Thursday to prepare hastily for a public rehearsal on Friday and a concert on Saturday. Even then, the concerts in Chicago might have gone better if the programs had been the same as those out of town *and* if the same players had been used. But Thomas traveled with just sixty musicians, mainly his "imports," and added the less-experienced local members for the Chicago concerts, even though they were the ones who needed more experience in ensemble playing. Complaints by Chicago's few responsible critics about the orchestra's deficiencies in this regard were therefore justified. Fortunately, the orchestra's playing improved in the second year, because out-of-town concerts were confined to specific periods and ample rehearsal time was allotted for all concerts. The musicians also worked together in summer concerts under Max Bendix's direction, and as the "imports" and "locals" got to know each other better, any uncomfortable feelings between them gradually disappeared.

For the orchestra's second year, Thomas grudgingly compromised in his programming: six subscription concerts were billed as popular, a substantial increase, and he gave a special working people's concert series. Yet there were still meaty programs: two all-Wagner concerts and one all-Beethoven. Unlike the opening concert of the first season, the second season's was pure gold. The highlight of the evening was the first American performance of Tchaikovsky's *Nutcracker* Suite, which met with unqualified approval (Tchaikovsky was now as popular as Brahms and Dvořák). George Upton of the *Tribune* said that it was "melodious and rhythmic and combined in color and sensuous beauty. . . . Its charm is due generally to the skill displayed in orchestration, odd and bizarre effects being frequently employed."[26]

The soloists were also better chosen in 1892–93. Thomas, who could smell out gifted young artists better than most conductors, had the brilliant Ferruccio Busoni, still in his twenties, as soloist in Beethoven's Piano Concerto no. 4 for the season's third concert. The Italian-German musician was not only a virtuoso performer in the Liszt tradition but an "intellectual" musician whose musical taste was above reproach. Busoni, delighted with Thomas, wrote him later about their work together and of the two happy evenings he had spent socially with Thomas's "marvelous family."[27] (Apart from his several weeks of touring, Thomas was able to lead a relatively normal home life in Chicago during the winter season.) Busoni would meet Thomas later that fall, in Toronto, to do Liszt's Piano Concerto no. 2—without rehearsal.

Another soloist who gave Thomas much satisfaction was Ignacy Jan Paderewski. Considered the successor to the aging Rubinstein as the reigning giant of the piano, Paderewski played with the Chicago Orchestra in its first two seasons. After a matinee concert on March 3, 1893, at which he did his own

Concerto in A Minor—the matinee and the next evening's concert drew the largest houses of the season—John Glessner hosted a party at which the pianist and Thomas ate and drank together with gusto. As musicians are prone to do, the two men gossiped about other musicians. Paderewski, chuckling, told how Walter Damrosch had foolishly beat time without letup while he played a lengthy cadenza with the orchestra. Both men, according to Frances Glessner, then agreed that Hans von Bülow was "not a musician." Thomas reminisced about his first meeting with Ole Bull, who said, "At last two great mountains meet." After dinner, Thomas ceremoniously presented Paderewski with a large cigar wrapped in a gold leaf and declared, "The great Polish prince, the world's pianist, shall smoke that." Paderewski declined: "I shall leave it for King Thomas." Alas, neither Paderewski nor Thomas would bask for long in the triumph of their performances together that spring.[28]

During these first two years of the Chicago Orchestra, Thomas would tour regularly, to Milwaukee, Omaha, Kansas City, St. Paul–Minneapolis, and St. Louis. He also went south sporadically and to the west coast. During a four-day Nashville festival in the spring of 1892, he wrote to his wife of typical travel misfortunes, summer heat, no hotel rooms, and lost baggage, but then recounted happily meeting with "a recent convert of the evangelist Moody," who had evidently seized Thomas's hand at the end of the first concert and asked, "Mr. Thomas, are you a Christian?" Using Rose for refuge, Thomas murmured, "My wife went to church," which seemed to satisfy the man, who said, "I just wanted to make sure that the Lord had some of your kind on his side." The following day, Thomas attended a picnic in his honor at Andrew Jackson's famous residence, the Hermitage. Alas, the same religious zealot was there, asking, "Brother Thomas, will you ask the blessing?" Thomas recounted: "I was so taken aback at this unexpected request to officiate in the role of priest, that I believe I would have said my *Vater unser*, in German, as the nearest approach to a grace that I could command, had not a quick-witted woman extricated me from the dilemma by hastily replying for me, 'I think as we have a descendant of General Jackson here with us today, it would be more appropriate to ask him.' And so it was arranged!"[29]

The Chicago Orchestra closed its second season with a deficit of more than $50,000.[30] Income from the Chicago concerts had risen $10,000 compared to the first season, but proceeds from tour concerts were down. Cancellations of Chicago performances by the Italian Opera Company, which had had its season disrupted by a major fire at the Metropolitan Opera House in New York, caused additional losses—eight weeks of opera were written into the orchestra players' contract, which the association had to pay, work or not. A drive at the beginning of the season to secure 500 associate members, each to contribute $100 annually for the support of the orchestra, was only partially successful: 175 new members. Ticket sales, admittedly better than the first year, had not come up to expectations. Still, the guarantors lived up to their obligations and once again made up the deficit. The Orchestral Association's executive even had a dinner for Thomas on April 14, when it gave him a splendid Norwegian tankard for work well done.

What impact had the orchestra made on Chicago in its first two years? Thomas had given the city orchestral music since before the Great Fire, and his summer concerts and festivals had attracted thousands. Where, in heaven's name, he now wondered, was the public? The orchestra had improved steadily, the programs were chosen more judiciously, and although he was discouraged by the poor reception, he was not yet ready to quit. Thomas conducted the season's final subscription concert, an all-Wagner program, on April 15. Two weeks later the orchestra would play at the opening of the world's fair. In those two weeks, all hell broke loose.

11

Debacle at White City

On April 28, 1890, President Benjamin Harrison signed an Act of Congress "to provide for celebrating the four hundredth anniversary of the discovery of America by Christopher Columbus, by holding an International Exhibition of arts, industries, manufactures and the products of soil, mine and sea in the City of Chicago in the State of Illinois."[1] It would be America's greatest fair to date.

Two American fairs had preceded Chicago's: a small one in New York in 1853, and the Philadelphia Centennial Exhibition in 1876, the success of which led to the World's Columbian Exposition. Since 1876, several major cities had been lobbying to be host, with Chicago the most vocal and persistent. The city had risen dramatically from the ashes of the Great Fire of 1871 to become America's second city and the commercial capital of the Midwest, and it felt that it deserved the honor. Chicago's entrepreneurs—ambitious, resourceful, and ruthless—had made millions from its factories and stockyards and had built its skyscrapers, the Auditorium, museums, schools, and universities. The Windy City was a "microcosm of America," the best and the worst, the exemplification of a raw and burgeoning country. Now it wanted to show the world what it had done.

As early as 1885, Chicago's Interstate Industrial Exposition Corporation, responsible for local fairs at the Exposition Building where Thomas gave his summer concerts, had put forward a strong case with the federal government to host the Columbus commemoration. The corporation's facilities, a good downtown location, and experience in operating large expositions were cited.[2] But the federal government, up until 1888, had not decided whether there would even be a Columbian Exposition, much less where.

The Paris Exposition of 1889, with its magnificent Eiffel Tower and the acclaim it brought France, convinced the United States to proceed with its fair. Members of the press of the two contending cities, New York and Chicago, manned their battle stations to expound on their respective city's virtues while denigrating the opposition. According to the *Chicago Tribune*, New York was not an "American" city, being neither patriotic nor "national," but was the "meanest city" and lacked public spirit; whereas Chicago was a "model" of American progress and industry.[3] The New York papers declared that the Lake Michigan city was a frontier town without traditions and culture and that its being so far from Europe was certain to discourage visitors from the Old World.[4]

In the end, Chicago out-lobbied New York by cultivating its friends in high places and placating its enemies. It maintained that Congress had unduly neglected the West in the past and that Chicago was not as "wild" as easterners claimed. The government in Washington, D.C., needing western votes to stay in power, chose Chicago, which, in turn, promised $10 million to the fair. The decision came too late for an 1892 fair, so the government prudently announced that the fair would be dedicated in October 1892 but would not be open to the public for another six months.

Daniel Burnham (who would become a close friend of Thomas) and his brilliant partner, John Root, were selected to design the exposition. They had been responsible for Chicago skyscrapers like the Rookery (1886) and the Monmadnock Building (1891), which had helped make the city a world leader in commercial urban architecture. The two men, showing rare collegiality, invited a number of important American architects to meetings in Chicago in January 1891 to share ideas and arrive at a plan for the fair's physical layout and general style. Once that was done, architects would be assigned to design specific buildings.[5]

Shortly after the meetings began, Root took ill and died. With him, it seems, went the plan for functional and uncluttered American exhibit buildings. Instead, the group decided upon pseudoclassical, Greek/Roman-style buildings, with a dash of Renaissance thrown in, the antithesis of the best American architecture. Only Louis Sullivan, designer of the Chicago Auditorium, objected—like Root, he felt that Chicago's style expressed America's strength, vitality, and distinctiveness. His design for the Transportation Building was markedly different from other exposition buildings and, ironically, was the only one to win an international architecture prize.[6]

The fairgrounds, a fantasyland of pillared white buildings that resembled ancient Greece more than late nineteenth-century America, was eventually given the sobriquet "White City." The concept was escapist and unreal, pretty, illusory, and genteel, yet formal, academic, and even monumental—the last hypocritical and ambivalent gasp of the Gilded Age. No matter, it was impressive. With special thanks to landscaper Frederick Law Olmsted of Central

Park fame, Burnham made effective use of Jackson Park, 700 acres of re-claimed swampland on the shore of Lake Michigan, eight miles south of downtown Chicago, for the exposition site. Artificial waterways, basins, and lagoons were created, and, in the end, the exposition's harmony, symmetry, order, and sheer grandiosity gave it a sense of occasion that contributed to its ultimate success.

Soon after Thomas first agreed to direct the Chicago Orchestra, the ex-position's executive committee approached him with a firm offer to be its musical director. Between March and May 1891 he mulled it over, the mem-ory of his misfortunes at the centennial celebration fifteen years earlier still fresh in his mind. Although national celebrations would not be the place to perform great music, Thomas's enthusiasm for all things Chicagoan clouded his judgment. Some of the same men who had helped to finance his new orchestra were on the fair's executive committee, and he trusted them, confi-dent that they would do right by him and his players. At meetings to discuss music buildings at the exposition, he was influenced powerfully by Burnham's imagination, drive, and resolve. The committee was prepared to spend up to an impressive half-million dollars on music. All it needed to finalize its plans was Thomas's assent.[7]

Convinced that Chicago would not be another Philadelphia, a sanguine Thomas formally accepted the offer on November 18, 1891. Col. George R. Davis, director-general of the exposition, wrote to the executive committee that Thomas "accepts this position without compensation at the present time, and when it shall be deemed necessary that a salary shall be paid this officer it will be reported to the Board for their approval."[8] This extraordinary com-munication—no pay, approval to come—did not concern Thomas, and he moved ahead, engaging the competent William M. Tomlins, choral director of the Chicago Apollo Musical Club, as his second-in-command and George F. Wilson, editor of Boston's *Musical Herald*, as executive secretary. The triumvirate, called the "Bureau of Music," would report to the exposition's Committee on Liberal Arts, which, in turn, reported to the executive com-mittee of the fair. Ultimate authority for major exposition policy matters was shared between the executive committee, mainly prominent Chicagoans, and a national commission appointed by Congress, to which Davis reported. The administrative structure of the fair was ambiguous at best and would cause Thomas much travail.[9]

Vested with the appropriate authority and Burnham's promise of excellent music buildings, Thomas made the Chicago Orchestra the resident musical group for the fair. The benefits were obvious: it would play together steadily for six months, learning repertoire, improving its ensemble playing, and, at the same time, earning good wages. (The cost was budgeted at $175,000, the bureau's single largest expense.) Augmented to approximately 130 players, the exposition orchestra would give free daily noon-hour concerts of a "popular educative character" and be broken into two groups for free light evening concerts in different parts of the fair.[10] The full orchestra was scheduled to play some special evening concerts of serious music—ultimately, they were given in the afternoon—that would be much like those given by the Chicago Orchestra during its season and for which admission would be charged. There would also be international concerts, with Brahms, Joachim, Tchaikovsky, Massenet, Saint-Saëns, Sir Alexander MacKenzie, Verdi, Mascagni, and Giovanni Sgambati in attendance as observers or performers; other possible invitees included Dvořák, Gounod, Rubinstein, Arthur Sullivan, Hans Richter, and the critic Eduard Hanslick.

With the hundreds of thousands of people expected at the fair, Thomas anticipated no difficulty in attracting audiences for such concerts, and he even believed that the concerts would more than pay the orchestra's costs. That such large-scale plans for serious music at a world's fair would first be realized not in London or Paris or New York but in Chicago spoke well for Thomas's influence on the ruling elite of the Windy City.

Secretary Wilson set out for Europe in March 1892, and when he returned two months later, he had firm commitments from only Saint-Saëns and MacKenzie.[11] Brahms, Joachim, and Rubinstein were honored to be asked but declined because of the long voyage. Verdi said that he was too old but hinted that he might compose a hymn for the fair. Dvořák said that his contract with Jeannette Thurber's National Conservatory, which he would direct, might forbid fair attendance. Wilson was unable to track down Tchaikovsky; Arthur Sullivan was ill. Gounod and Massenet said yes, then no, and so it went. Clearly, Thomas should have gone himself or sent another musician, someone with more persuasive powers than Wilson, a journalist by vocation, to entice the great names of music to Chicago. He had mistakenly thought that his personal invitation to such an important event, borne by his emissary, would suffice. By September, it appeared that music at the exposition would not be very international, and the plans for these concerts were dropped. It was the first of many disappointments Thomas would experience at White City.

Another setback concerned the performance of American music at the fair. Here, Thomas was more directly at fault. The bureau, in its first announcements, had patronizingly declared that American composers "have benefitted by the best foreign association and have returned to us wholesome, elevated and creditable. It is fitting that these men should be honoured at the Exposition." Yet, a year before the fair was to begin, it had done nothing to implement this noble pronouncement. A feeble gesture was made on June 30, 1892, when the bureau invited those American composers who wished to have their works performed at the exposition to submit them by October 15 to a special (as yet unnamed) committee for consideration. The invitation was repeated in September, at which time the committee's membership was named —several leading American musicians plus MacKenzie and Saint-Saëns—and the deadline was moved back a month. The press considered the proposal an insult and asked if European music were judged in similar fashion (which, of course, it was not). In all, twenty-one composers submitted thirty-one works, of which three were ultimately performed. Most American composers of stature ignored the whole process.[12]

Thomas did commission John Knowles Paine and George Chadwick each to write a short piece for the dedicatory ceremonies; and, a few months prior to the fair's opening, he formally invited Paine, Chadwick, Edward MacDowell, Arthur Foote, George Bristow, and Templeton Strong to name works of their own for presentation. These and compositions by Arthur Bird, Charles Converse, Frederick Grant Gleason, Henry Schoenfeld, Harry Rowe Shelley, and Arthur Whiting were, in due course, performed during the exposition. But considering the number of serious and light concerts given in the first three months of the fair—usually two a day—it was a sorry showing for American composers. That there were practically no commissions was scandalous.

The Bureau of Music did better when it came to engaging bands. Thomas was keen on the subject and helped Adolph Liesegang form a Chicago Exposition Band, which, along with Michael Brand's Cincinnati Band, played at White City for the duration of the fair. The bureau also booked the Sousa Band,[13] which would play at the dedicatory services, and the Gilmore, Pullman, and Innes bands for shorter engagements. Foreign bands were invited, but few were able to attend. In the last two months of the fair, other American bands were brought in to fill the many bandstands dotted throughout the grounds.

The exposition was generous to a fault in its grants to music. This was nowhere more evident than in its two music buildings, Music Hall and Festival Hall, which together cost over $230,000. Music Hall, designed by the fair's architect in chief, Charles Atwood, had two auditoria, one seating 2,000 for symphony concerts and the other 600 for smaller recitals and meetings. It was situated next to the Corinthian "Peristyle," which graced the major exposition entrance facing Lake Michigan. Festival Hall seated 4,000, with standing room for 2,000. Designed by Chicago architect Francis M. Whitehouse, it was a circular building modeled after a Greek theater, 250 feet in diameter and adorned on three sides with Doric porticos. The names of notable musicians were inscribed on the exterior borders of both buildings, along with decorative sculptured female figures traditionally associated with music. Notated themes from great musical works were also engraved on the interior supporting arches on the third floor of Music Hall.

For quite inexplicable reasons, Thomas told the press little of his exposition plans. He seems to have deliberately dragged his feet in booking other orchestras—everyone expected the New York Philharmonic, the New York Symphony Society, and the Boston Symphony to be invited—perhaps out of concern that they would outshine his Chicago Orchestra. Walter Damrosch suggested bluntly that Thomas looked down upon other conductors and did not want any of stature at the exposition (he meant Seidl and Nikisch). He contrasted Thomas's behavior with that of Burnham and Root, who had unselfishly brought the best architects from the East to share in planning the fair—which, after all, belonged to the nation, not to Chicago. Damrosch claimed that Thomas singlehandedly controlled the fair's music, and he urged his fellow musicians to protest loudly.[14] Some did, even the usually temperate Anton Seidl.

Finally, in September 1892, while in residence at Fairhaven, Thomas disclosed that he had asked the New York Philharmonic and the Boston Symphony to appear at the exposition. Damrosch, who had assumed that his own New York Symphony Society would be one of the invitees, was infuriated. (Ironically, Damrosch's group played at the exposition after the Philharmonic was unable to find suitable dates.) Later in the month, Thomas quite arrogantly told the *Chicago Tribune* that the country would be pleased with his plans and that the criticisms of Damrosch and others were "pique and jealousy." New York should trust him; his reputation spoke for itself. He claimed to have no time for nasty allegations and accusations made by other musicians.[15]

William Tomlins did better with his responsibilities as second-in-command. He arranged for sixteen western choirs to participate in a three-day massed choral festival as well as each giving a concert on its own. A festival of twenty eastern choirs was also planned, as was a festival to celebrate Bach and Handel. As additional plans took shape, the press and other musicians eased up on Thomas and the Bureau of Music.

It should be mentioned, too, that not all of the fair's musical activities were entrusted to Thomas. Mrs. Potter Palmer, wife of the real estate and hotel magnate and uncrowned queen of Chicago society, had been appointed director of the Board of Lady Managers, a national group of 115 women, to run the Woman's Building. Having a woman in such a senior executive position was extraordinary for the times, and Mrs. Palmer was determined to prove that she was up to it. She had toured Europe the preceding year to obtain exhibits for the Woman's Building, which had been designed by a woman, Sophia G. Hayden. The building would be a center for women's activities in the arts, sciences, and professions, a place where women could discuss issues of concern and give concerts, with works by women composers singled out for inclusion. The board underscored its mission by commissioning the talented twenty-five-year-old Amy Beach to write a *Jubilate* for orchestra and chorus for the building's opening ceremonies. In June, the Recital Hall of the Music Building would be the site of a three-day national convention of thirty-four women's amateur musical clubs, chaired by Rose Thomas. The clubs would take the "opportunity to measure themselves with each other" by giving concerts in the form of "a friendly competition for honors." A jury would be appointed and chaired by Theodore Thomas.[16]

Ceremonies to dedicate the exposition lasted a full week, starting with special church services to commemorate Christopher Columbus. On October 19, Columbus Day, there were celebrations in the local schools and an evening reception and ball at the Chicago Auditorium. A huge parade that brought out the entire city was held the next day. Flags and streamers adorned downtown buildings, and groups from all over the country marched in a colorful procession estimated to be ten miles long.[17] On October 21, an extravagant dedicatory ceremony was held on the fairgrounds in the newly built Hall of Manufacturers and Liberal Arts. The structure, which covered twenty-four acres and was four city blocks long, was reputedly the largest building in the world. (Rose Thomas said that its platform was as large as the entire Metropolitan Opera House.)[18] Thomas's 190-piece orchestra and his largest choir yet—5,700 voices from twenty-four American and eighteen German choral societies—would provide the music. The Sousa Band, a local band, and a drum corps of 50 would add to the festivities as required.

Thomas had rehearsed choir and orchestra a few days before at the Auditorium, where every seat on the floor and the entire stage was used; a dress rehearsal had taken place at the fair on the morning of the actual ceremony. He feared a repetition of the Philadelphia Centennial celebration, and by the end of the dress rehearsal, he knew it would be precisely that: the music he and thousands of others would play and sing would be lost to all but those closest to the platform. With amplification technology still a few years away, the dedication would be a musical fiasco and a portent of worse to come.

The ceremony itself went off fairly well, with close to 150,000 people in attendance. Vice President Levi P. Morton presided; members of the U.S. Supreme Court were there, as was former President Rutherford B. Hayes. The speeches suffered the same fate as the music—they were heard by only a few—and Thomas himself had to communicate with those on the speaker's platform by telephone.

Director-general Davis extolled Chicago as "the greatest city of modern times," and Mrs. Palmer proclaimed that this was a historic moment for American women: "Women can now take their place beside men in endeavors like education, art and industry. . . . Government has just discovered woman."[19] Awards were presented to those who had helped to bring the fair into being, including Thomas, who was too far away to go up and personally accept his plaque. In fact, distances were so great and the din of the crowd was so loud that Thomas had to get the attention of his musical forces with lengthy rolls on the snare drums, and he cued the orchestra and chorus entries by waving a handkerchief. Paine's and Chadwick's works attracted little attention; as at Philadelphia, the "Hallelujah Chorus" was the hit of the program. Following the speeches, 7,000 people were invited to a free lunch, which turned into something of a brawl as they fought to reach the food tables.

And so the world's fair was dedicated in much the same way as the centennial celebration had been, with hullabaloo, good and bad addresses, and inaudible music. Would the Columbian Exposition be just another large and expensive fair, or would it be indicative of the progress of a great nation? Of greater concern was whether the fair would indeed be ready. Burnham's White City was rising from Lake Michigan's mud, but with only six months left until it was open to the public, it still seemed a long way from completion.

With the dedication over, the Bureau of Music moved quickly to complete its scheduling of concerts before the May opening. Understandably, Thomas was concerned about the public response to the music he was planning. Were there too many serious concerts, too many costly events? Was the fair an appropriate place to continue his lifelong campaign to bring great music to the people? He worried, too, about Davis, who meddled in bureau business even though the bureau was technically responsible to the liberal arts committee, not to the national commission, which he headed.[20]

The big day approached, and reports from Jackson Park were discouraging. Although Burnham had pushed his workers to their limit, not all the exposition buildings, including Festival Hall, would be completed in time. Construction had been slowed by an unusually severe winter, and in the rush to finish the job, the exteriors of the buildings were being faced with flimsy white stucco, provoking the architectural critic Russell Sturgis to call it "schoolboy work . . . the adoption of what was easiest and quickest done," another manifestation of America's ongoing conflict between sheen and substance, between the material and the artistic.[21]

Nowhere was this conflict more evident than in the wretched "piano war," in which certain exposition officials sided with western piano makers and, aided by Chicago's infamous yellow press, viciously attacked Thomas's integrity and provided an open season for Thomas-haters from mid-April until August. Periodicals with long-standing grudges and professional musicians who, at one time or another, had suffered rebuffs or worse from the old warrior, fanned the flames that engulfed Thomas just as he was about to embark on what he had hoped would be one of his greatest achievements. The piano war shattered him like nothing else in his long career, damaged music at the fair, and was a sorry commentary on the ethics of the fair's officials and members of the piano-making industry.

What was this piano war all about? American piano production had expanded enormously after 1890. Over 100 American manufacturers vied for a major place in the market, and, although eastern companies led the field, a number of western firms were becoming increasingly competitive. The Columbian Exposition would be an important advertising outlet for piano firms, as their exhibits were to be attractively housed at the huge Manufacturers' Building. Eastern piano makers felt that from the beginning the fair had assigned the most advantageous exhibit spaces to its western rivals,[22] and thus, on February 1, 1893, New York's Chickering Company canceled its exposition exhibit. On February 11, Steinway followed suit, but not without donating $20,000 to the exposition and $5,000 to the city of Chicago, recompense for any inconvenience its withdrawal might have caused.[23] The latter pleaded insufficient exhibit space and, more significant, indicated its disapproval of the exposition's piano manufacturers' competition, which proposed to select the best instrument from among those exhibited (all exhibitors were expected to compete). Steinway's cancellation letter reminded fair authorities: "Some time ago 90 percent of the piano manufacturers in this country sent a petition to the managers of the Exposition asking that no awards at all be made." The petition and the reminder were ignored.

Sixteen eastern firms followed Chickering and Steinway and withdrew their exhibits. The western companies, including Chicago's Kimball Piano Company, were upset and asked Davis to urge the easterners to reconsider. When they refused, Davis suggested that they be allowed to exhibit without competing, which the western companies found unacceptable. It would be a hollow victory indeed for a western firm to win a competition without the participation of prominent eastern firms. But the fairness of the competition was called into question when it was learned that Dr. Florenz Ziegfeld, director of the Chicago Musical College, would be the sole judge and that W. W. Kimball, president of the Kimball Piano Company, was a member of the board of directors of Ziegfeld's school. Davis nevertheless insisted on continuing with the competition, and when he heard that some eastern piano companies planned to exhibit in their own state buildings rather than in the Manufacturers' Building, he decreed that they must exhibit in the Manufacturers' Building and compete or not exhibit at all. John Thacher, director of the competition, unabashedly declared that easterners wanted to avoid competing with western piano makers because they knew that the westerners made cheaper and better pianos.[24]

Failing to sway the eastern companies as a group, Davis proceeded to promise Steinway's preferred exhibit space to Chickering, and he approached other eastern manufacturers with similar offers. Again he was unsuccessful.

The western companies next persuaded Davis to invoke the regulation that only pianos made by exhibiting companies could be played at the exposition, and at this point the fair's musical director entered the fray. Thomas obviously believed that exhibiting pianos commercially had nothing to do with artists selecting pianos for concerts. It was an unwritten law, even in the highly competitive piano world of the 1890s, that musicians would play on instruments of their choice. He had already booked a number of pianists who, he knew, preferred instruments that the exposition would ban if it implemented its exclusion policy. Thomas protested to Davis, who ignored him. Serious trouble was imminent. Matters came to a head over Paderewski and his role at the exposition.

Ignacy Jan Paderewski, a star pupil of the great Leschetizky, was, at thirty-two, already the most sought-after pianist alive. An expressive and brilliant player, he was also personally attractive, the closest thing to a matinee idol in the musical world of the time. The Steinway Company had sponsored his first American tour in 1891, as it had Rubinstein's almost two decades earlier, both of them successful. When Paderewski played with Thomas and the Chicago Orchestra in March 1893 for the second season in a row, Thomas invited him to be soloist at the exposition's first two concerts. Not only did Paderewski agree, but he insisted on playing for no fee (he usually got upwards of $5,000 per concert). This largesse was his way of thanking the United States for the warm reception it had given him, to contribute something to an American fair of historic importance, and to enhance the work of one of his favorite conductors. The two men sealed the engagement with a handshake; no formal agreement was deemed necessary.[25]

Paderewski played a Steinway piano, but, unlike Rubinstein, he was not under contract to play it exclusively. Rather, he had a gentleman's agreement, an *Übereinkommen*, with Steinway not to use or endorse any other piano while in North America. Although he never mentioned this—he claimed that he played a Steinway for artistic reasons only—he had no intention of breaking the agreement.[26] Unfortunately, Davis was determined to enforce his ill-conceived policy, even if it led to cancellation of Paderewski's generously donated performance at the fair's first concert.

Soon the press got wind of the dispute and blew it out of proportion. Leading the pack were the *Chicago Herald* and the *Evening Post*, both owned by the same publisher, one of whose most influential backers was the Lyon & Healy Music Company, which did not sell Steinways. The two papers, in front-page stories, reported that Thomas preferred Steinways because he was an old friend of William Steinway, who had helped Thomas financially early in his career.[27] They accused the musical director of conspiring to get Steinway pianos onto the fairgrounds despite regulations to the contrary, which was disloyal to Chicago, to its industries, to its people, and to its exposition.

Toward the end of April, Davis created a special investigating committee to review the matter, deliberately bypassing the local executive committee, which totally disapproved of his policy. The investigating committee demanded that Thomas explain his position, which he refused to do, saying that he reported to the executive committee only. As a result, the investigating committee supported Davis and threatened to remove any unauthorized instrument from the fairgrounds "at the point of a bayonet if necessary."[28] The executive committee, which was committed to the Paderewski concerts, executed a series of ingenious bureaucratic maneuvers to delay Davis's national commission from acting before opening day, when it would be distracted by the formal ceremonies and related events. Meanwhile, Burnham got his workers to move Paderewski's Steinway onto the fairgrounds in the dead of night and left instructions that it was not to be removed without his approval. Once the national commission learned what was going on, it was too late to stop Paderewski from playing on his Steinway.

Ensconced with cook, valet, and servants in his private railway car just outside Jackson Park, Paderewski was clearly stunned by the entire affair. He had had an arduous season and had made a special trip from New York at his own expense to be at the exposition. Although one of his fingers had become infected, and he half-froze in the unheated and damp Music Hall, Paderewski played his own concerto as scheduled at the first concert, and Schumann's Concerto on the second night. It was a dreary experience and left him too exhausted to play his next engagement—an Actors Fund Benefit Concert in New York. Years later, he said, "It took all the energy and skill and tact of Theodore Thomas and all his friends to obtain the agreement of the committee to my playing on a Steinway piano."[29] If he had only known the half of it.

Thomas's troubles were only beginning, for the piano war was to spread to harps. Miss A. Breitschuk, a section harpist in the exposition orchestra, had written to the Lyon & Healy Company: "This morning [May 1] Theodore Thomas gave us notice that he would not allow us to play Lyon & Healy harps at the fair. With the harp I myself was delighted which you so kindly sent to my disposition, but, as you know, yourself, we must do what Theodore Thomas wants."[30] If this were true, it meant that Thomas was being selective in practicing what he preached, that the great Paderewski could do as he wished but not an ordinary harpist from Chicago. The national commission wasted no time in releasing Breitschuk's letter to the press and appointing a committee of six to investigate this attack on yet another of its loyal exhibitors.

Thomas was at breakfast with the executive committee on May 8 when he received a summons to appear before the committee to speak to "alleged abuses in the music department detrimental to the welfare of the World's Columbian Exposition." The *Herald* reported that "[Thomas's] lips curled ironically as he gave his assent." Edmund Schuecker, principal harpist of the Chicago Orchestra, and Breitschuk would also be present.[31]

Thomas treated the committee contemptuously at its meeting that afternoon, where it was revealed that all the harpists in Thomas's orchestra preferred the Érard, a French instrument, and that its North American agent was none other than the Chicago agent for Steinway—Lyon, Potter. As for the allegation of favoritism, it seems that Lyon & Healy had approached Schuecker in 1891, asking him to endorse its harps in exchange for a free instrument and a 10-percent commission on every Lyon & Healy harp he sold to his pupils. Schuecker agreed to the plan. However, in the fall of 1892, after one of his pupils bought a Lyon & Healy harp, the company refused to pay Schuecker, claiming that the student had planned to buy the harp before the commission deal had been made. Schuecker canceled his endorsement, and Lyon & Healy retaliated by having a sheriff seize the harp that it had given him. Schuecker now made it clear that Thomas had never dictated what harp he should use, and Breitschuk also changed her story and said that it was Schuecker, not Thomas, who had told her not to use a Lyon & Healy harp.

A vengeful *Herald* reporter pulled out all of the stops on May 11, declaring that Thomas "should have been the leader of a barrack band in a mountainous camp in North Germany," that he was "a small despot by nature; a dull and self opinionated man . . . a constitutional want of generosity . . . and a thrift that has looked out for himself no matter who suffered in consequence. . . . He is rough-shod; that with hood of hussar he tries to ride down all that is opposed to his vanity, his selfishness and his caprices."[32] Gathering strength from the press, the national commission demanded Thomas's resignation. Commissioner P. H. Lannon of Utah, chairman of the investigating committee, pleaded ignorance "of the divine art or the qualities that go to make a good musical conductor. I know, however, when I am sat upon and defied. The commission is authorized by Congress to deal justly with the exhibitors who are displaying their wares here and I insist that they shall be treated justly. . . . It was necessary to call [Mr. Thomas] down from his pedestal. . . . He refused to obey our orders and we adopted the only course open to us—that of getting a man who would obey."[33] J. R. Higginbotham, chairman of the executive committee, said firmly, "They will have a sweet time getting it [the resignation]."[34] Thomas ignored the demand, and the commission did not repeat it.

But what damage had been done! Music critic Mathews told the commission that the imbroglio had discredited the United States in the eyes of other nations, that "our cultivation [is] only skin deep. . . . The treatment of Mr. Paderewski is a disgrace to America and the city of Chicago." Musicians from everywhere rose to Thomas's defense, and the New York newspapers attacked the "yahoo" Chicago press. *Freund's* reminded its readers of Thomas's "glorious record" and said that cries for his resignation were "insane."[35]

There were other problems as well. Music Hall, which seemed so promising in the construction stage, was an acoustical disaster, an echo chamber beyond belief; drapes were hung and rugs were laid, to no avail. Thomas, still recovering from the piano war and the national commission's harassment, could not hide his disappointment and was promptly labeled an ingrate by fair officials. To make matters worse, May's weather was poor, with fierce winds from Lake Michigan chilling performers and spectators alike in the unheated hall. Paderewski had drawn poor houses, and it would be the same for the rest of the month, indeed, for nearly all of the serious concerts for the next three months.

From the outset, the exposition orchestra's free noon-hour light concerts played to packed houses of 3,000 or more, while the more serious admission concerts played to only a few hundred. Obviously, the public would not pay for orchestral concerts if free ones were available; nor was it interested in hearing symphonies by Beethoven on warm summer afternoons. In addition, band concerts lured music lovers away from orchestral concerts. The Boston Symphony and the New York Symphony each gave two concerts in May, with the box-office receipts for all four totaling $964; the Kneisel Quartet's three concerts at the Recital Hall grossed $83.[36]

Thomas had another setback, a comparatively minor one, but vexing nonetheless. He had assembled a magnificent exposition orchestra, the Chicago Orchestra augmented by some thirty hand-picked players from other cities and abroad, but in doing so he had imported musicians without union permission. On May 11, in the midst of the commission's inquiry, Thomas was formally censured by the Federation of Musicians at its national convention in Milwaukee.[37]

Festival Hall opened on May 22 with an all-Wagner program. Acoustically, the space was an improvement over Music Hall, but, even with Amalie Materna as soloist, the chorus and orchestra outnumbered the audience. The small houses continued for the three choral events led by William Tomlins. A nationwide financial panic that had begun in May cast a pall over the land, and with hundreds of thousands of Americans losing their jobs, many who had planned trips to Chicago in the spring now had to cancel them. As attendance sagged and the summer dragged on, Thomas asked himself if he had unwittingly taken advantage of the well-meaning executive committee. Almost half a million dollars for two halls and an orchestra seemed to have gone down the drain. Should he not have known better, advised the committee more wisely? Had his experience as a professional musician for over forty years taught him nothing? The total income from the thirty-two admission concerts from May through July was $15,135; fair officials had expected to gross ten times that amount.

Davis and the national commission had anticipated the concert attendance problem as early as the second week of May and demanded Thomas's resignation—for this reason as much as for his defiance of their authority. The commission's principal targets were Thomas's and the musicians' salaries. At the end of July, the executive committee, which had been consistently loyal to Thomas, stepped in and proposed cutting the music program's costs, to which Thomas grudgingly agreed. Concerned that the committee might terminate the musicians' contracts immediately, he suggested a compromise: that the orchestra give concerts only until September 1, rather than October 30, thus giving members time to make new plans as well as one more month of income. While the committee was considering this proposal, Thomas took it to the players, who turned it down, insisting that fair officials live up to the original contract. Normally, Thomas would have agreed with them, but how could he fight the very people who had given him all he wanted for music at the fair and shielded him from the national commission's attacks in April and May? (Several committee members were also among the fifty Chicago Orchestral Association guarantors.) The committee countered by proposing that the orchestra work for a percentage of the box office rather than for salaries, but Thomas would have none of that.

Exhausted physically, mentally, and emotionally, Thomas resigned at the beginning of August. He recommended that "for the remainder of the Fair music shall not figure as an art at all, but be treated merely on the basis of an amusement. More of this class of music is undoubtedly needed . . . , and the cheapest way . . . is to divide our two fine bands into four . . . for open-air concerts, and our Exposition orchestra into two . . . , which can play such light selections as will please the shifting crowds . . . and amuse them."[38] It was a melancholy but realistic assessment of the fair's musical needs and quite prophetic, for future American fairs would use music in just that way.

Thomas said nothing publicly to reveal how sick at heart he was, but those in the press who held him in high esteem did it for him. The *Chicago Tribune* pointed a finger at Davis, who, it said, had affronted Thomas and had, on two separate occasions, held back his salary. The *Mail* reported that Thomas was "sick of Chicago" and would return to New York, being "thoroughly dissatisfied with his treatment here. . . . The readiness with which his resignation was accepted has not added to his good opinion of the city." The *New York Times* used his resignation to urge that "those who were saddened and aggrieved by

Mr. Thomas' departure from New York . . . take steps to bring him back again so soon as his Chicago contract expires, and to establish, once and for all, the permanent orchestra which New York so urgently needs." [39]

Fair attendance spurted a few days after Thomas's departure, and by the end of August, it looked as if Americans would attend the World's Columbian Exposition, hard times or not. Most of those who went were thrilled and urged others to see the fair. White City, a capsule version of the make-believe America that people loved, or at least thought they did, triumphed in the end —as a fair should, it entertained and amused. The American writer Hamlin Garland said that it should not be missed. Henry Adams thought it chaotic, "a Babel of loose and ill-joined . . . vague and ill-defined and unrelated thoughts and half-thoughts and experimental outcries." [40] Taking the middle ground, one could say that the fair had something for everyone, that it marked the end of an era and the beginning of a new one, that the Gilded Age, as expressed in the fair's chintzy white exhibit buildings, was over, and that America's march into the twentieth century—the fabulous Midway, with its unbridled spirit, as an example—had begun. It was at the Midway that Scott Joplin, the black pianist, played a new kind of music called "ragtime," the most "American" music at the fair.

In mid-August, the executive committee wired Thomas at Fairhaven and asked him to return to his post, as did the exposition orchestra. [41] But Thomas, ill with a bronchitis that he had contracted earlier in the summer and that was fast becoming chronic, had not recovered from the insults he had received from Davis and others. His exposition plan, stated so grandiloquently, had been to give "for the first time in the history of the world a perfect and complete exhibition of the Musical Art in all its branches." He had tried to do this, but Americans neither wanted it nor were ready for it. His disappointment was great and led to a loss in self-confidence, even will. Thomas could not again face Davis, the national commission, the press, or the fair. For the first time, he decided not to do battle. He had his permanent Chicago Orchestra; it was enough.

Thomas wired his refusal to the committee the next day. [42] Then he wrote to the orchestra:

> When asked to resign . . . last May I did not do so because the orchestra needed my protection. In August when the financial crisis came . . . I could not protect the orchestra any more. . . . The members were not willing to listen to any compromise. I resigned my position. Now you must not blame me if I do not care to make a third attempt to continue as conductor of the Exposition Orchestra. . . . I intend to return to Chicago in November, to

carry out the remainder of my contract with the Chicago Orchestral Association, when I hope to meet you all again. With love to you all and best wishes for your prosperity.[43]

Concertmaster Max Bendix too eagerly took over the orchestra, marking the beginning of Thomas's antagonism toward him. Thomas thought of Bendix as the ringleader of the "malcontents" who had disagreed with his compromise proposal in August.[44] Under its new conductor, the orchestra played light music, charged low admission prices, and attracted small audiences. It also devised a cooperative plan with the exposition management, along the lines proposed to Thomas, that enabled it to function until September, when it disbanded.

The executive committee and the Chicago Orchestral Association both regretted the pain Thomas had endured that summer and wrote him a joint letter at the end of August to reaffirm their support for his work at the fair and to commend him for his honesty in the piano war.[45] They even praised his thrift, noting that the orchestral players had been engaged for 40 percent less than normal and the local bandsmen at minimum fees. (Thomas had paid the exposition players on a per service basis, the fairest way considering their heavy schedule; however, their total fees were between $70 and $150 per week, far more than orchestral players usually earned—hence the accusations that he was milking the fair for the sake of his orchestra.) Thomas's fees added up to $6,000 for his directing duties—not unreasonable—and $4,000 for the use of his library. (The *American Art Journal* had reported $12,000 and $8,000 respectively.)[46] So much for alleged extravagances and greed, about which the *Herald* and the *Evening Post* made so much capital. As for his "serious music" policy, his supporters wrote that to maintain such an orchestra in order to play popular music only "would be as ill-advised as to purchase a Krupp gun for shooting sparrows."

The letter, which was publicized widely, helped to restore the public's faith in Thomas, but he, personally, had been damaged irreparably. Rose Thomas later wrote: "He was growing old now, and the many hardships and disappointments of life had left their mark and taken away from him the buoyant, indomitable spirit with which he had hitherto faced the world. . . . He was never afterwards the man he had been before. His courage was gone, and for the rest of his life he would drop into despondency and be ready to give up at any little untoward happening."[47] C. E. Russell believed that Thomas was never able to shake the memory of the fair:

> Thomas had neither the strange egotism that sustains some public men in great crises nor the cynical philosophy that enables others to shed troubles as a mantle sheds rain. Always after this experience he showed the usual countenance of composure and self-command. To his friends and his family

he was not less genial, kindly, self-effacing and entertaining. He laughed and joked as before. But there was now perceptible an undercurrent of melancholy . . . a touch of bitterness. . . . For a time his mental state affected his work. He was still the great conductor after that fiery ordeal, still the conscientious artist, giving to the interpretation of great works all of his best of insight and devotion. But the old masterly confidence and spiritual serenity were gone, and I think with them went much of the joy in his art.[48]

The World's Columbian Exposition, like the Centennial, the Cincinnati College of Music, the American Opera Company, and his failure to found a permanent orchestra in New York, was one of the great disappointments of Thomas's life. Not only had he suffered personal abuse, but he now saw clearly that the music he thought was important was still alien to most Americans. There was much to be done to fulfill his self-appointed mission, and as those closest to Thomas observed, he feared he might not be up to it.

James Ellsworth, chairman of the exposition's liberal arts committee and an unswerving supporter of Thomas and the Chicago Orchestra, received the auditor's report on the Bureau of Music in October. As expected, the report noted a significant loss, some $220,932. Ellsworth declared that the word "loss" was not applicable since one of the purposes of the fair was the "exemplification" of music as an art: "The result will justify it as much and more than the dollars and cents. . . . [I am] thankful indeed that during a period of three months at least music received the recognition that it more than deserved."[49] Ellsworth also took the opportunity to thank Thomas eloquently for his work.

Good music at the fair, although an honorable failure, had aided the cause of good music generally. Thousands of amateur and professional musicians, music teachers, and choristers from all parts of the continent had met and shared musical experiences and ideas through hearing and participating in the works of Bach, Handel, Beethoven, and other greats, and they returned to their communities with renewed spirit and zeal. American concert bands, encouraged as they were by the public, reached new standards of excellence. Although no substitute for orchestras, at least in some music lovers' minds, these bands did bring light music and transcriptions of the classics to audiences where orchestras were as yet nonexistent. Young American artists also benefited from performing at recitals to small but critical audiences at other fair sites throughout the summer.

By the time the fair closed on October 30, over twenty-seven million people—almost three times more than for the Philadelphia exposition—had paid to see its 65,000 exhibits. Gross receipts totaled almost thirty million dollars, again far surpassing the centennial celebration.[50] Little remained of White City by 1894, but Americans basked in its glory for years to come. As for the exposition's music buildings, the ill-fated Music Hall burned down soon after the fair, and Festival Hall was demolished later in the year.

In truth, a younger man not involved in developing a new orchestra and not fatigued by the rigors of promoting good music in North America for so long would have been more appropriate than Thomas as the exposition's musical director. The Orchestral Association had given him the opportunity to leave an indelible mark on Chicago's—and the country's—musical life, in itself a considerable challenge. It was unfortunate that Thomas had succumbed to the lure of the fair, and even more unfortunate that he had to pay such a heavy price because of it.

Theodore Thomas in his Chicago study, circa 1897. The desk is at Orchestra Hall and still in use. (Courtesy of the Newberry Library)

Charles Norman Fay, without whose help the Chicago Orchestra might never have been started. (Courtesy of the Newberry Library)

Rose Fay Thomas, second wife of Theodore Thomas. (Courtesy of the Newberry Library)

Members of the Chicago Orchestra, 1895. (Courtesy of the Chicago Symphony Orchestra)

An informal snapshot of Thomas, circa 1903. (Courtesy of the Newberry Library)

AN APPROPRIATE COMPOSITION FOR THEODORE THOMAS TO PLAY AT PRESENT.

A cartoon from the *Chicago Tribune*, March 5, 1904, reacting to an announcement by the Orchestral Association that $650,000 had been raised to build Orchestra Hall. (Courtesy of the Newberry Library)

Orchestra Hall, circa 1925. (Courtesy of the Chicago Symphony Orchestra)

THEODORE THOMAS

A bronze relief of Theodore Thomas by Chicago artist George Piper, completed shortly before Thomas's death. (Courtesy of the Chicago Symphony Orchestra)

12

Mission Accomplished

The calm, familiar surroundings and clear sea air at Fairhaven made Chicago seem far away indeed. In nearby Boston, Arthur Nikisch, although admired by his orchestra and the public, was locked in battle with the city's music critics. An impressive group, they were conservative in outlook and disliked the brilliant conductor's personal (in their view) interpretations of the classics; they wanted Haydn, Mozart, Beethoven, Schubert, and Brahms presented conventionally, as Gericke, and before him Thomas, had done. The Boston press also complained that the orchestra was not the disciplined group it had been under Gericke, which was probably true.[1] Using a contractual dispute with Henry Lee Higginson as a pretext, Nikisch left Boston for Europe, not to return to the United States for almost twenty years.

And so, while Thomas was licking his wounds at Fairhaven, Higginson invited him to take over the Boston Symphony, a truly tempting offer.[2] The orchestra was unquestionably the best in the United States, its programs were as rigorous and uncompromising as the New York Philharmonic's, and it played to equally mature audiences. Most important, it was a *permanent* orchestra with well-paid players and no musicians' union with which to contend. Boston had other attractions for Thomas: its proximity to Fairhaven, its historic setting, its cultivated life-style, and the composer friends he had there —Paine, Chadwick, Foote, and Horatio Parker—with whom he spent many happy hours at St. Botolph Club, a gathering place for people in the arts. As if that were not enough, his wife's family had roots in New England (although most of the Fays had moved to Chicago). Like her husband, Rose Thomas felt at home in Boston and found its winters, while not the most congenial, still less trying than Chicago's. Thomas blamed Chicago for the rheumatism in his right arm, which was affecting his conducting, and for his chronic bronchitis. (He was also growing bald, needed glasses, and felt his physical powers —renowned in the musical world—waning in general, even though he was not yet sixty.)[3] If he had but a few years left, he preferred to spend them in Boston rather than Chicago.

Another reason not to return to Chicago was the press. Thomas dreaded facing the *Evening Post* and the *Herald,* which would probably shower new abuse on him and with which he doubted he had the strength to cope. Chicago had also been jolted by the economic depression, probably more so than any other American city because of the thousands who had gone there to work at the fair and were now jobless and homeless, many of them camping out in the crumbling exhibition buildings. Would Chicago's music lovers want to attend concerts in such times? Would they have the money to do so? Thomas feared that if he returned, he would have to compromise his programming still more to bring in large audiences. The coming season was the third and final one for the Orchestral Association's fifty guarantors, and no one seemed to know whether or not they would renew their support after May 1894.

In the end, however, Thomas said no to Boston. Rose Thomas wrote, eighteen years later: ". . . when he thought of his Chicago friends, of the large sums of money they had already given, the hard work they had done, their earnest desire to create a truly great musical institution . . . and [that they had] given him the means to restore his art, when his career had seemed ruined beyond all hope of recovery, he knew that . . . he could not honorably leave them until the Chicago Orchestra was either established or abandoned."[4] A disappointed Higginson, after trying to get Hans Richter, engaged the German conductor Emil Paur, who had succeeded Nikisch at Leipzig when the latter had gone to Boston. Paur liked the orchestra, but the players were slow to reciprocate; and his conducting seemed pallid after Nikisch's.[5]

Fortuitously, the start of the Chicago Orchestra's third season had been delayed until November 25, which gave Thomas time both to prepare for it and to recuperate from the arduous summer which had so drained him. He renewed his commitment to serious programming at Chicago, for he had not gone there to give pop concerts, nor had the association expected him to. The 1893–94 season would be the final test.

To everyone's surprise, the press welcomed Thomas back to Chicago and spent the entire season praising his conducting skill and his untiring efforts to bring great music to Americans. Hoping to capitalize on the press's positive mood, Thomas wrote a lengthy piece for the *Tribune* about the orchestra's financial difficulties and why Chicagoans, if they had any civic pride at all, must support their orchestra. (For the next three generations, other American orchestras would follow Chicago's example and routinely use civic pride to garner support from townspeople.) He said again, as he had in the past, that a city needed cultural institutions like a symphony orchestra, and in Chicago's case, he wished to see the level of support increase:

> I have not yet heard one murmur of discontent . . . from anyone who has given liberally in either money or time toward the support of this institution. [The] Chicago spirit . . . had created . . . the Art Institute, the Chicago University, the World's Fair and the Field Columbian Museum, and which thinks only of establishing something ennobling and refining in our great Western metropolis, to temper the influences of the daily struggle of life and to lighten its sordid cares. . . . Such a spirit does not seek to cramp its artistic standards within the limits of the means provided, but rather to enlarge the means to meet the requirements of the standards.[6]

Thomas went on to explain that Chicago was too far from other large centers for his orchestra to do profitable run-out concerts, and extensive tours lost money because the orchestra's travel, hotel, and meal costs were high. Chicagoans therefore had to "bear the whole burden alone," support of the arts being a duty, not a pleasure.

Barely a week later, Charles Norman Fay, discouraged with the persistently poor houses at the Chicago Auditorium, wrote to Charles L. Hutchinson, a wealthy Chicagoan who reportedly gave away half of his income each year to the arts. Fay suggested drastic changes in the orchestra's operation if the association agreed to an 1894–95 season: to increase the number of weekly concerts, to give concerts on Sundays, to move the concerts from the Auditorium to the much smaller Central Music Hall, and to reduce the orchestra from eighty-three to sixty-nine players.[7] No mention was made of Thomas's limited use of soloists, especially those in the "name" category, who would have attracted large audiences.[8]

In March 1894, members of the Orchestral Association, increasingly pessimistic about the orchestra's future, read in the *New York Daily Tribune* that a plan was afoot to "induce" Thomas to return to New York, which he was willing to do if the conditions were right. Thomas had not yet signed his contract with the Chicago Orchestra for the next year,[9] but he squelched all speculation by stating that under no circumstances would he leave Chicago. "People there have too many claims on me," he told a reporter. "While New York people are most liberal in their offers, do not think Chicago people any less so. I have had every privilege accorded me and I have been given great freedom of action."[10] Privately, Thomas doubted New York's sincerity, based on its lack of support in the past, and he feared the reception he might get there because of his bitter parting words about the great city's musical life. Perhaps as important, he felt that the local critics loved only Seidl, and he was not interested in being second best.

The topic surfaced again—and the outcome was the same—when a committee of New Yorkers traveled to Cincinnati for the May Festival with the avowed intention of convincing Thomas to return to the Empire City *with* the Chicago Orchestra.[11] It was not a good time to (re)propose new schemes, for Thomas's position at the festival was being threatened by the newly formed Cincinnati Symphony Orchestra, which had been incorporated in April and, as the city's resident orchestra, was expected to play at the festival.[12] He need not have worried, however, for his performances were so impressive that the Cincinnati Music Festival Association said categorically in its annual report that Thomas and his orchestra—the Chicago Orchestra—and no other would play at future festivals.[13]

An important reason behind Thomas's growing enthusiasm for Chicago, despite its poor concert attendance and economic difficulties, was its cultural and educational development. In 1892, the University of Chicago, located just north of the exposition grounds, had opened its doors to some 600 undergraduate and graduate students. The university owed its existence to enormous subventions from John D. Rockefeller, who chose as its first president his friend William Rainey Harper, a brilliant biblical scholar. Commenting that "a college teaches; but a university teaches—and also learns," Harper hired a faculty of 120, including 9 former university presidents, gave all of them generous salaries, and kept their teaching loads to a minimum so that they had time for research.[14] The university quickly became a leader in the humanities, in the natural and social sciences, and, led by John Dewey, in the study of education. Its role in community life was also not neglected: it established a junior college and gave extension courses for adults.

As for music, in May 1894, John J. Glessner asked Harper to find a way to "make a musical department in the university and call Theodore Thomas to take charge of it."[15] It was a casual proposal: Glessner did not understand what a university music department connoted and had not carefully thought out what role Thomas would play in it, other than that he supposed Thomas could lead a university chorus. If Harper was interested in engaging Thomas, Glessner promised to contribute $1,000 annually for three years toward his salary. Nothing came of the scheme, but Harper would return to it a few years later, for what was a great university without an equally great music school led by one of America's foremost musicians?

Also in the spring of 1894, Thomas, who had much respect for women and their ability to get things done, welcomed the appointment of the bright and energetic Anna Millar to direct the coming orchestra season's subscription campaign. Millar established the Fund for the Support of the Orchestra and ran an unusual subscription sales campaign, enticing potential subscribers to pledge in the spring and summer but not pay until October—one of the first "buy now, pay later" schemes used by a cultural organization. Unfortunately, many Chicagoans were in no mood for ticket buying, thanks to the Pullman strike, which had tied up the railroads and led to federal troops being called in, despite Illinois Governor Altgeld's objections. But Millar shamelessly cajoled potential customers until, by the end of the summer, she had 30,000 pledges, only 10,000 of which were ultimately honored.[16]

Thomas spent the summer at Fairhaven, where he engaged in an unpleasant exchange of letters with concertmaster Max Bendix. Although Thomas had always allowed himself the last word, he prided himself on his player relations and the fact that he paid the best salaries in the profession. Like most benevolent despots, he resented subjects who were dissatisfied with him or his organization, who grieved, no matter what the cause. He was the typical self-righteous, autocratic conductor, the first of a long line that would include Toscanini, Koussevitsky, Stokowski, Reiner, and Szell. (Only in the United States did conductors—and, by extension, supporting boards—have such power, despite frequent intervention by local musicians' unions. The situation continued until the third quarter of the twentieth century, and some say it is still the case.)

Bendix had disagreed with Thomas as to the course to be taken by the orchestra for the Columbian Exposition once the executive committee had terminated its contract with the group in August 1893. During his next season with the Chicago Orchestra, Bendix had been tardy at rehearsals, had even missed several, and had been, according to Thomas, a careless concertmaster. Thomas had known the violinist since his youth at the Cincinnati College of Music and had grown to dislike him because of his brashness and conceit; he preferred that Bendix not play solos or conduct the orchestra any more than absolutely necessary. When Bendix asked Thomas to relent and raise his salary, Thomas took the opportunity to state his personal credo: total discipline was essential in an orchestra, and "everyone must have the same aim and cause at heart"—art and loyalty to one's organization were paramount. Bendix played only one complete concerto with the orchestra during the next season, did not conduct at all, and left the group two years later.[17]

The Chicago Orchestra clearly showed progress in its fourth season, with attractive and varied programs that included first Chicago performances of Dvořák's Symphony from the New World and Richard Strauss's *Death and Transfiguration* (Seidl had given their American premieres with the New York Philharmonic). There were fine soloists, too, including the Belgian violinist Eugene Ysaÿe, playing Saint-Saëns's Concerto no. 3 and Bruch's "Scottish Fantasy," op. 46. (Ysaÿe, well over six feet tall, emphasized his height by standing on a platform during the performance, thus towering over both conductor and orchestra.)[18] Rafael Joseffy, who had played at the orchestra's first concert three years earlier, returned to do Brahms's Concerto no. 2. Thomas gave five popular and two request concerts; although there were no exclusively Beethoven or Wagner nights, as in previous years, the ninth and the twentieth concerts were both devoted to Beethoven *and* Wagner.

The *Tribune* carried a full-page feature story on Thomas in February to celebrate his sixtieth year and his fiftieth in the United States. It included a telling description of Thomas's conducting: "His gestures are always quiet and reserved, but his face is constantly changing in expression, more frequently than not directing without the music. Although the score lies open upon the desk, each man must feel the scrutiny fixed upon him. There is a quick movement of the head, a frown, or a smile. Eyes meet eyes, and the result is more effective than the baton, which Madame Nordica [the noted American soprano] describes as 'a little black stick dancing wildly in the air with everything at its mercy.'"[19]

The Orchestral Association marked the occasion with a meaningful gift: the 1895–96 Chicago concert season would be extended to twenty-two weeks, thanks to an improved box office and a deficit of only $30,000, which was 40 percent less than that of previous years. Anna Millar, now promoted to manager, announced that the Chicago Orchestra would play in New York City in February 1896, giving Thomas the opportunity to show his old city what his new city's orchestra could do and to see how it measured up to the Philharmonic and the Boston Symphony.[20] The press, too, was caught up in the pervasive good feeling and optimism. W. S. B. Mathews wrote that Thomas's hold on Chicago was "something wonderful" and that the trials of the orchestra's early years and the abuse that Thomas had personally suffered at the fair were now history. To prove his point, Mathews cited an unidentified Chicago musician: ". . . there are a hundred men in this town who would go down in their pockets to the tune of a thousand dollars a year each rather than have [Thomas's] work here cease. They are proud of him, believe in his artistic sincerity, and take him for what he is, one of the greatest musical artists now living."[21]

In May, Thomas was feted by the association board to mark his jubilee year. Board members' wives showed their appreciation by presenting him with a punch bowl—it seems that Thomas's punch had gained some notoriety in Chicago society for both its flavor and its potency.[22] The event moved Thomas to reciprocate the following November by mounting a special concert for the women, performed by members of the orchestra at Chicago's Steinway Hall.[23] After the concert, Thomas ceremoniously christened the punch bowl with much champagne. Earlier in the month, Charles Norman Fay told Frances Glessner that Thomas had been a "changed man" since the board's party the previous spring.[24] He was looking for appreciation and had gotten it in abundance. Having conducted the 1894–95 season without a contract,

Thomas never again asked for one and never again talked of leaving Chicago. His orchestra had become what he had said it would be, a Chicago institution.

Theodore and Rose Thomas spent almost five months in Europe in the summer of 1895, listening to a great deal of music, visiting churches and galleries, and generally getting the Old World out of Thomas's system forever (future summers would be spent in New England). Thomas had a particularly happy visit with Lilli Lehmann, his friend and staunch admirer in Austria, with whom he had worked frequently in New York and, since then, had maintained a steady correspondence.[25] Home again on October 10, he showed a startling lack of sophistication in talking to the press about European fine art:

> There were pictures there that I had never seen and I wanted to see. I cannot truthfully say I like any other form of art quite so much as music, but I do love pictures. You cannot appreciate the great masters until you have seen their pictures in these old world galleries. Take Rubens. His best paintings are in the Cathedral at Antwerp. They will never be moved. The works of art that give us the best appreciation of the genius of the masters never find their way to this country, but are purchased and kept in the picture galleries of Europe.[26]

Fortunately for Thomas, the attending reporters did not ask him if he had seen the holdings of the Art Institute of Chicago, just a few blocks from the Auditorium, where people like Charles Hutchinson and Martin Ryerson were building one of the finest collections of Dutch, Flemish, Spanish, and French paintings to be found outside Europe. Thomas disagreed—justifiably so—with those who believed that European music was, as a matter of course, performed better in Europe than in the United States, but he was typically American in not giving credit to American connoisseurs of European paintings and other works of art or to their collecting skills. As for music, he considered the Paris Opera's production of *Die Walküre* the best he had ever seen of that work, adding: "The singing [was] far above the average of operatic singing in Paris. Indeed, I have heard some very poor singing there."[27] Forever on the lookout for new music, Thomas acknowledged that he had brought back a wide assortment of new works which, as was his way, he would first try with the orchestra before telling the press what they were.

The *Evening Post* brought its readers up-to-date on Chicago's newsworthy conductor in an illuminating piece, "As He Is":

> Not a picturesque personality, he looks more like a substantial banker than one of the four most renowned conductors in the world. [He has] repressed force and . . . latent power. . . . As a conductor he seems never to equal, not

to say surpass, himself. So far from putting on wings, he puts on chains, as if in dread of his unfettered talents. . . . The high condition of discipline of the Chicago Orchestra is the result not only of Thomas' organizing faculty, but of his own strict subordination of the artistic element in his temperament to the practical. . . . Accused of being a martinet, irreconcilable, a hard man, reaping where he has not sown and gathering where he has not strewn . . . the trouble has not been with him, but with his accusers, themselves impracticable and unable to understand his direct and simple methods.

The article continued with some astute observations of Thomas on the podium:

You will find it difficult to detect the least outward symptom of an inward change even in the most sharply contrasted music. . . . The composition, the orchestra, the performance are merely so many incidents of the day's experiences. He lays down the baton as calmly as he takes it up, acknowledges applause with the imperturbability of a Melba and goes on his way serene and passionless, wondering, doubtless, how long it will be before the public he is educating even against its whim—like a pedagogue his refractory pupils—will get within gunshot of his own ideals of a community musically cultured.[28]

A popular program, a change from previous years, opened the 1895–96 season, and both subscription and single-ticket sales were up. There were new faces in the orchestra, including the violinist-violist Frederick Stock of Cologne, whose appointment would have long-range significance; only twenty-three years old, Stock had been a member of the Cologne Orchestra for four years. There was also added excitement because of the New York concerts. How would Thomas's "new" orchestra be received there? Eager to show New York what he could do with a permanent orchestra after a five-year absence, yet apprehensive of what the press might say, Thomas began rehearsing the New York repertoire early in the fall and first performed all of it at Chicago concerts. When the complete orchestra of 100—not the usual touring group of 60—headed east in February, it was thoroughly prepared and, Thomas hoped, in mint condition. Seven programs would be given at the Metropolitan Opera House, two at the Brooklyn Academy of Music, and one at the American Academy of Music in Philadelphia.

The Chicago Orchestra played to large and enthusiastic audiences while on tour, but in New York it got nasty reviews. The *Times* led the pack, calling the orchestra "a well-trained organization of mediocrities" and declaring, "Only Thomas' ability as a conductor [made possible] so good an exhibition with so ordinary an exhibit. . . . It is deficient chiefly in unity. . . . Its attack is generally uneven. The result is a general roughness, a lack of polish and an absence of finesse in nuances." Conceding that Thomas's reading of Tchai-kovsky's Pathétique Symphony was "masterly," the reviewer asked, somewhat arrogantly, why the orchestra had come to New York: "We have nothing to learn from this orchestra except that Chicago is getting good music fairly well played. No doubt that is unto the edification of Chicago." A vicious attack of a few first-desk players followed, along with comments about the weak violins and Thomas's deficient reading of Dvořák's Symphony from the New World.[29] Most of the other New York papers wrote in a similar vein, Henry T. Finck of the *Evening Post* being the sole exception. He informed the *Times* that "Thomas would not lead a band of mediocre players," that the orchestra was "versatile" and the programming offered surprises at every concert.[30]

The box-office returns were proof enough that bad reviews did not matter when Theodore Thomas headed up a concert; the orchestra made a comfort-able profit and planned a return visit. Yet Thomas took the reviews to heart, as always, even though he perceived that the press was motivated more by antipathy toward him for saying that the city failed to honor good music than by the results achieved. He had many old enemies, this blunt man with the indomitable, unyielding will, and like him they did not forgive easily.[31]

Thomas agreed that the orchestra needed more polishing, but how was he to cope with those who preferred Seidl's romantic interpretations to his apparently more prosaic efforts? He was simply not that kind of conductor, and it would be false for him to try to be. He did what the score said, and the results were clean and clearly stated. Admittedly, he lacked Seidl's dynamic stance on the podium—too many listeners let their eyes rather than their ears lead them—and avoided exaggerated gestures, since he knew that they did little for the orchestra. Thomas might not have been so upset by the reviews if he had known that New York's taste in conductors would always be erratic, that it would madly adore Toscanini and dislike Mahler and Furtwängler, that a mediocre conductor like Walter Damrosch could have a long career (1885–1928) in the great metropolis, or that an equally mediocre conductor, Josef Stransky, would conduct the Philharmonic from 1911 to 1923.

Bad reviews aside, there were some fine moments for Thomas in New York. Not only was his loyal public glad to see him, but so were many of the city's leading musicians. At the second concert, he was given a handsome, inscribed silver drinking horn that proclaimed him "a true man and a faithful friend." It was a gift from Ignacy Paderewski, who had played with Thomas in Chicago just prior to the eastern tour. At the final concert, several friends, including Walter Damrosch, gave Thomas a handsome silver bowl "as a testimonial of their esteem."[32]

After returning to Chicago, Thomas engaged a new principal flute and principal horn. He also insisted that the orchestra be allowed to rehearse in the Auditorium in order to improve its concert performances. But the Auditorium was not always available, which soon led to discussions about the orchestra having its own hall, one much smaller than the Auditorium.[33] It was suggested that the orchestra move to the new fine arts facility being built on Michigan Avenue adjacent to the Auditorium, with a hall seating 1,200, as well as studios and meeting rooms.[34] George C. Curtis, its director, was eager for the building to house the Chicago Orchestra and a University of Chicago music school.[35] But the Orchestral Association and the university decided against it, primarily because the fine arts building would be too small and because the Auditorium depended heavily on the orchestra's rental fees.[36]

Another important change was made in September 1896, when Ernest Wendel, a young German violinist and protégé of Joseph Joachim, replaced Max Bendix as concertmaster. Bendix, well known among Chicago's musical community, did not leave without spewing out half-truths about his relations with Thomas, about how he had been the orchestra's assistant conductor for years but had never been "honored" with the actual title, about how he had "taken no guff" from the "autocratic" conductor. (In truth, he was dismissed from the orchestra for poor behavior.[37]) Wendel lasted a year and was followed by Leopold Kramer, who held the post for more than a decade.[38]

The 1896–97 season, the orchestra's sixth, had some important first performances, including Strauss's *Also Sprach Zarathustra*; like his *Til Eulenspiegel*, premiered the year before, it pleased some and upset others. Dvořák's Cello Concerto was played by England's Leo Stern. The *Chicago Tribune* called it "the work of a fluent, versatile writer who has attained the most finished method of saying things well, but no longer has them to say."[39] Posterity would not agree. Fine soloists that year included Lillian Nordica and Teresa Carreño. Particularly memorable was the fourteen-year-old violinist Bronislav Huberman, whose performance of Mendelssohn's Concerto drew unanimous praise. Clearly, he was no mere prodigy but a mature young artist.

In April, the orchestra reluctantly agreed to play for its own fund-raising costume ball (it thought such work demeaning). Another economic depression had set in during the winter, harming single-ticket sales and wiping out the financial gains of the previous year. A concerned Thomas told the association that if his severe programs were to blame, he would resign forthwith. According to his wife, the board "simply scoffed at the idea of popularizing the programmes" and would not hear of his resigning.[40] Instead, it brought the people of Chicago into the picture by publishing summaries of donations and deficits. As a result, by the fall of 1897, $57,000 in subscriptions had been sold for the coming season, compared to sales of $48,767 for the previous year (and $17,540 in 1891–92). It was an impressive record; but large deficits would continue until 1903, when, as we shall see, a "final solution" was proposed.

Shortly after the New Year, the Chicago Orchestra did its second eastern tour. Manager Anna Millar, determined that it be a success, had booked

Josef Hofmann, Lillian Nordica, bass Pol Plançon, and Eugene Ysaÿe as tour soloists. She had convinced Thomas that they were necessary guarantees if the orchestra were to fill houses and please critics. Hofmann's appearances would be a coup, his first in the United States since he dazzled audiences at the Metropolitan Opera House a decade earlier, as a lad of eleven. Thomas remembered well how he had played to poor houses at Steinway Hall because the public had flocked to hear the young pianist, and he looked forward to joining forces with the grown-up Hofmann.

The New York press greeted Thomas more cordially than it had two years before. The *Times* praised the improved orchestra yet took Thomas to task for his "cold and polished style." It conceded that "Thomas at his best is not to be surpassed and hardly to be equaled by any living conductor. . . . The balance of the various parts [Brahms's Second Symphony] was so exquisite that not a single significant phrase of any instrument was obscured." There was "delicious clearness . . . beautiful transparency and reposeful finish. This kind of playing is obtained by careful and properly directed rehearsals and that is where the work of the conductor is done. . . . Mr. Thomas' reading . . . was one of the best if not the very best ever heard in New York." However, his Prelude to Act 1 of *Tristan* was "one of the worst."[41]

This second eastern tour included several concerts in Boston, where the musical public, which had feasted on the Boston Symphony for so long, eagerly awaited Thomas's return after a long absence. Reviews by the city's three leading critics tell us much about the mature Thomas at the height of his powers. Philip Hale of the *Home Journal*, the most articulate, discerning, and erudite music critic in the United States at the time, went so far as to call Thomas the "dominating" musical figure in nineteenth-century America: "The years have frosted his hair, but his figure is as erect, his bearing as graceful, his quiet authority as supreme as when he first visited us. I know of no conductor who has such despotic control over his men and at the same time commands so imperceptibly. His repose is absolute . . . but a look at his men brings forth a nuance when another would indulge in semaphoric gestures. . . . Mr. Thomas reminds them he is there; the army is eager to follow the general."[42]

Hale knew what Thomas's superlative musicianship, as exemplified in his conducting, was about:

> He is a master of the phrase, as well as a master of rhythm. . . . If the phrase is piano, it is played piano without unmeaning expression. The beauty of the phrase makes its way without the aid of rhetorical extravagance. And with what finish and subtlety is the phrase ended! How carefully are crescendos and diminuendos made, and yet with what apparent spontaneity! How clear is the dialogue between instruments! . . . In the stormiest of passages there is

the feeling of reserve strength. The repose of this orchestra is never soporific; nor is it ever feverish; it is the repose of intelligence and confidence. . . . Mr. Thomas gave an object-lesson in the art of conducting that should not be disregarded or speedily forgotten.

The *Herald*'s Benjamin Woolf praised Thomas's "ease, unobtrusiveness . . . relentless self-repression, warmth and flexibility" and perceptively observed that "the enthusiasm of the players was not dampened because they were not goaded." Of Brahms's Second, he noted: "Beauty of phrasing seems to be instinctive with Thomas. . . . He preserves the flow of the music, its meaning always clear, instead of confusing it by hysterical spasms of pseudo-emotion." Woolf condemned romantic excess, where New York critics cherished it, praising Thomas's rendering of Beethoven's Fifth: "Purity and simplicity, [no] vagaries in *tempi*, rubato, modernism generally. . . . The individuality of the conductor was permitted to disappear and that of the composer to predominate. In this reading Fate did not knock at the door, as if it was inspired by an angry desire to batter down a portal of bronze; nor did it linger long enough between its assaults to give time for the repairing of whatever damage it might have done." Under Thomas's baton, said Woolf, "Wagner is always sane, and the conductor is a better friend to the composer than are the most pronounced Wagnerphile conductors themselves. The *Meistersinger* Prelude had a broad sweep . . . a oneness. . . . Where the several themes are combined, there was not the usual ragged and disjointed effect; the prominence [was] given to the prize song, relegating the other parts to their due subordinate places as ingenious contrapuntal accompaniments to a main theme."[43]

The *Evening Transcript*'s William F. Apthorp, Boston's most senior critic, complimented Thomas's tempos: "[They] were always in place, always to the point; not because they were sudden or gradual, strongly marked or delicate, but solely and simply because they seemed artistically inevitable and not dictated by any mere whim of the conductor. [There was] conviction . . . an inner necessity . . . [and] the music could not go otherwise."[44]

Cheered by his Boston concerts, Thomas returned to New York, where the *Press* interviewed him, "a grim grizzled Teuton warrior, [an] unusually self-contained and reserved man with sensitive spots, which cause him to withdraw into his shell whenever they are touched. Yet, underneath all, there is a kindly tolerance, a comprehensive sympathy, a reasonable way of looking at things that make him as valuable as he is rare as a subject for the interviewer. The vein of humor in his composition relieves somewhat the tension caused by his reserve." When asked about his relations with the Orchestral Association, Thomas replied that they were "voluntary and unfettered." He did not plan to leave Chicago, where appreciation and enthusiasm for good music were growing; neither would he alter his philosophy, which had prevailed for forty years—"I do not adapt my work to audiences, they must adapt themselves to the music."[45]

Thomas went on to blame New York's lack of a permanent orchestra squarely on opera's "precedence," recklessly adding that "opera is not music. It is antagonistic to it. The opera is realistic, music is ethereal. . . . Wagner did not call operas music; he called them dramas, and there is where they belong." (Here, he showed how badly he misunderstood the composer he had advocated for so many years, perhaps because he could not forget that Damrosch and then Seidl had been chosen to do Wagner at the Met, not him.) Thomas scolded New Yorkers for being slaves to fashion, for being more interested in showing off their wealth than in developing a symphony orchestra, which, as he had said many times before, "shows the culture of a community."

The *Press* interviewer then changed the subject, asking about music in other countries. Thomas predicted that Russia, a developing world power, would soon "come to the front in music, as well as in other things," and added that he had introduced the music of Rimsky-Korsakov, Balakirev, and, most recently, Glazunov, to the United States; Tchaikovsky, whom he admired, was "no more Russian than Rubinstein." As for German music, Thomas warned that "we are not through with Germany yet, politically or musically." According to the reporter, the glow of loyalty to his native land shone in Thomas's face as he continued: "Political power and national prestige go hand in hand with artistic ability. . . . The history, the traditions, the power and even the geographical conditions of a man's native land determine to a large extent the character of his talent and work." This was why German music thrived in Germany, he said, implying that America's history, traditions, power, and geographical conditions were still inimical to musical growth. Thomas believed that the easiest way to speed up that growth would be to impose Europe's musical culture on the United States. Few would have disagreed with him.

This was the last time that Thomas conducted in the Northeast. En route to Chicago, he and his orchestra were in a serious train accident east of Buffalo, narrowly escaping with their lives.[46] Many instruments were destroyed, including Bruno Steindel's 1742 Bergonzi cello and all of the orchestra's double basses. It could have been much worse, however, for the head-on collision with another train occurred just 100 feet from a high bridge.

The day before the train crash, on March 28, Anton Seidl lunched with friends at a fashionable New York restaurant; a few hours later, he succumbed to acute ptomaine poisoning.[47] His premature death at age forty-six was a great loss to New York and to Thomas, who had had friendly relations with Seidl for almost two years. With the lackluster Paur in Boston, there was again no other conductor in America of Thomas's stature. As expected, Seidl's death renewed the cry to bring Thomas back to New York, but nothing came of it. The Philharmonic engaged Paur, and Henry Lee Higginson's favorite, the conservative Gericke, returned to Boston for eight more years.

Thomas's Chicago grew ever more rapidly from 1898 to 1903, as did its appreciation of both the arts and sciences and its orchestra. Thorstein Veblen, a lecturer at the University of Chicago, explained in *Theory of the Leisure Class* why the acquisitive rich behaved as they did. John Dewey, who started the University Elementary School Laboratory that helped bring about a revolution in American education, showed that children learn best through experience, when they do things that interest them and stimulate their imaginations. In the sciences, Albert Michelson's work on electromagnetic theory made him the first American to win the Nobel Prize. Other University of Chicago scientists included physiologist Jacques Loeb, botanist John Merle Coulter, and neurologist Henry H. Donaldson.

Brilliance in city planning and architecture was also evident. Daniel Burnham proposed a full-scale improvement of the city's lakefront—the "Chicago Plan"—and today's magnificent downtown was the ultimate result. Architect Frank Lloyd Wright learned his art at the side of Chicago's Louis Sullivan. As the century drew to a close, the Windy City's liberally disposed citizens—a decidedly select group—could point with pride at Jane Addams, also a Nobel Prize winner, and Julia Lathrop, who worked unselfishly for the poor; at the deposed governor, John Peter Altgeld, Henry Demarest Lloyd, and their legal voice, Clarence Darrow, who fought for social reform; and at Henry Blake Fuller and Robert Herrick, who wrote tellingly of Chicago life, and Theodore Dreiser, whose masterpiece *Sister Carrie* was published in 1900.

Theodore Thomas, builder of musical enterprises for almost four decades, was in good company. Like these men and women, his accomplishments were the stuff of American life. He himself had grown musically in Chicago, as had his followers, both in number and in comprehension of the music he brought them. Yet, they did not turn out in large numbers to buy tickets for concerts, despite the Orchestral Association's mighty efforts to convince them that they must. It remained for the rich to support the orchestra, and this they did handsomely. A November 1898 fund-raising dinner at the Chicago Club produced $30,000 in half an hour, which wiped out the current deficit, and in the next half-hour, another $17,500 was pledged for a reserve fund, bringing the grand total of all donations since the orchestra's inception to $255,000.[48] By 1900, however, the orchestra was again in financial trouble.

Tours continued, with their usual trials and tribulations. In Atlanta, Thomas raised a furor by refusing to play "Dixie," informing the dumfounded audience "that no popular music of any kind was included in his programmes," not even the South's unofficial anthem.[49] In St. Paul, he told the *Dispatch* that the West was making "amazing" progress in musical appreciation and that Chicago "is the only city in the world which can support a series of forty very classical orchestra concerts . . . and turn out 4,000 people to each concert." He credited Chicago's women with having made its musical life what it was: "They have more time to study and perfect themselves in all the arts. They come together in their great clubs and gain ideas. Then they travel abroad. They hear the best and become competent to judge. . . . Then the commonplace has no charms for them."[50]

For the 1899–1900 season, the association gave the sixty-five-year-old Thomas a private rail car to make touring more comfortable;[51] and to lighten his work load, Frederick Stock conducted a few tour concerts.[52] Chicago critics blamed the orchestra's financial woes on its programming, arguing that it should play more popular music, but Thomas was in no mood for compromise; he knew his mission and would accomplish it. In a fit of pique, he submitted his resignation to the Orchestral Association on November 14, 1899, but withdrew it soon afterward.[53]

If anything, Thomas's programming became more interesting and profound. In the 1900–1901 season, he did a four-concert Beethoven cycle, beginning with the "Eroica" and ending with the Ninth Symphony. In the next season, he gave a cycle of historical programs, six in all. The first concert included the music of Giovanni Gabrieli, Purcell, Rameau, Handel, J. S. Bach, C. P. E. Bach, Gluck, and Haydn. The second was devoted to Mozart, Spohr —the great Fritz Kreisler was the violin soloist in Concerto no. 8—Weber, and Schubert. For the sixth and final program, a lengthy one, he conducted Brahms's Fourth Symphony, Saint-Saëns's Piano Concerto no. 2, with Harold Bauer as soloist, and Tchaikovsky's *Pathétique*. He also gave twenty-two pairs of concerts and two young people's programs that season. A variety of soloists was used: in 1898, pianists Teresa Carreño, Moriz Rosenthal, and Emil Sauer, violinist Lady Hallé (Wilma Neruda), and soprano Marcella Sembrich; the next year, Paderewski and pianists Mark Hambourg and Leopold Godowsky; and in 1900–1901, pianists Ossip Gabrilowitsch and Ernst Von Dohnányi, along with violinists Fritz Kreisler and Maud Powell.

In August 1899, Edouard Colonne, director of the Colonne Concerts in Paris, invited Thomas to conduct—with or without the Chicago Orchestra —at the 1900 Paris Exposition. His elegant letter of invitation also suggested that if Thomas were unable to attend, he lend his name to the list of patrons for the concerts.[54] After careful thought, Thomas replied to Colonne: "I regret sincerely that circumstances have so changed of late that as an American, who loves justice and liberty, I am prevented from visiting the Metropolis of France next summer."[55] He was referring, of course, to the Dreyfus case, which he considered a "monumental injustice."[56] Thomas might have overreacted, since Colonne's invitation was neither official nor government-sponsored, yet one had to admire his sentiments. It was not until two months later that Chicago heard about the invitation and Thomas's reply, for which he was damned more than praised: "[It] shows that Theodore's heart is all right, but it does not reflect great credit on his head. He should not have allowed his sympathy for Dreyfus to stand in the way of the advancement of his own fame and that of his celebrated orchestra. The Dreyfus incident and the Exposition are not in any way related." [57]

The Orchestral Association lost Anna Millar that year as the result of a minor scandal involving the *Musical Courier*. Millar had bought extravagant advertising space in the *Courier* the year before, in return for good reviews of the orchestra's New York concerts. When the association heard of the deal, it refused to pay the bill, until the *Courier* threatened legal action. Millar was asked to resign, which she did promptly for "reasons of health." [58]

Theodore Thomas and Daniel Burnham had been good friends since the World's Columbian Exposition; they were kindred spirits, planners and builders who saw things through. It was with rare intuition, then, that Thomas's first act on New Year's Day 1900 was to write a personal note to Burnham, the man upon whom much of his professional fate would depend for the next four years, expressing his pleasure at seeing the last year of the nineteenth century in, "not only alive, but kicking." [59] Almost two years later, Burnham would write to Thomas: "I am here in Washington with Olmstead, McKim and St. Gaudens. We have talked of you constantly and wish you were with us and you have come in and taken part almost as if present in body as well as spirit. The Senate has appointed us to improve the park system. . . . Again has come the joy of creating nobler things. . . . And you have been with us, and we all think of how our power to dream truly we owe to you, dear friend and comrade." [60] Thomas and Burnham were destined to embark on still another "dream."

In Chicago, Thomas had many acquaintances and warm professional associates like George Upton, but other than Burnham and Glessner, and, of course, the Fay family, there were no close friends. He wrote letters to musicians in other parts of the country and received many more in return, but they were mainly brief and uninformative. There was a steady flow of requests from composers to perform their works, and it appears that Thomas invariably replied to them politely and even went to some bother to consider their scores fairly and perform them, as he should have, when warranted. However, these letters tell us much more about the writers than about Thomas, who was only slightly susceptible to their flattery, which came even from his composer friends in New England. Thomas wrote more personal letters to Lilli Lehmann, but their relationship was too much that of *Meister* and solo artist for him to open up to her. His letters to his wife, Rose, are a treasure trove— many of them are reproduced in her *Memoirs of Theodore Thomas*—although one suspects that she did not show the world all of them, especially those that might tell us what he thought of others. Put simply, Thomas was not one for close friendships, which made his relationship with Burnham so exceptional. (Unfortunately, just before Thomas's death, he seems to have had a falling out with Burnham's wife, which cast a shadow over their friendship.)

Thomas did have one old (literally and figuratively) friend, William Mason, whom he had hardly seen since leaving New York. About this time, *Century Magazine* was preparing to publish Mason's memoirs, in which, of course, there would be a good deal about Thomas in his early years. Mason asked Thomas to verify his recollections of the Academy of Music in 1859 and of his first conducting experiences there.[61] Letters were exchanged, and the men eventually met in New York in October 1901. Mason, who had been looking forward to the reunion for a full year, invited Thomas and his wife to stay with him. Alas, Thomas was not interested in getting close to Mason and turned down the invitation, keeping their meeting woefully brief.[62]

A Christmas party for the orchestra and the association board, hosted by Thomas, was to follow a concert on December 21, 1901. Shortly after the program began, Daniel Burnham and Charles D. Hamill, a member of the board, received a telegram that Thomas's eldest son, Franz, only in his thirties and crippled for many years, had just died in Florida.[63] The two men went to the Glessners' box to seek advice: should they tell Thomas at intermission or wait until after the concert? Then they asked Rose Thomas, who said that her husband must know immediately. Frances Glessner wrote that when Burnham gave Thomas the news, "he turned white as a sheet and afterwards showed much emotion when John [Glessner] spoke to him. Thomas told them that they 'must not mention it to a soul,' and he would go through the concert as though nothing happened, which he did." Aware that the players would call off the party if they heard of his misfortune, he said nothing. The party included a lot of in-house skits and lampooning, and Thomas managed to behave as if nothing untoward had occurred. Such was his rigorous sense of duty that Thomas did not even go to his son's funeral in New York because it clashed with a concert: "'I have no right to make the public mourn with me. . . . I have never missed a concert in my life. My duty is to stay here.' He led his concert that afternoon at the very hour when he knew his son's body was being laid in the earth."[64]

What of Thomas's other children? Marion, the youngest, had accompanied her father and his new wife to Chicago in 1891. Minna and Hector joined them in 1894 and stayed with the family intermittently thereafter; Hector married in 1896, Minna in 1899. Hermann's activities are unknown, other than that he traveled a good deal, was high-spirited, and later married and had two sons. Marion also married. The Thomas children frequently joined their father and stepmother at Felsengarten, yet in her *Memoirs*, Rose Thomas makes no mention of the children whatsoever during the Chicago years.

In February 1900, Thomas, thinking of posterity, bequeathed copies of nearly all of the orchestral concerts he had conducted since 1862 to Chicago's Newberry Library. In announcing the gift, he said that the programs, which he had retained religiously through thick and thin, "practically show the history of music in the United States." (He had never really believed that there was other good music besides orchestral music!)[65] He gave, in addition to this invaluable collection, manuscripts, scores, books on music, and other memorabilia to the Newberry.

Thomas's markings on his scores have left us some clues as to his interpretations of them. He inserted them tidily and in moderation, rarely cluttering the music with cues for different instruments because he knew his scores too well and, in his last years, conducted more from memory than not. He marked bowings and tempos in Beethoven's symphonies in colored pencil, leaving no room for doubt; and on occasion, he would double the winds and horns. His score of Mozart's Symphony in G Minor—the frequent performances of which drew rave comments—has few bowings but important phrasing marks for the winds; it is a light, unromantic conception. Thomas's phrasing of the rapid section of the Overture to *The Magic Flute* suggests much slower tempos than is customary now. An advocate of uniform bowing, he was also keenly aware of balance between the different sections of the orchestra and rarely added loud or soft markings or accents to scores and parts. There are timings for large works: Brahms's Second Symphony at forty-four minutes, his Third Symphony at thirty-four, and his "German" Requiem at seventy. Thomas never made a recording, but it is hard to think of him doing anything in excess, whether it be a Beethoven symphony or a Strauss tone poem.

Thomas used both good and bad editions of standard works for choir and orchestra. For the *Messiah*, he preferred the questionable Novello 1859 version, in which he inserted his own tempo markings. His fast tempos in oratorios, for which he was often criticized, would, if anything, be on the slow side today, and his phrasing marks in some solo arias could make them difficult to sing. Thomas did take major liberties with Gluck's *Orfeo*, both in the order of scenes and its orchestration.

Of the transcriptions available for perusal, many seem dated, although some could be done today at serious symphonic concerts. Thomas's varied treatment of the strings shows studied craftsmanship, and he used a wide variety of bowing techniques and mutes for effects. His accompaniments to Schubert's *Der Erlkönig, Am Meer,* and *Der Doppelgänger* are impressive, as is his arrangement of Mendelssohn's "Spring Song." His most successful transcription is undoubtedly Chopin's *Marche funèbre*, particularly because of his original use of percussion and tympani.

On October 15, 1900, Boston's new Symphony Hall opened its doors. It cost some $750,000 and had a seating capacity of 2,625. Modeled after the rectangular Leipzig Gewandhaus, it was an acoustical as well as an architectural triumph, due in no small part to the work of acoustician Wallace C. Sabine, a member of the Harvard physics department. (This was the first time an acoustician had worked closely with architects in designing a music hall in the United States.)[66] The beneficial effects of the hall on the Boston Symphony were not lost on Thomas, who pressed the Chicago Orchestral Association more urgently for a similar hall. The Auditorium simply did not measure up to his standards.

The remodeling of Felsengarten was also completed in 1900. The cottage —Thomas called it a "shack"—that he and Rose had built in the White Mountains of New Hampshire for brief summer stays since 1895 had been remade into a substantial house, which they soon considered their home. Thomas cleared land around it, planted a garden (upon which he showered attention), and built furniture and other needed items. He cherished the total escape from the trials of the musical season that Felsengarten provided and took extended summer holidays there. Following one long New Hampshire stay in 1902, Thomas proudly showed his callused hands to a *Chicago Tribune* reporter and laughingly remarked: "Those didn't come from conducting. I added a small piece of property to my 'farm' this year and as the cold which I took with me from Chicago didn't seem inclined to depart, I concluded to get rid of it and cultivate my new land at one and the same time. I therefore got me a pick and shovel, and every afternoon I was at work. I didn't dare begin in the morning, for if you once get outdoors in the country, you know how it is—you don't go in again."[67]

When Thomas was asked to comment on the English composer Edward Elgar, whose "Cockaigne" Overture and "Enigma" Variations he had done with success the previous season, he stated categorically that Elgar was the leading orchestral writer of the day, a violinist who knew how to write for strings but was equally proficient with all instruments. The interviewer then asked, "Do you consider him equally eminent from a creative viewpoint?" Here, Thomas held back: "We are too near him to judge positively. Time has to settle that." He maintained that, although Richard Strauss had more orchestral technique, Elgar (whose two symphonies and other substantial works for orchestra were yet to come) knew more than Strauss about the orchestra's possibilities and limitations. Then Thomas went out on a limb, claiming that the English composer's *Dream of Gerontius* was the finest choral work of the nineteenth century, bar none. He called the orchestral score and the text "tremendous" and "remarkable."

What eluded Thomas in his enthusiastic appreciation of Elgar's music was its uniquely English character: it had shaken off the Germanicism that had enveloped Britain's musical life and stifled its composers for the entire nineteenth century. American music had suffered the same malaise, yet Thomas was insensitive to it. He leaned, as always, toward conservative, mainstream German music, which explained his on-again, off-again attitude toward Wagner and now Strauss. He applauded Slavic music on occasion and considered French and Italian music generally lighter and more frivolous. After finding Elgar, Thomas discovered Sibelius, but he never knew Debussy, Ravel, or Mahler. Yet his taste had broadened over his forty years as a conductor. A breakdown by nationality of the Chicago Orchestra's repertoire for its first fourteen years, 1891–1904, reveals that 64 percent of the works were Austro-German in origin, 12 percent Russian, 11 percent French, 4 percent Czech (Dvořák, Smetana), 3 percent American, 2 percent Scandinavian, and 2 percent British. When Thomas had conducted the New York Philharmonic, 82 percent of the music he programmed had been Austro-German, 9 percent Russian, and 5 percent French. He conducted Beethoven fifty-six times; Wagner, thirty-four; Schumann, twenty-seven; Schubert, twenty; Mozart, seventeen; Rubinstein, seventeen; Brahms, sixteen; Bach, thirteen; Liszt, twelve; Berlioz, eleven; and Weber and Dvořák, ten each.[68]

A proposal to link the Chicago Orchestra with the University of Chicago to develop a music school was reopened in 1900, when William Rainey Harper formally requested that the association meet to discuss it. In a sense, the urgent need for such a school had passed. Northwestern University in Evanston, a suburb north of Chicago, had started a music school in 1895, and the unaffiliated music colleges were all prospering: the Chicago Musical College, the oldest one, founded in 1867; the American Conservatory of Music; and the three-year-old Sherwood Music School. Harper told the association that Thomas had written to him expressing "his willingness to take the directorship, upon certain conditions," and he noted Thomas's view that "the time is ripe for the establishment of such an institution."[69] Both the university president and Thomas obviously saw the need for a school of indisputable excellence.

Protracted correspondence and meetings among Harper, Thomas, and the association followed. Thomas wrote "A Plan for a Musical University," stating the case for a tuition-free school for professional students only—aspiring instrumental soloists, orchestral players, composers. Members of "the best obtainable [orchestra] in the world"—the Chicago Orchestra—would teach at the school, which would share the same building and administration with the orchestra.[70] Harper disliked the scheme and argued for a broader program that would deal with piano and voice and have music courses of a more general nature for all university students. This so irritated Thomas that he wrote testily to Harper in February 1901: "We have had several meetings, but either you do not understand my views on the subject or, I rather think, you do not want to understand me and wish to persuade me to take your view of the case—which is impossible."[71]

In 1902, Harper announced that he was ready to adopt Thomas's plan, including the proposal that the orchestra and the school share the same quarters at a downtown location, not at the university campus in south Chicago. He also confirmed that the university would take partial financial responsibility for the orchestra.[72] Yet, as his enthusiasm grew, Thomas's waned. The latter was now concerned that an endowed university school would compete unfairly with Chicago's independent music schools, particularly in piano and voice instruction, and that the school's future success would be so dependent on the support of the university's president that a change in administration could spell disaster for an otherwise thriving music school. Thomas had not forgotten his Cincinnati experience. As recently as 1898, Frank Van der Stucken, director of the Cincinnati College of Music, had been viciously attacked by the college's trustees without substantive cause.[73] The same thing could happen in Chicago.

As for the Orchestral Association, it was concerned that university affiliation, while helping the orchestra financially, might not, in the long run, be in the orchestra's best interests, since the university, not the association, could well dictate the orchestra's future. Perhaps the overriding reason for the failure of the scheme, however, was that Thomas was simply too old to muster enough energy to take on a completely new project. His golden years were reserved for his orchestra, and he must see those years through. He still had "unfinished business."

13

A Building for the Future

On February 13, 1903, Chicagoans awoke to read a dramatic headline in the *InterOcean*: "Chicago Orchestra May Be Abandoned—Only Endowment of $750,000 for New Hall Can Save It." The *Tribune* put it differently, but with the same thrust: "Crisis in Big Orchestra." The *Evening Post* proclaimed: "Orchestra in Danger." Only the *Journal* seemed calm about a fundamentally positive association announcement: "Home for Orchestra —Chicago Association Trustees Practically Ask Patrons to Contribute for a Building for Thomas."[1]

The news did not take the city by surprise. Earlier in February, there had been reports of mounting dissatisfaction with the Auditorium and claims that it was the principal cause of the orchestra's chronic deficit. Was the rent too high, the hall too uncomfortable, the acoustics too poor? Not really. The problem with the large hall was the same as it had been ten years earlier: size. It was simply too easy for the public to buy single tickets for preferred concerts, which hurt subscription sales, the orchestra's "bread and butter." Indeed, the number of subscribers had increased only marginally over the years.[2]

The Orchestral Association's deficit at the end of its eleventh season, 1901–2, had reached a sizable $30,000, as in 1897–98.[3] A membership drive was launched, with modest results, forcing the directors to conclude that a move to a smaller hall—it would have to be a new building—was the only solution. With this in mind, the association's president, Bryan Lathrop, on the advice of Daniel Burnham, laid out a deposit for the Payne Livery Stable lot on South Michigan Avenue in downtown Chicago. Although the negotiations with the University of Chicago were in full swing (see Chapter 12), the two men wanted this piece of land as insurance, should the talks break down (which, of course, they did).

Having obtained an ideal site, the association next sought the funds to build a new hall. On February 12, 1903, the enthusiastic Lathrop got thirteen association trustees to sign a public letter, bannered in the daily press the next day, that explained why a hall was needed and what it would cost—$750,000, the same amount as Boston's Symphony Hall. Without a new hall, the letter stated, the association preferred to "end [the orchestra's] honorable career now, while it is at the very height of its perfection, before financial weakness shall bring decadence and perhaps disaster."[4] (Whether the association meant what it said is conjectural, but it did touch the heart of every civic-minded and music-loving Chicagoan.)

The letter, prepared by Charles Norman Fay, went on to explain that the hall would be "simple and beautiful," ideally situated, and, most important, owned and controlled by the orchestra. Where, it asked, would Harvard College or Chicago's own Art Institute be without "dignified and noble seats" rather than "hired quarters"? A "fixed site and a monumental building" would have a "lasting influence upon musical art . . . from generation to generation . . . [of] the highest professional distinction." As for the new hall's practical advantages, there would be no rent to pay and subscription sales would increase because the hall would be smaller than the Chicago Auditorium and prices would remain the same. The new facility would, of course, be rented to outside groups when the orchestra was not using it, especially during the off-season, to help meet its maintenance and operating costs. The association promised that the seating capacity would be in "proper relation" to the "average audience," as at Carnegie Hall in New York and Symphony Hall in Boston.

Details followed. The lot was 105 feet wide and 171 feet deep, its limited depth ruling out a rectangular Boston-like hall, and would cost $450,000; the music hall, with seating for 2,500, would be an additional $300,000. If $750,000 were not raised, the association would sell the lot for "commercial purposes" at a $50,000 profit, discharge its deficit, and disband the orchestra. It was pointed out that since 1891 expenses had totaled $1,383,000, concert income had amounted to $1,012,000, and donations received had come to an impressive $300,000. In closing: "If among those who have listened to the Orchestra all these years, there are voices to raise in its behalf, now is the time to raise them. If there is money to give, now is the time to pledge it."

Thus began one of the most brilliant fund-raising campaigns in the history of the arts in North America. The association at first sought seventy-five subscribers, each to give $10,000; but by the end of February, it decided to ask all Chicagoans to contribute.[5] Donors could pledge set amounts but would not have to honor them for a year; if the target were not reached, the pledges would be canceled. The press, cooperating fully, wrote story after story about the orchestra and its needs. Association members gave speeches at clubs, churches, factories, and banks, wherever there might be an audience with money. Orchestra concerts were no exception: one association member began his plea at a matinee with a dramatic, "All of us know how magnificent Chicago can be in a crisis; Chicago that once built a city out of ashes and another out of dreams."[6]

To aid the drive, the association's Chicago Orchestra Auxiliary Committee prepared a fund-raising manual for its members, a "Suggested Outline of Method of Work."[7] Committee members were advised to send a personal letter to potential donors along with an information packet containing "Auxiliary Committee Appeal," "Plan and Description of the Building," "Press Comments from Chicago Papers," "Press Criticisms on the Orchestra," and "Auxiliary Committee Subscription Blanks." Prospective donors should be told that they would be called on in a few days and that time was short. The manual cautioned against asking for too little—"a small contribution might excuse a donor from giving a large one"—but added that "all subscriptions according to means should be appreciatively accepted." Avoid "possible subscribers of the $10,000 class, unless the person approaching them feels confident that he is the best person to solicit the subscription."

The appeal emphasized why a new hall was needed: an art-educational institution would never be self-supporting, a permanent endowment for a hall would free the orchestra from the annual deficit "menace," the new hall would be better for concerts than the Auditorium, ticket prices would remain the same, and the orchestra was of great importance to Chicago. Burnham had provided drawings of the building's exterior, auditorium, and foyers along with explanatory comment: "Its architecture will be . . . Italian Renaissance, that noble and well settled style, approved by the experience of centuries for external repose, dignity and effective decoration, and for internal elegance and charm." The stage in the five-story building would be well forward "so as to obtain perfection of tone delivery. . . . Between the curtain wall surrounding the stage and outside walls are proper air spaces for sonorousness, and the contour of the walls and ceiling of the hall proper, as well as the material, will conform to the best obtainable expert advice on acoustics." Temperature-controlled tuning and storage rooms would be under the stage.

Within a month, $225,000, almost one-third of the targeted sum, had been pledged by nearly 700 donors, with much more to come.[8] Thomas himself took an active role in the campaign, holding press interviews and even giving the occasional short address. The *InterOcean's* feature—including an impressive, large photo of Thomas—predicted that if the orchestra broke up, another would soon be formed in its place, but it "would have to begin where we began twelve years ago." It repeated one of Thomas's battle cries—"Does Chicago want to take the backward step or keep in the van of American cities as a musical center?"—then quoted Leonard Liebling of the *Musical Courier* as having said that the Chicago Orchestra ranked higher than Boston's "merely because I consider Thomas a greater leader than Gericke and because I think his control of his men is more immediate and effective." [9]

The *InterOcean* reporter described Thomas as not looking a day over fifty, an encouraging observation in view of his constant chest complaints and rheumatism: "Ruddy of cheek, springy of step, and erect of stature, his entire bearing and his forceful authoritative gestures indicate that he is at the zenith of his power, and that Chicago is now receiving the full fruition of his life of righteous living and earnest endeavor in the world of music. Lucky orchestra, Lucky Chicago." Three weeks later, Thomas told an interviewer that he preferred to talk about the future and that his orchestra was not a "one-man" show. With typical American braggadocio, he called his "the most thoroughly trained [orchestra] in the world." He wanted his players to "advance themselves, to find the soul in music . . . that is everything." [10] Yes, he did "drill" them, but with their full cooperation; without drill there could be no precision, unity, and coherence. Thomas explored and exploited the capacity of his players, excited their interests, pushed their talents to the limit —and worked them no harder than he worked himself.

Recalling his own youth, Thomas predicted that the children of the diverse "foreign" groups in Chicago would become music lovers after reaping the benefits of an American upbringing and education, for "immigrant Europeans have in their blood the true passion for melody." As for audiences in general, "I care not from what station in life come the thousands who sit before me. Beethoven will teach each according to his needs, and the very same cadence that may waft the thoughts of one to drowsy delight or oblivion, may give another hope in his despair, may bring to yet another a message of love." He continued passionately: "The power of good music! Who among us can tell or measure it? Who shall say how many hearts it has soothed, how many tired brains it has rested, how many sorrows it has taken away? It is like the power of conscience, mighty, immeasurable."

Unusually relaxed and talkative, Thomas described to the *Record-Herald* reporter his intuitive responses to "the character of the audience" and "the 'condition' of the orchestra" at his concerts:

> Before the first note is played there is a something in the air that whispers what sort of a concert we are going to have. Sometimes I breathe it in, and know that the night is going to be a triumph, and that every man waiting to respond to the baton is determined to find the true meaning in every note he plays. Then again there are times when the music, though technically correct, is mechanical, the audience restless and unsympathetic

—an indefinite, intangible something hovering over everybody that says as plainly as if it had a human voice, "You cannot win hearts tonight, Theodore Thomas. Nature is out of sorts."

Thoroughly caught up in the campaign, Thomas agreed to another interview with the *Record-Herald*. Frederic H. Griswold, the newspaper's music critic, wrote that Thomas, in an introspective mood, spoke with "epigrammatic power" throughout the meeting. "In art the first rule is system and form. In art you cannot count your time. We don't work for the penny. The world is moving in music; we must keep pace with the change. By permanent work alone can we accomplish our purpose. For artistic work the surroundings must be artistic." [11]

The fund-raising drive indirectly helped ticket sales, as the season's receipts totaled $10,000 more than in 1901–2. [12] On April 27, 1903, the association granted a reprieve: it would contract the Auditorium and orchestra for one more year—but no more, unless it had the required funds. Of course, this had been the strategy from the outset. The goal could not be reached in two months—realistically, it would take six months to a year—and the threat to disband the orchestra before the 1903–4 season was only a ploy used to urge Chicagoans to dig into their pockets swiftly rather than slowly.

The 1902–3 programs had been adventurous in the choice of both music and soloists. There were a number of brilliant pianists: Ossip Gabrilowitsch, Mark Hambourg, Frederic Lamond, Raoul Pugno, Fanny Bloomfield-Zeisler, and Rudolph Ganz. Another soloist was the American Horatio Parker, who played his own Concerto for organ and orchestra, which, despite many rehearsals, made little impact. Thomas also did works by Paine and by Charles Loeffler, a leading member of the Boston Symphony's violin section. There were premieres of compositions by now-forgotten or nearly forgotten European composers: Siegmund von Hausegger, Armas Jarnefelt, Anton Urspruch, Hugo Kaun, Samuel Coleridge-Taylor, Alexander Ritter, Fritz Volbach, Charles-Marie Widor, Frederic Cowen, Eugen d'Albert (best remembered as a pianist), and Thomas's old favorite, Raff. New works by Saint-Saëns, Humperdinck, and Sibelius were programmed, and Richard Strauss's music was played at five of the twenty-four concerts. There were also two programs for young people.

On October 23, the thirteenth and "final" season of the Chicago Orchestra at the Auditorium opened auspiciously with Beethoven's Seventh Symphony, short works by Berlioz and Wagner, and two premieres: *Messidor*, by the French composer Alfred Bruneau, and *Variations on a Russian Theme*, a collaboration by six composers—Nicholas Artciboucheff, Joseph

Wihtol, Anatol Liadov, Rimsky-Korsakov, Nikolai Alexandrevitch Sokolov, and Glazunov. The large and enthusiastic audience of 3,500 prompted a delighted Thomas to say effusively to a reporter: "Ten years ago such appreciation and such musical understanding would have been unlikely. . . . I fully expect that the orchestra will eclipse its previous best efforts."[13]

During the season, Thomas had tried a new orchestra seating plan: the cellos, normally to the right of the conductor, changed places with the violas and moved toward the center of the orchestra; the woodwinds were moved further to the left of the conductor, behind the first violins, with the double basses behind them. Although no great change in sound was noted, W. L. Hubbard of the *Tribune* felt compelled to praise the orchestra's tone: "[It has a] rare purity, richness and power—a tone such as is heard from but a few orchestras of the world, and these few the greatest."[14] Chicago's musical press, in general, thought that the orchestra—old or new seating plan—had never been better. Twelve seasons of work had finally produced true excellence.

As for the fund-raising drive, pledges had reached $410,000 by November, still a far cry from the required $750,000. The Orchestral Association gravely announced that unless something were done in the next few weeks to find more money, the orchestra would eventually disappear "like a wreath of smoke."[15] On November 30, Lathrop, Burnham, and Glessner obtained a trust deed of $450,000 from the Northern Trust Company (this included Lathrop's deposit of $100,000 which had secured a hold on the property) and took title to the desired "lots 165 to 168" on behalf of the association.[16] A month later, the fund reached $600,000, prompting the association to suggest that if donations reached $650,000, it would somehow find the remaining $100,000 over the next year. All eleven Chicago dailies dutifully reported this latest development, which encouraged still more donations. The first act of this musical-financial drama then came to an end on March 2, 1904, when the press trumpeted the news that the new music hall *would* be built and that the orchestra's future *was* assured. The interim goal of $650,000 had been reached. The *Sunday American* headlined the story: "Chicago Workers and Millionaires, United, Save Orchestra, World's Unique Institution." Other newspapers were equally dramatic.

The campaign was a singular achievement—in one year, Chicagoans had raised an enormous sum for a hall that many felt unnecessary and some actively opposed. After all, Sullivan and Adler's Auditorium, but fifteen years old, was considered one of the great theaters nationally and internationally. Yet the public believed Thomas: he had said that his orchestra needed a proper home and that there must be no compromise, and there it was. Thomas had conducted in Chicago for thirty-five years, been praised and pilloried, honored and scorned, and now he could say that "the object for which I have worked all my life is accomplished. . . . I see in my seventieth year the realization of the dreams of my youth. But I trust I may still live long enough to show my gratitude to the men and women who have made this possible." [17]

Confident that the trustees would find the still-required $100,000, the 8,000-plus pledgers gave their approval to the association to proceed. Buildings currently on the Michigan Avenue lots would be razed as soon as possible, with construction to begin on May 1. Burnham, formally assigned as hall architect—he later contributed his fee to the orchestra—promised that the hall would be ready for occupancy by October 1. He added: "The intention is to build a perfect music hall for orchestral music. There will not be so many seats that many persons would be too far removed from the orchestra to enjoy the softest strain. The seating capacity will not exceed 2,500." [18] Because Chicagoans were very conscious of safety—during Christmas week 1903, almost 600 people, mainly women and children, had lost their lives in a fire at a matinee performance of *Mr. Bluebeard* at the new Iroquois Theater— the new hall would be built of "fireproof material throughout." [19] The orchestra's final concerts on April 29 and 30 would be its last at the Auditorium, and a special dedicatory concert would formally open the orchestra's permanent home in October.

In the midst of all this activity, Thomas appointed Frederick Stock assistant conductor—a sound choice, as it turned out, although many wondered at first if he had enough talent and ability for the post. In December 1903, Thomas gave an all-Berlioz program to commemorate the centennial of the composer's birth, and much was made of Thomas's meeting with Berlioz in 1867. [20] Then, a week later, Thomas did an all-Beethoven program. Further into the season, French violinist Jacques Thibaud and Bohemian-born contralto Ernestine Schumann-Heink made their first appearances as soloists with the orchestra, and Busoni played again after a long absence.

The major attraction of the year, however, was the first guest conductor in the orchestra's history, Richard Strauss. Indebted to Thomas for his early championing of his music, Strauss was especially delighted to be in the Windy City. Although the Chicago Orchestra already had a considerable reputation in Europe, Strauss, himself an outstanding conductor, was quite overwhelmed when he actually heard it. After his first rehearsal, he told the players that theirs was "an orchestra of artists, in whom beauty of tone, technical perfection and discipline are found in the highest degree" [21] (Thomas had rehearsed the program thoroughly before Strauss's arrival). After his first concert, Strauss spoke in a similar vein to Walton Perkins of the *InterOcean*: "The Chicago Orchestra is one of the two great orchestras of the world. I have never led an orchestra that responded more quickly to my wishes than does this one." He praised Chicago, a city "not more than fifty years old," for having such an orchestra and for having such intelligent and responsive audiences, adding that "it was a pleasure to appear before them."[22] Chicagoans returned the compliment, filling the house for Strauss's concerts, all of which ended with standing ovations. The orchestra, clearly on its mettle, applauded him as much as the audiences did.

To Thomas's credit, the critics agreed that Strauss's interpretations of *Also Sprach Zarathustra*, *Death and Transfiguration*, and *Til Eulenspiegel* were much like Thomas's. The six-foot tall Strauss was described as "slight to the point of spareness in build. In conducting he is vigorous rather than dignified. The man vibrates in unison with the music, his arms extended and swaying, the muscles now contracted, now relaxed; bending at the knees, the body is lowered and raised in rhythmic sweeps until the climax is gained." (Strauss toned down his "vigorous" approach in his later years, wittily remarking that conductors should never perspire, only audiences.) Another press comment about Strauss tells us much about Thomas: "We who are so accustomed to the wonderful calm that Theodore Thomas maintains are inclined to deem a leader who displays outward signs of fire as an eccentric. We have learned that the frills are totally unnecessary, and hence we believe that the leader who indulges his emotions is needlessly demonstrative, if not given over to mannerisms. But in Richard Strauss there is nothing of the poseur. . . . He is sincere. . . . [He] wielded the baton like a man inspired."[23]

The press also reported Strauss's views on Beethoven, the symphonic form, and the tone poem:

> The tone poem simply has come in the course of the logical development of music. I believe that when Beethoven composed a symphony he started with a distinct poetic idea . . . [which] gave life to the symphonic . . . form. Since Beethoven that form has been an empty outline, a mere dead shell.
>
> The various preludes to Wagner's works . . . all differ from each other in form. Their form was governed entirely by their contents, not their contents by their form. If you will examine my tone poems you will discover the same thing. No two of them are alike in form, otherwise they would be written according to a formula, and that is something I detest.
>
> It would be much more comfortable for me to compose symphonies. A symphony is just so many empty jars into which I could pour anything I might want to. But with a tone poem it is different. Once you start with a poetic idea it must be logically developed.[24]

Strauss's visit could not have come at a more opportune time. The remainder of the season sold well, and in May, as promised, ground was broken for the new hall. As for Thomas, he was granted one last delight in this most pleasureable of years. E. Francis Hyde, still president of the New York Philharmonic, asked him to conduct a subscription concert the following year, either to open the season or on a date of his choosing. Hyde closed his letter of invitation: "You are first in all our hearts, and we trust that you will give us the supreme pleasure of seeing you once more in the place where for many years we loved to see you—at the conductor's desk of the Philharmonic Society of New York." [25] But Thomas feared that he would have insufficient rehearsal time with his old orchestra, which might lead the press to say that he was no longer the conductor he once was, and so declined the invitation. Undeterred, the Philharmonic sent its concertmaster, Richard Arnold, to Chicago to urge Thomas to change his mind. (The two were old friends; Arnold had played with Thomas for many years.) After such a gesture, Thomas had to accept, and the dates were fixed—March 25 and 26, 1905.

Thomas's family had been urging him since 1898 to give up the May Festival in Cincinnati. Conducting seven concerts in four days, several with choir, had simply become too great a strain for him. After each festival, he would retire to Felsengarten, where, Rose Thomas said, he would sit all day in his chair, "idle, and so exhausted that every few minutes his head would drop forward in a lethargic sleep. . . . He could neither read nor write nor even work out of doors." [26] Yet, because of his loyalty to colleagues like Lawrence Maxwell, and the artistic satisfaction the festival gave him, he would not leave it.

By 1904, the festival had been cut to five concerts in four days, more reasonable for a conductor approaching his sixty-ninth birthday. This would be the sixteenth festival in thirty-one years and would include Bach's Mass in B Minor, Elgar's *Dream of Gerontius*, Bruckner's Ninth Symphony, Brahms's *Rhapsodie* for contralto, chorus, and orchestra, and, at the final concert, Beethoven's *Missa solemnis* and Ninth Symphony. The program notes listed the major choral-orchestral works that the May festivals had presented since 1873; few great ones had been omitted, from those of Bach and Handel to the present. Other cities had given festivals from time to time, only to abandon them, and Cincinnati remained "the one city in the United States on which rests the responsibility of maintaining national music festivals. . . . [They] have become to America what the ancient and celebrated Lower Rhine Festivals have long been to Germany. . . . The spirit of Theodore Thomas' life is reflected in them. It is the 'honor of music,' and every act of the Festival Directors serves this end." [27]

It was Thomas's finest festival. The chorus of 500 and the soloists, which included Ernestine Schumann-Heink and a quartet of British singers who had sung with Richter the previous year at the Birmingham Festival— Agnes Nichols, Muriel Foster, William Green, and Watkin Mills—were uniformly outstanding. Chicagoan Philo Adams Otis, who had been listening to

Thomas's music since the 1870s, nonetheless remarked that, although chorus and soloists were excellent, the "strength of the Festival" continued to be Thomas and the Chicago Orchestra. Alas, Thomas was forced to admit that, as rewarding as this festival was, it must be his last.[28] He had accomplished his "mission" in Cincinnati, and there were still other important projects to complete that would need all of his remaining strength.

One such project was a set of essays, none of them particularly original, analyzing Beethoven's nine symphonies.[29] The pieces he was able to complete were typically romantic explanations of the symphonies' "spiritual" quality and how the composer had breathed "soul" into them and endowed them with "philosophy." Thomas saw the "Eroica"—the subject of his most interesting essay—as "a perfectly legitimate step forward, a logical sequence in [Beethoven's] normal development, [not an] unexampled advance . . . beyond his previous symphonies." Beethoven had already achieved "technical mastery," and what followed was the "dawn of modern music, written in a definite mood, giving expression to the soul through colour and contrast rather than attempting to illustrate a specified programme." Thomas dissociated the symphony from Napoleon, likening it rather to a Greek tragedy—a literary form that, he maintained, Beethoven ardently admired—and described its four movements accordingly: the first represented the "character and great qualities of the Hero"; the second, the "funeral rites of the Hero and lamentations of the people"; the third, "an interlude"; and the fourth, "public games in honour of the Hero and his final translation into the abode of the immortals." The "heroic portion of the symphony consisted of the first two movements only," whereas the final two movements were in conventional symphonic form and had no dramatic intent.

About the Fifth Symphony, Thomas wrote that its first movement "represents a struggle and the will power of a great soul" yet is only an introduction to the work. The second "represents the emotional side of the same soul and is a temporary rest." The third is "struggle again and leads to a great triumph of unusual strength and happiness in the fourth." Thomas maintained that this was not "programme music," in spite of his "representations," and he concluded that Beethoven showed "the psychological side of human nature in a manner so strong and full of meaning that he has only been equalled in this respect by one other creative mind—Shakespeare." Unfortunately, Thomas never finished the project.

During the summer of 1904, Thomas also wrote a short autobiography —"Life Work"—as part of the first of two volumes of his concert programs that George P. Upton was editing for publication the following year.[30] It is a short, impersonal account, some 35,000 words in length, of the major events in Thomas's life but says little of his family—he would not "thrust his family affairs upon people"—friends, and enemies. However, as Leon

Stein perceptively noted, it has "the salient characteristic of its writer—it is completely honest." Not "ghost-written," it is vintage Thomas—direct, terse, even brusque.[31]

Volume 2 includes a complete (though error-filled) list of works that had been given their first North American performance by Thomas and an "Introduction," prepared by the conductor, that explains his principles of program making. The latter discusses Beethoven, "the nearest to us in spirit," and why Thomas almost always included Beethoven's music in his concerts in his early years, preferably at the beginning. Wagner, with his "modern spirit and his effective scoring," was best done at the end to provide the needed climax to the evening. There is also good advice on program building: "Time your works, have each piece prepare for the one to follow, observe a steady crescendo, never allow an anti-climax, and 'keep a trump' for the last."

In the "Introduction," Thomas notes that he responded to "one-sided" public demand in his early days with two favorites, *Träumerai* and the *Blue Danube Waltz*, but his public had outgrown them. His objective was "to enlarge the repertoire of the public and broaden its conceptions. I have never wished to pose as an educator or a philanthropist, except in so far as I might help the public to get beyond certain so-called 'popular music'—which represents nothing more than sweet sentimentalism and rhythm on the level of the dime novel." As for his two pet peeves, the "Encore Habit" (in Thomas's day, encore meant a true repetition) and the latecomer, he had this to say: "The effect of a repetition is never so good as that of a first performance"; it prolongs a program and puts its final works at a disadvantage. The latecomer is simply inconsiderate, and he wondered why so much as one listener should have to be disturbed, even between movements of a symphony (which was why he avoided starting programs with symphonies).

Thomas next addressed the "practical effects of music. . . . Music is restful to the human being, because faculties are called into action and appealed to other than those he ordinarily uses, and also because it absorbs all his attention and frees him from worldly cares. [Instrumental music] appeals to his imagination and intellect, and permits his own interpretation to the extent of his experience." He recommended music listening as a salve for the businessman, who, he felt, needed respite from his trying work in the busy, material society of turn-of-the-century America. Chicago, with its hectic pace, was, in Thomas's view, where music was needed most.

On the subject of opera, Thomas explained that he did fewer operatic excerpts than in his early years because more operas were being staged. Although he did not say it in so many words, he could not—indeed, would not—put opera, in excerpt form or completely staged, on the same pedestal as symphonic music. To make his point, he focused on Wagner, "[whose] music always aims at a climax, and at times uses means which are too realistic for the concert stage but perfectly legitimate for the operatic stage, for which they were intended. . . . While the brain is engaged with dramatic action, the eye can take in scenery, color, etc. and still not hinder the ear from taking in the tone-flood prepared by the composer and justified by the situation, so as to saturate the whole human system. All may be in keeping with the dramatic action, and yet be at the expense of music and without soul." Thomas went so far as to claim that an operatic orchestra need not play every note in a difficult passage. (He was thinking of the demanding string parts in the "Ride of the Valkyries" and other excerpts from Wagner's operas.) In theatrical music, the effect, the general impression, is all-important, he said, whereas in the concert hall, "accurate execution, tone quality and expression are the first requisites and are of more importance than [in] descriptive music."

The first successful "descriptive" work, according to Thomas, was Beethoven's Pastoral Symphony. The works of Berlioz, Liszt, and Wagner were "natural evolutions of their time," yet the descriptive efforts of the first two were unsuccessful. Berlioz understood Beethoven, "but the soul or spirit expressing the deepest humanity [Beethoven's] he hardly understood. . . . [His] music and text do not harmonize, although his works were interesting for a time." Similarly, Liszt "was never able to reach the heights to which he so ambitiously aspired." Then the Victorian Thomas, explaining Wagner in this context, pronounced his last—dare I say confused?—words on music, morality, and sensuality: "[He] understood Beethoven principally from the intellectual side, and adopted and expanded everything, but also without soul. His text and music, however, blended. He made a great impression on the world by his combination of intellect and passion, or sensuousness. He touched greatness in 'Siegfried's Death March,' but even in this chiefly by his intellect. Wagner did not care for humanity, but in his later life he became sentimental, as is shown in his 'Parsifal'—though the Flower Maiden scene shows that he remained sensuous to the last."

According to Thomas, Wagner and Liszt both went unappreciated for a good part of their lives because their "expanded scores" had to wait for larger halls and opera houses. Now, however, with "enlarged and larger concert halls, Mozart and Beethoven have ceased to be effective." Performing Beethoven's Ninth in the immense halls of Chicago, New York, and Cincinnati, Thomas said, is "an injustice both to the work and the audience." He recalled the excitement that the Ninth had generated at the first Cincinnati festival, when it was given "in a wooden hall of moderate size," and observed that such excitement had never been repeated. (He apparently had forgotten that 6,000 people were at the memorable Sänger Hall concert.) Thomas concluded: "When I speak of a large hall, I mean large in the European sense of the term. Our monster American halls and theaters are fit only for mass meetings and horse shows." What he had failed to note was that, in the United

States, box-office returns help in great part to support orchestras. Thus, large halls—2,500 seats and up—continue to be the norm in most large North American cities.

Thomas had struggled with the "Introduction" and part of "Life Work" at Felsengarten. The Glessners, who had introduced Thomas to the area, visited him in early June and noted how tired he seemed. He was unshaven and "wore smoked glasses," and he didn't have on his wig—Thomas's vanity had led him to wear one in public.[32] His catarrh had become deeper, and he was now completely deaf in one ear and partially blind in one eye. Rose Thomas said that heart trouble had also developed and kept him from working outdoors: "He could only walk quietly about, saw in hand, and do a little light pruning. It was pathetic to see the old, sick lion, wandering slowly through the woods where he had been wont to roam in all the glory of abounding health and strength, or trying to spur his jaded energies on to meet the tasks of the coming winter."[33]

In the middle of the summer, Thomas left Felsengarten to direct a *Sänger-fest* in Milwaukee. He had trouble with the orchestra, the chorus, the festival's manager, and the press.[34] Perhaps the only reason he undertook the trip was to check en route the progress of his new hall (which clearly would not be ready for the October opening). He returned to Felsengarten, where he remained until September 28, then, on his way back to Chicago, made an unusual number of personal visits—to his children in New York, to his old friend Karl Klauser at Miss Porter's School, where he had met his first wife, to other friends in Boston and Philadelphia, and even to his devoted gardener in Fairhaven. Significantly, he stopped at the Mount Auburn Cemetery near Cambridge, Massachusetts, which he and Rose had designated as their final resting place.[35]

Seven years earlier, in 1897, Thomas had written "Notes on the Construction of Music Halls" for Russell Sturgis's *Dictionary of Architecture*. (Thomas deserved the assignment—he may have known more than any other musician of the time about concert hall acoustics—but there were family connections too: Sturgis's daughter Margaret had married Hector Thomas the year before, and Thomas's daughter Minna would marry Sturgis's son Newton in 1899.) Now Thomas hoped to see his ideas come to fruition in the new hall. He had said that soft wood, not plaster, should be used wherever possible and that there should be no uncovered brick. "The hall should be a separate structure, built within and separated from the outer walls and roof of the building," and it should be built on soft soil, not rock, with no other hall beneath it, to avoid "unpleasant vibration." "Walls and ceiling should be connected by a continuous curve which will allow the sound waves to move unhindered. . . . The ceiling of the entire hall should slope gradually down towards the stage. . . .

Limiting the height of the hall above the stage [to thirty-five feet] preserves the integrity of the tone. If the ceiling is too high the tone loses something before it reaches the audience; also, in orchestral performances, the various choirs cannot blend."[36]

The orchestra's seating plan was also important. Brass and percussion should be on raised platforms at the rear of the orchestra, but not so close to the rear wall of the stage as to resonate excessively. As for sounding boards, Thomas felt that they belonged only outdoors or in very large auditoria. He added some miscellaneous observations: "A high and deep gallery is good because the tone waves can run out and disappear gradually," but, since seats under the gallery are never good for listening, "the upper gallery should be a continuation of the hall, built over the foyer of the second story." A hall with too much vibration muddles complex rhythms; an empty hall should have resonance but no echo. Orchestra aisles should be covered with thin carpet and kept "unoccupied," for an orchestra loses some of its brilliance in a full hall.

The same man who had commissioned Thomas to write about concert hall acoustics now wrote about the "Thomas Music Hall" while it was under construction in the summer of 1904. He was not worried about the acoustics, since, as he said, Thomas was attending to them, and he liked the building's façade, despite criticism to the contrary (some had called its marked simplicity "commonplace"). Burnham, "not a fancy architect," had deliberately made it unpretentious in order to economize and, Sturgis concluded, although it was no "work of art," it would at least be "decent and somewhat elegant," located as it was on the finest street in "Thomaston"—as Sturgis jocularly called Chicago. But, economy aside, was the façade what Burnham really wanted or was he simply unimaginative? Compared to the monumental Art Institute facing it on Michigan Avenue, the new music hall was another Chicago tribute, admittedly with a vengeance, to modest functionalism. It was, as Sturgis said, a "design which grows, or seems to grow, out of the absolute requirements of the situation."[37]

Thomas returned to Chicago in October to begin the 1904–5 season at the Auditorium, not at his new hall. He hovered about the construction site a few blocks away and finally had to admit that the hall was a compromise— neither the arrangements of the stage, which would not be enclosed behind a proscenium arch, nor its shape were what he had expected. In most cases, iron and plaster were used instead of wood, which would inevitably harden tone quality. Had Burnham built him a poor hall? One thing was certain: it was *not* the hall Thomas had hoped for.

November was a particularly difficult month for the aging conductor, due to construction delays and his own deteriorating health, both of which made him irritable and impatient.[38] He remembered his premonition at Felsen-garten—that he would not spend another summer at his beloved cottage—and he now wondered whether he would live to see the new hall completed and to conduct in it. December came, and the hall's interior was still a mess. The smell of drying plaster was everywhere, the floors were littered with building materials, doors would not shut, and the heating system was not working as it should.

Earlier, the Orchestral Association had committed itself to a dedicatory concert in the new hall on December 14. Thus, on December 6, the restive Thomas called a "test" rehearsal in the drafty, unfinished building. He began with the Overture to *Tannhäuser* and, at its conclusion, danced a short jig on the podium, shouting to Charles Norman Fay, Lathrop, and a few other trustees seated in the boxes, "Your hall is a success, gentlemen, a great suc-cess." He then wired Burnham in Manila: "Hall a complete success. Quality exceeds all expectations."[39] Three days later, after an Auditorium matinee concert, he said exuberantly,

> The acoustic properties are all that we expected. The sound fills the hall and there is no echo. I had some misgivings for a time as the material used in the interior is all hard. The floor is concrete, the walls are hard plaster, the fronts of the balconies are iron, and there would seem to be nothing in the material to give resonance, but it is there.
>
> The construction of the stage is such that the orchestra really sits in the hall, and when you are all there in the audience the music is all around you, and you hear the instruments perfectly. Even in the greatest fortissimos of the full orchestra the fine tones of the violins are heard as plainly as the loudest brasses, and in the pianissimos the perfect nuances are heard in a beauty which it is hard to describe.[40]

Thomas could now look forward to the dedication concert. The orchestra would do the Overture to *Tannhäuser, Death and Transfiguration*—it had become one of Thomas's favorites—and Beethoven's Fifth. He would also bring in the choirs of the Apollo and Mendelssohn clubs to sing "Hail! Bright Abode" from *Tannhäuser* and the "Hallelujah Chorus" from the *Messiah*. Alas, he would have to rehearse the program in the Auditorium, for work was still going on at Orchestra Hall.

C. E. Russell, who was at the Beethoven rehearsal, noted that Thomas no longer stood before his players, preferring to sit on a kind of "wooden horse with a back to it." "It seemed to me that he was sadly depressed, a fact that made me wonder when I thought of the triumph that awaited him in a few days. When they reached the last movement, he did not stop [the orchestra] anywhere but let them play on as if at a concert, clear to the end, a thing most unusual for him. When it was over he lingered an instant, and I thought he was going to say something, but he only laid down his baton, made his little bow of thanks and dismissed them heavily."[41]

On December 11, W. L. Hubbard of the *Tribune* wrote an article on the new hall, praising Thomas, the association, and the people of Chicago but warning that the acoustics could not be judged until the hall was completed and tested at length. Personally, he liked the Chicago Auditorium and claimed that soloists who had appeared there said it was "one of the most perfect, if not the most perfect, acoustically in the world. Mr. Thomas has said himself repeatedly that in no other hall in which an orchestra of his has ever played has every instrument come out so completely and perfectly in the tonal mass as in the Auditorium." Since Thomas himself had pronounced the new hall "acoustically ideal," Hubbard skeptically concluded that "its success . . . is assured."[42]

To prepare the public for Chicago's biggest musical event since the opening of the Auditorium fifteen years earlier, the *Evening Post* did a more positive and prideful feature piece:

> The platform is an oval, 72 feet long and 32 feet wide at the west end of the building. . . . The 23 boxes . . . are beneath the first balcony and above the parquet, forming a distinct balcony across the hall. Each box seats six persons. On the main floor are 1,000 chairs, in the balcony 916 and 500 in the gallery. [There is] an artistically designed vestibule. Then comes the grand staircase . . . to the second floor grand foyer. This commodious room, two stories high, is as long as the building is wide and extends back from the Michigan Avenue windows to the main auditorium. It is finished in Louis XV style, the work having been done by a Parisian artist. . . . In Europe, the music halls where the opera and the art in music and acting are preserved are built by government funds. In other American cities some local Carnegie contributes funds and has his name carved in stone at the entrance. Here in Chicago the millionaires and the toilers have jointly contributed.[43]

The triumphant hour arrived when Thomas would conduct his "permanent" orchestra, one of the finest in the world, in its "permanent" home. He had finally achieved his life's goal, something he could leave to future generations. Few people could ask for more. Still, he was worried: Was the hall as good as he said it was? Was it even ready for concerts? Had he rushed the opening? How serious would a short delay have been when he had waited for this moment for a lifetime? All was forgotten as he mounted the podium, however, "a pink carnation the size of a cauliflower in his buttonhole." The "fashionable" audience of 2,500 "cheered, waving hands and handkerchiefs, while the veteran conductor, with tears in his eyes, bowed and bowed again." Past-president George Adams spoke on behalf of the association, praising the

8,000 Chicagoans from all walks of life who had helped build the hall to show their love of music and civic pride. He added: "Mr. Thomas and gentlemen of the Orchestra, we hope and believe that it will stand for generations to come, but if it stands for centuries it will not outlast the beneficent influence which you have bestowed on the higher life of the American people." More cheering followed, which Thomas terminated by "tapping his baton for the opening of the Tannhäuser Overture." His conducting was as "undemonstrative as ever . . . in the same dignified and modest manner long familiar to the 'family.'" The concert went well, closing with the "Hallelujah Chorus."[44]

Most of the musical press either praised the hall's acoustics or asked for more time to evaluate them properly—except for Hubbard of the influential *Tribune*. He wrote that the orchestra's sound during rehearsal in the empty hall—which he claimed to have liked—differed from its sound when full. He had sat in various places in the hall during the concert, from the fourth row center of the orchestra to the rear of the balcony, but found essentially the same defects everywhere. At times, the brass "completely swallowed up the rest of the orchestra," the quality of the strings when heard alone "was hard, and wanting in the warmth and vitality which had heretofore been their distinguishing characteristic," and the woodwinds were "prominent" but lacking in "beauty." The orchestra sounded "small. . . . It was as if the number of men had been divided in half, and the quality and nobility and refinement seemed to have suddenly vanished. For the first time since the Chicago Orchestra has been heard it sounded common."[45]

Hubbard's views were contagious. Following a Beethoven "Anniversary Program" a few days later, it was Walton Perkins's turn to be negative. He wrote in the equally influential *InterOcean* that the "universal verdict" of those who had heard the orchestra in the new hall was "undisguised disapproval. The query 'Have we lost the orchestra?' is frequently met with." Perkins complained that the hall had been built on too short notice, the plaster and mortar were still damp, and the heat used to dry both had caused excessive humidity. He disliked the narrow seats and the limited space between rows, which forced people to get to their places slowly and clumsily. The hall seemed crowded after the "spacious aisles, wide seats and generous amount of room" at the Auditorium, and he asked whether the public would ever get used to it after having known "perfect accommodations."[46]

At first, Thomas was unperturbed. He had expected some negative press, and such remarks about the hall were more or less typical of the responses to other Thomas projects in past years. The press would never fully appreciate him and his work, he felt, and so he defended the hall: "I have either played or been an auditor in every prominent hall in the world [actually, Europe and North America], with the exception of the new one in Leipzig and one or two others recently constructed, and not one of these famous places is the equal of our building. Why, they can't do such things abroad. They haven't money enough, and what money there is doesn't go to musicians."[47] He praised the clarity of the double basses, which were, like the woodwinds and brasses, undeniably heard to better advantage in the new hall.

The *Record-Herald*, which had sought out Thomas for his views, quizzed P. C. Lutkin, dean of the music school at Northwestern University, who commented:

> The regular patrons of the orchestra are in a position somewhat similar to that of a man who has been looking through the wrong end of a pair of opera glasses for years. The glasses are now in the correct position, so that we see things as they should be seen, and it all looks queer to us. A little time is necessary before we can adapt ourselves perfectly to the new condition. There is a difference between the familiar effects and those heard in the new hall . . . a lack of finish to which we have become accustomed. The gain however is much greater than any possible loss.[48]

Lutkin added that Orchestra Hall's "intimacy" in itself was an improvement over the Auditorium, that the listener was in "close touch" with the performance and heard inner parts more clearly. Balance between woodwinds and strings was also much better. He concluded, "When the new conditions have become familiar we will find that we have ample cause to be thankful."

The main problem with Orchestra Hall was its curved walls and ceiling, which caused sound to reverberate differently in different sections of the auditorium.[49] Depending on where one sat, the sound could be either too reverberant or too dry, with a great deal "in-between." The fact that the shoe-box-shaped Boston Symphony Hall had a more consistent, even sound did not mean that Chicago's new hall had a poor one; rather, seat location was paramount for the Chicago listener who wanted to hear music a certain way. Once Chicagoans wearied of blaming Thomas for his latest "wrongdoing," they would get to know their hall and choose their seats accordingly.

It is difficult to say whether or not Thomas *really* liked Orchestra Hall.[50] Certainly, he was dismayed and upset by the stinging criticism of Hubbard and Perkins. He should have had a number of rehearsals in the hall, even private concerts, so that he and the players could get used to it before exposing it to a critical public that would inevitably compare it to the Auditorium. Also, he had come to terms with the hall's structural features because he could not alter them even if he wanted to. How could he respond to those who said nastily that the hall was actually a theater without a curtain, not a concert hall? And what could be done about the fact that the orchestra's sound would forever be slightly muffled to those seated under the balcony, or that the sharp angle of the balcony and gallery made some listeners slightly giddy? Did he know that the hall had been built on a lot too small for a shoe-box hall—undeniably the best kind for symphonic music? Perhaps the association had put cost and location first.

Thomas caught a cold at the dedicatory concert, and it soon developed into grippe. He should have stayed home, but instead, for the ten days until Christmas Eve, he worked at fever pitch, rehearsing the orchestra, rearranging its seating plan, balancing its choirs, and urging its solo instruments to play softer or louder than at the Auditorium—in effect, doing all the things that he should have done before the first concert. He was determined to convince the public that it had a hall of which it could be proud, but he was exhausting himself. Rose Thomas remembered that they spent Christmas Eve together at home, roasting oysters: "'How good these taste,' he exclaimed. 'It is the first time anything has tasted good to me since we got into the new hall. Come, we must drink Brüderschaft together, German fashion, to celebrate the day'. . . . All at once he seemed to wilt. His laughter died and his spirits fell. 'I am so tired, so tired,' he said wearily, 'I must go to bed.'"[51]

On Friday, December 30, Frederick Stock conducted the Chicago Orchestra at Orchestra Hall. Thomas was stricken with pneumonia, and for the first time in his long career, he had to miss a concert because of illness. He was critically ill, but reports said only that "alarm is felt . . . [but] there is no immediate danger of death."[52] On Monday, he seemed to improve, and on Tuesday morning, when Frances Glessner went to his home at 43 Bellevue Place, she found him seeking comfort from his family—nearly all of whom were there—and holding hands with them. He asked his wife, "Would you be content to live with me in the country on what we have?" to which she replied, "Yes, any place on anything, so long as it is with you."[53] Later, Thomas asked his son Hermann to get a rare bottle of wine, a gift from Charles Hutchinson, to drink with friends and family. It seemed that, with his iron constitution, he might be able to fight back. By nightfall, however, he had a relapse, and it was clear that the end was near.

Rose Thomas wrote that during her husband's last days, he bore the "torturing illness . . . without a murmur," but Frances Glessner did not recall Thomas being that stoical.[54] A few hours before his death, he had a vision of his beloved Felsengarten and then drifted off into unconsciousness. With his wife and two sons at his bedside, he died peacefully in the early morning of January 4, 1905. Mrs. Glessner had "never seen death more solemn, more majestic." The next day "he lay in his coffin dressed in his doctor's gown with a single rose and his baton in his hand—'his wife and his art,' said Rose, 'clasped together over his heart.'"[55]

During Thomas's illness, all of Chicago was at his bedside in spirit, hoping for his recovery. When death came, people everywhere reacted with shock and disbelief. Two generations of Americans had attended his concerts. His was a household name; he was a part of their lives, indestructible. Even before his death was announced in the papers, the public heard the news over the phone: operators were saying "Theodore Thomas is dead" before the customary "number please."[56] Lengthy obituaries followed in cities across the land, everywhere he had conducted. Telegrams of condolence were received from New York, Cincinnati, Philadelphia, Boston, and many European cities. Nikisch wired Rose Thomas from Berlin: "Not only Americans, but we all owe Theodore Thomas enormous thanks. Without his indefatigable pioneer work we musicians of the Old World could never have had such success in the United States." From Vienna came Gericke's message: "It is impossible to exaggerate the great loss. . . . His position was unchallenged: the greatest orchestra conductor in the world. He had no equal. There is none to take his place." Strauss wrote from Berlin: "What we Germans owe him shall be held in everlasting remembrance."[57]

Lilli Lehmann's letter was particularly reverent: "Beside yourself, dear Mrs. Thomas, there are few people who appreciated him, his character, and all that he did, so highly as I. I never met a musician who equaled him. I hope he was buried like the King that he was."[58] Composer George Chadwick wrote of Thomas the man and his efforts on behalf of American composers:

> I have never had any other teacher or friend in my whole career, from whom I absorbed so much in knowledge, in stimulation, or in courage to fight for a high standard and for an ideal. It was impossible to come into his presence without feeling his magnetism and the force of his great personality. . . . One felt at once that here was a *man* . . . intolerant of everything that was against the principles of eternal truth and beauty.
>
> He alone, of all the American conductors, has treated American composition as a dignified and serious effort. . . . Not, on the one hand, as the work of incompetent amateurs to be scoffed and sneered at; nor, on the other, as an infant industry to be coddled and shielded from all opposition. He produced the works of American writers side by side with the classic, and also the modern masters, so that they could be compared with their contemporaries, and could stand or fall by their own intrinsic value—the only position a real artist cares to occupy.[59]

The *New York Times* editorialized on America's debt to the man who had developed the public's taste for good music. His concerts at Irving Place, Terrace Garden, and Central Park Garden "saw the line of ignorance and indifference steadily pushed back, the standard gradually, almost insidiously, raised." Most of Thomas's concerts had to be given up, the *Times* wrote, but they had all "borne good fruit. 'Tis not the grapes of Canaan that repay, but the high faith that fails not by the way.'"[60] Henry Krehbiel of the *Daily Tribune*, who had known Thomas for thirty years, laid him to rest with ambivalent praise in ambiguous prose:

> Thomas had many friends, who saw only his good qualities as a man and were blind to his defects as an artist, because, chiefly, they did not know wherein artistic merit lay. He had enemies, who saw only his personal and social infirmities, and persisted in confounding those with artistic short-comings. To the first he gave his friendship, and they were helpful to him in his great achievements; to the second he gave indifference or contempt. . . . He was in many enterprises, but never in one the success of which would not have redounded to the honor, advantage and glory of art.[61]

His departure from New York was not a "calamity," Krehbiel asserted, for the seeds he sowed there had sprouted: "Others were at hand to nourish the sturdy plants, and the flowers are now fragrant, the fruits glorious."

There were many musical tributes as well. The New York Philharmonic played the *Marche funèbre* from the "Eroica" on January 6 to honor its greatest conductor.[62] There was a memorial concert at the Metropolitan Opera House on January 8; among the soloists was Max Bendix, now concertmaster of the Met orchestra.[63] Fritz Scheel changed the Philadelphia Orchestra's program on January 6 to a memorial concert.[64] The Chicago Orchestral Association, the Cincinnati Music Festival Association, the Brooklyn Philharmonic, the Chicago Musicians' Union, the Aschenbrödel Verein, and other organizations with which Thomas had worked all paid their respects. In fact, not until Toscanini's death over half a century later did a conductor's passing attract as much attention. (Toscanini's fame in his later years was aided by radio and records; Thomas's fame stemmed from the several thousand concerts he had led across the length and breadth of America, from whistle stops to great metropolises.)

Thomas's "religious" approach to great music and his unceasing efforts to spread its moral benefits, however secular in their basis, had long struck responsive chords among the clergy. The popular Chicago minister Frank Gunsaulus spoke of Thomas the idealist, of his "spiritual force" and "the effects he produced on man's higher being." For both Chicago's Protestant and Jewish clergy, Thomas represented "the kinship between religion and music."[65]

The funeral took place on Friday, January 6, at 11 A.M. at St. James Episcopalian Church. Association trustees and honorary pallbearers preceded the funeral cortège; eight members of the orchestra were the pallbearers. It was a simple service with no eulogies. Bach and Beethoven were played on the organ and by a wind choir from the orchestra. The subscription concerts scheduled for that afternoon and the next evening were postponed, but Stock led a memorial concert, for subscribers only, at Orchestra Hall at the normal Friday time. Another concert, for donors, was held at the Auditorium on Sunday afternoon, and for once the hall was too small to accommodate the public, many of whom remained outside in the blistering January cold in silent tribute. Stock chose a Bach chorale, the first two movements of the "Eroica," the "Funeral" March from *Die Götterdämmerung*, and *Death and Transfiguration*. The funeral and both concerts were solemn, beautiful occasions. Final interment was, as planned, at the Mount Auburn Cemetery, in Cambridge, Massachusetts, on March 4, 1905.

Not long afterward, the Chicago Orchestra was renamed the Theodore Thomas Orchestra, as a lasting tribute to its founder. (In 1912–13, it officially became "The Chicago Symphony Orchestra, Founded by Theodore Thomas.")[66] On January 10, 1905, the association trustees met and voted that "hereafter, the Friday afternoon and Saturday evening concerts falling nearest the anniversary of his death shall be a memorial to the honored founder and leader of the Chicago Orchestra, Theodore Thomas."[67] President Lathrop then read a letter from Rose Thomas bequeathing her husband's entire orchestra library, other than the material earmarked for the Newberry Library, to the Chicago Orchestra.[68] (In 1913, she angrily withdrew some of the most valuable scores, because she objected to the orchestra's change in name, and gave them to the Newberry.)[69]

A bronze statue of Theodore Thomas was unveiled on May 3, 1910, in the foyer of his "other" hall, Music Hall in Cincinnati. President William Howard Taft, a native of the city, spoke glowingly of "this man, who made an ideal of his art and lived up to it."[70] Some fourteen years later, on April 24, 1924, a statue commemorating Thomas was unveiled by his daughter, Minna Thomas Sturgis, in the south garden of the Art Institute of Chicago, opposite Orchestra Hall. Charles H. Hamill, then president of the Chicago Symphony, praised Thomas for his unerring taste, "the last refinement of artistic judgement." The memorial's inscription, written by Paderewski and chiseled in stone, reads: "Scarcely any man in any country has done so much for the musical education of the people as has Theodore Thomas in this country. The nobility of his ideals and the magnificence of his achievements will assure him everlasting glory."[71]

In 1941, Charles Norman Fay, who had moved to Boston—he was in his early nineties—wrote an article for the Chicago Symphony's fiftieth anniversary program. The passage of time had not diminished his ebullience when referring to Thomas and his orchestra: "There were presidents from Grant to Theodore Roosevelt; Generals Sherman and Sheridan; Statesmen Root and Hay; Inventors Edison, Bell, McCormick . . . financiers . . . industrialists . . . all of them men of great achievement. But by far 'bigger' than any of them— the most powerful personalities I have known—*men as great as their work*—

were two musicians: Ignace Paderewski and Theodore Thomas." Toward the end of the piece, Fay wrote of his delight at hearing the Chicago Symphony at Symphony Hall in Boston and at "the warmth and admiration of that educated audience, for the masterly continuation of the Thomas tradition by Dr. Stock [who was still conducting after 35 years]. *Brilliance* their own Boston orchestra has, indeed, and unsurpassable technic, but not the quality, the tenderness, the balance and reserved emotion of *our* [!] orchestra."[72]

Rose Fay Thomas died in 1929. She once said that if her husband had known of the high esteem in which he was held, "it would have glorified and inspired his declining years. But very little of all this came to his knowledge, for while he was the recipient of many honors during his life, they came chiefly from special sources, and of the popular reverence and love he realized very little."[73] But Thomas had neither sought nor expected love or reverence; and more than what he got would have embarrassed him. What he really wanted was critical and professional acclaim, and he had had that in no small measure, certain New York critics notwithstanding. What he resented was being considered an outdated conductor as he grew older.

How good a conductor was Thomas? How did he compare to Habeneck and Mendelssohn before him, to contemporaries like von Bülow, Richter, and Seidl, to younger contemporaries like Nikisch, Mahler, and Toscanini, not to mention later greats of the twentieth century—Furtwängler, Stokowski, Koussevitsky, Von Karajan, Solti, and Bernstein? Without recordings for reference, our judgments must depend on written accounts. Musical criticism was in its infancy and of variable quality in the Gilded Age, but enough good critics heard Thomas in New York, Chicago, Boston, and Cincinnati— conducting too was a young art—to leave us valid assessments of his work.

Thomas conducted with economy of motion, quiet control, and with no choreographic embellishments, all of which led to his being accused of lacking feeling and excitement; and his reserved demeanor off the podium helped to reinforce this "unemotional" image. Yet nothing could be further from the truth. Thomas simply did not wear his heart on his sleeve. He throttled emotional display because it got in the way of the music; he did not conduct to show off, to be a "star" (he would probably not have known what the word meant). Yet, despite his restraint, in his own unobtrusive way he was a joy to behold as well as to listen to when he was in front of an orchestra. Sidney Lanier, in a well-known piece on Thomas, said that his baton was "alive, full of grace, of symmetry; he made no gestures, rarely looked at his score, seeth everybody, heareth everything, warneth every man, encourageth every instrument, quietly, firmly, marvelously." No nonsense, no affectations. "He taketh the orchestra in his hand as if it were a pen and writeth with it."[74]

Like Toscanini and Reiner, Thomas strove relentlessly for accuracy in rehearsals and performances; like Stokowski, he sought blend and tone color; like Furtwängler, he masterfully brought to light the intentions of the great masters. He may have lacked the imagination of Furtwängler, the dynamism of Von Karajan and Solti, the frenzied emotion of Bernstein, and the special gift of Nikisch, but he did establish the Chicago "tradition" that Fay wrote of on the orchestra's fiftieth anniversary—mellow, refined, and graceful. The orchestra may not have had the finish of the Boston Symphony, the sensuality of the Philadelphia Orchestra, or the brash brilliance of the New York Philharmonic, but it had a memorable life and style of its own.

Going to a symphonic concert today is tantamount to going to a museum. We want and get the standard works of the eighteenth and nineteenth centuries, along with a number of "acceptable" works of this century, but very little new music. North American symphonic audiences want no surprises. How long they will continue to attend concerts, given this mentality, is anyone's guess, although the danger signs are there and must be heeded. Thomas, like other conductors, cultivated the public's love for this museum repertoire. But he constantly performed new works along with old, constantly stretched his public's ears with music that could be unpopular—Berlioz, Wagner, and Liszt—in the programs of the Theodore Thomas Orchestra, the Philharmonic, with all of its conservatism, and the Chicago Orchestra. Thomas's programming in fourteen Chicago seasons was devoted not only to the classical and the early and mid-nineteenth-century composers but to "contemporaries" like Brahms, Tchaikovsky, Dvořák, Elgar, and Richard Strauss. That much of their music is now part of the museum repertoire is not surprising; however, it was Thomas who recognized its merit and promoted it. He set an example for serious and enterprising conductors who followed him.

Thomas's efforts were not confined to great contemporaries: he played the music of many now-forgotten composers. The nineteenth century was rich—but no richer than the twentieth—in composers writing for orchestra. Look, for example, at Thomas's season of crisis, the season after the fair, 1893–94. He did the American premiere of Gustave Charpentier's *Impressions d'Italie* at the first concert, the Overture "Count Robert of Paris" by Horatio Parker at the second, the American premiere of a new symphony by Christian Sinding at the third. Going to a Thomas concert was always an adventure, and even when it could have meant life or death for the Chicago Orchestra, he did not cater to the box office. The Chicago millionaires who so admired this courageous, tenacious, and self-made man of music never asked him to.

Unlike today's conductors, Thomas not only had to assemble an orchestra, train it, and conduct it well, but he had to create the opportunities for it to perform in a country not yet ready to listen. He strove and he sacrificed, this "Johnny Appleseed of Music," and coped with each new setback in turn. He could be stubborn, egotistical, and even selfish, learning to compromise only in his later years. Conducting, lifting a stick, and having 100 players and 500 voices respond is a giddy experience for any musician. While such power can go to one's head, it did not in Thomas's case: he used it wisely, showed more good judgment than bad, and treated his players with respect, as he did boards, sponsors, and friends.

There were many nineteenth-century "captains of industry," but Theodore Thomas was the only real "captain of musical enterprise." With his competence, drive, and ambition, he undoubtedly would have been successful in any kind of work. Victorian morality inhibited him personally but fueled the missionary zeal that spurred him on to great deeds and accomplishments. His was a successful and fulfilled life. Daniel Burnham once said, "Make no little plans, they have no magic to stir men's blood."[75] Was he thinking of Thomas, who had the vision to make big plans and bring them to life? What Thomas did for music in the United States is all around us. The people of his time said that his work would be appreciated for generations to come. They were right.

Chronology

1835   Theodore Thomas born on October 11 at Esens, East Friesland, Germany

1845   Emigrates with his family to New York City

1848   Joins the navy band in Norfolk, Virginia, with his father, Johann Thomas

1850   Returns to New York

1852   Featured as violin soloist at Dodworth band concert

1854   Elected to the Philharmonic Society of New York; joins first violin section

1855   Mason-Thomas chamber concerts begin in New York

1859   Conducts Donizetti's *Lucrezia Borgia* at New York's Academy of Music on April 20

1862   Directs first orchestral concert at New York's Irving Hall on May 14

1863   Matinee series at Irving Hall begins on October 24

1864   Soiree symphonic concerts begin on December 3; marries Minna Rhodes

1866   Appointed musical director of the Brooklyn Philharmonic Society; Theodore Thomas Orchestra gives summer concert series at New York's Terrace Garden

1867   Hears European orchestras; meets Berlioz, Dvořák, Joachim, and von Bülow

1868   Directs first of eight consecutive summer concert seasons at New York's Central Park Garden

1869   Leads inaugural tour of Thomas Orchestra on "Thomas Highway"

1873   Conducts Rubinstein-Wieniawski concerts; founds Cincinnati May Festival

1876   Directs Philadelphia Centennial concerts

1877   Elected conductor of the Philharmonic Society of New York; gives first season of Summer Night Concerts at Chicago's Industrial Exposition Building

1878   Cincinnati's Music Hall is completed and opens for Third May Festival on May 14; appointed director of the newly founded Cincinnati College of Music and moves to Cincinnati

1879   Resumes conductorship of Philharmonic Society of New York

1880   Leaves Cincinnati College of Music and moves back to New York

1882   Conducts tri-city festival in New York, Cincinnati, and Chicago

1883   Conducts "Ocean to Ocean" festival tour

1884   Conducts Wagner festival tour

1885   Becomes director of newly organized American Opera Company

1887   American Opera Company folds

1889   Minna Thomas dies

1890   Marries Rose Fay

1891   Leaves New York to found the Chicago Orchestra, directing its first concert at the Chicago Auditorium on October 17; appointed musical director of the 1893 World's Columbian Exposition

1896   Chicago Orchestra plays in New York for first time

1903   Drive to build Chicago's Orchestra Hall begins

1904   Orchestra Hall is dedicated on December 14

1905   Theodore Thomas dies on January 4

Notes

The following abbreviations are used:

CT   *Chicago Tribune*
CHS   Cincinnati Historical Society
DJM   *Dwight's Journal of Music*
FC   Felsengarten Collection
GJ   Glessner journals, Chicago Historical Society
MC   *Musical Courier*
NL   Newberry Library
NYDT   *New York Daily Tribune*
NYH   *New York Herald*
NYPL   Library and Museum of the Performing Arts, New York Public Library at
        Lincoln Center
NYPS   New York Philharmonic Society minutes and bylaws, NYPL
NYT   *New York Times*
RFT   Rose Fay Thomas, *Memoirs of Theodore Thomas* (New York: Moffat Yard
        and Co., 1911)
TT   Theodore Thomas, *A Musical Autobiography*, ed. George P. Upton, 2
        vols. (Chicago: A. C. McClurg & Co., 1905)
TTCP   Theodore Thomas concert programs, Theodore Thomas Papers, NL
        (TTCP refers to fifty-one volumes of programs and a few press clippings
        that Thomas bequeathed to the Newberry Library. The programs are in
        chronological order, from February 20, 1852, until May 31, 1903.)

Introduction
1. "Music Palace Opens," *Chicago Evening Post*, Dec. 14, 1904.

Chapter 1
1. Partisans of the American actor Edwin Forrest mobbed performances by the English actor William Macready at the Astor Place Opera House. Militia were called to the scene and fired on the mob, killing twenty people.

2. H. Earle Johnson, "The Germania Musical Society," *Musical Quarterly* 32 (Jan. 1952), 75–93.

3. "Josef Gungl on Musical Taste in America," *DJM* 2 (Dec. 18, 1852), 83–84, reprinted from *Neue Berliner Musikzeitung*.

4. Joseph Wandel, *The German Dimension of American History* (Chicago: Nelson Hall, 1979), pp. 2–5; Edward K. Spann, *The New Metropolis: New York City, 1840–1857* (New York: Columbia University Press, 1981), p. 24.

5. Letter from Marschner to Thomas, 1860, NL. Thomas, who saw Marschner in Paris in 1860, where they spent time together, did not mention this trip in his autobiography.

6. TT, vol. 1, p. 22.

7. TT, vol. 1, pp. 29–30.

8. Thomas Ryan, *Recollections of an Old Musician* (London: Sands & Co., 1899), pp. 74–75.

9. *NYH*, Aug. 30, 1852.

10. "William Mason's Reminiscences of Theodore Thomas," *Chicago InterOcean*, Jan. 15, 1905.

11. "Musical Correspondence," *DJM* 2 (Dec 1, 1855), 68.

12. William Mason, *Memories of a Musical Life* (New York: The Century Co., 1901), p. 201; *NYT*, Apr. 21, 1859.

13. George P. Upton, *Musical Memories: My Recollections of Celebrities of the Half Century, 1850–1900* (Chicago: A. C. McClurg & Co., 1908), p. 181.

14. TTCP, vol. 135.

15. Quoted in H. Earle Johnson, *First Performances in America to 1900—Works with Orchestra* (Detroit: College Music Society, Information Coordinators, 1979), p. 377.

16. "The Concert of Mr. Theodore Thomas," *NYDT*, May 15, 1862.

17. Quoted in T. C. Russell, "Theodore Thomas: His Role in the Development of Musical Culture in the United States, 1835–1905" (Ph.D. diss., University of Minnesota, 1969), p. 33.

18. TTCP, vol. 135.

19. The renovation is described in "Music in New York," *DJM* 22 (Sept. 27, 1862), 205; reprinted from *NYDT*, Sept. 20, 1862.

20. Ibid.

21. Ibid., p. 204.

22. TT, vol. 1, p. 50.

23. Apr. 30, 1857, NYPL. The society was incorporated on May 5, 1857.

24. Marta Milinowski, *Teresa Carreño: "By the Grace of God"* (New York: Da Capo Press, 1977), p. 34.

25. Richard Hoffman, *Some Musical Recollections of Fifty Years* (New York: Charles Scribner's Sons, 1910), pp. 133–34. Gottschalk had given several of his own concerts in New York earlier in the week.

26. See note 10.

27. RFT, p. 31.

28. "English Opera in Brooklyn," *New York World*, Jan. 6, 1864.

29. This performance of Fry's opera was part of a Central Fair in aid of the U.S. Sanitary Commission, a volunteer organization that helped nurse and rehabilitate maimed and disabled Civil War victims. Thomas was responsible for planning and conducting the fair's musical programs: *Bohemian Girl*, *Maritana*, Haydn's *Creation*, and several miscellaneous concerts.

30. "Musical Correspondence," *DJM* 24 (Nov. 12, 1864), 343–44.

Chapter 2

1. Announcement card, TTCP, vol. 135.

2. "New York," *DJM* 24 (Dec. 24, 1864), 363–64; "Symphonic Soirees of Theodore Thomas," *NYH*, Dec. 4, 1864; "Amusements," *NYT*, Dec. 11, 1864; see also TTCP, vol. 135.

3. "Musical Portraits: Theodore Thomas," *The Playbill*, Jan. 11, 1865.

4. *The Orpheus*, Mar. 3, 1866.

5. For transcriptions, see NL and FC.

6. "Theodore Thomas' Symphonic Soirees," *NYH*, Jan. 9, 1865; *Watson's Weekly Art Journal*, Jan. 14, 1865.

7. "Theodore Thomas' Second Symphonic Soiree," TTCP, vol. 135.

8. "Symphony Soiree," newspaper clipping, ibid.

9. Ibid.

10. "Amusements," *NYT*, Feb. 12, 1866.

11. T. C. Russell, "Theodore Thomas," p. 68.

12. *NYH*, Aug. 6, 1866.

13. TT, vol. 1, p. 54.

14. *NYH*, Sept. 3, 1866.

15. Quoted in Lilli Lehmann, *My Pathway through Life*, trans. Alice Seligman (New York: G. Putnam and Sons, 1914), p. 344.

16. "Musical Notes," *NYDT*, Nov. 12, 1867. In the fall, the society replaced the silver baton with an ebony baton tipped with gold.

17. NYPS business meeting minutes, May 25, 1867, NYPL.

18. RFT, pp. 36–45. Thomas kept a diary of the trip.

19. T. C. Russell, "Theodore Thomas," p. 66.

20. TTCP, vol. 137.

21. "Mason and Thomas Conservatory" (advertisement), *NYDT*, Sept. 28, 1867.

22. Letter from NYPS, Apr. 18, 1868, NYPL.

23. Newspaper clipping, Aug. 19, 1868, TTCP, vol. 137.

24. "Garden Concerts," *NYH*, May 28, 1868; see also "Thomas's Concerts," *NYDT*, May 27, 1868; ibid., May 21, 1868; Edwin T. Rice, "Thomas and Central Park Garden," *Musical Quarterly* 26 (Apr. 1940), 43–51.

25. "Opening of Steinway Hall," *NYDT*, Oct. 22, 1868.

26. "Theodore Thomas and His Orchestra," *DJM* 29 (Nov. 1869), 134.

27. Both articles, dated Nov. 1, 1869, reprinted in RFT, p. 55.

28. Philo Adams Otis, *The Chicago Symphony: Its Organization, Growth and Development, 1891–1924* (Chicago: Clayton F. Summy Co., 1924), p. 11.

29. *Cleveland Plain Dealer*, Nov. 23, 1869; *Buffalo Express*, Nov. 20, 1869; *Detroit Free Press*, Nov. 26, 1869; see also RFT, pp. 57–58.

30. Reprinted in RFT, pp. 58–59.

31. Quoted in Harvey S. Whistler, "The Life and Work of Theodore Thomas" (Ph.D. diss., Ohio State University, 1942), pp. 94–96.

32. Quoted in TT, vol. 1, p. 118. Upton helped Thomas write his autobiography and then wrote an appreciation of Thomas to accompany it. He also collated all of Thomas's orchestral programs, covering a forty-three-year span, as well as the Mason-Thomas programs.

33. "Theodore Thomas's Concerts," *DJM* 30 (Oct. 22, 1870), 334–35.

34. "The Thomas Concerts," *Cincinnati Daily Gazette*, Dec. 2, 1870; see also unpublished notes of Joseph E. Holliday, University of Cincinnati, concerning visits by the Thomas Orchestra to Cincinnati.

35. "Theodore Thomas," *NYDT*, Jan. 28, 1871.

36. Quoted in Walter Damrosch, *My Musical Life* (New York: Charles Scribner's Sons, 1926), p. 22.

37. Cited in Florence Ffrench, *Music and Musicians in Chicago* (Chicago: by the author, 1899), pp. 18–19.

38. TT, vol. 1, p. 56.

39. "Music," *Atlantic Monthly* 29 (Feb. 1872), 248.

40. *Atlanta Constitution*, Feb. 9, 1872; *New Orleans Picayune*, Feb. 20, 21, 1872; see also *Charleston Daily Courier*, Feb. 2, 1872.

Chapter 3

1. See TT, vol. 1, pp. 78–79. Their first meeting was probably in March 1872.

2. Ibid., vol. 2, p. 18.

3. Quoted in ibid., vol. 1, p. 133.

4. *Philadelphia Evening Bulletin*, July 17, 1872; reprinted in "Thomas' Garden Concerts," *DJM* 32 (Aug. 10, 1872), 284.

5. See TT, vol. 1, pp. 61–62.

6. "Thomas and His Orchestra at Steinway Hall," *DJM* 32 (Nov. 30, 1872), 34.

7. "Some Rubinstein Reminiscences [Maurice Grau]," *NYH*, Nov. 25, 1894; "Personal Reminiscences of Anton Rubinstein as Related by William Steinway," *Freund's Musical Weekly*, Nov. 30, 1894, p. 5.

8. "The Rubinstein Concerts," *NYT*, Jan. 1, 1873.

9. "Rubinstein," *NYDT*, Apr. 1, 1873.

10. "Rubinstein's Farewell," *DJM* 33 (May 31, 1873), 30–31.

11. "Some Rubinstein Reminiscences [Maurice Grau]," *NYH*, Nov. 25, 1894.

12. "Personal Reminiscences . . . William Steinway," *Freund's Musical Weekly*, Nov. 30, 1894, p. 5.

13. TT, vol. 1, pp. 63–64.

14. "Testimonial Dinner for Theodore Thomas," *MC*, Apr. 29, 1891, pp. 416–20; see also note 9.

15. "Genius and Mediocrity," *NYT*, Apr. 26, 1873.

16. See Charles Hamm, *Music in the New World* (New York: W. W. Norton, 1983), esp. p. 310, for a concise account of Gilmore's festivals.

17. "Circular of Invitation," Nov. 12, 1872, CHS; "The May Musical Festival," *Cincinnati Daily Gazette*, Oct. 24, 1872.

18. "The May Musical Festival," *Cincinnati Times and Chronicle*, Nov. 6, 1872; *Cincinnati Daily Gazette*, Oct. 24, 1872.

19. Letters from Thomas to Nichols, Jan. 20, Feb. 7, Mar. 3, Mar. 10, 1873, CHS.

20. *Cincinnati Commercial*, May 6, 1873; see also *NYDT*, May 7, 1873, for orchestra statistics.

21. "Cincinnati May Musical Festival," *Cincinnati Commercial*, May 5, 1873.

22. "Music," *NYDT*, May 7, 1873.

23. "The Cincinnati Festival," *Detroit Tribune*, May 11, 1873.

24. "Cincinnati," *Chicago Times*, May 11, 1873.

25. "Cincinnati," *CT*, May 10, 1873.

26. "Cincinnati," ibid., May 9, 1873.

27. "Why It Was a Failure," *Chicago Times*, May 10, 1873.

28. *Detroit Free Press*, May 11, 1873.

29. "Cincinnati," *CT*, May 10, 1873.

30. "The Cincinnati Musical Festival," *Indianapolis News*, May 10, 1873; "The Cincinnati Festival," *Detroit Tribune*, June 2, 1873.

31. TTCP, vol. 143; see also "Central Park Garden," *NYT*, May 21, 1873.

32. Essays dated May 14, 1873, and May 21, 1873, ibid.

33. Essay dated June 4, 1873, ibid.

34. Essay dated Sept. 3, 1873, ibid., vol. 145.

35. See RFT, pp. 96–99.

36. Letter from von Bülow, Aug. 11, 1872, quoted in ibid., pp. 78–79; TT, vol. 1, p. 62.

37. See RFT, pp. 81–82.

38. Quoted in "Music," *NYDT*, Apr. 26, 1874.

39. Letter, Mar. 20, 1874, TTCP, vol. 146 (Apr. 1874).

40. Howard Shanet, *Philharmonic: A History of New York's Orchestra* (Garden City, N.Y.: Doubleday & Co., 1975), p. 144.

41. Quoted in Johnson, *First Performances*, p. 81.

42. "Letter from the Celebrated Franz Liszt," *Cincinnati Commercial*, May 14, 1874.

43. Newspaper clipping, Sept. 19, 1874, George Ward Nichols Scrapbook, CHS.

44. Ibid.

45. "A May Festival," *NYT*, Apr. 11, 1875.

46. "The Cincinnati Musical Festival," *Baltimore Bulletin*, May 12, 1875; reprinted in *DJM* 35 (May 29, 1875), 25.

47. Ibid.

48. *Cincinnati Daily Gazette*, May 14, 1875.

49. Letter from Springer to John Shillito, May 1875, reproduced in the *First Annual Report of the Cincinnati Music Hall Association*, Apr. 30, 1877, pp. 3–5, CHS.

50. Ibid.

51. *Dictionary of American Biography*, vol. 9, ed. Dumas Malone (New York, Charles Scribner's Sons, 1958), pp. 482–83.

52. "Gilmore's Concert Garden," *NYT*, May 30, 1875.

53. "Law Reports," *NYT*, Apr. 2, 1876.

54. See George Martin, *The Damrosch Dynasty* (Boston: Houghton Mifflin Co., 1983), p. 33.

55. Sam Franko, *Chords and Discords: Memories and Musings of an American Musician* (New York: Viking, 1938), pp. 62–63. Franko founded the American Symphony Orchestra in New York in 1894, gave "Concerts of Old Music" between 1900 and 1909, and taught violin at the Stern Conservatory in Berlin from 1910 to 1915. He then returned to the United States, where he died in 1937.

56. Hans von Bülow, *Briefe*, vol. 6 (Leipzig: Breitkopf and Härtel, 1904), pp. 299–301.

57. Letter to Cosima Wagner, Feb. 6, 1876; see Klaus Liepmann letter in *High Fidelity* 26 (Mar. 1976), 6–7, and Siegmund Levarie, "Hans von Bülow in America," *Institute for Studies in American Music Newsletter* 11 (Nov. 1981), 8–10.

Chapter 4

1. Bernard A. Weisberger, *The Life History of the United States*, vol. 7 (New York: Time, 1964), p. 8.

2. William Dean Howells, "A Sennight at the Centennial," *Atlantic Monthly* 38 (July 1876), 106–7.

3. RFT, p. 109.

4. "Music at the Centennial," *NYDT*, Sept. 8, 1875.

5. "Music at the Centennial," *Watson's Art Journal*, Nov. 20, 1875, p. 43.

6. Quoted in "The Centennial Music," *NYT*, Jan. 31, 1876.

7. RFT, pp. 111–17. Rose Fay Thomas probably translated this correspondence.

8. Quoted in Klaus Liepmann, "Wagner's Proposal to America," *High Fidelity* 25 (Dec. 1975), 70–72.

9. "Opening of the Fair," *NYDT*, May 11, 1876.

10. *NYH*, May 11, 1876.

11. "The Music," *NYDT*, May 11, 1876.

12. "Inauguration," *Philadelphia Press*, May 11, 1876.

13. "The Music," *NYT*, May 11, 1876.

14. See note 11.

15. Quoted in "Inaugurated," *Philadelphia Inquirer*, May 11, 1876.

16. Abram Loft, "Richard Wagner, Theodore Thomas and the American Centennial," *Musical Quarterly* 37 (Apr. 1951), 184–202; see also *American Musician*, June 9, 1886, pp. 234–35.

17. See Loft, "American Centennial," pp. 195–96.

18. Ibid., pp. 198–99.

19. "The Garden Concerts," *NYDT*, June 8, 1876.

20. Jacques Offenbach, *Orpheus in America: Offenbach's Diary of His Journey to the New World*, trans. Lander MacClintock (Bloomington: Indiana University Press, 1958), p. 166; see also *Musical Times* 18 (Apr. 1, 1877), 167–69.

21. Offenbach, *Orpheus in America*, p. 191.

22. Ibid., pp. 122–23.

23. Loft, "American Centennial," p. 200.

24. C. E. Russell, *The American Orchestra and Theodore Thomas* (Garden City, N.Y.: Doubleday, Page & Co., 1927), p. 103.

25. RFT, p. 108.

26. Shanet, *Philharmonic*, pp. 133–35.

27. Ibid., pp. 152–53. Strong's diaries are an invaluable account of cultural life in mid-nineteenth-century New York.

28. Program dated Oct. 4, 1876, TTCP, vol. 154.

29. NYPS business meeting minutes, May 18, 1877, NYPL. Later meetings in June and July resolved matters.

30. Shanet, *Philharmonic*, pp. 160–61.

31. "A Great Concert Hall," NYDT, May 12, 1877; RFT, pp. 123–25.

32. See C. Norman Fay, "The Theodore Thomas Orchestra", *The Outlook*, Jan. 22, 1910, pp. 159–69. The building was so large that during the Pullman strike of 1877, federal troops camped at one end without disturbing concerts at the other end.

33. See RFT, pp. 123–25.

34. TT, vol. 1, p. 171.

35. Otis, *Chicago Symphony*, p. 15.

36. Letter to Wirt Dexter and others, July 28, 1877, in RFT, p. 132.

Chapter 5

1. See Robert Thomas Gifford, "The Cincinnati Music Hall and Exposition Building" (Master's thesis, Cornell University, 1973), p. 115. The local press wrote voluminous accounts of the hall's features; see especially "The Cincinnati Music Hall Organ," *Cincinnati Daily Gazette*, Apr. 11, 1878.

2. "The May Festival," *Cincinnati Commercial*, Apr. 10, 1878.

3. Ibid., May 15, 1878; see also ibid., May 9, 1878; "Third Biennial Festival at Cincinnati," CT, May 13–14, 1878, reprinted in DJM 38 (May 25, 1878), 236–37.

4. "Springer's Remarks," *Cincinnati Enquirer*, May 15, 1878.

5. "Third Biennial Festival," DJM 38 (June 8, 1878), 244–45.

6. RFT, pp. 144–51.

7. "Mr. George B. Carpenter," *Cincinnati Enquirer*, Mar. 8, 1880.

8. "Theodore Thomas," NYDT, Aug. 26, 1878.

9. "Cincinnati Takes Thomas," NYT, Aug. 27, 1878.

10. Reprinted in "Go West Young Man, Go West! And He Went," DJM 35 (Sept 14, 1878), 301.

11. Martin, *Damrosch Dynasty*, p. 47.

12. Quoted in NYPS business meeting minutes, Aug. 30, 1878, NYPL.

13. Shanet, *Philharmonic*, p. 160. Forty-six members voted for Neuendorff, twenty-nine for Damrosch. Damrosch's supporters contested the results, and for a while it looked as if the society would break up because of the dispute. In truth, the Philharmonic might have been better off with Damrosch, for Neuendorff's season would be the worst in Philharmonic history. Box-office receipts fell to around $7,000, 10 percent lower than the year of the Damrosch fiasco.

14. "Brooklyn Philharmonic Society," NYT, June 7, 1878. The society generously agreed to let Beale repay the sum in a "reasonable length of time," which he never did.

15. Damrosch, *My Musical Life*, pp. 25–26.

16. *NYH*, Oct. 4, 1878.

17. "Thomas's Farewell Concert," *NYDT*, Oct. 4, 1878.

18. "Theodore Thomas's Farewell Concert," *NYT*, Oct. 4, 1878.

19. College publication, Oct. 1878, CHS.

20. Thomas suggested this in March 1880. See RFT, pp. 123–25.

21. Letters from Gemünder to Thomas, Sept. 30, Oct. 11, 18, 23, 1878; July 27, 1879, NL. According to Whistler, "Theodore Thomas," pp. 948–53, the conductor tried to help Americans develop an appreciation of fine violins. Whistler cites Jay C. Freeman's piece on Thomas in *Who Is Who in Music* (Chicago: Lee Stern Press, 1941) to verify this; a Chicago luthier, Freeman knew Thomas personally. Thomas also wrote an introduction in 1904 for Lyon & Healy's "Hawley Collection of Violins," which addressed instruments made by master Italian violin makers of the seventeenth and eighteenth centuries.

22. Louis R. Thomas, "The Glorious Drunk," *Cincinnati Historical Society Bulletin* 33 (Oct. 1975), 222–39.

23. Quoted in ibid.

24. Ibid.

25. "Prize of One Thousand Dollars Offered for a Musical Composition," a CMFA announcement "for the information of Editors," signed by Thomas and the board of directors, CHS; see also "The Cincinnati Musical Prize," *NYT*, Feb. 13, 1879.

26. "The May Festival Prize," *Cincinnati Daily Gazette*, Jan. 30, 1880.

27. "A Prize Musical Competition," *NYT*, Jan. 30, 1880; see also ibid., Mar. 20, 1880, for hints of foul play.

28. "The Cincinnati Prize," *NYDT*, Apr. 3, 1880; "May Festival Prize," *Cincinnati Daily Gazette*, Apr. 15, 1880.

29. NYPS business meeting minutes, Apr. 29, 1879, NYPL; see also "The Philharmonic Society," *NYT*, Apr. 30, 1879.

30. Thomas gave his account of subsequent proceedings in press interviews. See especially "An Interview with Theodore Thomas," *Cincinnati Enquirer*, Mar. 5, 1880; "Colonel Nichols Resigns," *Cincinnati Daily Gazette*, Mar. 6, 1880; "Theodore Thomas Back," *NYDT*, Mar. 12, 1880; "Theodore Thomas Returns," *NYH*, Mar. 11, 1880.

31. The board published "Correspondence Connected with the Withdrawal of Mr. Theodore Thomas from the College of Music of Cincinnati" (Cincinnati: Press of Robert Clarke & Co., 1880). It commences with Goshorn's letter of Feb. 25, 1880, and concludes with the board's letter to Nichols on Mar. 5, 1880.

32. "Colonel Nichols Resigns," *Cincinnati Daily Gazette*, Mar. 6, 1880.

33. "Theodore Thomas Must Go," ibid., Mar. 9, 1880; "An Interview with Theodore Thomas," *Cincinnati Enquirer*, Mar. 9, 1880.

34. "At the Mass Rehearsal," *Cincinnati Commercial*, Mar. 10, 1880.

Chapter 6

1. "Arrival in New York City," *NYT*, Mar. 15, 1880.

2. CMFA minutes, May 6, 11, 1880, CHS.

3. "Why Otto Singer Was Superseded," *Cincinnati Commercial*, May 25, 1880.

4. RFT, p. 198.

5. "Serenade in New York City," *NYT*, May 26, 1880.

6. Quoted in RFT, pp. 179–88.

7. Franko, *Chords and Discords*, p. 56.

8. RFT, p. 182.

9. Ibid., p. 183; "The Handel Festival," *Musical Times* 20 (July 1, 1880), 338–39.

10. RFT, pp. 187–92. Maxwell replied on July 9, 1880, suggesting that London might be more attractive to Thomas than America; but, should Thomas stay in London, Maxwell hoped he would continue to conduct the May Festival (see letter, FC).

11. RFT, p. 184.

12. Ibid., p. 186.

13. *NYH*, Aug. 16, 1880. See also "What Theodore Thomas Says," *Musical Record*, Aug. 28, 1880, p. 753, and "Concerning a Proposition from P. T. Barnum," *The Musical and Dramatic Courier* (later the *Musical Courier*), Aug. 20, 1880, p. 243.

14. "Theodore Thomas," *NYDT*, Sept. 20, 1880. The paper omitted mention of the college course.

15. Shanet, *Philharmonic*, p. 166. Joseffy did receive a fee in the 1889–90 season, his last appearance with the Philharmonic. He later played with Thomas and the Chicago Orchestra.

16. Theodore Thomas, "Musical Possibilities in America," *Scribner's Monthly* 21 (Mar. 1881), 777–80.

17. "The Orchestral Problem Well-Nigh Solved," *DJM* 51 (Apr. 9, 1881), 58.

18. RFT, p. 204.

19. David Swing, "Notes from Address," *Chicago InterOcean*, Aug. 20, 1881.

20. "A Perverted Singing School," *NYT*, Jan. 27, 1881.

21. Negotiations began with a wire from Thomas to Maxwell on Nov. 5, in FC. Other wires and letters related to the engagement are in FC and CHS.

22. Quoted in *Cincinnati Enquirer*, Dec. 30, 1881.

23. *Cincinnati Commercial*, Dec. 30, 1881.

24. "The Cincinnati Opera Festival," *NYT*, Feb. 20, 1882; "Maretzek Abandons His Post," ibid., Mar. 11, 1882; "No More Pork for Max," ibid., Mar. 14, 1882.

25. Damrosch, *My Musical Life*, pp. 30–34; Martin, *Damrosch Dynasty*, pp. 56–59.

26. *NYH*, Mar. 31, 1882.

27. RFT, pp. 221–22; TT, vol. 1, p. 90; "The Music Festival," *NYDT*, Apr. 28, 1882.

28. "Frau Materna in This City," *NYDT*, Apr. 23, 1882.

29. Ibid.

30. "The May Music Festival," *NYT*, Mar. 12, 1882; "Arrangement of the Concert Room," *NYDT*, Apr. 29, 1882; RFT, pp. 225–26.

31. "The May Music Festival," *NYT*, Mar. 26, 1882; "Auction Sale of Festival Seats," *NYDT*, Apr. 18, 1882.

32. TTCP, vol. 161.

33. "The Music Festival," *NYH*, May 6, 1882.

34. George William Curtis, "The New York Festival of 1882," *Harper's New Monthly Magazine* 65 (July 1882), 306–8.

35. CMFA annual meeting minutes, June 17, 1882, CHS.

36. *Chicago InterOcean*, May 20, 1882.

37. Ibid., May 26, 1882.

38. Ibid., May 27, 1882.

Chapter 7

1. NYPS business meeting minutes, Apr. 15, 1882, NYPL.

2. "Trying to Corner Musicians," *NYT*, Nov. 13, 1882; "Dr. Damrosch in the West," ibid., Dec. 3, 1882.

3. *Freund's Weekly*, Feb. 14, 1884.

4. See *History of the Liederkranz of the City of New York, 1847–1947, and of the Arion, New York* (New York: Drechsel Printing Co., 1948), p. 19.

5. Ibid., pp. 15–16.

6. RFT, pp. 216–18.

7. Quoted in "Important Musical Decision," *NYT*, Jan. 24, 1883.

8. Letter from Buck to Thomas, Jan. 28, 1883, NL.

9. *The Musical Record*, Feb. 24, 1883, p. 406.

10. "The Wagner Memorial Concert," *NYDT*, Apr. 15, 1883. The tone quality of Thomas's orchestral bells drew great praise. One well-traveled critic said that they were better than Bayreuth's.

11. Newspaper clipping, TTCP, vol. 163.

12. "Thomas Continental Trip," *NYDT*, Apr. 1, 1883.

13. See W. S. B. Mathews, "Educational Bric-a-Brac," *Music* 19 (1900), 153–54.

14. TTCP, vol. 164.

15. Ibid.

16. *San Francisco Chronicle*, June 10, 1883.

17. TTCP, vol. 164.

18. *San Francisco Chronicle*, June 14, 1883.

19. Quoted in Richard McCandless Gipson, *The Life of Emma Thursby* (New York: The New-York Historical Society, 1940), pp. 336–39.

20. CMFA Chicago meeting minutes, July 13, 1883, CHS.

21. RFT, pp. 253–56.

22. *NYT*, Nov. 22, 1883.

23. "Theodore Thomas Concerts for Young People," ibid., Sept. 23, 1883.

24. "The Second Young People's Concert," *Freund's Music and Drama* 1 (Jan. 17, 1884); "Theodore Thomas Concerts for Young People," *NYT*, Jan. 13, 1884.

25. NYH, Feb. 25, 1884; *New York Evening Post*, Feb. 25, 1884; "The *Sun* and Music for the People," *Freund's Music and Drama* 1 (Apr. 10, 1884); "Theodore Thomas Concerts for Working Men," *NYT*, Mar. 31, 1884.

26. *New York Evening Post*, Feb. 25, 1884.

27. "The *Sun* and Music for the People," *Freund's Music and Drama* 1 (Apr. 10, 1884).

28. RFT, p. 261.

29. "The Boston Wagner Festival," *NYDT*, Apr. 15–16, 1884; "Boston Wagner Festival," *MC*, Apr. 23, 1884, p. 261.

30. Charles Dudley Warner, "Wagner's *Parsifal*," *Atlantic Monthly* 51 (Jan. 1883), 75–86. Reprinted in part in TTCP, vol. 165.

31. "Philadelphia Wagner Festival," *MC*, May 7, 1884, p. 300.

32. See "Boston Wagner Concerts," ibid., May 14, 1884, p. 317.

33. "Justice and Lawlessness," *NYT*, Mar. 31, 1884.

34. CMFA financial statements, FC.

35. CMFA annual report, June 17, 1884, CHS.

36. "Closed Is the Sixth of the Brilliant May Festivals," *Cincinnati Enquirer*, May 25, 1884.

37. See "Cincinnati's Musical Festival," *Chicago Morning News*, May 21, 1884.

38. "Sixth Cincinnati May Festival," *MC*, Mar. 26, 1884, p. 195.

39. See "The May Festival," *Chicago Evening Journal*, June 2, 1884; "The May Festival," *CT*, May 31, 1884.

40. "Chicago's May Festival," *Chicago Morning News*, May 28, 1884.

41. "May Music," *CT*, May 28, 1884.

42. "The May Festival," ibid., May 29, 1884; *Chicago Morning News*, May 30, 1884; see also *Chicago Times*, May 30, 1884, and *CT*, May 30, 1884.

43. "The May Festival," *Chicago Evening Journal*, June 2, 1884.

44. "The Overdone Musical Festivals," *Chicago Morning News*, June 19, 1884; "Musical Matters," *Chicago Saturday Evening Herald*, May 31, 1884.

45. "Quatrième et Cinquième Concert de l'Orchestre Thomas," *La Patrie*, June 30, 1884; see also *Montreal Star*, June 22, 1884. Despite entreaties that the public attend, houses were less than half full.

46. See "Mr. Gye to Succeed Mr. Abbey," *NYT*, Mar. 11, 1884.

47. Damrosch, *My Musical Life*, p. 52.

48. See "German Opera at the New House," *NYT*, Aug. 14, 1884.

49. TT, vol. 1, p. 94; RFT, pp. 276–78. The *Musical Courier* (July 9, 1884, p. 18) reported that Thomas might give Wagner's principal operas "a complete stage presentation in this city, perhaps next season, or the season after." That was less than a month before Damrosch's appointment.

50. "Opera at the Metropolitan," *NYDT*, Nov. 18, 1884.

51. See "Will Opera Houses Coalesce?," ibid., Jan. 18, 1885.

52. Quoted in "The Last Tributes Given," *NYT*, Feb. 19, 1885.

53. "Damrosch Obituary," *Freund's Music and Drama* 2 (Feb. 21 1885; Mar. 21, 1885); see also "The Philharmonic and the Funeral," *NYDT*, Feb. 20, 1885.

54. TT, vol. 1, p. 151. Gross income was greater; a dividend was worth $223.

55. See "Music in America," *Musical Times* 20 (May 1, 1885), 272–73. Van der Stucken later became director of the Cincinnati College of Music, the Cincinnati Symphony, and, after Thomas's death, the Cincinnati May Festival.

56. See "The Rose of Sharon," *NYDT*, Apr. 17, 1885.

57. Joseph Bennett, "Observations on Music in America," *Musical Times* 26 (June 1, 1885), 319–22; 26 (May 1, 1885), 255–56.

58. James Henry Mapleson, *The Mapleson Memoirs*, ed. Harold Rosenthal (London: Putnam, 1966), pp. 178–79. It was not until 1920 that an American orchestra, the New York Symphony conducted by Walter Damrosch, performed in Europe.

59. Lehmann, *My Pathway through Life*, pp. 344–46.

60. RFT, pp. 270–73.

61. See "Thomas and the Philharmonic," *NYT*, Feb. 22, 1885.

62. See Abram Loft, "Musicians' Guild and Union: A Consideration of the Evolution of Protective Organizations among Musicians" (Ph.D. diss., Columbia University, 1950), pp. 303–10. Similar union regulations prevail a century later.

63. Ibid.

64. Ibid.

65. See "Discord among Musicians," *NYT*, Nov. 4, 1885.

66. See "Discordant Musicians," ibid., Nov. 11, 1885; "Mr. Thomas' Oboe Player," ibid., Nov. 12, 1885; "Thomas and the Musical Union," ibid., Dec. 3, 1885.

67. See note 62.

68. Ibid.

69. Seventeen-year-old Amy Marcy Cheney (later the composer Mrs. Beach) was the piano soloist at the first concert.

70. See "The Thomas Concerts," *San Francisco Chronicle*, June 4, 1885.

Chapter 8

1. "A Project for American Opera," *MC*, Mar. 8, 1885, p. 148; "An American School of Opera," *Freund's Music and Drama* 3 (Mar. 14, 1885), 7.

2. "The American Opera Company's Plans," *MC*, Sept. 16, 1885, p. 165.

3. "School of Opera," *NYT*, Dec. 18, 1885.

4. "Patrons of American Opera," ibid., Dec. 29, 1885.

5. "Academy of Music," ibid., Jan. 5, 1886; "The American Opera," *NYDT*, Jan. 7, 1886.

6. Frederick Archer, "Opera Sung by Americans," *Keynote* 9 (Jan. 9, 1886), 2–3; "Opening of the Season of Opera Sung by Americans," *American Art Journal* 44 (Jan. 9, 1886), 196; *Freund's Music and Drama* 4 (Jan. 16, 1886), 5.

7. Quoted from *NYH* and *NYT*, in TTCP, vols. 169–70.

8. "A Supper in Honor of Herr Seidl," *MC*, Jan. 13, 1886, pp. 18, 21.

9. *NYT*, Apr. 11, 1886.

10. Henry E. Krehbiel, *Review of the New York Musical Season, 1886–1887* (New York and London: Novello, Ewer, 1887), pp. 203–4.

11. Quoted in TTCP, vols. 169–70.

12. "The German Lohengrin Sung by Americans in English," *American Art Journal* 44 (Jan. 23, 1886), 234.

13. Ibid. 44 (Jan. 30, 1886).

14. *Sylvia* was billed as a "spectacular ballet."

15. "Certain Uncertainties," *MC*, Aug. 25, 1886, p. 114.

16. "Opera in the Vernacular," *Boston Evening Transcript*, Apr. 20, 1886; "Music and the Drama," *Boston Traveler*, Apr. 29, 1886.

17. "Music and the Drama," *Boston Advertiser*, Apr. 26, 1886.

18. Quoted in "The American Opera Company in the Flying Dutchman," *Boston Herald*, Apr. 24, 1886.

19. "The American Opera," *Philadelphia Press*, Apr. 20, 1886.

20. See "Criticism in Baltimore," *MC*, May 26, 1886, p. 332.

21. *St. Louis Post-Dispatch*, May 14, 1886.

22. "The Ballet," *New York Sun*, June 13, 1886.

23. "Mme. Hastreiter's Woes," *NYT*, June 7, 1886.

24. American Opera Company, Circular, *MC*, July 28, 1886, p. 51.

25. "American Opera," ibid., Aug. 11, 1886, p. 85.

26. "The American Opera," *NYT*, July 19, 1886.

27. *MC*, Aug. 4, 1886, p. 66.

28. "A Controversy over Opera," *NYDT*, Aug. 9, 1886.

29. "The American Opera Company Wins," *MC*, Sept. 1, 1886, p. 134.

30. "Mrs. Thurber's Venture," ibid., Sept. 29, 1886, p. 194.

31. "A Musical Pilgrimage," *NYDT*, July 1, 1886.

32. "Paris in Midsummer Time," *NYT*, Aug. 20, 1886.

33. See *Freund's Music and Drama* 4 (June 5, 1886), which contains a reprint of an editorial in the *Cincinnati Commercial-Gazette*, May 26, 1886; see also *NYT*, May 22, 1886; CMFA annual meeting minutes, June 21, 1886, CHS.

34. Quoted in Johnson, *First Performances*, p. 99; see also *NYT* and *NYDT*, Nov. 14, 1886.

35. "National Opera in Philadelphia," *NYDT*, Nov. 16, 1886.

36. "The American Opera," *Philadelphia Times*, Nov. 21, 1886.

37. *Cincinnati Enquirer*, Nov. 8, 1886.

38. "Members of the Church Requested to Keep Away from the Opera," *St. Louis Republican*, Nov. 30, 1886; "Rubinstein's Ballet," *St. Louis Post-Dispatch*, Dec. 2, 1886.

39. "Ballet Coryphées," *St. Louis Post-Dispatch*, Dec. 1, 1886.

40. "Fursch-Madi in Tears," *NYT*, Dec. 1, 1886.

41. "Table Was the Cause," *CT*, Dec. 1, 1886.

42. "DeVivo Did It," *St. Louis Post-Dispatch*, Dec. 2, 1886.

43. "Mrs. Thurber's Grief," *St. Louis Evening Chronicle*, Dec. 1, 1886.

44. "Fursch-Madi Coming Back," *NYT*, Dec. 3, 1886.

45. "Hasty Hock," *St. Louis Post-Dispatch*, Dec. 1, 1886.

46. "Fursch-Madi's Victory," ibid., Dec. 3, 1886.

47. "Grand Opera Once More," *CT*, Dec. 9, 1886.

48. "The Change in Lakmé," ibid.

49. "Preachers at the Ballet," *NYT*, Dec. 17, 1886.

50. "St. Louis Ministers Shocked," *CT*, Dec. 19, 1886.

51. "Alone in the World," *Chicago Morning News*, Dec. 15, 1886.

52. "National Opera Troubles," *NYT*, Dec. 14, 1886.

53. "Will It Disorganize," *CT*, Dec. 14, 1886.

54. "The Members of the Company All Satisfied," ibid., Dec. 15, 1886.

55. "The New Opera Company," *NYT*, Jan. 1, 1887.

56. "Keeping Down Expenses," ibid., Jan. 2, 1887.

57. "Mrs. Thurber Its Saviour," *New York World*, Jan. 10, 1887.

58. "The Big Success of Nero," ibid., Mar. 16, 1887.

59. "A Review of the American Opera Company's Work," *Washington Post*, Feb. 6, 1887.

60. "Anton Seidl Goes," *MC*, Feb. 16, 1887, p. 104.

61. "Theodore Thomas Talks," *NYH*, Feb. 20, 1887.

62. "The Boston Orchestra," *NYT*, Feb. 15, 1887.

63. "Thomas Popular Concert," *NYDT*, Feb. 25, 1887.

64. "Count Hochberg's Subterfuge," *MC*, Apr. 20, 1887, p. 254.

65. NYPS business meeting minutes, June 22, 1887, NYPL.

66. "The National Opera Company," *NYDT*, Mar. 8, 1887.

67. "The Big Success of Nero," *New York World*, Mar. 16, 1887.

68. "Nero a Great Success," ibid., Mar. 15, 1887.

69. "Woeful Waste," *New York Graphic*, Mar. 19, 1887.

70. "Fursch-Madi's Victory," *NYT*, Apr. 3, 1887.

71. "Starting for the Wild West," ibid., Apr. 4, 1887.

72. "The National Opera Company Hangs Up the Fiddle," *Omaha World*, Apr. 14, 1887.

73. Quoted in RFT, pp. 300–301.

74. The sad ending of the NOC was not disclosed immediately; see the *New York World*'s cheerful account, "National Opera Returns," June 21, 1887.

75. "NOC Closes," *Freund's Music and Drama*, July 30, 1887; "National Opera Company," ibid., July 9, 1887. Thomas's letter of June 29, 1887, was reprinted in full.

76. TT, vol. 1, p. 95.

Chapter 9

1. See RFT, p. 303.

2. Ibid., p. 302.

3. Ibid., pp. 331–32.

4. Ibid., pp. 317–20; see also "Theodore Thomas Retires," *NYDT*, Sept. 22, 1888.

5. "A Public Calamity," *NYT*, Oct. 8, 1888.

6. Telegram from W. A. Hobart to Thomas, Dec. 31, 1888, FC.

7. "Mr. Thomas's Orchestra," *NYT*, August 5, 1888; Johnson, *First Performances*, pp. 85–86; "Thomas Concert," *MC*, Jan. 9, 1889, p. 23.

8. Johnson, *First Performances*, pp. 288–89; "Mr. Thomas's Matinee," *NYT*, Feb. 15, 1889.

9. Quoted in RFT, p. 316.

10. Letter from Thomas to MacDowell, Jan. 6, 1889, Edward MacDowell Papers, Rare Book and Manuscript Library, Columbia University; "The Fifth Thomas Concert," *NYDT*, Mar. 6, 1889.

11. "A New Music Hall," *NYT*, Mar. 15, 1889.

12. "New Music Hall," ibid., Mar. 22, 1889.

13. "New Music Halls," *MC*, Apr. 10, 1889, pp. 285–86.

14. "Von Bülow Comes Again," *NYT*, Mar. 28, 1889.

15. "Death of Mrs. Theodore Thomas," *NYDT*, Apr. 9, 1889.

16. J. M. Rogers, "Theodore Thomas—An Appreciation," *Booklovers Magazine* 5 (Apr. 1905), 530.

17. RFT, pp. 326–37.

18. "Many Music Lovers," *NYDT*, Apr. 22, 1889.

19. RFT, pp. 335–37.

20. Ibid.
21. "A Thomas Testimonial Tour," *CT*, May 19, 1889.
22. RFT, p. 339.
23. "The Thomas Orchestra," *NYT*, Oct. 10, 1889.
24. "Live Musical Topics," ibid., Oct. 13, 1889.
25. RFT, p. 343.
26. Ibid., p. 341.
27. Ibid., p. 347.
28. Ibid.
29. Ibid., 348–49.
30. Ibid.
31. Ibid., p. 350.
32. "Thomas Will Wed," *CT*, Feb. 13, 1890.
33. "Theodore Thomas Gets a License," *NYT*, Apr. 26, 1890.
34. "Marriage of the Famous Musician to Miss Rose Fay," *CT*, May 8, 1890.
35. Ibid.
36. NYPS business meeting minutes, May 1890, NYPL.
37. "Notes and Comments," *The Presto*, June 5, 1890, p. 294, cited in Whistler, "Theodore Thomas," p. 425.
38. "A Great Home of Music," *NYDT*, May 14, 1890.
39. "A Brilliant Audience," *NYT*, June 17, 1890.
40. "Strauss Orchestra at Madison Square Garden," ibid., June 17, 1890.
41. Quoted in "Theodore Thomas from Chicago," ibid., July 8, 1890.

Chapter 10

1. "Theodore Thomas Plans to Shake the Dust of New York from His Feet and Settle in Chicago," *NYT*, Nov. 7, 1890; see also "He Will Have a Great Orchestra," *CT*, May 8, 1890; "An Orchestra Needed," ibid., July 27, 1890.
2. C. Norman Fay, "The Theodore Thomas Orchestra," *The Outlook*, Jan. 22, 1910, pp. 159–69.
3. "Chicago's Musical Wants," *NYT*, Dec. 19, 1890.
4. RFT, p. 356.
5. Ibid., pp. 357–58.
6. NYPS business meeting minutes, Jan. 2 and 27, 1891, NYPL.
7. "For a Permanent Orchestra," *NYT*, Feb. 6, 1891.
8. *CT*, Feb. 14, 1891; see also "Can't Have Thomas," *Chicago Evening Post*, Feb. 11, 1891.
9. NYPS business meeting minutes, Apr. 1, 1891, NYPL.
10. Quaintance Eaton, "Great Opera Houses—Chicago," *Opera News*, Jan. 7, 1961, pp. 28–30.
11. "Will Not Play for Thomas," *NYT*, Mar. 11, 1891; see also *CT*, Mar. 6, 18, 20, 1891.
12. "Mr. Thomas in the City," *CT*, Mar. 22, 1891; see also "Theodore Thomas Version," ibid., Mar. 25, 1891.
13. "Testimonial Dinner to Theodore Thomas," *MC*, Apr. 29, 1891, pp. 416–20.

14. "It Stood the Test Well," *NYT*, May 6, 1891; Martin, *Damrosch Dynasty*, pp. 115–17. Wm. Knabe & Co. helped defray Tchaikovsky's expenses.

15. "Thomas' New Creation," *CT*, Oct. 17, 1891.

16. "It Was Thomas' Night," ibid., Nov. 8, 1891.

17. Otis, *Chicago Symphony*, p. 38.

18. W. S. B. Mathews, "The Chicago Orchestra Commercially Considered," *Music*, May 1892, pp. 574–81.

19. John Russell, *Erich Kleiber* (London: André Deutsch, 1957), p. 48; David Wooldridge, *Conductor's Art* (London: Barrie & Rockliff, 1971), p. 111; Ferdinand Pfohl, *Arthur Nikisch* (Hamburg: n.p., 1925).

20. "Editorial Bric-a-Brac," *Music*, Feb. 1898, pp. 485–86.

21. "Theodore Thomas on Musical Critics," *Chicago Herald*, Mar. 30, 1892.

22. Otis, *Chicago Symphony*, p. 38.

23. GJ, box 3, Oct. 18, 1891–June 26, 1892, pp. 104–5.

24. "Play with Thomas," *CT*, Dec. 20, 1891.

25. *Memorandum of Agreement* between the Orchestral Association and Fritz Dreibrodt, double bass player, Apr. 30, 1892, Chicago Symphony Orchestra archives.

26. "Music Hath Charms," *CT*, Oct. 23, 1892.

27. Letter from Busoni to Thomas, n.d., NL.

28. GJ, box 3, Feb. 28, 1893–Sept. 24, 1893, pp. 17–18.

29. RFT, pp. 372–74.

30. Otis, *Chicago Symphony*, p. 43; see also "Its Second Year a Success," *CT*, Apr. 16, 1893.

Chapter 11

1. Reid Badger, *The Great American Fair: The World's Columbian Exposition and American Culture* (Chicago: Nelson Hall, 1979), pp. 133–36. The House of Representatives selected Chicago on Feb. 24, 1890; the Senate verified the choice on April 21.

2. Ibid., p. 48.

3. Ibid.

4. Emmett Dedman, *Fabulous Chicago* (New York: Random House, 1953), p. 221. Charles Dana of the *New York Sun* spoke of the "nonsensical claims of that Windy City," and the sobriquet stuck.

5. Badger, *Great American Fair*, pp. 63–73.

6. David F. Burg, *Chicago's White City of 1893* (Lexington: University Press of Kentucky, 1976), p. 139; see also Stephen Longstreet, *Chicago 1860–1919* (New York: David McKay Company, 1973), who quoted Sullivan: "The damage wrought by the World's Fair will last for half a century . . . if not longer. It has penetrated deep in the American mind, effecting lesions significant of dementia" (p. 272). Important, too, is Ray Ginger, *Altgeld's America: The Lincoln Ideal versus Changing Realities* (Chicago: Quadrangle Books, 1965), pp. 15–25, for a reasoned negative view of White City. Ironically, the 1933 Chicago Fair—the committee secretary was Daniel Burnham, Jr.—was the epitome of modern architecture.

7. Letter from Burnham to Thomas, May 19, 1891, NL. The meetings were held May 25–26.

8. Letter from Davis to William T. Baker, Nov. 18, 1891, FC.

9. "Official Report of the Bureau of Music," Mar. 31, 1894, NL.

10. Ibid.

11. Wilson and his wife wrote a number of letters to Thomas from Europe; see FC.

12. See note 9; see also "Music for Visitors," CT, Mar. 27, 1892; "Music for the Fair," ibid., June 30, 1892. The *Tribune* carried two other lengthy stories on July 3. See "World's Fair Music," CT; "Chicago Trying to Shine," NYT, Sept. 18, 1892; "World's Columbian Exposition," MC, Mar. 8, 1893, p. 7. Fifteen works by seven American composers were listed as scheduled for performance at the fair; works by three other composers were to be selected.

13. The American bandmaster John Phillip Sousa, a Thomas admirer, described him as "one of the greatest conductors who ever lived. He gave Wagner, Liszt and Tschaikowsky in the belief that he was educating his public; I gave Wagner, Liszt and Tschaikowsky with the hope that I was entertaining my public. Thomas was primarily an educator, and nothing turned him aside from his purpose. It made him lose his sense of proportion, and at times brought him into sharp conflict with his public." Sousa, *Marching Along: Recollections of Men, Women and Music* (Boston: Hale Cushman and Flint, 1928), pp. 132–33.

14. NYH, Sept. 4, 1892. See also "The Kettle May Boil Over," MC, Sept. 13, 1892, p. 3; "Music at the World's Fair," NYT, Oct. 2, 1892; "Music at the Columbian Exposition," MC, Oct. 8, 1892, pp. 8–9.

15. CT, Sept. 29, 1892.

16. The official report (see note 9) summarized activities at the Women's Building. The National Federation of Women's Musical Clubs evolved from the fair.

17. Burg, *White City*, p. 101.

18. Letter from Rose Thomas to Amy Fay, reprinted in MC, Nov. 16, 1892, pp. 9–10.

19. Badger, *Great American Fair*, p. 84.

20. Letter from Thomas to Davis, Mar. 30, 1893, FC.

21. Longstreet, *Chicago 1860–1919*, p. 272.

22. Paul Hume and Ruth Hume, "The Great Chicago Piano War," *American Heritage* 21 (1970), pp. 16–21; see also Ignacy Jan Paderewski and Mary Lawton, *The Paderewski Memoirs* (New York: Charles Scribner's Sons, 1938); see note 25 below and note 28, chap. 10, for descriptions of meetings between Thomas and Paderewski.

23. "Piano Men Disgusted," NYT, Feb. 12, 1893; "Will Not Exhibit at the Fair," ibid., Feb. 15, 1893.

24. "The Steinway Piano: A Detailed Report of All Matters Concerning the World's Fair Controversy," *The Presto*, May 4, 1893.

25. Ibid. *The Presto* reported that W. S. B. Mathews explained to the national commission "that at a banquet a couple of months ago, following a concert . . . Thomas laughingly asked Paderewski why he didn't come and play at the World's Fair. The necks had been knocked off several bottles of extra dry and the whole crowd was in consequent good humor. With a graciousness befitting a genial frame of mind, the great pianist announced his entire willingness to play . . . the only thing in the nature of a contract between Mr. Thomas and the pianist."

26. Hume and Hume, "Piano War," p. 20.

27. See "Wrangle over Music," *Chicago Evening Post*, Apr. 30, 1893; "Thomas Ungentlemanly Act," ibid., May 4, 1893; "Thomas to Be Tried," *Chicago Herald*, May 9, 1893.

28. Hume and Hume, "Piano War," p. 21.

29. Reprinted in ibid. A few days after Paderewski played, the *Chicago Herald* ran a full-page advertisement for Lyon, Potter, a local music store that held the Steinway franchise. The advertisement denied, tongue-in-cheek, that the store had been paying the *Evening Post* for free publicity about the wicked Steinway piano and invited the curious to visit its showrooms to see "the merits of . . . superior musical instruments." Paderewski's own instrument was on display, "and for days crowds stretched around the block waiting for a chance to file by and look at it. In the end [the piano] was the only real winner in the Great Chicago Piano War."

30. C. E. Russell, *American Orchestra*, p. 227.

31. Ibid., pp. 221–25.

32. Ibid., p. 228.

33. "The Bureau of Music," *The Presto*, May 25, 1893, pp. 19ff.

34. C. E. Russell, *American Orchestra*, p. 227.

35. Ibid., pp. 228, 230–31.

36. See note 9. The bureau sponsored 197 concerts from May until the end of August—137 pay and 55 free concerts. Among them were 32 pay and 58 free concerts by the exposition orchestra, 27 pay choral concerts, and 62 pay organ recitals. Admission for reserved seats at choral and orchestral concerts was usually one dollar; organ recitals cost twenty-five cents. Other concerts were given by visiting concert groups, some not sponsored by the bureau.

37. *Chicago Herald*, May 12, 1893.

38. RFT, p. 411. The letter suggests that it was written on August 12, but Thomas actually wrote it on August 1, the executive committee reviewed it on August 9, and the resignation was made official on August 12; see FC.

39. "Thomas Gives It Up," *CT*, Aug. 4, 1893; "Mr. Thomas Going," *Chicago Mail*, Aug. 12, 1893; "Art and Chicago," *NYT*, Aug. 12, 1893.

40. Ginger, *Altgeld's America*, p. 21; Henry Adams, *The Education of Henry Adams* (1918; rpt. Boston: Houghton Mifflin, 1961), p. 340.

41. Telegrams from Ellsworth to Thomas and Bendix, Dietrich, and Sachleben to Thomas, Aug. 21, 1893, FC.

42. Telegram from Thomas to Ellsworth, Aug. 22, 1893, FC.

43. RFT, pp. 415–16.

44. See note 9.

45. Ibid.

46. Sandy R. Mazzola, "Bands and Orchestras at the World's Columbian Exposition," *American Music* 4 (Winter 1986), 411–15; *American Art Journal*, Aug. 12, 1893, p. 413.

47. RFT, p. 416.

48. C. E. Russell, *American Orchestra*, pp. 235–36.

49. See note 9.

50. Ibid.

Chapter 12

1. Mueller, *American Symphony Orchestra*, pp. 86–87.

2. RFT, pp. 423–24.

3. Whistler, "Theodore Thomas," pp. 455–56, cites an article in the *Metronome* (reprinted in *MC*, Nov. 24, 1886, p. 324) that claimed that Thomas was indeed concerned about any signs of aging when on the podium. According to C. E. Russell, *American Orchestra*, pp. 268–69, Thomas covered his bald spot in rehearsals, first with a jockey cap, then with a black silk cap, and finally, in 1898, with a wig. The first time he wore it at rehearsal, "he marched out before [the orchestra's] astonished gaze and turned his back. 'Now laugh,' said he, and added with a peculiar emphasis, 'once!'"

4. RFT, p. 424.

5. Mueller, *American Symphony Orchestra*, p. 87.

6. TT, vol. 1, pp. 275–79.

7. Letter from Fay to Hutchinson, Feb. 1, 1894, NL.

8. T. C. Russell, "Theodore Thomas," p. 154, has observed that from 1891 to 1904, Thomas's final year as conductor, he gave 26 percent of his concerts without a soloist, 18 percent with soloists from the orchestra, and 56 percent with soloists from outside the orchestra, at a cost of but 4 percent of the orchestra's total budget for the fifteen seasons. Yet, when the soprano Lillian Nordica was soloist in the 1895–96 season, for example, single-ticket sales jumped from an average of $300 to $2,000 per concert.

9. "Trying to Get Theodore Thomas Back," *NYDT*, Mar. 6, 1894.

10. "Thomas May Give Concerts Here," *NYT*, Mar. 19, 1894.

11. Otis, *Chicago Symphony*, p. 58.

12. "Theodore Thomas's New Plans," *NYDT*, May 24, 1894; "Mr. Thomas's New York Plan Dropped," ibid., May 25, 1894.

13. Louis R. Thomas, "A History of the Cincinnati Symphony Orchestra to 1931" (Ph.D. diss., University of Cincinnati, 1972), pp. 99–127. The Ladies Music Club had organized the symphony and its first board was composed entirely of women.

14. Dedman, *Fabulous Chicago*, p. 199.

15. Letter from Glessner to Harper, May 14, 1894, President's Papers, ser. 1, University of Chicago Archives.

16. Otis, *Chicago Symphony*, pp. 59–61; Ginger, *Altgeld's America*, p. 159.

17. Letters between Bendix and Thomas, June and July 1894, private collection of Dr. Leon Stein.

18. "M. Ysaye Demands a High Perch," *CT*, Feb. 1, 1895.

19. "Theodore Thomas' Golden Jubilee," *CT*, Feb. 3, 1895.

20. Otis, *Chicago Symphony*, pp. 73–74.

21. "Editorial Bric-a-Brac," *Music* 9 (Oct. 1895–Apr. 1896), 538.

22. GJ, box 3, Apr. 28, 1895–Mar. 18, 1896, p. 3.

23. Ibid., pp. 43–44.

24. Ibid., p. 41.

25. Letter from Lehmann to Thomas, Nov. 13, 1895, NL.

26. "Mr. Thomas Saw Art," *Chicago Times-Herald*, Oct. 11, 1895.

27. "Trunk Full of Music," unidentified clipping, Oct. 11, 1895, Chicago Symphony Orchestra Scrapbooks, vol. 1, NL.

28. "Mr. Thomas As He Is," *Chicago Evening Post*, Dec. 21, 1895.

29. "Theodore Thomas Once More," *NYT*, Mar. 18, 1896; "Yesterday's Musical Doings," ibid., Mar. 28, 1896.

30. See RFT, pp. 444–45.

31. Richard Aldrich, *Musical Discourse* (New York: Oxford University Press, 1928), p. 302.

32. "Adieu to Theodore Thomas," *NYT*, Mar. 29, 1896.

33. Otis, *Chicago Symphony*, p. 80.

34. Ffrench, *Music and Musicians*, pp. 77–80.

35. *Prospectus*, n.d.; letter from Richard Waterman to William Rainey Harper, Oct. 23, 1896, see note 15.

36. Otis, *Chicago Symphony*, p. 82.

37. "Max Bendix Drops Out," *NYT*, Sept. 18, 1896; *Chicago Record-Herald*, Sept. 19, 1896; "Interview with Mr. Max Bendix," *Music* 14 (May–Oct. 1898), 71–76.

38. Otis, *Chicago Symphony*, p. 85.

39. Johnson, *First Performances*, p. 130.

40. RFT, pp. 455–57.

41. "Music," *NYT*, Mar. 15, 1898; "The Thomas Concerts," ibid., Mar. 15, 1898.

42. RFT, pp. 468–79.

43. Quoted in ibid.

44. Quoted in ibid.

45. "Theodore Thomas Talks of Music in New York," *New York Press*, Mar. 20, 1898.

46. "Artists in a Wreck," *CT*, Mar. 30, 1898.

47. Henry T. Finck, ed., *Anton Seidl: A Memorial by His Friends* (New York: Chas. Scribners & Sons, 1899).

48. Otis, *Chicago Symphony*, pp. 104–7.

49. "Trouble in Dixie," *Chicago Chronicle*, Apr. 20, 1899.

50. "The Orchestral Chief and the Western Advance in Music," *St. Paul Dispatch*, Dec. 2, 1898.

51. RFT, p. 485.

52. Otis, *Chicago Symphony*, p. 118.

53. Ibid., p. 114.

54. Letter from Colonne to Thomas, Aug. 15, 1899, NL.

55. Letter from Thomas to Colonne, Sept. 14, 1899, NL.

56. RFT, pp. 482–84.

57. Unidentified clipping, Chicago Symphony Orchestra Scrapbooks, vol. 2, NL.

58. Chicago Symphony Board minutes, Dec. 19, 28, 30, 1899, NL.

59. Letter from Thomas to Burnham, Jan. 1, 1900, Art Institute of Chicago.

60. Letter from Burnham to Thomas, Oct. 26, 1901, NL.

61. Letter from Mason to Thomas, NL.

62. Letters between Mason and Thomas, Oct. 7, 1900, Sept. 14, 27, Oct. 19, 1901, NL.

63. GJ, box 4, June 2, 1901–May 1, 1902, p. 52.

64. C. E. Russell, *American Orchestra*, p. 287.

65. "Announces Great Gift," *Chicago Evening Post*, Feb. 15, 1900; "Great Gift from Thomas," *Chicago Herald*, Feb. 15, 1900.

66. Philip Hart, *Orpheus in the New World* (New York: W. W. Norton, 1973), pp. 60–62.

67. "Theodore Thomas Home," *CT*, Oct. 1, 1902. Thomas failed to tell the reporter about the fiftieth birthday party he had given for his wife on September 4, a lively picnic at Felsengarten. The event began with a mock English royal procession, led by Thomas dressed as a drum major: "He wore white duck trousers, a Prince Albert coat, a black evening waistcoat (it was still morning), a four in hand tie and an opera hat with a large wreath of golden rod around it. He carried a baton of golden rod— and his scarf pin wore the metal head of a champagne bottle. He wore a charm made of champagne corks, and a large wooden medal from his children . . . inscribed 'to Theodore Thomas, who carried out water and brought in liquor' [Evidently, Thomas had worked out an effective drainage system for the house]." (GJ, box 4, May 18, 1902–Jan. 18, 1903, pp. 36–38) The guests—Frederick Stock, Bruno Steindel, several others from the orchestra, Hector Thomas and his wife, and, of course, the Glessners —were also dressed in outlandish garb. Rose Thomas spoke to the assembly in her role as Queen Victoria—the Thomases were not notable Anglophiles—which was followed by "God Save the Queen," "Home Sweet Home," and "The Last Rose of Summer," sung by all and played on an odd assortment of instruments. A string quartet then played Beethoven quartets. It was an extremely happy day.

68. Hart, *Orpheus*, p. 34. See also Shanet, *Philharmonic*, p. 439.

69. Letter from Harper to Fay, July 4, 1900, see note 15.

70. RFT, pp. 156–58.

71. Letter from Thomas to Harper, Feb. 26, 1901, see note 15.

72. Otis, *Chicago Symphony*, pp. 132–35.

73. "Against Van der Stucken," *Indianapolis News*, Feb. 11, 1898.

Chapter 13

1. *Chicago InterOcean, CT, Chicago Evening Post, Chicago Journal*, all Feb. 13, 1903.

2. "'In a Statement,'" *CT*; "Our Deficiency Orchestra," *Chicago Chronicle*; "Our Great Orchestra," *Chicago Evening Post*, all Feb. 8, 1903.

3. "Lose $30,000 on Concerts," *Chicago Chronicle*, May 2, 1902.

4. RFT, pp. 513–18.

5. "Public Can Aid Orchestra," *Chicago Record-Herald*, Feb. 28, 1903.

6. "Plea for Orchestra," ibid., Mar. 13, 1903.

7. Chicago Symphony Orchestra Papers, NL.

8. "Many Gifts to Orchestra," *CT*, Mar. 14, 1903.

9. "Has Chicago Grown Weary of Classical Music? Views of Theodore Thomas on the Future of the Chicago Orchestra," *Chicago InterOcean*, Mar. 1, 1903.

10. Ibid.; "The Chicago Orchestra," *Chicago Record-Herald*, Mar. 22, 1903.

11. "Plea for Orchestra," ibid., Apr. 12, 1903.

12. Otis, *Chicago Symphony*, p. 143.

13. "Chicago's Growth in Musical Taste Is Very Gratifying, Says Theodore Thomas," *Chicago InterOcean*, Oct. 24, 1903.

14. "Chicago Orchestra Concert," *CT*, Oct. 24, 1903.

15. "Thomas Orchestra at Crisis," *Chicago Evening Post*, Nov. 11, 1903.

16. "Give Orchestra New Life," *CT*, Dec. 1, 1903.

17. TT, vol. 1, pp. 107–8.

18. "Music Hall Assured," *Chicago Evening Post*, Mar. 2, 1904.

19. For brief accounts of the fire, see Dedman, *Fabulous Chicago*, pp. 218, 219; Longstreet, *Chicago 1860–1919*, pp. 415–18. The aftermath of the fire saw a series of new safety regulations for Chicago's theaters and concert halls: requirements for automatic sprinklers and proper ventilators, fireproof curtains, clearly marked, unlocked exit doors that opened outward, and minimal use of wood and other flammable material (the latter especially affected Thomas's and Burnham's building plans).

20. "Berlioz' Music Given," *Chicago Record-Herald*, Dec. 12, 1903; "The Chicago Orchestra," *Chicago InterOcean*, Dec. 12, 1903.

21. Quoted in RFT, p. 503.

22. "Dr. Strauss Leads Chicago Orchestra," *Chicago InterOcean*, Apr. 2, 1904.

23. Ibid.; "Music and the Drama," *Chicago Evening Post*, Apr. 2, 1904; "Richard Strauss Scores Triumph with Orchestra," *Chicago Record-Herald*, Apr. 2, 1904.

24. "Richard Strauss Believes in Himself," *CT*, Apr. 3, 1904.

25. RFT, p. 531.

26. Ibid., p. 480.

27. Sixteenth May Music Festival program, May 11–14, 1904, p. 2, CHS.

28. Otis, *Chicago Symphony*, pp. 147–48; RFT, p. 509.

29. Theodore Thomas and Frederick Stock, *Talks about Beethoven's Symphonies*, ed. Rose Fay Thomas (Boston: Oliver Ditson Co., 1930).

30. See RFT, p. 530. The "Life Work" was edited by George P. Upton and published in two volumes; see TT.

31. From the introduction by Leon Stein to the 1964 Da Capo Press reprint of Thomas's autobiography.

32. GJ, box 5, Jan. 1904–Aug. 1904, p. 72.

33. RFT, p. 530.

34. Whistler, "Theodore Thomas," pp. 620–27.

35. RFT, p. 534.

36. Ibid., pp. 520–24.

37. "An Architect's View of the New Thomas Music Hall," *Chicago InterOcean*, July 31, 1904.

38. RFT, p. 534.

39. Otis, *Chicago Symphony*, p. 130.

40. "Theodore Thomas Likes New Hall," *Chicago InterOcean*, Dec. 10, 1904.

41. C. E. Russell, *American Orchestra*, pp. 299–300.

42. "A Night of Pride," *CT*, Dec. 11, 1904.

43. "Music Palace Opens," *Chicago Evening Post*, Dec. 14, 1904.

44. "Orchestra in Its New Home," *Chicago Journal*, Dec. 15, 1904; "Thomas Welcomed to Orchestra Hall," *Chicago InterOcean*, Dec. 15, 1904; "Orchestra Hall Is Dedicated," *CT*, Dec. 15, 1904.

45. "Acoustics of Hall Defective," *CT*, Dec. 15, 1904.

46. "Have You Heard the Orchestra," *Chicago InterOcean*, Dec. 18, 1904.

47. "The Chicago Orchestra," *Chicago Record-Herald*, Dec. 18, 1904.

48. Ibid.

49. Unpublished paper by Richard Schulze, author's files.

50. CSO Librarian Lionel Sayers told me in 1974 that Eric De Lamarter, a young choirmaster when the hall opened and later assistant conductor of the CSO and conductor of the Chicago Civic Symphony, told Sayers that Thomas's disappointment with the hall "crushed" him. Yet, Alfred Barthel, Thomas's principal oboist in 1904–5, told Theodora Schulze, his student in the 1940s, that Thomas liked the hall very much.

51. RFT, p. 542.

52. "Theo. Thomas Very Ill," *Chicago Evening Post*, Dec. 31, 1904.

53. GJ, box 5, Aug. 8, 1904–Feb. 18, 1905, p. 73.

54. RFT, p. 543.

55. See note 53. Minna Sturgis and Marion (Mrs. Gale Carter) were both in New York and received news of their father's death by telephone.

56. "Demise of Thomas Is Keenly Felt," *Chicago Journal*, Jan. 4, 1905.

57. RFT, pp. 564–69.

58. Ibid.

59. Ibid.

60. *NYT*, Jan. 5, 1905.

61. "Theodore Thomas Dead," *NYDT*, Jan. 5, 1905.

62. "Safonoff Conducts the Philharmonic," *NYT*, Jan. 7, 1905.

63. "Throng at Thomas Concert," ibid., Jan. 9, 1905.

64. Frances Wister, *Twenty-Five Years of the Philadelphia Orchestra* (Philadelphia: Books for Libraries Press, 1970), p. 170.

65. RFT, p. 563.

66. Otis, *Chicago Symphony*, pp. 248–52. The change was made to strengthen the orchestra's relationship with the city that supported it and to prevent any other group from using the name "Chicago Symphony Orchestra."

67. Ibid., p. 156.

68. Ibid., p. 157. Rose Thomas did this with Hector and Hermann Thomas's approval. The library's value, she hoped, would make up for Thomas's small "contribution in money towards the new Hall." His will was filed for probate on Jan. 19, 1905. See "Music Library Is $150,000—All Other Property Left by Theodore Thomas Is Valued Only at Around $50,000," *CT*, Jan. 20, 1905.

69. GJ, box 6, May 1912–May 1913.

70. Otis, *Chicago Symphony*, pp. 219, 220; see also "The Memorial Statue of Theodore Thomas," program, May 1910, Municipal Art Society of Cincinnati.

71. "Theodore Thomas Memorial Dedicated," *Musical Leader*, May 1, 1924. See also Otis, *Chicago Symphony*, p. 372.

72. Charles Norman Fay, "Theodore Thomas, an Appreciation," CSO *Program Notes, Fiftieth Anniversary Program*, pp. 25–39.

73. RFT, p. 547.

74. Quoted in Harold C. Schonberg, *The Great Conductors* (New York: Simon and Schuster, 1967), p. 196.

75. Dedman, *Fabulous Chicago*, p. 301.

Bibliography

This bibliography, which is divided into three main sections, includes most of the items cited in the Notes and adds others used but not cited.

BOOKS AND THESES

By and About Thomas

Correspondence Connected with the Withdrawal of Mr. Theodore Thomas from the College of Music of Cincinnati. Cincinnati: Press of Robert Clarke & Co., 1880.

Russell, Charles Edward. *The American Orchestra and Theodore Thomas.* Garden City, N.Y.: Doubleday, Page & Co., 1927. (An affectionate account by a popular biographer who knew Thomas personally; includes some penetrating observations and insights about Thomas's character and goals.)

Russell, T. C. "Theodore Thomas: His Role in the Development of Musical Culture in the United States, 1835–1905." Ph.D. diss., University of Minnesota, 1969. (Deals best with Thomas's early years and criticizes his obsessive desire for a permanent orchestra.)

Thomas, Rose Fay. *Memoirs of Theodore Thomas.* New York: Moffat, Yard and Co., 1911; Freeport, N.Y.: Books for Libraries Press, 1971. (A long, informative, adoring memoir; includes extracts from important correspondence and other relevant documents.)

Thomas, Theodore. *A Musical Autobiography.* Edited by George P. Upton. 2 vols. Chicago: A. C. McClurg & Co., 1905. (Vol. 1 consists of Thomas's "Life-Work," a reverent "Reminiscence and Appreciation" by Upton, several articles by Thomas, and speeches and tributes given by others. Vol. 2 includes, among other items, Thomas's most important concert programs. Vol. 1 and Thomas's introduction to vol. 2 were reprinted by Da Capo Press in 1964, with a thoughtful introduction by Leon Stein.)

Thomas, Theodore, and Frederick Stock. *Talks about Beethoven's Symphonies.* Edited by Rose Fay Thomas. Boston: Oliver Ditson Co., 1930.

Whistler, H. S. "The Life and Work of Theodore Thomas." Ph.D. diss., Ohio State University, 1942. (Deals best with Thomas's Chicago years; includes an exhaustive bibliography.)

About Music, Musicians, and Musical Life

Aldrich, Richard. *Musical Discourse.* New York: Oxford University Press, 1928.

Arditi, Luigi. *My Reminiscences.* New York: Dodd, Mead & Co., 1950.

Aronson, Rudolph. *Theatrical and Musical Memories.* New York: McBride, Nast & Co., 1913.

Bowen, Catherine Drinker. *Free Artist: The Story of Anton and Nicholas Rubinstein.* New York: Random House, 1939.

Bülow, Hans von. *Briefe und Schriften,* vol. 6. Leipzig: Breitkopf and Härtel, 1904.

Carse, Adam. *The Life of Jullien.* Cambridge: W. Heffer & Sons, 1951.

———. *The Orchestra from Beethoven to Berlioz.* New York: Broude Bros., 1949.

Chase, Gilbert. *America's Music from the Pilgrims to the Present.* 3d ed. Urbana: University of Illinois Press, 1987.

Chicago Symphony Orchestra. *Biography of an Orchestra: An Affectionate Look at Eighty Years of Music and Life in Chicago.* Chicago: Chicago Symphony Orchestra, 1971.

———. *Chicago Symphony Orchestra—75th Anniversary Diamond Jubilee.* Chicago: Chicago Symphony Orchestra, 1966.

Damrosch, Walter. *My Musical Life.* New York: Charles Scribner's Sons, 1926.

Davis, Ronald L. *A History of Music in American Life.* Vol. 2, *The Gilded Years, 1865–1920.* Huntington, N.Y.: Krieger, 1980.

Early Histories of the New York Philharmonic (H. E. Krehbiel, 1892; James G. Huneker, 1917; John Erskine, 1943), with an introduction and notes by Howard Shanet. New York: Da Capo Press, 1979.

Eisler, Paul E. *The Metropolitan Opera: The First Twenty-Five Years, 1883–1908.* Croton-on-Hudson, N.Y.: North River Press, 1984.

Elson, Louis C. *The History of American Music.* 2d rev. ed., edited by Arthur Elson. New York: Macmillan, 1925.

Ewen, David. *The Man with the Baton.* New York: Thomas Y. Crowell, 1937.

Ffrench, Florence. *Music and Musicians in Chicago.* Chicago: by the author, 1899.

Finck, Henry T., ed. *Anton Seidl: A Memorial by His Friends.* New York: Chas. Scribner & Sons, 1899.

Finck, Henry T. *My Adventures in the Golden Age of Music.* New York: Funk and Wagnalls, 1926; New York: Da Capo Press, 1971.

Fiske, Stephen. *Off-Hand Portraits of Prominent New Yorkers.* New York: George R. Lockwood and Son, 1884.

Frank, Leonie C. *Musical Life in Early Cincinnati and the Origin of the May Festival.* Cincinnati: The Ruter Press, 1932.

Franko, Sam. *Chords and Discords: Memories and Musings of an American Musician.* New York: Viking, 1938.

Gifford, Robert Thomas. "The Cincinnati Music Hall and Exposition Building." Master's thesis, Cornell University, 1973.

Gillespie, Elizabeth Duane. *A Book of Remembrances*. Philadelphia: J. B. Lippincott Co., 1901.

Gipson, Richard M. *The Life of Emma Thursby*. New York: The New-York Historical Society, 1940.

Goldin, Milton. *The Music Merchants*. Toronto: Collier-Macmillan, 1969.

Graber, Kenneth Gene. "The Life and Works of William Mason." Ph.D. diss., University of Iowa, 1976.

Hamm, Charles. *Music in the New World*. New York: W. W. Norton, 1983.

Hart, Philip. *Orpheus in the New World*. New York: W. W. Norton, 1973.

Herz, Henri. *My Travels in America* (1866). Translated by Henry Bertrand. Madison: The State Historical Society of Wisconsin, for the Department of History, University of Wisconsin, 1963.

History of the Liederkranz of the City of New York, 1847–1947, and of the Arion, New York. New York: Drechsel Printing Co., 1948.

Hitchcock, H. Wiley. *Music in the United States: A Historical Introduction*. Englewood Cliffs, N.J.: Prentice-Hall, 1969.

Hoffman, Richard B. *Some Musical Recollections of Fifty Years*. New York: Scribners, 1910.

Horowitz, Joseph. *Understanding Toscanini*. New York: Alfred A. Knopf, 1987.

Howe, M. A. DeWolfe, and John N. Burk. *The Boston Symphony Orchestra, 1881–1931*. Boston: Houghton Mifflin Co., 1931.

Johnson, Ellis A. "The Chicago Symphony Orchestra, 1891–1942: A Study in American Cultural History." Ph.D. diss., University of Chicago, 1954.

Johnson, H. Earle. *First Performances in America to 1900—Works with Orchestra*. Detroit: College Music Society, by Information Coordinators, 1979.

———. *Hallelujah, Amen! The Story of the Handel and Haydn Society of Boston*. New York: Da Capo Press, 1981. Originally published in 1964.

Kaye, Joseph. *Victor Herbert*. Freeport, N.Y.: Books for Libraries Press, 1970. Originally published in 1931.

Kellogg, Clara Louise. *Memoirs of an American Prima Donna*. New York: Da Capo Press, 1978. Originally published in 1913.

Koury, Daniel James. "The Orchestra in the Nineteenth Century: Physical Aspects of Its Performance Practice." Ph.D. diss., Boston University, 1981.

Krehbiel, H. E. "Music in America." In *Famous Composers and Their Music*, vol. 6, edited by Theodore Thomas, John Knowles Paine, and Karl Klauser. New York: Merrill & Baker, 1901.

———. *Review of the New York Musical Season*. 5 vols. (1885–86, 1886–87, 1887–88, 1888–89, 1889–90). New York and London: Novello, Ewer & Co., 1886–90.

Krummel, D. W., Jean Geil, Doris J. Dyen, and Deane L. Root. *Resources of American Music History: A Directory of Source Materials from Colonial Times to World War II*. Urbana: University of Illinois Press, 1981.

Lahee, Henry C. *Annals of Music in America*. Boston: Marshall Jones Co., 1922.

Lang, Paul Henry, ed. *One Hundred Years of Music in America*. New York: G. Schirmer, 1961.

Lehmann, Lilli. *My Pathway through Life*. Translated by Alice Seligman. New York: G. Putnam and Sons, 1914.

Loesser, Arthur. *Men, Women and Pianos: A Social History*. New York: Simon and Schuster, 1954.

Loft, Abram. "Musicians' Guild and Union: A Consideration of the Evolution of Protective Organizations among Musicians." Ph.D. diss., Columbia University, 1950.

Mapleson, James Henry. *The Mapleson Memoirs*. Edited and annotated by Harold Rosenthal. London: Putnam, 1966.

Maretzek, Max. *Crochets and Quavers* (New York, 1855) and *Sharps and Flats* (New York, 1890) reprinted as *Revelations of an Opera Manager in 19th Century America*. New York: Dover Publications, 1968.

Martin, George. *The Damrosch Dynasty*. Boston: Houghton Mifflin Co., 1983.

Mason, William. *Memories of a Musical Life*. New York: The Century Co., 1901.

Mathews, W. S. B. *A Hundred Years of Music in America*. Chicago: G. L. Howe, 1889; New York: AMS Press, 1970.

Milinowski, Marta. *Teresa Carreño: "By the Grace of God."* New York: Da Capo Press, 1977. Originally published in 1940.

Moore, Edward C. *Forty Years of Opera in Chicago*. New York: Horace Liveright, 1930.

Mueller, John H. *The American Symphony Orchestra: A Social History of Musical Taste*. Bloomington: Indiana University Press, 1951.

Mussulman, Joseph A. *Music in the Cultured Generation: A Social History of Music in America, 1870–1900*. Evanston: Northwestern University Press, 1971.

Odell, George C. D. *Annals of the New York Stage: From Beginnings to 1894*. 15 vols. New York: Columbia University Press, 1937.

Offenbach, Jacques. *Orpheus in America: Offenbach's Diary of His Journey to the New World*. Translated by Lander MacClintock. Bloomington: Indiana University Press, 1958. Originally published in 1877.

Otis, Philo Adams. *The Chicago Symphony: Its Organization, Growth and Development, 1891–1924*. Chicago: Clayton F. Summy Co., 1924; Freeport, N.Y.: Books for Libraries Press, 1972.

Paderewski, Ignacy Jan, and Mary Lawton. *The Paderewski Memoirs*. New York: Charles Scribner's Sons, 1938.

Ritter, Frederic Louis. *Music in America*. New York: Charles Scribner's Sons, 1890.

Ryan, Thomas. *Recollections of an Old Musician*. London: Sands & Co., 1899.

Schonberg, Harold C. *The Great Conductors*. New York: Simon and Schuster, 1967.

Seltsam, William H. *Metropolitan Opera Annals: A Chronicle of Artists and Performances*. 2d ed. New York: H. W. Wilson, 1949.

Shanet, Howard. *Philharmonic: A History of New York's Orchestra*. Garden City, N.Y.: Doubleday & Co., 1975.

Sherman, John K. *Music and Maestros: The Story of the Minneapolis Symphony Orchestra*. Minneapolis: University of Minnesota Press, 1952.

Slonimsky, Nicolas. *Lexicon of Musical Invective: Critical Assaults on Composers since Beethoven's Time*. 2d ed. Seattle: University of Washington Press, 1965.

Smith, Mortimer. *Life of Ole Bull*. Princeton, N.J.: Princeton University Press, 1947.

Sousa, John Philip. *Marching Along: Recollections of Men, Women and Music*. Boston: Hale, Cushman and Flint, 1928.

Stebbins, Lucy Poate, and Richard Poate Stebbins. *Frank Damrosch: Let the People Sing*. Durham, N.C.: Duke University Press, 1945.

Steinway, Theodore E. *People and Pianos*. New York: Steinway & Sons, 1953.

Strong, George Templeton. *The Diary of George Templeton Strong*. Edited by Allan Nevins and Milton Halsey Thomas. 4 vols. New York: Macmillan, 1952.

Svorecky, Josef. *Dvořák in Love: A Lighthearted Dream*. Toronto: Lester and Orpen Dennys, 1983.

Thomas, Louis R. "A History of the Cincinnati Symphony Orchestra to 1931." Ph.D. diss., University of Cincinnati, 1972.

Upton, George P. *Musical Memories: My Recollections of Celebrities of the Half Century, 1850–1900*. Chicago: A. C. McClurg & Co., 1908.

Wells, Katherine Gladney. *Symphony and Song: The St. Louis Symphony Orchestra: The First Hundred Years, 1880–1980*. St. Louis: The Countryman Press, 1980.

Wister, Frances. *Twenty-Five Years of the Philadelphia Orchestra*. Philadelphia: Books for Libraries Press, 1970. Originally published in 1925.

Wooldridge, David. *Conductors Art*. London: Barrie and Rockliffe, 1970.

About the Gilded Age

Adams, Henry. *The Education of Henry Adams*. Boston: Houghton Mifflin, Co., 1961. Originally published in 1918.

Addams, Jane. *Twenty Years at Hull House, with Autobiographical Notes*. New York: Macmillan Co., 1910.

Andrews, Wayne. *Battle for Chicago*. New York: Harcourt, Brace & Co., 1946.

Badger, Reid. *The Great American Fair: The World's Columbian Exposition and American Culture*. Chicago: Nelson Hall, 1979.

Bergamini, John D. *The Hundredth Year: The United States in 1876*. New York: G. P. Putnam's Sons, 1976.

Burg, David F. *Chicago's White City of 1893*. Lexington: University Press of Kentucky, 1976.

Dedman, Emmett. *Fabulous Chicago*. New York: Random House, 1953.

Dickens, Charles. *American Notes for General Circulation*. Edited and with an introduction by John S. Whitley and Arnold Goldman. Harmondsworth, U.K.: Penguin Books, 1972. Originally published in 1842.

Douglas, Ann. *The Feminization of American Culture*. New York: Alfred A. Knopf, 1977.

Furnas, J. C. *The Americans: A Social History of the United States, 1587–1914*. Toronto: Longmans, 1969.

Ginger, Ray. *Altgeld's America: The Lincoln Ideal versus Changing Realities*. Chicago: Quadrangle Books, 1965. Originally published in 1958.

Grafton, John. *New York in the Nineteenth Century: 321 Engravings from Harper's Weekly and Other Contemporary Sources*. New York: Dover Publications, 1977.

Green, C. M. *American Cities in the Growth of the Nation*. London: The Athlone Press, 1957.

Hoogenboom, Ari, and Olive Hoogenboom, eds. *The Gilded Age*. Englewood Cliffs, N.J.: Prentice-Hall, 1967.

Kowenhoven, John A. *The Columbia Historical Portrait of New York: An Essay in*

Graphic History in Honor of the Tricentennial of New York City and the Bicentennial of Columbia University. Garden City, N.Y.: Doubleday & Co., 1953.

Longstreet, Stephen. *Chicago, 1860–1919.* New York: David McKay Co., 1973.

O'Conner, Richard. *The German-Americans.* Boston: Little, Brown & Co., 1968.

Perry, Bliss. *Life and Letters of Henry Lee Higginson.* Boston: Atlantic Monthly Press, 1921.

Ripley, Lavern J. *The German-Americans.* Boston: Twayne, 1976.

Wagenknecht, Edward. *Chicago.* Norman: University of Oklahoma Press, 1964.

Wandel, Joseph. *The German Dimension of American History.* Chicago: Nelson-Hall, 1979.

Weymouth, Lally. *America in 1876: The Way We Were.* Toronto: Random House, 1976.

Reference Books

Baker's Biographical Dictionary of Musicians. 4th ed., rev. and enl. New York: G. Schirmer, 1940; with 1949 Supplement by Nicolas Slonimsky.

Encyclopedia Brittannica. Toronto: William Benton, 1958.

Hitchcock, H. Wiley, and Stanley Sadie, eds. *The New Grove Dictionary of American Music.* London and New York: Macmillan, 1986.

James, Edward T., ed. *Notable American Women, 1607–1950: A Biographical Dictionary.* 3 vols. Cambridge, Mass.: The Belknap Press, 1971.

Malone, Dumas, ed. *Dictionary of American Biography.* New York: Charles Scribner's, 1958.

National Cyclopaedia. New York: James White & Co., 1892.

Sadie, Stanley, ed. *The New Grove Dictionary of Music and Musicians.* London: Macmillan, 1980.

U.S. Department of Commerce. Bureau of the Census. *Historical Statistics of the United States, Colonial Times to 1870,* Bicentennial Edition, pt. 1. Washington, D.C., 1975.

Willard, Francis E., and Mary A. Livermore, eds. *A Woman of the Century: Fourteen Hundred-Seventy Biographical Sketches Accompanied by Portraits of Leading American Women in All Walks of Life.* New York: Charles Wells Moulton, 1893.

MAGAZINE AND NEWSPAPER ARTICLES

There is rich material on Thomas in nineteenth-century music and nonmusic magazines, in more contemporary music magazines, and in the newspapers of his times. Listed here are the most significant articles, including major interviews but excluding concert reviews, many of which are cited in the Notes. The following journals were scanned: *Dwight's Journal of Music* in its entirety (1852–81), *Musical Courier* (1880–91), *Freund's Weekly* (1883–87), and *Music: A Monthly Magazine* in its entirety (1891–1902). The best sources for Thomas news were the *New York Daily Tribune,* the *New York Herald* and the *New York Times* for his New York period; the *Chicago InterOcean* and the *Chicago Tribune* for his Chicago period; and the *Cincinnati Daily Gazette* and the *Cincinnati Enquirer* for his college and festival periods.

Magazine Articles

Bennett, Joseph. "Observations on Music in America." *Musical Times* 26 (Mar. 1885), 125–28; (Apr. 1885), 193–96; (May 1885), 255–58; (June 1885), 319–22; (July 1885), 388–90; (Aug. 1885), 459–61.

Curtis, George W. "Farewell to Theodore Thomas." *Harper's New Monthly Magazine* 57 (Nov. 1878), 934–35.

———. "The New York Festival of 1882." *Harper's New Monthly Magazine* 65 (July 1882), 306–8.

———. "The Philharmonic under Thomas." *Harper's New Monthly Magazine* 56 (Feb. 1878), 462–63.

———. "Theodore Thomas's Farewell." *Harper's New Monthly Magazine* 83 (July 1891), 309–10.

Eyer, Ronald F. "America's Notable Orchestras: The Vision of Theodore Thomas Fulfilled." *Musical America*, Mar. 10, 1937, 6–8.

Fay, C. Norman. "The Theodore Thomas Orchestra." *The Outlook*, Jan. 22, 1910, 159–69.

"A Few of Our Representative Men." *The Holiday Visitor*, Jan. 1879, 7–14.

"Go West, Young Man, Go West! And He Went." *DJM* 35 (Sept. 14, 1878), 301.

Gungl, Joseph. "Josef Gungl on Musical Taste in America." *DJM* 2 (Dec. 18, 1852), 83–84.

Hassard, J. R. G. "Theodore Thomas." *Scribner's Monthly* 9 (Feb. 1875), 458–66.

Holliday, Joseph E. "The Musical Legacy of Theodore Thomas." *Cincinnati Historical Society Bulletin* 27 (Fall 1969), 191–205.

Hume, Paul, and Ruth Hume. "The Great Chicago Piano War." *American Heritage* 21 (1970), 16–21.

"An Interview with Theodore Thomas." *The Presto*, Oct. 2, 1902, 9.

Krehbiel, H. E. "Cincinnati and Its Music Festival." *Harper's Weekly* 38 (May 12, 1894), 440–42.

Loft, Abram. "Richard Wagner, Theodore Thomas and the American Centennial." *Musical Quarterly* 37 (April 1951), 184–202.

Mason, William. "The Nestor of American Musicians: Dr. William Mason's Reminiscences." *The Etude*, Oct. 1901, 351–52.

Mathews, W. S. B. "The Chicago Orchestra Commercially Considered." *Music*, May 1892, 574–81.

———. "Editorial Bric-a-Brac." *Music*, Feb. 1898, 485, 486.

———. "A Study of Theodore Thomas." *The Etude*, Feb. 1905, 54.

Mazzola, Sandy. "Bands and Orchestras at the Columbian Exposition." *American Music* 4 (Winter 1986), 411–15.

"Mrs. Theodore Thomas." *Ladies Home Journal*, Aug. 1895, 2.

"Musical Portraits—Theodore Thomas." *The Playbill*, Jan. 11, 1865.

"Return to Theodore Thomas Mountain." *Symphony News*, Feb.–Mar. 1974, 7–8.

Rice, Edwin T. "Thomas and Central Park Garden." *Musical Quarterly* 26 (Apr. 1940), 43–51.

Saerchinger, Cesar. "Musical Landmarks in New York." *Musical Quarterly* 6 (Apr. 1920), 69–90; (July 1920), 227–56.

Schiel, Wendel. "Theodore Thomas v. Singing in the Public Schools of America." *The Cincinnati Public School Journal*, Apr. 1881, 81–83.

Seidl, Anton. "The Development of Music in America." *The Forum*, May 1892, 386–93.

Steinway, William. "Personal Reminiscences of Anton Rubinstein as Related by William Steinway." *Freund's Musical Weekly*, Nov. 30, 1894, 5.

Stone, James H. "Mid-Nineteenth-Century American Beliefs in the Social Value of Music." *Musical Quarterly* 63 (Jan. 1957), 38–49.

"Testimonial Dinner for Theodore Thomas." *MC*, Apr. 29, 1891, 416–20.

"Theodore Thomas: A Sketch by an Old Admirer." *Music: A Monthly Magazine* 20 (Apr. 1901), 96–104; (May 1901), 167–72.

"Theodore Thomas: The Man and His Work." *MC*, Nov. 9, 1935, 6, 23.

"Theodore Thomas' Arrival." *MC*, Apr. 17, 1880, 155.

"Theodore Thomas' Interview in the New York Herald." *MC*, Mar. 2, 1887, 141.

"Theodore Thomas Memorial Dedicated—Chicago Symphony in Superb Program—'Spirit of Music' Statue in Grant Park Unveiled." *Musical Leader*, May 1, 1924.

"Theodore Thomas on Popular Music." *The Etude*, June 1899, 229.

"Theodore Thomas on Wagner's Death." *The Musical Record*, Feb. 24, 1883, 406.

"Third Biennial Festival at Cincinnati." *DJM* 38 (May 25, 1878), 236–37. Reprinted from *CT*, May 13, 14, 1878.

Thomas, Louis R. "The Glorious Drunk." *Cincinnati Historical Society Bulletin* 33 (Fall 1975), 222–39.

Thomas, Theodore. "Musical Possibilities in America." *Scribner's Monthly* 21 (Mar. 1881), 777–80.

"Thomas' Garden Concerts." *DJM* 32 (Aug. 10, 1872), 284. Reprinted from Philadelphia *Evening Bulletin*, July 17, 1872.

"Three Impressions of Theodore Thomas." *The Outlook*, Feb. 4, 1905, 316–18.

"A Tribute to Mrs. Theodore Thomas." *Music News*, May 10, 1929, 27.

Upton, George P. "Recent Development of Musical Culture in Chicago." *Harper's New Monthly Magazine* 96 (Feb. 1898), 473–78.

Waters, Edward N. "John Sullivan Dwight, First American Critic of Music." *Musical Quarterly* 21 (Jan. 1935), 69–88.

"What Theodore Thomas Says." *Musical Record*, Aug. 28, 1880, 753–54.

Newspaper Articles (arranged chronologically)

"100th Anniversary Year: Cincinnati May Festival." *Cincinnati Enquirer* (souvenir edition), May 18, 1973.

"Opening of the Fair," *NYDT*, May 11, 1876.

"An Interview with Theodore Thomas," *Cincinnati Enquirer*, Mar. 5, 1880.

"Colonel Nichols Resigns," *Cincinnati Daily Gazette*, Mar. 6, 1880.

"An Interview with Theodore Thomas: He Sees His Way Clear And Will Go," *Cincinnati Enquirer*, Mar. 9, 1880.

"Theodore Thomas Talks," *New York Herald*, Feb. 20, 1887.

"Mr. Thomas's Changed Symphony Readings," *NYDT*, Nov. 6, 1887.

"Mr. Thomas as a Leader," *Chicago Times*, Aug. 5, 1888.

"The Great Musical Conductor in the Role of Politician," *Chicago Daily News*, Aug. 7, 1890.

"Theodore Thomas Plans to Shake the Dust of New York from His Feet and Settle in Chicago," *NYT*, Nov. 7, 1890.

"Mr. Thomas in the City," *CT*, Mar. 22, 1891.

"Thomas' New Creation: Chicago's Orchestra the Peer of Any in the Land," *CT*, Oct. 17, 1891.

"It Was Thomas Night: The Director Presented a Baton by the Germania Club," *CT*, Nov. 8, 1891.

"Theodore Thomas on Musical Critics," *Chicago Herald*, Mar. 30, 1892.

"His Services Free: Mr. Thomas Presents a Plan for Economy in Music at the Fair," *CT*, Aug. 5, 1893.

"Thomas May Give Concerts Here: Movement on Foot to Secure Abbey's Theatre for Next Season," *NYT*, Mar. 19, 1894.

Grau, Maurice. "Some Rubinstein Reminiscences," *NYH*, Nov. 25, 1894.

"Theodore Thomas' Golden Jubilee: Fifty Years in America of a Great Orchestra Leader," *CT*, Feb. 3, 1895.

"Mr. Thomas Saw Art, Returns from Visit in Europe," *Chicago Times-Herald*, Oct. 11, 1895.

"Mr. Thomas as He Is: Strongest Personality in Our World of Music," *Chicago Evening Post*, Dec. 21, 1895.

"Adieu to Theodore Thomas: He Gets a Very Large Present and Makes a Very Small Speech," *NYT*, Mar. 29, 1896.

"Theodore Thomas Talks of Music in New York," *New York Press*, Mar. 20, 1898.

"Announces Great Gift," *Chicago Evening Post*, Feb. 15, 1900.

"Theodore Thomas Home, Tells Plans for Season," *CT*, Oct. 1, 1902.

"Has Chicago Grown Weary of Classical Music? Views of Theodore Thomas on the Future of the Chicago Orchestra," *Chicago InterOcean*, Mar. 1, 1903.

"The Chicago Orchestra," *Chicago Record-Herald*, Mar. 22, 1903.

"Plea for Orchestra: Theodore Thomas Talks of the Movement in Behalf of Music," *Chicago Record-Herald*, Apr. 12, 1903.

"Chicago's Growth in Musical Taste Is Very Gratifying, Says Theodore Thomas," *Chicago InterOcean*, Oct. 24, 1903.

"Theodore Thomas Likes New Hall: After a Preliminary Trial, Acoustics in Home for Orchestra Are Pronounced Satisfactory by the Conductor," *Chicago InterOcean*, Dec. 10, 1904.

"Orchestra Hall Is Dedicated: Big Audience Attends Formal Opening of New Home of the Theodore Thomas Organization," *CT*, Dec. 15, 1904.

Perkins, Walton. "Theodore Thomas' Life a Chronicle of Great Talents Splendidly Developed," *Chicago InterOcean*, Jan. 5, 1905.

"Thomas' Memory Lives in Praise of His Admirers," *Chicago InterOcean*, Jan. 6, 1905.

Hubbard, W. L. "Theodore Thomas Unique in the Music World," *CT*, Jan. 8, 1905.

"Glowing Tributes Paid Dead Maestro," *Chicago InterOcean*, Jan. 9, 1905.

"William Mason's Reminiscences of Theodore Thomas," *Chicago InterOcean*, Jan. 15, 1905.

Willis, Thomas. "Mr. Martinon's Mountain Theme," *CT*, Oct. 31, 1965.

ARCHIVAL MATERIALS

The Art Institute of Chicago
Letters between Thomas and Daniel Burnham, Daniel H. Burnham Collection.

Chicago Historical Society
Glessner journals, providing interesting accounts of Chicago's musical and social life from 1883 to 1905, including revealing material about Theodore and Rose Fay Thomas.

Chicago Symphony Orchestra
Complete collection of its programs since inception; photos, other memorabilia.

Cincinnati Historical Society
Early correspondence of the CMFA, including letters between Thomas and George Ward Nichols, Lawrence Maxwell, and other CMFA trustees.
Reports and minutes.
Financial records and reports, employee records, ticket sales information, various other material.
George Ward Nichols Scrapbook, with clippings about musical life in Cincinnati from the early 1870s until Nichols's death in 1885.
Other relevant scrapbooks, including Lucien Wulsin's.
Histories of the CMFA and the May Festival by Sylvia Kleve Sheblessy (1973) and Susan S. Stanley and Joan B. Bissell (1971).
Pictures, drawings, and posters from early May festivals.

Columbia University Rare Book and Manuscript Library
Edward MacDowell Papers, including letters between Thomas and Edward MacDowell.

De Paul University
Leon Stein's private collection of letters between Thomas and Max Bendix.

Felsengarten Collection
Fourteen volumes, in sixteen cartons, of orchestral and vocal scores, miscellaneous music, manuscripts of Thomas's orchestral transcriptions and orchestrations, books, Rose Thomas's horticultural collection, photographs, prints, and miscellany, and several hundred letters, mainly between CMFA members and Thomas, dealing with Cincinnati affairs between 1880 and 1904, and between George Wilson and other World's Columbian Exposition officials and Thomas. This collection was kept at Felsengarten by Rose Thomas and is now in the custody of Richard and Theodora Schulze, Fort Lauderdale, Florida. A catalog of its holdings is at the Newberry Library.

Isabella Stewart Gardner Museum
Letters between Mrs. Gardner and the Thomases.

Library and Museum of the Performing Arts, New York Public Library at Lincoln Center
Minutes and bylaws of the Philharmonic Societies of New York and Brooklyn. Available on microfilm.
Jeannette Thurber Scrapbook, including clippings from newspapers in cities where the

American Opera Company appeared from April 1886 until the summer of 1887. Available on microfilm.

Library of Congress

Theodore Thomas Notebooks, including a collection of informal notes made by Thomas about programs and other matters.

Newberry Library

Chicago Orchestra minutes.

Chicago Symphony Orchestra Scrapbooks, the first four volumes of which contain clippings from the *Chicago Chronicle, Daily Journal, Daily News, Evening Post, Examiner, InterOcean, Record-Herald,* and *Tribune* about orchestra activities from 1894 until Thomas's death. Available on microfilm.

Felsengarten Collection catalog.

Frederick Grant Gleason Papers, comprised of fifteen volumes of clippings, programs, and other miscellaneous material about early musical life in Chicago, arranged chronologically from 1878 to 1903. Available on microfilm.

Theodore Thomas Collection, including autographed scores and his personal library of printed books and scores.

Theodore Thomas Concerts/Programs, comprised of fifty-one volumes, including nearly all of Thomas's programs in chronological order from January 1852 until May 1903. Available on microfilm.

Theodore Thomas Papers, comprised of approximately 630 letters to and from Thomas, photographs, and miscellany, including the "Official Report of the Bureau of Music," March 31, 1894. Available on microfilm.

Steinway & Son Archives, Long Island City, N.Y.

Diary of William Steinway, 1861–93.

University of Chicago Archives

President's Papers, Series 1, including letters between William Rainey Harper, Thomas, and trustees about a music school at the university.

University of Cincinnati

Joseph E. Holliday's unpublished notes concerning visits by the Thomas Orchestra to Cincinnati.

Yale University

Letters between Thomas and Horatio Parker.

Index

Abbey, Henry, 137, 138, 169
Academy of Music, 13–14, 16, 18, 23, 28, 53, 124–25, 130, 137, 145, 148, 152, 157
Adams, George, 249
Adams, Henry, 209
Adler, Dankmar, 185
Adler, Felix, 131
Aiken Theater, 50
Albani, Emma, 124
Albani, Marietta, 9
Albany, N.Y., 35, 41
Albert, Eugen d', 19, 238
Albert Hall, 85
Alhambra Theater, 77
Allemand, Pauline l', 151–52
Altgeld, John Peter, 217, 226
Alvary, Max, 162
American Academy of Music (Philadelphia), 22, 174, 220
American Conservatory of Music, 232
American Guild of Organists, 171
American Opera Company (AOC), 1, 2, 147, 152
—Americans-only policy, 148, 154
—appearances in: Baltimore, 153; Boston, 152, 161–62; Brooklyn, 151; Buffalo, 165; Chicago, 154, 160; Cincinnati, 158; Philadelphia, 152, 157–58; St. Louis, 153, 158, 165; San Francisco, 165; Toronto, 165; Washington, D.C., 153, 162
—ballet and morality, 153, 158, 160

—board membership, 148
—collapse, 165–67, 274
—contractual disputes, 155
—European response, 156
—fees, 161
—financial difficulties, 155, 160, 164–65
—Fursch-Madi suspension, 158–60
—local chapters, 154, 161
—McVicker lawsuit, 154–55, 161
—and National Opera Company (NOC), 155, 161, 170
—New York seasons, 149, 164
—opera school, 147–48, 154
—prospectus, 148
Andersen, Vigo, 191
Andrews, Judge, 145
Anschütz, Carl, 14, 16, 22, 27
Apollo Musical Club, 119, 197
Apthorp, William F., 46, 224
Archer, Frederic, 149
Arctiboucheff, Nicholas, 238
Arditi, Luigi, 14
Arion Society, 28, 45, 122, 139
Arnold, Richard, 242
Art Institute of Chicago, 215, 219, 235, 247, 255
Aschenbrödel Verein, 187, 254
Astor Place Opera House, 4
Atlanta, Ga., 47, 220
Atwood, Charles, 199
Auber, Daniel, 28

Auditorium Theater, 1, 183–85, 188, 190, 201, 215, 221–22, 231, 235–36, 238–40, 247–48, 255

Bach, C. P. E., 17
Bach, Johann Sebastian, 24, 26, 39, 83, 103–4, 179, 200, 232, 254-55
—*Magnificat*, 64
—*Mass in B Minor*, 156, 242
—*St. Matthew Passion*, 63, 118
Balakirev, Mily, 225
Balfe, Michael, 21–22
Baltimore, Md., 40, 68, 126, 133
Baltimore Oratorio Association, 115
Barnum, Phineas T., 6, 107–8
Barthel, Alfred, 282
Barus, Carl, 55
Bassett, Charles, 158
Bauer, Harold, 227
Bauer, S., & Co., 41
Bayreuth Festival, 60, 72, 93, 104, 116, 148
Beach, Amy, 201, 272
Beale, J. C., 91, 268
Beecher, Henry Ward, 69, 138
Beethoven, Ludwig van, 12, 18, 23–24, 26–28, 30, 34, 36, 43, 51, 62, 79, 83, 104–5, 110–11, 138, 192, 207, 218, 230, 232, 237
—all-Beethoven concerts, 10, 38, 44, 177, 250
—Beethoven cycle, 227
—metronomic markings, 150–51
—*Missa solemnis*, 102, 117, 242
—symphonies, 19–20, 25, 32, 38–39, 53–55, 57, 59, 64, 66–67, 86–87, 103, 116, 131–32, 141, 156, 179, 186, 188, 224, 238, 242, 245, 248, 254
Bellini, Vincenzo, 13, 22
Bendix, Max, 93, 171, 188, 191, 210, 217, 222, 254
Bennett, Joseph, 140–42
Berger, Emma, 155
Bergmann, Carl, 11–13, 15, 30, 51, 59, 78–79, 81, 94, 104, 186, 262
Bergner, Frederick, 13, 27
Bériot, Charles de, 39
Berlin, Ger., 5, 52, 89, 106
Berlin Philharmonic Orchestra, 45, 90
Berlin State Opera, 9, 162–63
Berlioz, Hector, 19, 24–25, 29, 34, 38, 43, 79, 87, 156, 187, 232, 238, 240, 257

Bernstein, Leonard, 256–57
Bibeyan, Mamet, 158
Bilse, Benjamin, 30, 90
Bird, Arthur H., 199
Birmingham Festival (1882), 123
Blaine, James G., 73, 187
Booth Theater, 76
Boston, Mass., 5, 10, 19, 40–44, 46, 48, 52, 90, 111, 133, 146, 213
Boston Conservatory, 36
Boston Musical Instrument Company, 43
Boston Symphony Orchestra, 110–11, 145–46, 157, 163, 168, 183, 186, 200, 207, 213, 218, 231, 257
Boston Third Triennial Festival (1874), 63
Bouhy, Jacques, 157
Bour, Felix, 144–46, 191
Brahms, Johannes, 12, 38, 63, 83, 91, 95, 140, 171, 189, 198, 224, 230, 232, 242, 257
Brand, Michael, 57, 199
Breitkopf & Härtel, 171
Breitschuk, A., 205
Bristow, George F., 33–34, 108, 199
Brooklyn Academy of Music, 18, 32, 53, 130, 176, 220
Brooklyn Philharmonic Society, 18, 33, 35, 40, 51, 61–62, 81, 91, 96, 99, 103, 111, 124, 168, 254
Bruch, Max, 38–39, 217
Bruckner, Anton, 157, 242
Bruneau, Alfred, 238
Buck, Dudley, 66, 71, 74, 95, 123
Bull, Ole, 5, 42, 193
Bülow, Hans von, 34, 45, 60–61, 67–68, 173, 193, 256
Buffalo, N.Y., 40–42, 165, 225
Burlington, Iowa, 126
Burnham, Daniel H., 196–97, 200, 202, 205, 226, 228–29, 234, 236, 239–40, 247–48, 258
Busoni, Ferruccio, 192

Caecelian Society of Philadelphia, 115
Campanini, Italo, 116–17
Candidus, William, 151, 161
Carl Rosa Opera Company, 29, 149, 152
Carnegie, Andrew, 148, 172, 175, 180, 184
Carnegie Hall, 37, 172, 179, 184, 187, 235
Carpenter, George, 63, 82, 90

Carreño, Teresa, 18–19, 171–72, 222, 227
Cary, Annie Louise, 57, 86, 108, 112–13, 116–17, 119
Central Music Hall, 215
Central Pacific Railroad, 165
Central Park, 30, 36–37
Chadwick, George W., 189, 199, 202, 213, 253
Charleston, S.C., 47
Charpentier, Gustave, 257
Cherubini, Luigi, 38
Chicago, Ill., 7, 40, 43, 45, 50, 55, 81–82, 84, 90, 96, 111, 157, 184, 196, 216, 226, 228
—Chicago Plan, 226
—Great Fire, 2, 46, 50, 60, 170, 195
Chicago Academy of Music. *See* Chicago Musical College
Chicago Art Institute. *See* Art Institute of Chicago
Chicago Civic Symphony, 282
Chicago Exposition Band, 199
Chicago Music Festival Association: 1882, 119, 120; 1884, 128
Chicago Musical College, 36, 90, 232
Chicago Musicians' Union, 185–86, 254
Chicago Orchestra, 1–2, 187–93, 214, 216–17, 220, 222, 232, 238, 243, 257. *See also* Orchestra Hall; Orchestral Association
—auditions and selection of members, 175, 185–86, 191
—founding, 175, 181–83
—memorial concerts, 255
—New York concerts, 220, 222
—programming, 188–89, 192, 215, 220, 227
—renaming, 255, 283
—soloists, 188, 192, 279
—touring, 193, 220–21, 223–25, 227
—train wreck, 225
Chicago Symphony Orchestra, 256–57
—Thomas monument, 255
Chicago University. *See* University of Chicago
Chickering & Sons, 68, 117, 171, 173, 203
Chickering Hall, 117, 171
Chopin, Frédéric, 12, 25, 43, 51, 174, 186, 230
Cincinnati, Ohio, 6, 40, 42, 44, 48, 51, 70, 81, 83, 91–92, 96, 101, 111, 127, 146, 170, 179

Cincinnati Art Museum, 48
Cincinnati Chamber of Commerce, 86–87
Cincinnati College of Music, 2, 95, 112, 128, 217, 233
—American Opera Company collaboration, 158
—dispute with Thomas, 97–103, 268
—opera school, 112
—Queen City Club "Musical Mash," 93–94
—Thomas appointment, 88–89, 112
—Thomas directorship, 89, 92–93
Cincinnati Conservatory of Music, 36, 48
Cincinnati Exposition Building, 48, 54–55, 86
Cincinnati Festival Chorus, 55, 100, 134
Cincinnati Grand Orchestra, 93
Cincinnati May Festival, 1, 48–49, 54–59, 63, 85–88, 101–3, 118, 133, 135, 154, 156, 180, 183, 216, 242
Cincinnati Music Festival Association (CMFA), 63–64, 87, 102, 114, 118, 128, 133, 216, 254
—composers' competitions, 95, 118
—finances, 133–34
—*Messiah*, 102, 111–13, 119
Cincinnati Music Hall Association, 65
Cincinnati Opera Festival, 112–14, 118
Cincinnati Symphony Orchestra, 216, 279
Cincinnati World's Columbian Exposition band, 199
City Assembly Rooms, 12
Cleveland, Ohio, 40, 42, 111
Coleridge-Taylor, Samuel, 238
Colonne, Edouard, 107, 142, 227
Columbia College, 115
Columbia Theater, 155
Columbus, Ohio, 126
Conservatoire National de Musique orchestra (Paris), 52, 186
Converse, Charles C., 199
Converse, Frederick S., 63
Costa, Sir Michael, 105, 141
Couture, Guillaume, 136
Covent Garden, 104, 137
Cowen, Sir Frederic, 140, 238
Crimmins, John D., 172–73
Crosby Opera House, 45–46
Crystal Palace, 105
Curtis, George C., 222
Curtis, George W., 115, 118, 175, 186

Damrosch, Leopold, 45, 67–68, 80–81, 91, 94–95, 108, 114–16, 121–23, 130, 137–39, 147–48, 167, 173, 225, 268, 271
Damrosch, Walter, 139, 147, 168, 172, 184, 187, 193, 200, 221, 271
Davis, Col. George R., 197, 201–5, 208
Decker Bros., 126
De Lamarter, Eric, 282
Delibes, Léo, 151, 160
Delmonico's Restaurant, 91, 182
Denver, Colo., 128
Detroit, Mich., 40, 42
DeVivo, Signor, 159–61
Dexter, Emma, 56
Dexter, Julian, 88
Dodworth, Harvey, 27
Dodworth Music Festival, 9
Dodworth's Band, 30, 83
Dohn, Adolph, 43
Dohnányi, Ernst von, 227
Donizetti, Gaetano, 16, 22, 27, 30
Doremus, R. Ogden, 33–34, 78
Dreyfus case, 227–28
Drury Lane Theatre, 149
Dütsche, Hermann, 191
Dvořák, Antonin, 140, 150, 188, 198, 217, 221, 232, 257
Dwight, John S., 41, 44, 52

Eckert, Karl, 9
Eddy, Clarence, 179
Edward Schuberth Co., 43
Edwin Forrest estate, 74
Eisfeld, Theodor, 15, 18
Elgar, Sir Edward, 232, 242, 257
Eller, Joseph, 144
Ellsworth, James, 211
Emerson, Ralph Waldo, 177
English Opera Company, 21–22, 27
Érard harp, 206
Esens, Ger., 7

Fairhaven (Thomas's house), 146, 200, 209, 213, 217, 246
Fay, Amy, 129, 179
Fay, Charles Norman, 129, 155, 179, 181, 184, 215, 218, 235, 248, 255, 257
Fay, Rose. See Thomas, Rose Fay
Fay family, 179, 213, 228
Feder, Otto, 12

Federlein, Otto, 72
Felsengarten (Thomas's house), 231, 246, 248, 252
Festpielhaus, 60–61, 72, 116
Finck, Henry T., 63, 132, 151, 221
Foote, Arthur, 63, 171, 199, 213
Forrest, Edwin, 261. See also Edwin Forrest estate
Forrest Art Gallery, 75
Forrest Mansion, 76–77
Foster, Muriel, 242
Franko, Sam, 67, 105, 176, 266
Franz, Robert, 64
Freeman, J. C., 268
Freund, John C., 122
Friedrich, Karl, 116
Fry, William Henry, 22, 262
Fursch-Madi, Emmy, 146, 158–61, 164
Furtwängler, Wilhelm, 221, 256–57

Gabrilowitsch, Ossip, 227, 238
Gade, Niels, 20, 38–39, 43
Galassi, Antonio, 188
Ganz, Rudolf, 238
Garland, Hamlin, 209
Gebhart, Otto, 191
Gemünder, George, 93, 110, 268
Gericke, Wilhelm, 111, 145, 163, 213, 226, 237, 253
German influence, 6, 26, 48, 58, 60, 62–63, 86, 94–95, 116, 122, 137–38, 140
German Opera Company, 137–38, 147–49, 152
Germania Club, 188
Germania Musical Society, 5, 8–9, 11, 41
Gerster, Etelka, 116
Ghys, Joseph, 83
Gilchrist, William Wallace, 118
Gillespie, E. D., 70, 78, 174
Gilmore, Patrick S., 53, 70, 115
Gilmore's Band, 66, 75, 199
Gilmore's Garden, 66, 76, 81, 107. See also Theodore Thomas Orchestra, summer series
Glazunov, Alexander, 225, 239
Gleason, Frederick Grant, 189, 199
Glessner, Frances, 190, 218, 229, 252
Glessner, John, 190, 193, 216, 228–29, 239
Glessner family, 246, 281
Glinka, Mikhail, 38

Gluck, Christoph, 86–87, 124, 149, 188, 230
Godowsky, Leopold, 227
Goetz, Hermann, 148
Goldbeck, Robert, 18
Goldmark, Karl, 79
Goshorn, A. T., 98–99
Gottschalk, Louis, 19
Gounod, Charles, 30, 83, 123, 134–35, 157, 198
Grace, William R., 143
Grant, Ulysses S., 69, 73–74
Grau, Jacob, 50
Grau, Maurice, 50–51
Green, William, 242
Grieg, Edvard, 139
Grisi, Giulia, 9
Gungl, Joseph, 5–6, 8, 10, 19, 38
Gunsaulus, Frank, 254
Gye, Ernest, 137

Habeneck, François, 52, 256
Hale, Philip, 223
Halévy, Jacques, 16
Hall of Manufacturers and Liberal Arts, 201, 203
Hallé, Sir Charles, 140, 142
Hallé, Lady (Wilma Neruda), 227
Hallgarten, Julius, 104
Hambourg, Mark, 227, 238
Hamerick, Asger, 95
Hamill, Charles D., 229
Hamill, Charles H., 255
Hamilton College, 115
Handel, George Frideric, 28, 41, 53, 56, 85, 87, 117, 134, 138, 200, 242
—*Messiah*, 67, 74, 111–13, 202, 230, 248, 250
Handel and Haydn Society, 28, 41, 53, 59, 63, 115
Handel Festival (London), 105
Hanover, Ger., 7
Hanslick, Eduard, 198
Harrison, Benjamin, 184, 195
Harmonic Society, 48–49, 55
Harper, William Rainey, 216, 232
Harrison, L. F., 27
Hartford, Conn., 41
Harvard University, 63, 231, 235
Hassard, J. R. H., 70, 88
Hastreiter, Helene, 150, 154, 161

Hauk, Minnie, 33
Hausegger, Siegmund von, 238
Hayden, Sophia G., 200
Haydn, Franz Joseph, 17–18, 20, 28, 63, 103, 110, 156
—*Creation*, 41, 56–57, 135, 156, 263
Hayes, Rutherford B., 103, 201
Heller, Stephen, 12
Henschel, Georg, 110–11, 116
Herbert, Victor, 171, 175, 177–78
Hermitage, The, 193
Herz, Henri, 5, 13
Higginbotham, J. R., 206
Higginson, Henry Lee, 110, 145, 161, 213, 226
Hill, Edward B., 63
Hiller, Ferdinand, 38
Hippodrome, The, 66, 107
His Majesty's Theatre, 149
Hoch, William, 155, 158–59
Hoffman House, 150
Hofmann, Josef, 168, 223
Howells, William Dean, 69
Hubbard, W. L., 249–51
Huberman, Bronislav, 222
Humperdinck, Engelbert, 238
Hutchinson, Charles L., 215, 219, 252
Hyde, E. Francis, 179, 183–84, 241

Industrial Exposition Building (Chicago), 82–83, 111, 114, 119, 135–36, 157, 182
Innes Band of New York, 199
Inten, Ferdinand von, 39
Interstate Industrial Exposition Corporation (Chicago), 195
Iroquois Theater, 240, 281–82

Jackson, Andrew, 193
Jackson Park, 197, 202, 205
James, Henry, 209
Jarnefelt, Armas, 238
Joachim, Joseph, 88, 106, 198, 222
Joplin, Scott, 209
Joseffy, Rafael, 108, 122, 175, 188, 217, 269
Juch, Emma, 122, 132, 146, 150, 154, 157, 161
Jullien, Louis Antoine, 9–10, 12, 19–20

Kalisch, Paul, 177
Kansas City, Mo., 126–27, 193

Karajan, Herbert Von, 256, 257
Kaun, Hugo, 238
Kéler-Béla (Albert von Kéler), 30, 38
Kellogg, Clara Louise, 33
Kimball, W.W., & Co., 203
King, Frank, 126
Klauser, Karl, 20, 246
Knabe, William and Co., 275
Kneisel, Franz, 145
Kneisel Quartet, 207
Koch, Edward, 29–30, 66
Koussevitsky, Serge, 217, 256
Kramer, Leopold, 222
Krehbiel, Henry Edward, 117, 134–35,
     150–51, 156–58, 172, 254
Kreisler, Fritz, 227

Lachner, Franz, 24
Lamond, Frederic A., 238
Lamoureux, Charles, 107
Lanier, Sidney, 71, 74, 256
Lanner, Joseph, 38
Lannon, P. H., 206
Lathrop, Brian, 234–35, 239, 248, 255
Lehmann, Lilli, 142–43, 162, 177, 219, 228,
     253
Leipzig Conservatory, 118, 139, 148
Leipzig Gewandhaus, 231
Leipzig Gewandhaus Orchestra, 38, 89, 186
Lennon, J. G., 123
Levy, Jules, 39
Liadov, Anatole, 239
Liebling, Leonard, 237
Liederkranz, The, 28, 122, 132, 177, 187
Liesegang, Adolph, 199
Lind, Jenny, 6, 9, 51, 113
Listemann, Bernhard, 145
Liszt, Franz, 11, 29, 32, 38–39, 43, 45, 50,
     63–64, 78, 86, 106, 108, 140–41, 169,
     171, 192, 232, 245, 257
Locke, Charles, 125, 127–28, 133, 135, 146,
     152–55, 159, 164–65
Locke, Seymour, 125
Loeffler, Charles Martin, 238
Loewe, William, 191
London, Eng., 38, 52, 104–5, 107, 112, 156
Louisville, Ky., 40, 55
Ludwig, William, 157
Lutkin, P. C., 251
Lyon, Potter Co., 206
Lyon & Healy, 204–6, 268

MacDowell, Edward, 171–72, 199
Mackenzie, Sir Alexander, 140, 198
Macon, Ga., 47
Macready, William, 261
Macready-Forrest riots, 4
Madison Square Garden, 173–74, 180, 187
Mahler, Gustav, 221, 256
Manns, Sir August, 38
Mapleson, Col. James Henry, 113, 116, 124,
     137–38, 142
Maretzek, Max, 27, 94, 112–14
Mario (Giovanni de Candia), 9
Marschner, Heinrich, 7, 262
Mascagni, Pietro, 198
Mason, Daniel Gregory, 63
Mason, Lowell, 11
Mason, William, 11–12, 16–17, 20–21, 27,
     36, 43, 186, 229
Mason and Bergmann Concerts, 11
Mason & Hamlin Co., 43
Mason-Thomas Concerts, 11–13, 20, 93, 186
Massé, Victor, 151, 157
Massenet, Jules, 198
Materna, Amalie, 116–17, 119, 129, 132–33,
     136, 138, 146, 186, 207
Mathews, W. S. B., 189, 206, 218
Matzka, George, 11, 35
Maxwell, Lawrence, 106, 209
Mechanics Institute, 131
Mees, Arthur, 134, 157
Mehlig, Anna, 43–44
Melba, Nellie, 220
Memphis, Tenn., 126
Mendelssohn, Felix, 10, 12–13, 22, 28, 30,
     38–39, 53, 64, 67, 83, 95, 111, 131, 141,
     222, 230, 256
Mendelssohn Glee Club (N.Y.), 11
Mendelssohn Union (N.Y.), 39
Metropolitan Hall, 9
Metropolitan Opera House, 124–25, 130,
     137–39, 147–50, 157, 167–68, 171, 181,
     193, 220, 254
Meyer, Leopold de, 5
Meyerbeer, Giacomo, 17, 30, 138, 157–58
Millar, Anna, 216–18, 222, 228
Mills, Sebastian Bach, 25
Mills, Watkin, 242
Milwaukee, Wis., 111, 129, 193, 207, 246
Minneapolis, Minn., 126, 170, 175
Miss Porter's School for Young Ladies, 20,
     36, 246

Mollenhauer, Eduard, 19
Monitor and Merrimac Building, 172
Mormon Choir (Salt Lake City, Utah), 126
Morton, Levi P., 201
Mosenthal, Joseph, 11
Moszowski, Moritz, 146
Mount Auburn Cemetery, 246, 255
Mozart, Wolfgang Amadeus, 12, 18, 20, 24,
    28, 30, 38–39, 110, 117, 124, 151, 230,
    232
Music Festival Association of New York
    (1882), 114–18
Music Hall, 64–65, 70, 85–88, 135, 158, 267
Musical Club of Cincinnati, 93
Musicians Mutual Protective Union of New
    York (MMPU), 144–46

Nashville Festival (1892), 193
National Conservatory of Music of America,
    2, 147–48, 154, 198
National Opera Company (NOC), 155, 161,
    170
National Sanitary Commission, 70
Neuendorff, Adolph, 91, 267
New Bedford, Mass., 42
New England Conservatory, 36, 90
New Orleans, La., 47
New York City, 4–7, 12, 27, 36–37, 51, 81,
    84, 88, 100–101, 106, 127, 139, 146, 182,
    195, 205, 209
New York College of Music, 108
New York Exchange for Woman's Work, 124
New York Oratorio Society, 67, 114, 172
New York Philharmonic Society, 5, 10–13,
    15, 22–25, 33–34, 36, 38, 50–52, 59, 79,
    83, 125, 163, 200, 218, 226, 242, 254, 257
—Damrosch conducts, 79, 90
—finances, 78, 81, 103, 139, 267
—Thomas conducts, 79–80, 89, 91, 96,
    99, 103–6, 108, 111, 115, 121, 123–24,
    139–40, 142–44, 150, 157, 163, 168, 170,
    173, 178–79, 181, 183–84, 188, 232, 242
New York State Court of Appeals, 146
New York State Supreme Court, 145
New York Symphony Society, 91, 114, 121,
    137, 139, 172–73, 183–84, 187, 200, 207
New York's 400, 124, 171
Newberry Library, 230, 255
Niblo's Garden, 5
Nichols, Agnes, 242
Nichols, Col. George Ward, 48–49, 54–56,

86, 88–89, 92–93, 95, 97–103, 112–13,
    118, 158
Nichols, Maria Longworth, 48
Nicodé, Jean-Louis, 140
Nicolai, Otto, 12, 151
Nikisch, Arthur, 186, 189, 200, 213, 253,
    257
Nilsson, Christine, 129, 133–34, 136
Nordica, Lillian, 218, 222–23, 279
Northern Trust Company, 239
Northwestern University, 232, 251

Oberlin Conservatory, 35, 90
"Ocean to Ocean" Tour (1883), 125–28
Offenbach, Jacques, 30, 76–77
Offenbach Gardens, 77
Omaha, Nebr., 165, 193,
Olmsted, Frederick Law, 36, 196
Orange, N.J., 170
Orchestra Hall, 1, 234, 252, 255
—acoustics, 2, 247, 249–51, 282
—compared to Auditorium, 249, 251
—compared to Symphony Hall, 251
—dedication, 1–2, 248–50
—description, 236–37, 246–47, 249
—fund raising, 1, 235–36, 238–40
—purchase of land, 234
Orchestral Association, 1, 184, 187, 208–10,
    212, 214, 218, 222, 224, 226–28, 231,
    233–34, 239, 248, 252, 254
—players' contracts, 191
—Thomas's contract, 182–83
Osgood, George, 50
Osgoode, Aline, 117
Otis, Philo Adams, 83, 242

Paderewski, Ignazy Jan, 2, 192, 204–5, 207,
    221, 227, 255–56
Paganini, Niccolò, 39
Paine, John Knowles, 63, 71, 74, 171, 189,
    199, 202, 213, 238
Palestrina, Giovanni, 39
Palmer, Mrs. Potter, 200–201
Pappenheim, Eugenie, 86
Parepa-Rosa, Euphrosene, 29, 33
Paris, Fr., 15, 52, 106–7, 142, 156, 195, 219,
    228, 262
Parker, Horatio, 213, 238, 257
Park Theatre (Brooklyn), 21
Pasdeloup Jules-Étienne, 34, 38, 107
Patti, Adelina, 112–13, 119, 124, 150, 153

Paur, Agriol, 122
Paur, Emil, 226
Peabody Conservatory of Music, 35–36, 90, 95
Pendleton, E. H., 119
Perkins, Walton, 240, 250–51
Philadelphia, Pa., 22, 40, 52, 70, 75, 133, 170, 174
Philadelphia Centennial Exhibition, 1–2, 69, 73–74, 78, 170, 195, 201
—closing, 78
—concerts, 75–76
—Grand Centennial Chorus, 73–74
—inauguration ceremony, 73–74
—program plans, 70–71
—Wagner commission, 71–74
—Women's Centennial Executive Committee, 70, 74–76, 78
Philadelphia Orchestra, 254, 257
Philharmonic Society of Boston, 111
Philharmonic Society of London, 18, 105–6
Philharmonic Society of New York. *See* New York Philharmonic Society
Phillips, Adelaide, 33
Pierce, Charles, 129
Pittsburgh, Pa., 6, 40, 42, 170, 176
Pittsburgh Festival (1889), 173
Portland, Maine, 42, 133
Poughkeepsie, N.Y., 41
Potter, Bhp. Henry C., 187
Powell, Maud, 227
Pugno, Raoul, 238
Pulitzer, Joseph, 164
Pullman Band, 199
Pullman Strike: 1877, 182; 1894, 217

Quantz, Johann Joachim, 171
Quigg, Travis, 75–76, 78

Raff, Joachim, 24, 26, 38, 88, 106, 171, 238
Raymond, Fanny, 25
Reading Choral Society, 115
Reinecke, Carl, 38, 118, 139
Reiner, Fritz, 217, 256
Reinhold, Hugo, 140
Rheinberger, Josef, 140
Richardson, Florence Wyman, 153
Richmond, Va., 133
Richter, Hans, 104–6, 148, 198, 256
Rick, Henry, 38

Rimsky-Korsakov, Nikolai, 225, 239
Ritter, Alexander, 238
Ritter, Frederic, 24–25, 35
Rivé-King, Julia, 126
Royal Italian Opera Company (Covent Garden), 137
Rochester Festival (1888), 170
Rodenkircher, Christian, 191
Rollwagen, Louise, 86
Roosevelt, Hilborn, 137
Roosevelt, James, 137
Root, John, 196, 200
Rosa, Carl, 29, 156. *See also* Carl Rosa Opera Company
Rosenthal, Moriz, 227
Rossini, Gioacchino, 27, 30
Royal Philharmonic Society. *See* Philharmonic Society of London
Rubinstein, Anton, 38–39, 50–53, 62, 67–68, 102–3, 157, 164, 198, 204
Russell, C. E., 210, 248
Russell, T. C., 279
Ryerson, Martin, 219

Sabine, Wallace C., 231
Sachleben, Henry, 191
St. Botolph Club, 213
St. James Episcopalian Church, 254
St. Louis, Mo., 6, 40, 46, 55, 81, 152, 193
St. Louis Festival (1885), 146
St. Paul-Minneapolis, Minn., 193, 226–27
St. Petersburg, Fla., 50, 52
Saint-Saëns, Camille, 79, 106, 118, 198, 217, 238
Salt Lake City, Utah, 128
San Francisco, Calif., 125–27, 146, 165
Sänger Hall, 54–56, 64, 245
Sängerfesten, 6, 28, 46, 48, 56, 127, 246
Sauer, Emil, 227
Sayers, Lionel, 282
Scalchi, Sofia, 124
Scaria, Emil, 129, 132
Scheel, Fritz, 254
Schirmer, Gustav, 27
Schmitt, F. A., 87
Schoenfeld, Henry, 199
Schott, B., 72
Schreurs, Joseph, 191
Schubert, Franz, 12, 28, 38–39, 64, 86, 103–4, 110, 131, 186, 188, 230, 232

Schuecker, Edmund, 206
Schulze, Theodora, 283
Schumann, Robert, 12, 24, 26, 38, 42–43, 51, 95, 103, 131, 176, 188, 205, 232
Schumann-Heink, Ernestine, 240, 242
Schurz, Carl, 108
Schützen Corps, 7
Schwab, F., 151
Seidl, Anton, 139, 147–48, 150, 157, 162–64, 167–68, 171, 173, 176, 178, 184, 200, 215, 217, 221, 225, 256
Sembrich, Marcella, 227
Seventh Regiment Armory, 114, 116, 136
Seventh Regiment Band, 83
Sgambati, Giovanni, 198
Shanet, Howard, 62
Shelley, Harry Rowe, 189, 199
Sherwood Music School, 232
Sibelius, Jan, 232, 238
Sinding, Christian, 257
Singer, Otto, 39, 55, 59, 63–64, 86–87, 89, 95, 102
Smetana, Bedrich, 232
Society for Ethical Culture, 131
Sokolov, Nikolai Alexandrevitch, 239
Solfège, 109
Solti, Sir Georg, 256–57
Sontag, Henrietta, 9
Sousa, John Philip, 277
Sousa Band, The, 199, 201
Spohr Ludwig, 11, 141
Springer, Reuben, 64–65, 70, 85–88, 97, 99–100
Stadtmusicus, 7
Stanton, Edmund, 163
Stein, Leon, 244
Steindel, Bruno, 191, 225, 281
Steinway, William, 27–28, 38, 50–53, 66, 122, 132, 151, 173, 186, 204
Steinway & Sons, 32, 50–51, 126, 173, 203–4, 206
Steinway Hall (Chicago), 218
Steinway Hall (New York), 32, 45, 50–51, 91–92, 108, 139, 169–71, 177. *See also* Theodore Thomas Orchestra, winter series
Stern, Leo, 222
Stock, Frederick, 220, 227, 240, 252, 254–56, 281
Stokowski, Leopold, 217, 256–57
Strakosch, Max, 47, 94

Strauss, Eduard, 180
Strauss, Johann, Jr., 34, 38, 130
Strauss, Richard, 140, 217, 222, 238, 248, 253, 255, 257
—conducts Chicago Orchestra, 240–41
—views on music, 241
Strauss family, 20, 30, 83
Strong, George Templeton, 51, 78
Strong, Templeton, 199
Stucken, Frank Van der, 139, 168, 233
Sturgis, Minna Thomas, 229, 246
Sturgis, Russell, 202, 246–47
Sullivan, Louis, 185, 196, 198, 226, 276
Swing, David, 111
Symphony Hall, 230, 235, 256
Szell, George, 217

Taft, William Howard, 255
Tammany Hall, 181
Tausig, Karl, 45, 108
Tchaikovsky, Peter Ilyitch, 172, 187–88, 192, 198, 221, 225
Teutonic Choral Society, 16
Thacher, John, 203
Theodore Thomas Orchestra, 1, 27–28, 31, 33, 35, 37–39, 41–42, 45–47, 49, 51, 63, 66–67, 70–71, 73–75, 79–81, 91, 108, 116, 122, 124, 139, 142–43, 149, 170, 180, 257
—compared to European orchestras, 52, 104–5, 107, 115, 140–43, 186
—summer series: Belvedere Lion Park, 27–28, 30, 38; Central Park Garden, 2, 37–40, 44, 49, 52, 58–59, 61–62, 66, 75–76, 79, 130, 173, 176, 253; Gilmore's Garden, 83–84, 89; Highland House, 83, 96, 111; Madison Square Garden, 178; Summer Night Concerts, 82, 111, 137, 146, 154, 168, 170–71, 267 (*see also* Industrial Exposition Building); Terrace Garden, 29–31, 35, 37–38, 253
—Thomas Highway, 40, 44, 127, 152, 169
—touring, 39, 41–44, 47, 50, 61, 125, 127–29, 140, 146, 175–77, 227
—winter series: Chickering Hall, 171; Irving Hall, 16–19, 23, 32, 253; Lenox Lyceum, 172; Lyric Hall, 38; matinees, 19, 24; soirees, 24, 29, 39–40, 49; Steinway Hall concerts, 45, 51, 59, 61, 67, 78–79, 81, 168; Working People's Concerts, 130;

Theodore Thomas Orchestra (*continued*)
  Young People's Concerts, 60, 130, 168
Thibaud, Jacques, 240
Thomas, Ambroise, 77
Thomas, Franz (son), 229
Thomas, Hector (son), 229, 246, 281
Thomas, Hermann (son), 229, 252
Thomas, Johann August (father), 7–8
Thomas, Marion (daughter), 229
Thomas, Minna Rhodes (wife), 20–21, 170,
  173–74
Thomas, Rose Fay (wife), 20, 129, 131, 168–
  70, 176–78, 185, 190, 201, 210, 213, 219,
  228–29, 252–53, 255–56, 281
Thomas, (Christian Friedrich) Theodor(e)
—American music commissioned, performed, competitions, 22, 33, 41, 58,
  71–74, 95–96, 118, 189, 198–99, 253
—anecdotes, 31–32, 42–44, 111, 193, 279
—audience behavior, 32, 49, 62, 87, 135,
  237
—audience development, 16, 28, 32, 35, 58,
  60, 63, 88, 120, 131, 188, 227, 237, 239,
  244, 253, 277
—autobiography, "Life Work," 44, 243, 264,
  284
—character and personality, 3, 13, 25, 46,
  59, 61, 99, 101, 111, 113, 129, 143, 153–
  54, 157, 159, 172, 174–75, 200, 208, 210,
  227–29, 254, 257–58
—choral work, 16, 39, 53, 108, 122, 201
—compared to other conductors, 13, 67, 79,
  189, 221, 237, 256–57
—composer, 26, 44, 171
—conductor, 156, 177, 277; discipline, 13–
  15, 141, 159, 217, 223, 237; first North
  American performances, 16, 19, 22, 24,
  26, 29, 39, 46, 63, 73–74, 91–92, 118,
  140, 150, 157, 171, 192, 202, 222, 238,
  257; interpretation and temperament,
  2, 10, 19, 42, 113, 122, 186, 189, 223–
  24, 230, 241, 256; national preferences
  in programming, 232; offers from other
  orchestras, 105–6, 213–15, 269; opera,
  14, 16, 22, 149, 151, 156, 160, 166;
  player relations, 14, 31, 80, 121, 142–
  43, 163, 175–77, 185, 208–10, 217, 222;
  programming, 15–17, 20, 25–26, 29–30,
  38–41, 58, 64, 82, 111, 120, 127, 130,
  157, 188–89, 192, 218, 221, 227, 230, 232,

244, 257; rehearsals, 2, 15, 141–43, 156,
  172, 223, 257; score reading, 230; soloist
  relations, 43, 52, 54, 56, 86, 108, 112–13,
  116, 127–28, 154, 158–59, 172, 188, 192–
  93, 279; technique and musicianship, 2,
  20–21, 40–41, 103, 113, 141–43, 172, 189,
  218, 221, 223–24, 230, 239, 256; training,
  9, 13–15
—death, posthumous tributes, 252–56
—descriptions of, 20, 113, 127, 162, 169–70,
  218–20, 223–24, 237, 241, 256, 277–79
—encores, 49, 128, 244
—European visits, 33–34, 104–7, 137, 219,
  262
—family, 3, 7–8, 20–21, 47, 66, 99, 121,
  146, 174, 229, 246
—finances, 43, 46–47, 49, 61, 66, 75, 78,
  81, 88–89, 139, 161, 164–66, 168–70,
  173, 177, 183
—friendships, 11, 53, 129, 172, 182, 219,
  228–29
—health, 2, 163, 209, 213–14, 246–47
—honorary doctorates, 103, 115
—library, 78, 230
—marriages, 20–21, 179
—one-composer concerts, 82, 192, 194, 207,
  227, 240
—press relations, 21, 44, 54, 56, 102, 119,
  128, 155–56, 161, 175, 189–90, 200, 208,
  214, 218, 221, 236
—programs of orchestral concerts, 230
—religion, 20, 193
—rivalry with Leopold Damrosch, 45, 67,
  91, 114, 121–23, 130, 139, 167, 225, 271
—rivalry with Seidl, 148, 157, 162, 164, 167,
  178, 215, 221, 225
—social life, 94, 193, 277, 280–81
—support for permanent orchestra, 61, 83,
  143, 170, 174, 189, 214–15, 218, 227,
  236–37
—teacher, 36, 43, 97, 130–31, 171, 178, 277
—testimonials, tributes, 20, 27, 33, 104, 111,
  175–76, 186, 188, 194, 218, 221, 253–56
—transcriptions, 26, 42, 174
—unions, 144–45, 157, 185, 207
—views on: acoustics, 82, 246–247; American musical life, 17, 108–9, 163, 186, 189,
  253; American musical life compared to
  European musical life, 34–35, 105, 107,
  115, 219, 225, 250–51; audiences, 225,

237; Beethoven, 59, 178, 243–45; Berlioz, 245; competitions, 54; concert halls, 59–60, 81, 173, 245–46; copyright laws, 123; *diapason normal*, 123; Elgar, 231; fine arts, 219; German music, 225; Gluck, 124; Liszt, 245; music, 3, 109, 117–18, 163, 237, 245; musical education, 60, 90, 93, 101, 108–10, 130, 148, 232–33; opera, 107, 138, 162–63, 225, 244–45; Orchestra Hall, 247–51, 282; Protestant church music, 109; Richard Strauss, 231; Russian music, 225; theater music, 109; Wagner, 29, 59, 124, 162–63, 177–78, 225, 244–45; women, 97, 124, 201, 216, 227
—violinist, violins, 7–9, 12–13, 18–19, 22–23, 27, 36, 87, 92–93, 186, 268
Thomas Garden Concert Corporation, 81
Thurber, Francis B., 147
Thurber, Jeannette, 130, 147, 152–55, 159, 161, 164, 198
Thursby, Emma, 127–28
Titl, Anton Emil, 16
Tomlins, William M., 119, 197, 200, 207
Toscanini, Arturo, 217, 221, 254, 256
Tri-City Music Festival (1882), 114. *See also* Chicago Music Festival Association, 1882; Cincinnati May Festival; Cincinnati Music Festival Association; Music Festival Association of New York

Übereinkommen, 204
Ullman, Bernard, 13–14, 94
Union Pacific Railroad, 165
United States Circuit Court of Appeals, 123
United States Sanitary Commission, 263
University of Chicago, 216, 222, 226, 232–34
Upton, George P., 16, 42–44, 46, 49, 56, 70, 88, 192, 228, 243
Urso, Camilla, 33, 78
Urspruch, Anton, 238

Vanderbilt, Cornelius, 107
Varley, Nelson, 56
Vassar College, 35
Verdi, Guiseppe, 30, 72, 107, 116, 157, 160, 198
Victoria Skating Rink, 136
Vienna, 110
Vienna *Musikfreunde*, 26
Vienna Philharmonic, 34

Vienna State Opera, 9, 116, 148
Vieuxtemps, Henri, 5
Villa, Signor La, 92
Vittorio Emanuele Galleria, 81
Volbach, Fritz, 238
Volkmann, Robert, 039

Wagner, Cosima, 34, 68
Wagner, Richard 2, 12, 16, 19, 27, 29, 30, 34, 38, 45–46, 50, 59–64, 77–79, 83, 86, 93, 103–4, 106–7, 111, 116, 119, 130–32, 137, 139–42, 148–49, 151, 164, 169, 179, 186, 188, 192, 194, 207, 218–19, 224, 232, 245, 248, 255, 257. *See also* Philadelphia Centennial Exhibition, Wagner commission; Thomas, (Christian Friedrich) Theodor(e), views on Wagner
Wagner Tour, 129, 131–33, 135–37, 147
Wagner Union, 60–61, 72
Wallace, William Vincent, 22
Warder, George W., 126
Warner, Charles Dudley, 132
Washington, D.C., 40, 133, 196, 228
Washington inauguration centenary, 174
Waterbury, Conn., 41
Watson, Henry C., 70
Weber, Carl Maria Von, 20, 28, 30, 43, 131, 179, 232
Weber, Albert, 43
Weimar, Ger., 11, 106
Weimar Ducal Orchestra, 45
Wendel, Ernest, 222
White, Richard Grant, 62
Whitehouse, Francis M., 199
Whiting, Arthur, 199
Whiting, George, 95
Whitney, Myron, 57, 86, 116
Whittier, John Greenleaf, 71, 74
Widor, Charles-Marie, 238
Wienawski, Henri, 50–53
Wihtol, Joseph, 239
Wilde, Oscar, 119
Wilhemj, August, 93
Wilson, George F., 197–98
Winkelmann, Hermann, 129, 132
Wolfsohn, Carl, 26
Women's Christian Temperance Union, 158
Worcester County Musical Association, 115
World's Columbian Exposition, 1–2, 187, 195–212, 215, 276

World's Columbian Exposition (*continued*)
—American music and musicians, 198–99, 202, 211
—bands, 199, 211
—choirs, 200–201
—concert halls, 199, 207, 211–12
—concert plans, performances, 197–98, 200–201, 207, 278
—dedication, 201–2
—musical expenditures and income, 207–208, 210–11
—orchestra, 197–98, 201, 207, 209–10, 217
—piano war, 202–7, 277–78
—press difficulties, 190, 200, 202, 206–7
—Thomas's resignation, 208–12
—union problems, 207
—White City, 195–97, 202
—women's activities, 200–201

Yale University, 103
Ysaÿe, Eugène, 217, 223

Zandt, Jennie Van, 26
Zeisler, Fannie Bloomfield, 238
Zerrahn, Carl, 41, 53, 59, 63, 94–95
Ziegfeld, Dr. Florenz, 203
Zinsser, Dr. Franz, 78

A Note on the Author

Ezra Schabas has written and spoken widely on the symphony orchestra and its influence on Western life. A founder and first president of the Association of Canadian Orchestras, he was the first general director of the National Youth Orchestra of Canada (1960) and the Orchestral Training Program at the Royal Conservatory of Music, where he was Principal from 1978 until 1983. Schabas, a clarinetist, holds degrees from Juilliard and Columbia, and first taught at the University of Massachusetts and Western Reserve University. A professor at the University of Toronto since 1952, he headed its performance and opera department for ten years. He has been a consultant for the Canada Council, the Ontario Arts Council, and several Canadian universities.

Books in the Series
Music in American Life

Only a Miner: Studies in Recorded Coal-Mining Songs
Archie Green

Great Day Coming: Folk Music and the American Left
R. Serge Denisoff

John Philip Sousa: A Descriptive Catalog of His Works
Paul E. Bierley

The Hell-Bound Train: A Cowboy Songbook
Glenn Ohrlin

Oh, Didn't He Ramble:
The Life Story of Lee Collins as Told to Mary Collins
Frank J. Gillis and John W. Miner, Editors

American Labor Songs of the Nineteenth Century
Philip S. Foner

Stars of Country Music:
Uncle Dave Macon to Johnny Rodriguez
Bill C. Malone and Judith McCulloh, Editors

Git Along, Little Dogies:
Songs and Songmakers of the American West
John I. White

A Texas-Mexican *Cancionero*:
Folksongs of the Lower Border
Americo Paredes

San Antonio Rose:
The Life and Music of Bob Wills
Charles R. Townsend

Early Downhome Blues:
A Musical and Cultural Analysis
Jeff Todd Titon

An Ives Celebration: Papers and Panels of the Charles Ives Centennial Festival-Conference
H. Wiley Hitchcock and Vivian Perlis, Editors

Sinful Tunes and Spirituals:
Black Folk Music to the Civil War
Dena J. Epstein

Joe Scott, the Woodsman-Songmaker
Edward D. Ives

Jimmie Rodgers:
The Life and Times of America's Blue Yodeler
Nolan Porterfield

Early American Music Engraving and Printing:
A History of Music Publishing in America from 1787 to 1825
with Commentary on Earlier and Later Practices
Richard J. Wolfe

Sing a Sad Song: The Life of Hank Williams
Roger M. Williams

Long Steel Rail:
The Railroad in American Folksong
Norm Cohen

Resources of American Music History:
A Directory of Source Materials from Colonial Times
to World War II
*D. W. Krummel, Jean Geil, Doris J. Dyen,
and Deane L. Root*

Tenement Songs:
The Popular Music of the Jewish Immigrants
Mark Slobin

Ozark Folksongs
Vance Randolph; Edited and Abridged by Norm Cohen

Oscar Sonneck and American Music
Edited by William Lichtenwanger

Bluegrass Breakdown:
The Making of the Old Southern Sound
Robert Cantwell

Bluegrass: A History
Neil V. Rosenberg

Music at the White House:
A History of the American Spirit
Elise K. Kirk

Red River Blues:
The Blues Tradition in the Southeast
Bruce Bastin

Good Friends and Bad Enemies:
Robert Winslow Gordon and the Study of American Folksong
Debora Kodish

Fiddlin' Georgia Crazy:
Fiddlin' John Carson, His Real World, and the World of His Songs
Gene Wiggins

America's Music: From the Pilgrims to the Present,
Revised Third Edition
Gilbert Chase

Secular Music in Colonial Annapolis:
The Tuesday Club, 1745-56
John Barry Talley

Bibliographical Handbook of American Music
D. W. Krummel

Goin' to Kansas City
Nathan W. Pearson, Jr.

"Susanna," "Jeanie," and "The Old Folks at Home":
The Songs of Stephen C. Foster from His Time to Ours
Second Edition
William W. Austin

Songprints:
The Musical Experience of Five Shoshone Women
Judith Vander

"Happy in the Service of the Lord":
Afro-American Gospel Quartets in Memphis
Kip Lornell

Paul Hindemith in the United States
Luther Noss

"My Song Is My Weapon":
People's Songs, American Communism, and the Politics of Culture
Robbie Lieberman

Chosen Voices:
The Story of the American Cantorate
Mark Slobin

Theodore Thomas:
America's Conductor and Builder of Orchestras, 1835-1905
Ezra Schabas

"The Whorehouse Bells Were Ringing"
and Other Songs Cowboys Sing
Guy Logsdon

Crazeology:
The Autobiography of a Chicago Jazzman
Bud Freeman, as Told to Robert Wolf

Discoursing Sweet Music:
Town Bands and Community Life in Wayne County, Pennsylvania, 1897-1901
Kenneth Kreitner